Olmsted's Sudbrook

THE MAKING OF A COMMUNITY

BY MELANIE D. ANSON

FORWARD BY CHARLES E. BEVERIDGE

PUBLISHED BY SUDBROOK PARK, INC.

BALTIMORE, MARYLAND

Published by Sudbrook Park, Inc.,
Baltimore, MD 21208

First Edition

10 9 8 7 6 5 4 3 2

The initial publication of this book was funded in part by the
Maryland Humanities Council, through a grant from the National
Endowment for the Humanities, and by a grant from the Jacob and
Annita France Foundation and the Robert G. and Anne M. Merrick
Foundation (the France-Merrick Foundations). The Baltimore
County Historical Trust, Inc. also assisted in making possible the
initial publication of this book.

Library of Congress Catalog Card Number: 97-61916

ISBN 0-9661031-0-6

A portion of the profits from the sale of this book will go toward the
preservation of Sudbrook Park.

To obtain additional copies of this book, contact:
Sudbrook Park, Inc.
www.sudbrookpark.org
Baltimore, MD 21208
(410) 486-6814

What artist so noble…as he who, with far-reaching conception of beauty and designing power, sketches the outline, writes the colors, and directs the shadows of a picture so great that nature shall be employed upon it for generations, before the work he has arranged for her shall realize his intentions!

FREDERICK LAW OLMSTED, SR.

Contents

Foreword

Creation of community was the great concern of Frederick Law Olmsted's pioneering career as a landscape architect. His parks, the projects for which he is best known, were places where all members of an urban society could intermingle on ground they owned in common. In the villages and subdivisions that he planned, Olmsted likewise sought to foster a sense of community and communal life. Sudbrook, Maryland, stands as a prime example of his work in this area. As this book demonstrates, it illustrates the significant elements of Olmsted's community-making.

Olmsted was a dedicated advocate of the suburban movement, which offered the advantages of a "more openly built city" made possible by the separation of place of work from place of residence. In New York he condemned the crowding of the poor into tenements, while at the same time he criticized the row houses of the prosperous as an admission of "the impossibility of establishing a civilized residence" in that city. He watched apprehensively as commercial establishments spread uptown in Manhattan, constantly pushing residential areas northward. During the twenty years he resided in the New York area between 1855 and 1880 he had little chance to plan a neighborhood whose design would protect and perpetuate its residential character. His best opportunity came in the mid-1870s, when he collaborated with the engineer J. J. R. Croes in planning the street system of the eastern half of the Bronx. Their plan included a section of curvilinear streets in the three-mile-long Riverdale area that lies between the Hudson River and Broadway. The street plans they drew up, though officially adopted, were never carried out. In any case, the only element of community planning involved in this project was the siting of streets. The opportunity to create communities using the full range of means available to the landscape architect came in cities other than New York.

Olmsted's earliest significant commission was the planning of Riverside, Illinois, near Chicago, in 1868–70. On the sixteen-hundred-acre site he and his partner Calvert Vaux established most of the features that Olmsted would use to create communities during the next three decades. The streets displayed "gracefully-curved lines, generous spaces, and the absence of sharp corners," thus producing a sense of "leisure, contemplativeness and happy tranquility." They provided "comfort and convenience of movement" that contrasted strongly with the "eagerness to press forward, without looking to the right hand or the left" expressed by the "ordinary directness of line in town-streets." At the same time, Olmsted's curvilinear streets protected residential enclaves against the intrusion of cross-cutting delivery wagons and the encroachment of commercial enterprises.

The streets also served as a series of public landscapes running throughout the village. By various means, Olmsted sought to make the area in front of each residence a transition zone between private and communal space. Owners were to maintain trees in their front yards, while setback requirements for houses preserved the front yards as part of a continuous landscape open to public view. The setbacks also served to keep poor architecture from intruding too greatly on the sensibilities of other residents.

At Riverside, Olmsted began to develop the series of restrictions on which he would rely, in lieu of zoning ordinances, for creating and preserving the atmosphere of domesticity that was such an important element of suburban life. Fences and hedges no more than four feet high would define property lines and help to create privacy since Olmsted rejected the idea of a park-like community with houses set down in the midst of pastoral scenery that extended unbroken from house to house. At Riverside and elsewhere he also required purchasers of land to build houses quickly, forbidding them to hold the land on speculation and thus weaken the bonds of community.

Moreover, the heart of the community was not to be a downtown center for shopping and professional services. Residents would go elsewhere for such things, or have them delivered directly to their homes. Instead, communal facilities were the special mark of an Olmsted community. Most important was public open space, ranging from large scenic reserves to small neighborhood play areas in the triangles at the ends of blocks. There were also community-wide systems of water supply, gas lighting, and sewerage.

Olmsted's community plans also reflect an apparent desire for a considerable variety of economic standing among the residents. On the Sudbrook plan most of the lots ran from a half acre to an acre and a half, but along the railroad line there were to be forty-three lots measuring only 50 by 150 feet—whereby distinctly less prosperous people could benefit from the suburban amenities of the village. Olmsted included the same feature at Riverside. There, as at Sudbrook, the railroad provided a crucial connecting link to the nearby city, making possible frequent and rapid access to the economic and cultural institutions there.

While Olmsted sought to demonstrate the superiority of the new suburb over the old close-built city, such ventures were notoriously subject to the vagaries of the economic cycle. At Riverside the roads, sidewalks, and public spaces were laid out during the first few years. They then preserved the plan on the ground through the decades required for settlement to be completed. Most of the forty residential areas planned by Olmsted and his firm before his retirement in 1895 were likewise slow to reach completion, and in no major project was his plan fully carried out. Many of his commissions for year-round settlements were in fact subdivisions, part of larger suburbs. Of all the year-round communities in which Olmsted's direct participation can be documented, only Riverside, Sudbrook, and Druid Hills in Atlanta were in large part carried out. Sudbrook, then, is one of the few places where today one can see the shape of community as Olmsted envisioned it.

No full-length study has been made of any of Olmsted's communities that traces the origins of the project, the role of the Olmsted firm in its planning, and the relation of the plan to Olmsted's design principles, and further examines reasons for its success or failure. This book is the first of what I hope will be many such studies. The history of Sudbrook as related here is a fascinating story, developed with eye for significant detail, and showing an understanding of Olmsted's social and aesthetic thought. The author brings to her task the appreciation of a resident, the dedication of an activist, and the curiosity and indefatigable search for information of a true historian.

Charles E. Beveridge
Series Editor, The Papers of Frederick Law Olmsted
Department of History, American University

Preface

Although Sudbrook Park is a nationally significant example of community design, it has long been neglected as a subject of historical research and inquiry. Sudbrook was designed in 1889 by the most celebrated of all American landscape architects, Frederick Law Olmsted, Sr., assisted by his stepson John Charles Olmsted. More than a century later, Sudbrook still bears testimony to Olmsted's enduring principles of landscape design. Olmsted's gracefully drawn curvilinear roads, open greenspaces, and abundantly planted trees continue to give Sudbrook a sylvan atmosphere little diminished by the passage of time.

Despite Olmsted's renown as the father of landscape architecture in the United States, I had never heard of him when I moved to Sudbrook Park in 1970. My husband and I purchased a one-and-a-half-story cape cod in Sudbrook because it was affordable and conveniently located. But after living only a few years in Sudbrook Park, I experienced a sense of community unlike any I had ever known. Growing up as the child of an Air Force pilot, I had moved from base to base without establishing roots. Yet in Sudbrook Park I found multi-generational family ties: many young adults who had been raised in the community, and whose grandparents and parents still lived in Sudbrook, had themselves chosen to purchase their homes here. Neighbors seemed to know each other. The community association, then called the Sudbrook Club, sponsored holiday parades and events that regularly brought residents together. There was a community playground. A bucolic ambiance permeated the community — its landscape a kaleidoscope reflecting seasonal permutations in the colors and contours of nature. For me, as for many other residents, Sudbrook Park became far more than just a place to live.

Having helped the Sudbrook Club with some of its parades, I was asked to be its historian in 1977. Little did I know that the position would soon introduce me to the study of Olmsted and propel me into being a full-time community activist. For in July 1978, I was jolted by an article in the Sunday paper describing the intended construction of a rapid transit line through Sudbrook Park. I could not believe what I was reading. Although a transit line had been planned in conjunction with a six-lane expressway through the community, I — like most other residents — was under the impression that Sudbrook's 1973 listing on the National Register of Historic Sites and Places had negated both of these projects. After contacting the Maryland Historical Trust, the State Highway Administration, the Mass Transit Administration and elected officials, I learned that the expressway had been deleted but the rapid transit line was indeed coming through Sudbrook Park and, astonishingly, the Maryland Historical Trust had signed off on the detailed plans. This construction would, I felt, devastate the community as we knew it.

I soon found myself trying to reactivate a community that had already depleted its energy and spirit in a protracted expressway battle. Perhaps my personal outrage over the MTA's plan and the failure of responsible state agencies to halt or moderate it was sufficiently contagious to stir renewed interest, because the community rallied to fight again. It became a seven-year battle to preserve Sudbrook — a battle which was resolved with compromises that deflected much of the proposed devastation. In the course of this struggle, I met Charles McLaughlin and Charles Beveridge, co-editors of the Olmsted Papers Project and the acknowledged pre-eminent Olmsted scholars. Dr. Beveridge, in particular, guided me in researching Sudbrook's Olmsted history in an effort to expand the historic district boundaries.

I learned that Sudbrook's historic significance was bolstered by its status as one of only three surviving suburban villages designed by Olmsted, Sr., and the only one in Maryland. Sudbrook also was one of the earliest planned communities in Baltimore's nineteenth-century suburban movement. It was the first to incorporate a pattern of curvilinear roads, a rarity at that time. In addition, it introduced Baltimoreans to comprehensive deed restrictions governing such aspects as setbacks, lot size, residential use requirements, permitted heights for houses and prohibitions against subdividing. These land-use restrictions were important precursors of later zoning regulations.

The more I learned about Olmsted's design principles and their implementation in Sudbrook, the stronger became my resolve to fight to preserve as much of his design as possible. I began to look at Sudbrook in a new way. What I had seen previously as simply a lovely and cohesive community, I could now see as the intended result of a master planner. Today, not only is Sudbrook a well-preserved example of Olmstedian design principles, but it has stood the test of retaining much of its unique character and community cohesiveness through 108 years of change.

Like many persons who immerse themselves in a cause, I often had difficulty understanding why more people did not share my unbounded enthusiasm for preserving the important design elements of Sudbrook. But I came to realize that, just as I had once known nothing of Olmsted and his principles, few people had access to the information I had uncovered. Here was one of the few surviving communities designed by the founder of landscape architecture in this country and imbued with his vision. Yet, state and county planners had repeatedly proposed projects which, if implemented, would destroy the historic underpinnings of the community. Thus, I resolved to someday extend my research and to share what I had learned about Sudbrook's historic significance.

My sources included the papers of Frederick Law Olmsted and the Olmsted Associates records at the Library of Congress; Olmsted's working drawings at the Frederick Law Olmsted, Sr., National Historic Site ("Fairsted") in Brookline, Massachusetts; and the James Howard McHenry papers and the Blackford Record and Account Books at the Maryland Historical Society. The Blackford records, which have not been previously published and which I only stumbled upon in November 1995, contained almost four thousand letters written between 1891 and 1907 by Eugene Blackford, the manager of Sudbrook Park. These letters provided important new information about many aspects of the Sudbrook Company and the community's formation. I also researched deeds at the Baltimore Land Records office, corporate documents in the State Archives, newspaper articles dating back more than a century, and records of the Western Maryland Railroad. Important background information came from books about early Baltimore, unpublished accounts and memoirs of life in Sudbrook Park, and interviews with current and former Sudbrook residents, some of whom had the foresight to preserve photographs and artifacts. Surprisingly, there were very few newspaper articles about Sudbrook Park and almost none from 1907 into the 1960s.

Communities that are more than one hundred years old have many stories to tell. Inevitably, errors creep into the spoken and written records. Sudbrook Park is no exception — its current historical marker incorrectly states that the community was designed in 1891 as a rural summer resort. Actually, Olmsted designed it in 1889 for year-round residency. The marker and several written accounts also imply that a golf course and swimming pool were part of the original design. They were not proposed by Olmsted and were introduced well after the community was underway. Similarly, newspaper articles based on interviews with residents have sometimes erroneously attributed Sudbrook Park's development to officials of the Western Maryland Railroad; there was no such involvement.

It is my hope that this book will correct the historical record and focus attention on Sudbrook as the first and most important Olmsted suburb in the Baltimore region, to which all subsequent Baltimore area designs of the Olmsted firm — however noteworthy on their individual merits — are but successors. By disseminating accurate information about Sudbrook's origins and development, I hope that this book will increase appreciation for Sudbrook's historic significance and stimulate a renewed interest in preserving and restoring, when possible, important aspects of the original Olmsted plan. May residents, planners, landscape architects, Olmsted scholars, historians, environmentalists and others long continue to study, enjoy, preserve and treasure the Olmsted legacy in Sudbrook.

Acknowledgments

Although my desire to write a book about Sudbrook's history arose in the early 1980s, there was never time to devote to the effort. Finally in 1995, a window opened and I began work on this book. Any book whose genesis dates back seventeen years will owe a debt of gratitude to many people. The danger in attempting to acknowledge each individually is that I may unintentionally leave someone out. Yet this book came to publication only through the enthusiasm and combined efforts of numerous people. To each and everyone who helped with this effort, including anyone I may inadvertently fail to mention by name, my deepest thanks.

Initial work on this book, together with a related exhibit and symposium in the fall of 1996, was funded by the Maryland Humanities Council through a grant from the National Endowment for the Humanities. Sudbrook Park, Inc. assumed the role of sponsoring organization for this multifaceted project. A second grant from the Jacob and Annita France Foundation and the Robert G. and Anne M. Merrick Foundation made possible continued work and publication of this book. The Baltimore County Historical Trust, Inc. agreed to act as recipient and administrator for the second grant. I am deeply grateful to the Maryland Humanities Council and to the France-Merrick Foundations for their generosity in funding publication of this book, and to Sudbrook Park, Inc. and the Baltimore County Historical Trust, Inc. for the important role each has played.

Two historians served as consultants: W. Edward Orser, Professor of American Studies, University of Maryland Baltimore County, and Charles E. Beveridge, Series Editor of The Papers of Frederick Law Olmsted. Each contributed an invaluable perspective. Dr. Orser has a wide-ranging knowledge of the nineteenth-century suburban movement and local history. His input and suggestions on various versions of the manuscript guided me in several areas, and helped me to expand on Sudbrook's social history and to place the early community more accurately in the context of other late nineteenth-century Baltimore suburbs.

I met Dr. Beveridge in the late 1970s, and it would not be an overstatement to say that without his encouragement, assistance and direction, I would not have begun the Olmsted research that led to this book. Whether guiding me in research, providing me with additional relevant materials, helping me select illustrations, discussing concepts or reviewing multiple versions of the manuscript, Dr. Beveridge provided insight, expertise, and encouragement. Although I take responsibility for any errors in the manuscript, Dr. Beveridge's willingness to share with me his extensive knowledge of Olmsted has vastly contributed to the quality and comprehensiveness of this book.

A very special thanks to my dear friend, Dr. Leonard Frank. Without his able assistance and unwavering sense of humor, I surely would have given up long ago. I originally estimated that this book, together with the exhibit and symposium, would be completed within a year. Instead, this undertaking has consumed more than two years. Len, a biochemistry professor who mistakenly thought he had retired, not only agreed to serve as grant administrator throughout this time, but helped with all aspects of the project. He made my burden significantly lighter by handling a multitude of tasks from the most mundane to the most complex. No one read as many revisions of this manuscript as Len. It was a task that was arduous at best, yet Len managed to critique productively and always encouraged my sometimes faltering efforts. Whether running errands for supplies, taking and developing photographs, or helping me select illustrations and think through or revise difficult portions of the text, Len was indispensable — a steady support and a stellar asset.

Every writer knows how crucial a good editor is, and I was fortunate to have Barry Kessler in this key position. Not only did Barry's editing skills greatly improve the many rough edges of my manuscript, but he made the process smooth and painless. Despite his own hectic schedule, Barry also found time to answer my wide-ranging technical and substantive questions and provided clear direction to guide me in rewriting portions of the manuscript. His help was extensive and invaluable. Barry also served as advisor on the exhibit. Not only was it a pleasure to work with him, but the success of that component was due primarily to his curatorial expertise.

I would also like to say a special thanks to Sudbrook residents Peggy Feldman-Eskey and Boots Shelton for sharing their time, talents and photographic skills; to Darragh Brady and Ellen Kahan Zager for creating maps and graphics to illustrate the text; to John Leith-Tetrault, for reviewing the early manuscript and offering thoughtful suggestions; to Pat Leith-Tetrault for help organizing photographs; to Irma Frank, for general assistance as well as reviewing and commenting on portions of the manuscript; and to Dorothy Collins — friend, long-time resident and historian of Sudbrook Park, Inc. — for locating old photographs of Sudbrook for me, searching the community association's historical archives for information, cataloguing photographs and providing continual encouragement and practical support in myriad ways, always above and beyond the call of duty.

I am grateful to so many present and former Sudbrook residents who shared their professional expertise, personal knowledge, photographs or recollections with me, including Betty Ann Anton, James Barrett, Mrs. Robert Leland Bart, Rick Bauman, Priscilla Beachley, Delores Bennett, A. Hamilton Bishop, the late Matilda Bishop, Darragh and Ed Brady, Jackie and Newell Cox, Jr., Betty and William Cox, Mary Beth Betz Davis, Martha Dickey, Dorothy Diehl, Jack Dowell, Betty O'Connell Erwin, Sylvia Finifter, Sally Gracie, Stella Hazard, Bayard Hochberg, Roger Katzenberg, Martha Volz Kaufman, Tom Lewis, Dorothy Liebno, Edna Mae Loane, Brooke Lynch, Donna MacLean, Michael Mannes, Mary H. Mosner, Phyllis Moynahan, Joan Quisgard, Robert M. Schaller, Sr., Sarah Sener, Janet Singerman, Nita and Jeff Smith, Michael Sotir, Betsy and Tadd Stellmann, Jim Talbott, and Betty and Bill Traband. I am indebted to the late Edward B. Stellmann, whose tales of growing up in Sudbrook Park piqued my interest in the community's history before I knew anything about Frederick Law Olmsted; and to the late Mrs. Dorothy Cox, who shared with me her information and account of "life in the Park at the turn-of-the-century" — her enthusiasm for the community's history was contagious.

I am also grateful to Stewart McLean, for the use of the Merrick family photograph and his willingness to share his grandfather William Merrick's memoirs of life in Sudbrook Park — they added an important personal perspective; to Joan McHenry Hoblitzell for sending me news clippings and portions of the McHenry Family History for use in the book; to Elisabeth Corddry for sharing with me her research on Eugene Blackford and his family; to Arleyn Levee for reviewing and adding to my infor-mation about John Charles Olmsted; to Edward Straka for sending me relevant books, photographs and information about Riverside, Olmsted's first suburban design; to Laurie Blumberg and Barbara Johnson for their valuable research assistance; to Catherine Mahan, ASLA, for her counsel and expertise; to John McGrain, for forwarding to me relevant historical facts and news articles; to Judith Kremen for on-going encouragement and competent assistance; to Curtin Winsor IV, who provided me with historical background information on one of the original Sudbrook Company directors; to James Wollen, for sharing his architectural expertise and providing me with biographical information on several local architects; to Sandra Sparks, for her suggestions and general assistance early in the project; to Herb Harwood and Stewart Rhine for sharing their knowledge about Baltimore's early railroad and streetcar systems; to David Belcher, whose legal expertise helped me make sense of certain Sudbrook Company real estate transactions; to Frank Gorman, for legal advice on publication issues; to Jennifer Rossman, Sandra Crockett, Rich Krohn, and Bob and Maxine McKinney for practical advice and general support; to Beryl Frank, whose interest in Sudbrook Park reinforced my own; to the staff of the Maryland Historical Society, particularly the Manuscript Division and Prints and Photographs Department; to Joyce Connelly at Fairsted, the Frederick Law Olmsted National Historic Site, for her able assistance; to Richard Parsons, Baltimore County Public Library, for quickly locating photographs that I needed and arranging for their timely reproduction; to the Friends of Maryland's Olmsted Parks & Landscapes and the National Association for Olmsted Parks, for their contributions to this effort; to the helpful reference staffs at Baltimore's Enoch Pratt Library Maryland Room, especially Lee, and at the Library of Congress, especially Jeff Flannery; to Ellen Kahan Zager for her graphic design and layout of the book; to Deborah Patton for indexing the book; to Michael Early, for help with print production; to Marty Anson for his production expertise and the services provided by Bindagraphics, Inc.; and to the many Sudbrook Park residents and other friends who offered moral support and motivation.

Finally, a special thanks to my family, whose patient support and understanding were crucial throughout this long undertaking: to Gregory Anson, for research assistance and for cheerfully running countless errands so that I could concentrate on writing; to Matthew Anson, for research assistance and astute suggestions on portions of the manuscript; to Todd Anson, for research and general assistance as well as reading and thoughtfully critiquing much of the initial manuscript; to Scott Anson, for his suggestions and improvements to Chapter 1; and to Regee and Blair Anson, for their sustaining enthusiasm and encouragement from afar.

To all, my deepest thanks.

Author's Note about Street Names

The names of several streets in Sudbrook Park changed over time from the names shown on Olmsted's 1889 "General Plan of Sudbrook," but two in particular raised issues as to their treatment in this book.

1. The current Windsor Road was Winsor Road until about 1911, when the "d" was inadvertently added on several deeds and plats, eventually becoming the accepted spelling. I have retained the original spelling in this book up until the 1911 period, when I adopt the current spelling.

2. Sudbrook Lane did not appear as a street name within the community until the 1940s. Before that time, the current Sudbrook Lane had three designations; it was called:

(a) "Sudbrook Avenue" from Reisterstown Road to the entranceway bridge into Sudbrook Park;

(b) "Sudbrook Road" within Sudbrook Park from the bridge to what is now Olmstead Road (encompassing numbers 401 and 501 to 520 of what is now Sudbrook Lane and the 600 and 700 blocks of what is now Sudbrook Road); and

(c) "Monmouth Road" along the segment within Sudbrook Park going from what is now 517 Sudbrook Lane to Milford Mill Road (presently, 544 to 568 Sudbrook Lane).

In the 1940s, Monmouth began to be called "Sudbrook Lane" by some residents and "Sudbrook Road" by others. It was not unusual for immediate next door neighbors to list different street names. Houses numbered from 501 to 520 were designated "Sudbrook Road" until the early 1980s, when Baltimore County erected new signs designating that portion of the street "Sudbrook Lane." Even then, some along the street continued to use the Sudbrook Road appellation, while others adopted Sudbrook Lane. Today, only the 600 and 700 blocks of Sudbrook Road retain their original name; the 400 and 500 blocks (including what began as Monmouth Road) are called Sudbrook Lane.

To lessen confusion and avoid always having to insert dual or clarifying street names, I use the currently applicable designations of Sudbrook Lane and Sudbrook Road throughout this book, except when quoting from the Olmsted and Sudbrook Company letters. Direct quotes from these early letters either contain clarifying information in brackets or are self-explanatory in the context of the letter.

As a final point of clarification, while there is no "a" in the spelling of Olmsted's surname, Sudbrook Park's Olmstead Road, named after him, mistakenly contains one.

Chapter 1

FREDERICK LAW OLMSTED AND THE AMERICAN SUBURB

So accustomed are we to the existence of the suburbs that surround our cities, forming mile upon mile of metropolitan development, that it may be difficult even to imagine a time when American cities had no suburban extensions. Yet, only one hundred fifty years ago, the very concept of living in a suburb was novel.

Not that there had not been development on the edge of cities. That had gone on for thousands of years. Communities also had been labeled "suburban" before 1800. But even by the 1840s, suburbs were not distinct or recognizable entities apart from either the city or the farm. The outlying towns that did exist were little more than miniature cities.[1]

The primary force behind the suburban movement in the nineteenth century was rapid industrialization. The momentum of the industrial revolution created an unparalleled need for and influx of many thousands of people, swelling existing cities to the breaking point and producing metropolises where none had existed before. In 1840, the only cities in the United States with more than 125,000 residents were New York and Philadelphia. By 1890, many new cities such as San Francisco, Seattle and Atlanta had become major centers of population and industry. Baltimore's population rose from about 102,000 in 1840 to 434,400 in 1890. Chicago and Philadelphia by that time each contained about one million inhabitants, while New York ran a close second to London as the world's largest city.[2]

As the country filled with new arrivals — from adventurers and prosperous merchants anxious to reap the rewards of industry, to laborers and immigrants who arrived by the thousands looking for work — cities were hard-pressed to handle the problems their swelling populations created. There were not enough existing buildings to house everyone. City dwellers crowded into boarding houses; slums sprang up, congestion increased, and crime became more prevalent. Sanitation presented major new hurdles. Disease multiplied with poor sanitary practices and overcrowding. The city, once a center of civilized culture for those of wealth and refinement, became a hodgepodge of diverse nationalities and economic classes from which those who could afford it would seek to escape.

But escape to where? To what? Beyond the cities lay vast expanses of undeveloped land — the much-idealized agrarian America. The countryside did not have the problems of the cities, it was true, but rural life was extremely isolated in the days before improvements in transportation technology more closely linked outlying areas with the city. Despite the glorification of rural life by many nineteenth-century writers, those who thrived on intellectual and cultural stimulation often found unremitting rural life lonely and monotonous. Only the wealthiest could afford to maintain both city residences and country estates — permitting them to partake of the best of both worlds.

The relentless pace of industrialization in the nineteenth century brought to the boiling point urban-rural dichotomies that had been simmering: Americans had long had a love-hate relationship with their cities. For many theorists, cities were difficult to live with, but impossible to live without. Even in the eighteenth century, Thomas Jefferson reflected this ambivalence. Convinced that cities were "dangerous threats to republican institutions because they housed large numbers of the dependent poor," he also delighted in the cultural amenities of urban life and mingled comfortably in the most fashionable circles of Parisian society. Nevertheless, the idea that "agriculture was the most virtuous way of life and that cities were necessary evils" had deep roots in the American psyche and was reinforced by the chaos that grew out of rapid industrialization.[3]

By the 1850s there was a growing belief among a cultural elite that American cities needed the "civilizing" influence of open spaces and parks to temper the untoward social effects of oppressive congestion and high density building. Many could agree on the goal, but there was no consensus on how nature should be incorporated into expanding cities.[4] By accident or fate, the park movement was soon to be molded and propelled by a man who in many ways had not yet found himself, but would go on to found a profession that helped shape the American landscape.

Frederick Law Olmsted, by many measures, might have seemed an unlikely candidate to fill this role. His adult life began with many starts and stops, plans and detours. For years he seemed propelled by happenstance and whim, without apparent direction or purpose. But as often happens, his seemingly random adventures and misadventures contributed to expanding his intellectual vision. They provided him with the practical experiences he needed to mold a comprehensive landscape design theory that was imbued with democratic ideals and attuned to the psychology of esthetics. To Olmsted, naturalistic scenery was not just pleasing to the eye; it had the power to uplift and improve the condition and character of persons at all levels of society.

Olmsted was born in Hartford, Connecticut, on April 26, 1822. His father, John Olmsted, was a prosperous dry-goods merchant who transmitted his love of nature and beautiful scenery to Frederick. Young Frederick was taken at an early age on his father's "tours in search of the picturesque."[5] On horseback through the countryside around their home and on outings with his family through the White Mountains, up the Hudson River, and into the Niagara Falls region, Olmsted developed, as he later said, "an early respect for, regard and enjoyment of scenery… and extraordinary opportunities for cultivating susceptibility to the power of scenery."[6]

Sent away to be schooled at an early age and often left by his delegated caretakers to fend for himself, Olmsted did not have an especially happy childhood. But he developed a strong sense of independence that stood him in good stead in later life, and a close and sustaining relationship with his brother, John, whose family would later become his own.[7]

Just as he was ready to enter college, Olmsted developed a severe case of sumac poisoning, causing temporary partial blindness. His father took him to New York specialists who thought it best that he not strain his eyes by reading. For the next few years, Olmsted studied with a civil engineer, learning surveying, collecting rocks and plants, and drawing plans of imaginary towns. Unknowingly, he was gaining necessary tools for what would ultimately be his career.[8]

His father next sent him to learn about business by working in a dry-goods-importing firm. Olmsted disliked the life of a clerk and after a little more than a year, returned to Hartford.[9] At that time, Olmsted's younger brother John was about to enter Yale. Frederick, now a young man of 21, still did not know what he wanted to do with his life. So he signed up for sea duty on a ship to the Far East. It turned into another misadventure; he was sick most of the time.[10]

Realizing that he did not have sea legs and having disliked being a clerk, Olmsted decided to study scientific farming. Farming at the time was a popular occupation. The idea of improving the life and productivity of the farmer interested Olmsted. He signed up for special courses at Yale. Again, illness prevented him from finishing this course of study. Once again, his father rescued him, setting him up with a farm near New Haven. But soon Olmsted moved again, to another farm his father

Frederick Law Olmsted, Sr., 1860s. After trying his hand at several livelihoods, Olmsted found his calling as a landscape architect. His renown as co-creator of New York City's Central Park led to commissions for other major parks, college campuses, private estates, and suburban villages. COURTESY OF THE NATIONAL PARK SERVICE, FREDERICK LAW OLMSTED NATIONAL HISTORIC SITE.

financed on Staten Island. Although he would intersperse travel with farming, this became his home for seven years. Olmsted learned important skills during his years of farming that would help him later in constructing Central Park — he improved the landscape, got experience with drainage systems and supervised a team of farmhands.[11]

A trip to England, then in the beginning stages of a movement to convert portions of urban space into park land, further reinforced the foundation upon which Olmsted would later build. His travels brought him in contact with the "green, dripping, glistening" beauty of the English countryside. Joseph Paxton's 120-acre Birkenhead Park made a lasting impression. This lush People's Garden, in stark contrast to the squalor of much of industrial England in 1850, appealed to Olmsted's sensibilities.[12] Here, Olmsted observed citizens of all classes harmoniously sharing the lush, tranquil surroundings. The scene, which he saw repeatedly in his travels through England, helped form the foundation of his belief that picturesque public grounds were a necessary prerequisite to civilized urban living.

Returning from this trip, Olmsted added another venture to his growing list of hobbies-turned-professions: he embarked on a literary career. He wrote a book about his journey to England that was published in 1852. Through connections, Olmsted soon was hired by the *New York Times* as the paper's correspondent in the American South. Based on his travels in the slave-holding South over the next two years, Olmsted wrote "the most extensive and detailed study of southern society by any writer of the time."[13]

Olmsted became convinced that a free-labor society was superior to the South's slave-holding system. At the same time, however, it was apparent to Olmsted that northern industrial cities, far from being models of exemplary living, were spawning a new breed of citizens who lacked morals, manners and civility. Abhorring violence as a solution to the disparate ideologies and economic systems of the northern and southern states, Olmsted came to believe that the challenge of the northern system was to assure that free labor was demonstrably superior and thus a more desirable system than slave labor. These beliefs strengthened an imperative that Olmsted felt to find ways to elevate the spirit and improve the moral and cultural life of all the classes in a free-labor society.

Again, Olmsted stumbled upon an enlightenment of sorts in an unlikely spot. As he traveled through San Antonio, Texas, he was captivated by the scenery in the hill country there and was impressed by a German settlement that he discovered. Composed of educated and cultured Germans who had fled their homeland, the group had a small farm where, to Olmsted's surprise and delight, they performed parts of Mozart's *Don Giovanni* one evening to piano accompaniment. But that wasn't all. As Olmsted scholar Charles Beveridge has noted:

> Elsewhere [Olmsted] encountered teamsters camped on the prairie who
> repeated passages from Dante and Schiller "as they lay on the ground
> looking up into the infinite heaven of the night," and met people who
> quoted Hegel, Schleiermacher, Saint Paul, and Aristotle with familiarity
> and yet lived "in holes in the rock, in ledges of the Guadalupe…
> earn[ing] their daily bread by splitting shingles." Such a society of
> cultured laborers was, for Olmsted, a glimpse of the millennium.[14]

Although he was not yet to have a direct outlet for it, Olmsted was building the structure of his vision through experiences such as these. From impressions gathered visiting such diverse places as

England's People's Park and this German settlement, Olmsted was forming beliefs about the effectiveness of nature to uplift the spirit, soothe the ills of urban stress and elicit higher moral standards and behavior from people in all walks of life.

Olmsted moved to New York City in 1855 to be the editor of *Putnam's*. With money from his father, he also bought an interest in the firm that published the magazine. Two years later, the magazine and its publisher failed, leaving Olmsted in debt and without a job. That same year, Olmsted's brother John died of tuberculosis. It was a difficult time for Olmsted. As historian Charles McLaughlin observed:

> He was now 35 years old, and the parts of his life seemed to add up
> merely to the sum of those parts and nothing more. Yet Olmsted had
> acquired over the years — "without my knowledge, through living a
> somewhat vagabondish, somewhat poetical life" — a rather unique set
> of skills and interests. He was an engineer, a surveyor, a horticulturalist,
> a farmer. He enjoyed an instinctive rapport with "scenery" and had
> thought deeply about urban life. He was also a writer. This, oddly,
> proved decisive. As Olmsted later wrote, "If I had not been a 'literary
> man'…I certainly should not have stood a chance."[15]

Olmsted had to find employment. Again, fate or luck intervened. The movement to build a park in New York City had been launched and a superintendent for the monumental project was needed. Olmsted happened to encounter a City commissioner he knew who told him about the position and suggested he apply. Somewhat known through his literary reputation, Olmsted was supported by enough prominent people to get the job.[16]

Still bereft from losing his brother, Olmsted threw himself into his work. It was to be a formidable task. The proposed 770-acre park site was not much more than a wasteland in 1857, with its topography a mixture of barren rock and stinking swamp. Cows, pigs, goats, slaughterhouses and squatters had to be removed. Soon after the work of clearing the site began, the city announced a competition for the design of the park. Calvert Vaux, an architect and landscape gardener whom Olmsted knew, asked Olmsted to collaborate with him. In 1858 their plan, Greensward, was chosen from the competing entries. Now the real work would begin. To create Central Park's pastoral setting and lush landscape, Olmsted would oversee as many as four thousand men at a time and rearrange almost five million cubic yards of earth and rock. He also found himself frequently pitted against politicians and bureaucrats who threw up obstacles at every turn.

In 1859, still very much immersed in Central Park, Olmsted married his brother's widow, Mary Perkins. John's last request had been that Olmsted take care of her and their three young children.[17]

With the outbreak of the Civil War in 1861, Olmsted's administrative capabilities led to his appointment as executive director of the U.S. Sanitary Commission, an agency that was the precursor to the American Red Cross. After a few years, Olmsted tired of the bureaucratic hassles and resigned, but the experience proved fruitful for his later career. It impressed upon him the absolute necessity, for public health reasons, of insuring good sanitary conditions and providing for adequate drainage.

Having given up his Central Park and Sanitary Commission positions, Olmsted had to find employment.[18] In 1863, he became administrator of the 44,000 acre Mariposa mining estate near what is now Yosemite National Park in California. The lifestyle prevalent on the mining frontier — with its gambling, heavy drinking, rowdyism and every-man-for-himself attitude — was antithetical to Olmsted's values. But once again, this experience would have future application. Olmsted's Mariposa stay strengthened his belief that the most civilized values were associated with domesticity and community. Later, design aspects that promoted the ideals of "domesticity" — home, family and concern for neighbor — would become an integral part of Olmsted's suburban planning principles.[19]

The Mariposa Company collapsed within two years. The owners apparently had used Olmsted to bolster the company's reputation while they unloaded their stock. During his time in California, and on the weight of his Central Park reputation, Olmsted had obtained three landscape design commissions in California.[20] But Calvert Vaux convinced Olmsted to return to New York and work with him. Vaux had regained their position with Central Park and was also to carry out a plan for Prospect Park. Olmsted accepted his invitation.

In October 1865, Olmsted set sail for New York. At age 43, he had found his passion and direction. Over the next thirty years, Olmsted would continue and further expand his life's greatest work as a landscape architect, leaving an urban design legacy unmatched by anyone before or since.

The core principle underlying all of Olmsted's designs was his belief in the therapeutic power of beautiful scenery to uplift the spirit. His ideal was a democratic one — to enhance and employ nature to civilize and benefit every level of society. As a result of his travels in Europe, Olmsted realized that the history of Western civilization centered around people coming together to form great cities, but he also saw clearly the detrimental aspects of congestion and industrialization in America. His solution was to apply the ameliorative effect of naturalistic scenery to counteract the stress, noise and artificial surroundings of urban life — to ruralize cities by incorporating comprehensively planned parks or park systems. At the same time, he wanted to bring urban benefits — culture and tasteful design — to rural America, especially the sterile parts of the West.[21]

While Olmsted had no qualms about enhancing nature to achieve a heightened effect, he always respected the existing topography and the "genius of the place." According to Beveridge, Olmsted "wanted his designs to remain true to the character of their natural surroundings, and not clash with them."[22]

Olmsted became known for two primary styles — the pastoral and the picturesque — that had been used by English landscape gardeners in the late eighteenth century. As Beveridge has noted, Olmsted employed the pastoral style, the predominant mode of his park designs, "to create a sense of the peacefulness of nature and to soothe and restore the spirit." Olmsted used the picturesque style, inspired by the tropical scenery he had seen when crossing the Isthmus of Panama on his way to California, to heighten the sense of nature's mystery and bounteousness. To achieve the picturesque effect, he planted profusely and mixed "a variety of tints and textures of foliage that… created a constantly changing play of light and shadow."[23]

In defining the profession of landscape architecture that he had founded, Olmsted struggled to distinguish it from common "gardening." He did not incorporate decorative flowers in his landscapes, feeling that they would weaken the "unity of design" and psychological power of his work. As described by Beveridge, Olmsted "subordinated all elements of the design to the overall effect. He particularly sought to exclude objects that would call attention to themselves for their individual beauty or interest and distract from the landscape as a whole."[24]

Upon returning to New York in 1865, Olmsted worked in partnership with Vaux until 1874. While much of their expanding practice involved park planning, Olmsted was anxious for the opportunity to design a suburban development, believing as he did that "no great town can long exist without great suburbs."[25]

After the Civil War, cities had resumed their explosive growth patterns. Being the visionary that he was, Olmsted foresaw the movement toward suburban living before it became an established phenomenon. His fear was that without foresight and planning, these haphazardly formed suburbs would be little more than city extensions, eventually perpetuating the cities' problems.[26]

Over the years, Olmsted had given much thought to the trend toward the "removal to suburban districts... the end of which must be, not a sacrifice of urban conveniences, but their combination with the special charms and substantial advantages of rural conditions of life."[27] Olmsted received an opportunity to put his theories into practice in 1868, when he and Vaux were retained by the Riverside Improvement Company to design a suburban village nine miles west of Chicago.

Although Llewellyn Park in West Orange, N.J. (1853) is often cited as the first American romantic suburb,[28] Olmsted and Vaux's "Riverside" on Chicago's Des Plaines River may well be the most prominent. Both Olmsted and Vaux were involved in the Riverside project; however, most of the credit for the design goes to Olmsted, since he inspected the site, wrote the report and designed much of the plan while Vaux was out of the country in 1868.[29] Olmsted's design of Riverside was a work of art. The early implementation of a large portion of the Riverside plan in adherence to Olmsted's design principles firmly ensconced Riverside as the largest and foremost Olmsted suburb.

Olmsted went on to design numerous other communities and subdivision plans during his career.[30] Many of these were never implemented at all, some were not followed with any accuracy, and some, while executed along the lines of their design, nevertheless lack the separateness, integrity and cohesiveness required to categorize them as true "suburban villages." Today, Riverside (1869), Sudbrook (1889), and Druid Hills in Atlanta (designed by Olmsted in 1893 but not built until 1905) are recognized as the three most fully carried out and preserved examples of Olmsted's concept for a suburban village.[31]

On a smaller scale than Riverside, Sudbrook also artfully manifests Olmsted's design principles for a suburban village. The curvilinear road pattern is the most prominent design feature, whether one is looking at the "General Plan for Sudbrook" or traversing the community. As Baltimore author James Waesche has observed, Olmsted produced a plan whose roads "loop back upon themselves....They transform residential 'blocks' into paisleys, pods, and other globular forms. Because of them, maps of Sudbrook Park fairly leap from the grid-filled pages of contemporary atlases."[32]

In America today, a curving street may seem commonplace because, for more than a hundred years, developers have emulated Olmsted's curves. But at Riverside in 1869 and Sudbrook in 1889, the curvilinear form was nothing short of revolutionary. That was a time when the parallel and perpendicular grid pattern predominated everywhere. So innovative were Olmsted's curves in the Baltimore of 1889 that the Sudbrook Company found it almost impossible to find a surveyor to lay them out on the ground. Finally, the manager of the Sudbrook Company, who had some engineering knowledge, did the initial work himself.[33]

Olmsted's trademark curvilinear roads are not the kind of curving streets found in almost every modern subdivision, where a combination of tangents and curves produces a segment of straight-of-way that evolves into a curve.[34] Walk Olmsted's roads in Sudbrook and notice that Olmstedian curves contain no straight-of-way components; rather, they form an ever-continual bend, pulling pedestrians on while merging almost imperceptibly into the landscape. The allure of the Olmsted curve is

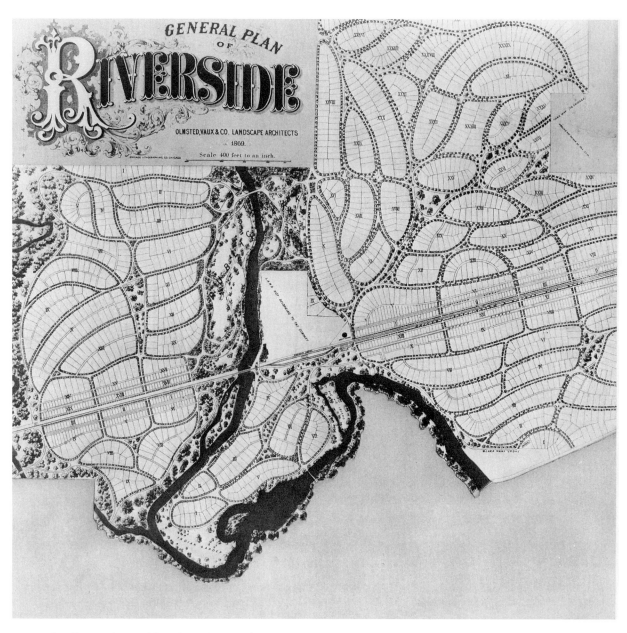

Riverside, Illinois, designed by Olmsted, Vaux & Co., 1869. Riverside was Olmsted's first and most famous suburban residential design. Its curvilinear streets imparted a sense of enclosure, while its open green spaces provided areas for residents to gather informally. Both design aspects fostered the sense of "community" that Olmsted sought to create in his suburban villages. COURTESY OF THE NATIONAL PARK SERVICE, FREDERICK LAW OLMSTED NATIONAL HISTORIC SITE.

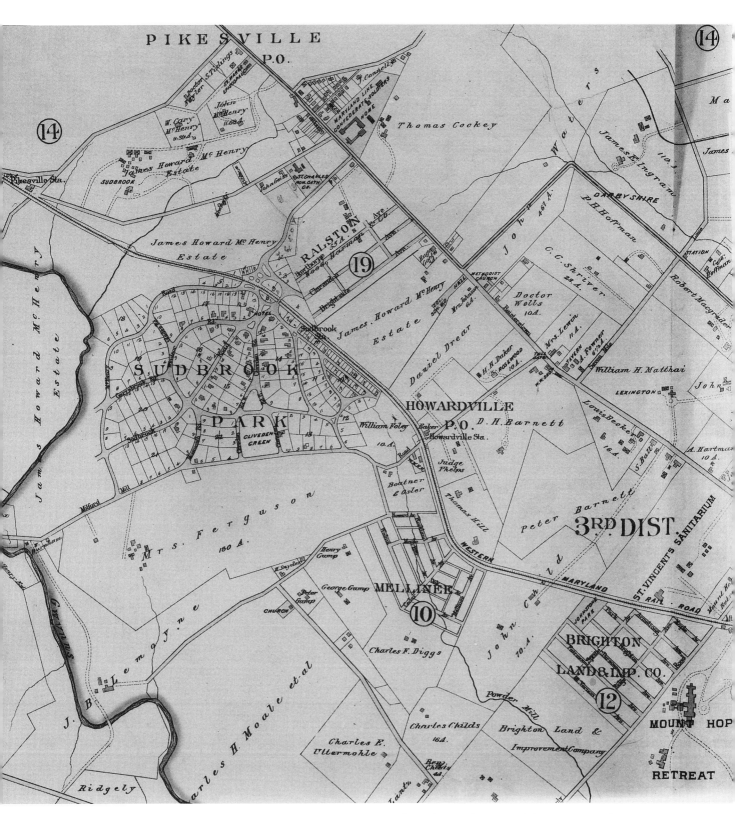

As can be seen by comparing Sudbrook with other 1898 developments, Olmsted's curvilinear road design contrasted starkly with the grid pattern that predominated. THE 1898 BROMLEY ATLAS OF BALTIMORE COUNTY, PLATE 14. COURTESY OF THE BALTIMORE COUNTY PUBLIC LIBRARY COLLECTION accentuated by the topography of the road, originally sunk in a slight depression to emphasize the visual impact of the landscape.

Curvilinear roads also promoted values that were important to Olmsted in a residential community. In his 1868 Preliminary Report on Riverside, Olmsted explained:

> [A]s the ordinary directness of line in town-streets, with its resultant
> regularity of plan would suggest eagerness to press forward, without
> looking to the right hand or the left, we should recommend the general
> adoption, in the design of your roads, of gracefully-curved lines,
> generous spaces, and the absence of sharp corners, the idea being to
> suggest and imply leisure, contemplativeness and happy tranquillity.[35]

As Beveridge has observed, Olmsted employed the curvilinear form not only for its beauty, but also because on a practical level, it discouraged through traffic and "enhanced the domestic atmosphere of the village by creating an enclosed, intimate space."[36]

Even gracefully curving roads would be of little value if they were not usable, and so Olmsted insisted that the roads in his communities be well paved, noting that "frost-proof, rain-proof wheelways and footways, let them cost what they will, should [be]…in planning a suburb, the first requirement to provide for."[37] In 1889, when Sudbrook was designed, "paved" usually meant macadam — crushed rock rolled firm and smooth with a steam roller. Olmsted also deemed cobblestone or turf gutters "absolutely indispensable" to keep his roads well-drained so that carriages could traverse them in good weather and bad, but stated that it must "be a chief object, if we desire [the community] to have a quiet rural character, to avoid anything like the ordinary high curb of the town streets, and to make the gutter as shallow and inconspicuous as…it can be."[38]

To Olmsted, sidewalks were necessary to provide access to scenery, and Sudbrook originally had them. The Sudbrook Company installed sidewalks on residents' property as soon as houses were built. These were described as wide, six-foot graveled walkways that were well-drained. Photographs of the original cottages show the sidewalks, but they are no longer visible in the older-house section. While it is possible that some were subsumed as roads were widened, others have been swallowed up by lawns over time.[39]

Olmsted's suburban designs always set aside a significant amount of public park land and open green space by recommending "the appropriation of some of the best of your property for public grounds.…Most of these should have the character of informal village-greens, commons and playgrounds, rather than of enclosed and defended parks or gardens. We would have, indeed, at frequent intervals in every road, an opening large enough for a natural group of trees.…" These open spaces were intended to promote neighborly cohesiveness and community spirit by providing an "open-air gathering for purposes of easy, friendly, unceremonious greetings…to which the people of a town, of all classes, harmoniously resort on equal terms." In addition, public areas were to be places for "occasional rural fetes and holiday recreations of families."[40]

Olmsted's plan for the 1,600-acre Riverside community provided for significant areas of public space, much of which has been preserved. Olmsted's plan for the 204-acre Sudbrook included an 8.5 acre public space called Cliveden Green. That area was eventually divided into lots and developed. Sudbrook has retained its configuration of open space triangles at its entranceway bridge, however, and some, but not all, of those that Olmsted provided elsewhere through the community. One of the larger entranceway triangles is still used for community gatherings and holiday events. In addition, an area along McHenry Road was never developed and has become a playground providing a large open recreational space for the community.

While Olmsted provided ample public room for communal activities, he was opposed to the creation of open "suburban parks" with houses in their midst and no indication of the boundary lines between properties. He favored fences or hedges to enclose private domestic space around the rear yard of each residence, creating what he called "private open-air apartments." In a letter to Edward Everett Hale,[41] Olmsted stated:

> The point I stand for is that no house is [a] fit place for a family that has not both public *& private outside apartments.* Consequently I am bound to regard the fence as a sort of outer wall of the house. I think that the want of fences, of distinct family separation out of the house, is the real cause of the ill-success or want of great success of…Llewellyn Park.[42] (Emphasis in original)

These photographs taken on Upland Road (left) and Sudbrook Lane (right) typify Sudbrook Park's "roads of continuous curvature." Olmsted drew his roads freehand, not using the tangent-curve-tangent method used in so many modern suburbs. PHOTOGRAPHS BY LEN FRANK.

The front yard between the road and the house, although private property, was to remain open. It would not only show the communal orientation of homeowners, but it would provide a transition between the two spaces — the public road and the private house.[43]

For the most part, Sudbrook follows Olmsted's intent as to fences and hedges, keeping front yards open as communal space and demarcating only rear and side boundaries. In good weather, residents out for a walk can often be seen talking to neighbors in their open front yards. As for its sense of neighborhood, Sudbrook has nurtured, from its earliest years, a sense of shared community. This is clear from the warm relationships that developed among residents, by numerous members of the same extended family choosing to reside in Sudbrook, by the early formation of a community association and its continuation in some form until the present, by the multiple generations of the same family that lived (and still live) in Sudbrook, and by the long-established holiday celebrations and parades that are still a part of Sudbrook's community life.

As a landscape architect *par excellence,* Olmsted placed great emphasis in his designs on the use and placement of trees and other vegetation, and usually selected certain types as necessary for the effect he desired. As Beveridge has noted, Olmsted created the picturesque style common in romantic suburbs by planting "profusely to secure greater richness and lushness of growth than nature would produce unaided."[44]

Early Sudbrook Park, viewed from the intersection of Cliveden Road and Sudbrook Lane, about 1893. Sidewalks along the road were an important component of an Olmsted suburb (they even traversed the triangle within the intersection), but none of Sudbrook's graveled sidewalks has survived. COURTESY OF THE COX FAMILY.

Olmsted's plans generally showed an overview of planting areas, but he usually also developed specific planting plans and sometimes nursery lists. Unfortunately, Olmsted's planting plans for Sudbrook have not been located. Neither the Olmsted firm correspondence nor the Sudbrook Company letters provides more than minor information. Yet, it is clear from seeing Sudbrook that it embodies Olmsted's characteristic planting scheme to a degree that could not have happened entirely naturally or by accident. Perhaps the planting plans will be found someday. Until then, various letters and Olmsted's cross-sections of roads give the only information we have about his landscaping intent for Sudbrook.

Whether designing a park or residential area, Olmsted separated or diffused the impact of different modes of transportation to keep distractions to a minimum and establish the tranquillity he sought to impart. In 1877, Olmsted's plan for local steam transit routes in parts of New York City called for placement of trains below grade at developed areas and streets. This was consistent with his solution to a similar problem years earlier in Central Park:

> The commissioners had stipulated that four commercial roads must traverse the park's width. To nullify that menace, Olmsted and Vaux decided to sink them below the level of the footpaths and carriage drives, which would pass over the roads by bridges blending so gently with the park that visitors scarcely would notice the four commercial incisions ….By keeping every form of locomotion independent and self-contained, Olmsted hoped…to relieve the park's visitors of "anxiety"….Irritation and fretfulness…were absolutely fatal to his fundamental principle: "to recreate the mind from urban oppression through the eye."[45]

In his residential communities, Olmsted often recessed the roads slightly, minimizing their intrusion on the landscape. In Sudbrook, both a pedestrian and a carriage bridge were planned to cross over the tracks of the Western Maryland Railroad, thus minimizing noise and inconvenience from the train. A grade crossing was placed near the Sudbrook Company's freight siding so that supplies and building materials could be unloaded conveniently.

Although Olmsted's suburban designs were primarily for the more affluent middle class, which comprised the market for developers who could afford to hire him, "he wished to extend the benefits of his planning concepts more broadly."[46] One way he achieved this was by deliberately placing smaller lots in his residential designs of Riverside and Sudbrook, in contrast to the prevailing social custom of separating residential areas for the wealthy from those for the not-so-wealthy. While the smaller lots were placed in a less desirable location along the railroad track, their mere inclusion was unusual for those times. The inclusion of smaller lots allowed younger and less affluent families to enjoy the beauty and benefits of an Olmsted community. These families might, as their size or means grew, move within the community to a larger home. In Sudbrook, this pattern has been repeated many times over and still continues.[47]

Another design element employed by Olmsted was to clearly demarcate the boundaries of a community to establish its separateness. Olmsted's plan for Sudbrook included an approach road from Pikesville (the current Sudbrook Lane) that led to the station. The station was to be used not only by residents, but would be available to persons living in the surrounding area. The main approach continued beyond the station around a curve to an entranceway bridge going over the tracks into the heart of the community. The constricted bridge was a design component of the community, beyond which five roads fanned out broadly like streamers, weaving and looping and tying the parts of the plan into a cohesive whole. Sudbrook's bridge and distinctive road pattern clearly delineated the community's boundaries.

One of the most important aspects of Olmsted's plans for residential communities was his insistence that developers incorporate deed restrictions to protect the master plan and moderate the impact of poor architectural design. In his Preliminary Report on Riverside, Olmsted previewed his still-developing thoughts on restrictions, noting:

> We cannot judiciously attempt to control the form of the houses which
> men shall build, we can only, at most, take care that if they build very
> ugly and inappropriate houses, they shall not be allowed to force them
> disagreeably upon our attention when we desire to pass along the road
> upon which they stand. We can require that no house shall be built
> within a certain number of feet of the highway, and we can insist that
> each house-holder shall maintain one or two living trees between his
> house and his highway-line.[48]

The deeds for the sale of property at Riverside required purchasers to build within a year (to guard against speculative buying), mandated that the house cost at least three thousand dollars (to establish a minimum standard of cost, if not design), and required that houses be situated at least thirty feet from the front of the lot line and that the front thirty feet be retained as an open court or "door yard" (to provide public space for the neighborhood and indicate the communal orientation of house owners).[49]

In planning Sudbrook twenty years later, Olmsted with his adopted son and partner, John Charles Olmsted, further expanded the number and scope of proposed restrictions. The Olmsteds suggested sixteen restrictions and the Sudbrook Company included these, with minor variations, in the deeds to the houses it sold. In addition to stipulating the minimum cost of a house, the restrictions governed lot size, detailed the required setbacks, the height and style of house and other permitted outbuildings, set up sanitary provisions as to sewerage and animal waste disposal, restricted the number and type of animals that could be kept, required residential use only and prohibited subdividing lots into less than an acre. The Olmsteds considered such restrictions "a part of a plan for a suburb as truly as certain lines on paper."[50]

Sudbrook's deed restrictions were intended to protect the master plan, to safeguard the residential character of the neighborhood, and to provide for water, sewerage and similar sanitary requirements by mutual agreement, since at the time there were no public utilities available for residents of Sudbrook. Sudbrook's restrictions, adopted by the Company in 1889 and incorporated in all early deeds, are believed to be the first comprehensive land-use requirements in Maryland.[51] Zoning regulations for Baltimore County were not adopted until 50 years later.[52]

A man ahead of his time, Olmsted intended his suburban designs to insure "permanent health-fulness and permanent rural beauty."[53] In the second half of the nineteenth century, healthfulness was almost synonymous with the use of appropriate sanitary practices. Pasteur had introduced his germ theory in 1862. A widespread cholera epidemic in 1866, as well as the spread of typhoid among clusters of residents in cities, made evident that public health was dependent, in large part, upon adequate water and sanitary sewage systems.[54]

Looking southwesterly on Sudbrook Lane, about 1890. Olmsted designed Sudbrook's roads to be sunk slightly below the land's surface, in order to minimize the intrusion on the landscape. (508 Sudbrook Lane is partially visible). FROM *SUDBROOK COMPANY BROCHURE. COURTESY OF ROGER KATZENBERG.*

Olmsted's experience as administrator of Central Park had introduced him to Col. George E. Waring, Jr., a well-known agriculturist and sanitary engineer. Waring had been responsible for constructing the "thorough drainage" system used in Central Park.[55] "Thorough drainage," according to Waring, was "of the sort employed in the agricultural improvement of land;" its intent was to keep fields, roads, walks, house foundations, cellars and the like dry.[56] When soil was not of a type to drain naturally and quickly, drainage could be accomplished by laying a subsurface system of agricultural tiles to carry water away.

Waring also advocated a complete system of house drainage, claiming that "the first aim of the householder himself should be to secure a perfect means for carrying safely beyond the walls of his domicile everything of a dangerous character that is generated or produced within it, and to secure his living-rooms against the entrance of any manner of foul air, impure water, or excessive dampness."[57]

Olmsted felt that the adoption of proper sanitary engineering principles was vital for the health of a community. His views were strengthened by his observations as executive director of the U.S. Sanitary Commission, when he saw firsthand the results of less-than-adequate sanitary provisions during the Civil War. Since early suburban communities often were not linked to city water or sewer systems, provisions for these systems had to be made. Olmsted favored communally provided facilities when possible, and at both Riverside and Sudbrook, the developers supplied these services. Sudbrook implemented house, sewer and ground water drainage systems developed by Waring.[58]

The residential suburbs that Olmsted planned were much more than just houses set amidst a bucolic landscape. As architect and urban designer Michael Robinson has noted, such suburbs "were

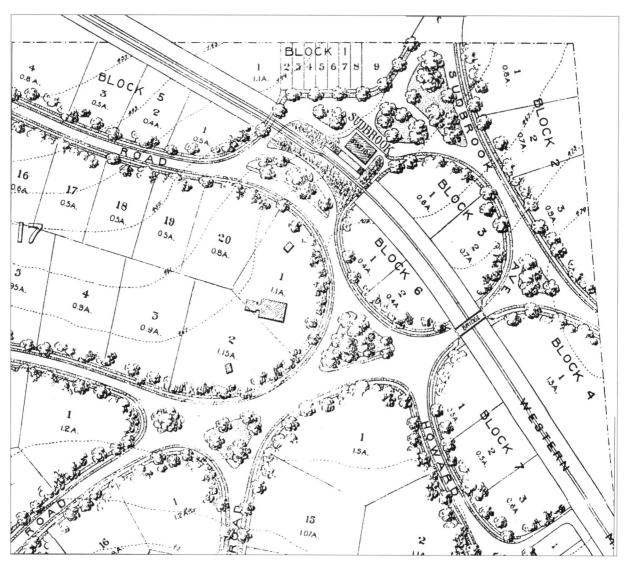

Detail of the 1889 Olmsted Plan for Sudbrook, showing (l–r), the location of the freight siding (which also served as a grade crossing), the railroad station, the pedestrian bridge between the railroad station and Block 3, and the carriage bridge between Blocks 3 and 4. COURTESY OF THE NATIONAL PARK SERVICE, FREDERICK LAW OLMSTED NATIONAL HISTORIC SITE.

distinctive because they were planned and developed as a total, harmonious unit." Not only is Sudbrook one of only three preserved examples of a suburban community designed by Olmsted, Sr., but its influence has had a ripple effect on later suburban development in the region.

In Sudbrook's surrounding area, suburbs such as Harden Heights, Cedarwood Estates, Gwynnvale, Dumbarton, and Stevenson employ a curvilinear street design that follows the natural contours of the land. Others, such as Colonial Village, Villa Nova and Lochearn include fewer curving streets, but clearly abandon the strict grid pattern and seem to adapt roads to the natural land contours. In addition, a number of suburbs designed and developed in the Baltimore metropolitan region soon after 1889 (such as Plat 1 of Roland Park designed by George Kessler; Ruxton Heights, Windsor Hills and Eden Terrace), and of course those developed by the Olmsted firm when Olmsted, Sr., was no longer active (Plats 2 and 3 of Roland Park, Guilford, Homeland, Dundalk, Northwood, Gibson Island),

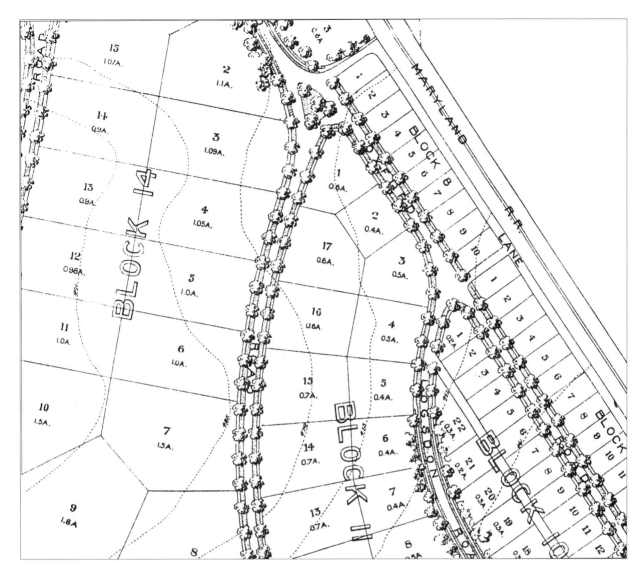

As can be seen in this detail of the 1889 Plan for Sudbrook, Olmsted included smaller lots of one-fifth of an acre along with lots of an acre or more. The area shown includes what is now Westover Road and a portion of Howard and Greenwood Roads. COURTESY OF THE NATIONAL PARK SERVICE, FREDERICK LAW OLMSTED NATIONAL HISTORIC SITE.

adopted one or more attributes identical or similar to those introduced by Sudbrook, including paved curvilinear streets, public green space, profuse plantings, use of the Waring system for sewers and drainage, and many of the same or similar deed restrictions.

While some similarities may be coincidental, Olmsted's influence can hardly be doubted. Olmsted was, after all, the pre-eminent landscape architect of his time. Included among his designs were parks or park systems for New York City, Buffalo, Rochester, Chicago, Boston, Montreal, and Louisville, Kentucky; residential communities such as Riverside, Sudbrook and Druid Hills; the United States Capitol Grounds; academic campuses such as Stanford University (whose Mission style was adopted by many subsequent California schools), Cornell College, American University, Gallaudet College and Yale University; scenic preservations, such as the Niagara Reservation and a plan to preserve the Yosemite Valley; and private estates, the most famous being Biltmore in North Carolina. After his retirement and death, his design legacy was carried on by his stepson and son in the firm he founded.[59]

Olmsted's plans and design principles for suburban communities, introduced at Riverside twenty years before Sudbrook, became the much-emulated model for nineteenth century romantic suburbs, aspects of which found their way into many twentieth century suburban developments. Olmsted's designs were influential in shaping the American landscape and its early suburban frontier. That Sudbrook played an important role as one of the earliest planned suburbs in the Baltimore region is certain.

The story of how Sudbrook came into existence is, in many ways, reminiscent of the pattern of Olmsted's early life — a series of starts and stops, plans and detours, adventures and misadventures, with just a touch of mystery for those who might like to probe further.

Chapter 2

JAMES HOWARD MCHENRY'S "SUDBROOK"

The 1877 Atlas of Baltimore [p. 20] shows a marked contrast between Baltimore City's darkly shaded grid of streets and the expanse of largely undeveloped land comprising Baltimore County's thirteen districts. To be sure, the county was by no means entirely undeveloped in 1877, but according to the Atlas' 1870 census figures, Baltimore City had 250,000 people residing in an area just over eleven square miles, while Baltimore County's combined thirteen districts had fewer than one-third as many people (65,346) residing in an area that was more than fifty-seven times larger.[1] As urban congestion increased in the second half of the nineteenth century, more and more Baltimoreans of means began looking toward the outlying areas to escape from crowded and often unsanitary conditions in the city.

One Baltimorean who purchased extensive acreage in the Pikesville area of Baltimore County in the 1850s was James Howard McHenry. McHenry came from a family that was well-known for its distinguished service to Maryland and the nation. His paternal grandfather, James McHenry (1753–1816), was a physician and a statesman. In the Revolutionary War, he served on the Marquis de Lafayette's staff, as secretary to General George Washington, and as a surgeon. He was in the Maryland legislature for thirteen years, sat in the Continental Congress, represented Maryland at the Constitutional Convention, and served as Secretary of War under Presidents George Washington and John Adams. Baltimore's Fort McHenry was named in his honor.[2]

McHenry's maternal grandfather, Col. John Eager Howard (1752–1827), was a Maryland Revolutionary War hero who later was elected to the Continental Congress and became the fifth governor of the State of Maryland, serving three one-year terms (1788–1791). Subsequently, he was elected to the United States Senate for nine years. The sixth of eleven children of Cornelius and Ruth (Eager) Howard, John Eager Howard was born and grew up on land that was settled by his grandfather and included the area now known as Grey Rock, near Pikesville.[3] Later, he inherited extensive sections of the west central section of the city from the Eager family, through his mother. His estate, "Belvidere," was located near what is now Calvert and Chase Streets; during his lifetime, his property was considered the outermost limit of the city and children were warned not to venture into or beyond "Howard's Woods." Col. Howard gave the city a 200-square foot parcel from his estate for its Washington Monument on Charles Street. In 1831, the four surrounding parks were created when Howard's heirs donated additional land to the city.[4]

Col. Howard's daughter Juliana married John McHenry, son of the famous statesman, in December 1819 at Belvidere. Their only child, James Howard McHenry, was born at Belvidere on

Shown as a young man, James Howard McHenry was a descendant of a distinguished Maryland family and a gentleman farmer. He amassed a large estate in the Pikesville area which he called "Sudbrook." COURTESY OF BALTIMORE COUNTY PUBLIC LIBRARY COLLECTION.

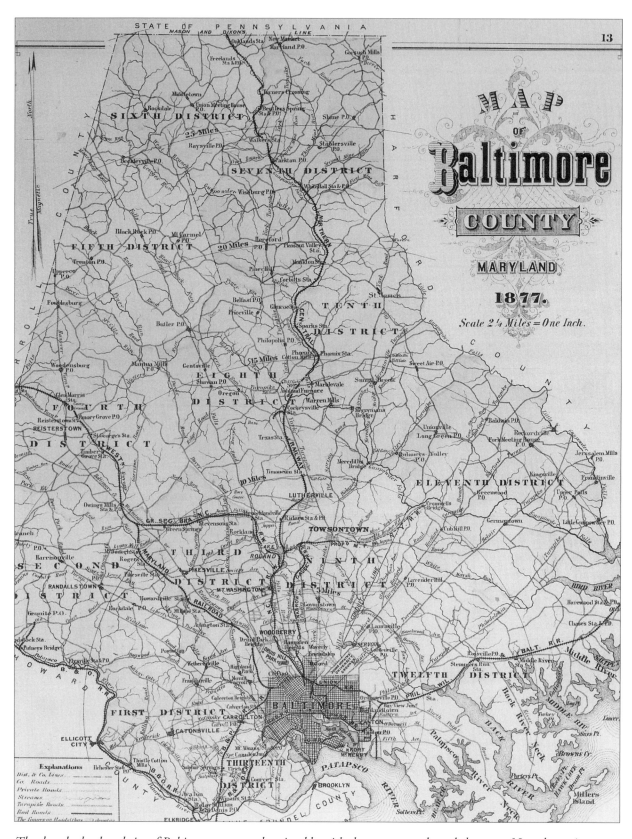

The densely developed city of Baltimore contrasted noticeably with the more sparsely settled county. Note the major railroad lines that linked outlying areas with the city. THE 1877 HOPKINS ATLAS, DETAIL OF THE THIRD DISTRICT OF BALTIMORE COUNTY. COURTESY OF THE BALTIMORE COUNTY PUBLIC LIBRARY COLLECTION.

Baltimore's Washington Monument, erected on land donated to the city by McHenry's grandfather Col. John Eager Howard, once grandly towered over the stately homes nearby and the city beyond. "View of Baltimore, 1850."
COURTESY OF MARYLAND HISTORICAL SOCIETY.

October 11, 1820. Seven months later, Juliana McHenry died at the age of twenty-five.[5] Five months after that, her thirty-one year old husband died of bilious fever.[6] Before the age of two, young J. Howard McHenry was left an orphan. He was raised by Mrs. John Ridgely of Hampton, his aunt, who sent him to school in Geneva, Switzerland. McHenry later graduated from Princeton University and Harvard Law School.[7] A passport issued when McHenry was almost twenty-five described him as five feet, eleven-and-a-half inches tall with hazel eyes, dark brown hair, oval face and ruddy complexion.[8]

After completing his formal education, McHenry traveled extensively. Journals from 1845 to 1852 relate his trips to South America, Marseilles, Paris, England, Italy, Constantinople, Malta and Cadiz.[9] Before embarking on his travels, McHenry sold property which he had inherited from his grandfather, Col. John Eager Howard, at No. 11 West Mt. Vernon Place.[10] In 1852, perhaps feeling that it was time to settle down, McHenry began to purchase

Sarah Nicholas Cary McHenry. Sally and James Howard McHenry had seven children, five of whom lived beyond early childhood. In addition to residing at their Sudbrook estate (which Sally sometimes complained was too isolated and remote from friends in the city), they often stayed in Baltimore city and lived abroad for a time. COURTESY OF THE BALTIMORE COUNTY PUBLIC LIBRARY COLLECTION.

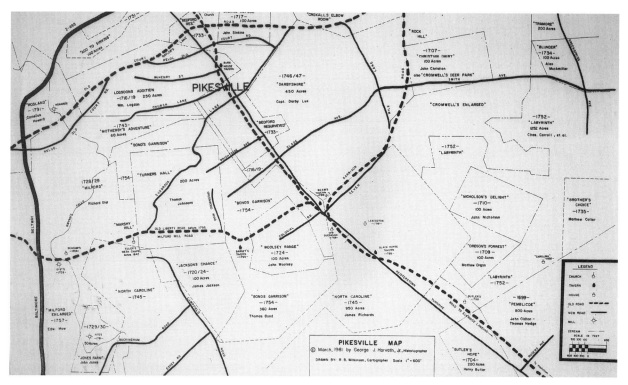

The Wilkenson 1799 map of Pikesville, with several major current roads superimposed to provide perspective. McHenry purchased land in Logsdons Addition, Motherby's Adventure, Bond's Garrison and Turner's Hall, among other sites.

COURTESY OF THE MARYLAND STATE ARCHIVES. SPECIAL COLLECTIONS (MARYLAND STATE ARCHIVES MAP COLLECTION) MSA SC 1427-778.

numerous parcels of land in the Pikesville area, eventually amassing an estate of 850 to 1,000 acres.[11] McHenry's estate, which he called "Sudbrook," was situated on both sides of Old Court Road southwest of the current Reisterstown Road.[12]

In June 1855, at the age of thirty-five, McHenry married Sarah Nicholas Cary. Sally, as she was called, was said to be "a cultivated, particularly charming lady, noted among other attributes for her infectious laugh."[13] Judging from receipts that McHenry retained, the newlyweds spent their first fall and winter in Europe.[14] Upon returning to Baltimore, McHenry had a home built on his Sudbrook estate.[15] When completed, the estate included "a large gray stone house…stables, hot houses, a grapery and all the requirements for a luxurious, hospitable country life….[McHenry also] had a passion for blooded stock and had the finest herd of Jerseys and Devons in Maryland."[16] Sally McHenry gave birth to seven children between 1856 and 1871 — Juliana, James (who died when he was ten months old), W. Cary, Ellen, John, Sophia and C. Howard.[17]

McHenry either did not keep journals between 1860 and 1870 or none survive, although his scrapbooks with news clippings, receipts, memoranda and correspondence during that period provide some insight into his life and travels. While there have been accounts that McHenry took his family abroad during the Civil War (1861 to 1865), McHenry's own papers and accounts of his activities indicate that he and his family remained in Baltimore during the war.[18] The McHenrys did, however, live abroad from November 1867 to July 1869, apparently in France and England.[19] It is clear from one of McHenry's letters during that time that he and his wife had sympathized with the South during the earlier conflict.[20] Writing to a physician whose house they appear to have rented in Brighton, McHenry stated:

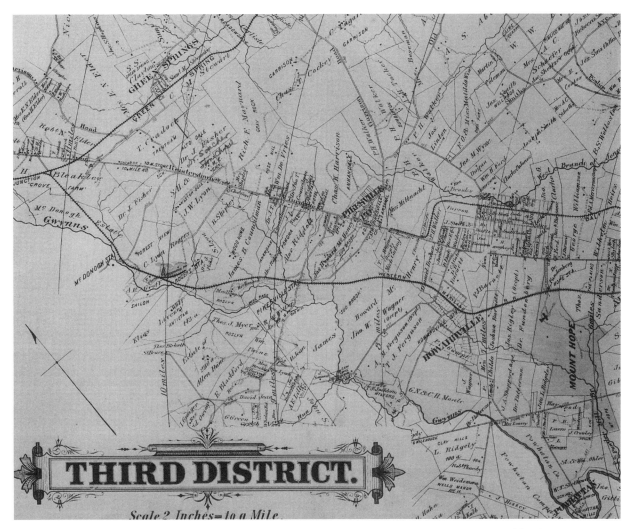

James Howard McHenry's "Sudbrook" estate contained over 850 acres. After 1873, it was traversed by the Western Maryland Railroad; the route of the horse-car line can be seen above and into Pikesville. Eugene Blackford, McHenry's friend and later manager of Sudbrook Park, owned a 100-acre estate, located southwest from Sudbrook. THE 1877 HOPKINS ATLAS, DETAIL OF THE THIRD DISTRICT OF BALTIMORE COUNTY. COURTESY OF THE BALTIMORE COUNTY PUBLIC LIBRARY COLLECTION.

I ought however to explain that whilst Mrs. McHenry and I claim to be Southerners in feeling, we do not come from those of the Southern States that were desecrated by the war. We are from Maryland, a state about centrally situated on the seaboard but one the large majority of whose inhabitants sympathized during the war with the South. The State government was however at an early stage of the game deposed by the Federal forces and the State thereafter remained nominally and apparently loyal, as it was called, to the Federal government. Very many young men joined the Southern armies…I therefore whilst not hesitating to avow my sympathies for the Southern cause in America, do not claim in the character of a sufferer by the war, immunity from

The McHenrys' home at Sudbrook. The house was designed by Baltimore architect Edmund Lind in the 1850s and was situated between what is now Old Court Road and Church Lane, north of Greenwood Road and south of Glenback Avenue. It no longer survives. COURTESY OF THE BALTIMORE COUNTY PUBLIC LIBRARY COLLECTION.

the usual obligations of society....[noting that he would remit the full amount of money owed].[21]

By August 1869 the McHenrys had returned to Sudbrook from England. J. Howard McHenry easily embraced the busy, multifaceted life of a gentleman farmer. An avid reader, McHenry compiled a personal library and subscribed to numerous periodicals, including *The Horticulturist, The Practical Farmer, Eclectic, Scientific American, The Nation, The Country Gentleman* and *Gardeners' Monthly.*[22] He regularly took the train to Philadelphia for meetings of the Jersey Cattle Club and to judge livestock exhibitions. He kept meticulous track of the horses and cattle that he purchased, bred, exhibited and sold. McHenry often had business in New York and on each visit he noted in his journal that he drove through Central Park. He also sat on a number of boards. For many years he was a trustee of the Maryland Agricultural College, on the board of the Maryland Home of Instruction for the Blind, and a director on the boards of both the Baltimore and Reisterstown Turnpike Road and the Baltimore, Pimlico & Pikesville Railroad Co. In addition to his directorships, McHenry owned a number of rental

The drawing room at Sudbrook. The McHenrys frequently entertained friends and visitors at their Sudbrook estate, which was decorated with fashionable and ornate furnishings purchased in their travels abroad. COURTESY OF THE BALTIMORE COUNTY PUBLIC LIBRARY COLLECTION.

properties in the city and in Pikesville.[23] These properties were managed by McHenry's agent and friend, Thomas Hill.

In addition to his other commitments, McHenry and his wife maintained an active social life. They regularly attended performances, balls and the opera in the city; entertained guests at their estate; and frequently visited relatives and owners of neighboring estates.[24] Although his writings seldom betray emotion, McHenry clearly was devoted to his own family as well as to a number of close relatives and friends.[25] He was intensely interested in the education and upbringing of his children.[26] The McHenrys enjoyed traveling: summer vacations took them to Cape May or Bar Harbor; they were known to visit White Sulphur Springs in West Virginia, and occasionally they traveled abroad.

At that time, the area around Green Spring Valley, Garrison Forest and Pikesville contained a number of large farming estates. Motivated by an interest in productivity and improved farming techniques, the owners of these estates formed an agricultural society called the Garrison Forest Farmers' Club in April 1874.[27] One of McHenry's long-standing friends and a fellow Farmers' Club member was

Eugene Blackford. Blackford, who owned a 100-acre farming estate called "Cleve" near Sudbrook, would later play a pivotal role in the development of Sudbrook Park.

McHenry's surviving correspondence, memoranda and journals — while extensive in many respects — leave gaps during certain time periods and contain a fair number of undated notes, lists and ruminations. Read in totality, however, they show a man intent on improving himself, his family, his farming estate and the world around him, as well as a man of vision who actively involved himself in important issues of the day. By 1870 McHenry showed an interest in the concept of a suburban village and worked to secure the transportation links between Pikesville and the city of Baltimore that would be necessary for such an enterprise to succeed — obviously hoping to benefit his own investments and property in the process.

In May 1869 Thomas Hill wrote to McHenry in London, enclosing a letter soliciting McHenry "to subscribe again to the Union Railroad" in an effort to obtain a rail line to Pikesville. Hill informed McHenry that all local railroad projects were at a standstill and that Hill doubted the ability of the solicitor to do what he proposed, adding: "If he can, I would help him or anybody else who can get a railroad made to Pikesville or near it."[28]

By March 1870 the prospect of a railroad link between Pikesville and the city had appeared, but the Union Railroad was not involved. Instead, officials of the Western Maryland Railroad and its new president began visiting McHenry, who had returned from abroad, at his Sudbrook estate. Discussions centered on "the location of the road," the lines to be run by surveyors and McHenry's "disposition as to right-of-way."[29] Initial surveying work on McHenry's estate got underway in June and resumed in December.[30]

As plans for the long-hoped-for railroad connection progressed, McHenry took the opportunity to view Olmsted's earliest masterpiece when he visited New York City's Central Park. Before returning to Sudbrook, McHenry went to Orange, New Jersey, "by invitation of Mr. Haskell, owner of Llewellyn Park, to drive with him through his Park which he has laid off into drives, walks and building lots and has made an attractive spot."[31]

Llewellyn Park began in 1853 as a forty-acre estate that was Haskell's own residence; by 1870 when McHenry visited, Haskell had enlarged it to almost 750 acres. One of the first and most influential suburbs in the United States to be planned according to Andrew Jackson Downing's precepts,[32] it included a large centrally-located park or open space, a gently curving road pattern and densely planted avenues of shade trees. The plan had sites to accommodate one hundred families (on lots varying in size from one to twenty acres). There were no fences separating the properties, giving it the effect of a single large landscaped estate.[33]

McHenry clearly entertained the idea of creating some kind of suburban village on his Sudbrook property, but he knew that the success of any venture so far removed from the city depended on there being convenient transportation linkages between Pikesville and Baltimore; at the time, there were none. McHenry's first journal entry of 1871 stated: "The opening year finds me and my family (my wife and five children) at Sudbrook." The children had lessons from Mademoiselle Naejely, who lived with them. To get into town, McHenry mentioned two forms of transportation — his private conveyances and the omnibus, a large four-wheeled carriage drawn by a team of horses that was available to the public. (The omnibus may have been noteworthy as the "first feeble attempt at mass transportation" but it has been described as "uncomfortable and slow."[34])

McHenry continued meeting with officials of the Western Maryland Railroad and in April, surveyors began working again on the line through Sudbrook. McHenry attended the daily inquisition by a jury summoned by the railroad to condemn the right-of-way through neighboring property owners' land, but reported that he had settled with the Western Maryland Railroad "very nearly on terms proposed by me."[35]

A pressing issue with the Western Maryland Railroad appeared to be the location of the station; McHenry had on-going meetings with railroad officials, as well as with Eugene Blackford and other neighbors to discuss the matter. The installation of the railroad line and station necessitated that the county road on McHenry's property be relocated and surveying work began on that. McHenry involved Blackford in many of his discussions regarding the location of the station and the opening and closing of various county roads. After much negotiation, McHenry reached an agreement with the railroad about the station, agreeing to locate it "near Gen. Howard's entrance gate" (which became the Pikesville or "Roslyn" station) if the railroad would change the line of the road and "induce others to agree to the closing of the County road in front of my house."[36] In September, McHenry traveled to New Jersey, New York, Rhode Island, and Boston.[37] While in Newport, he met with Col. George E. Waring, who had worked with Olmsted in designing the drainage system for Central Park.[38] At the time of McHenry's visit, Waring was a prominent agriculturist and drainage engineer, who managed Ogden Farm near Newport from about 1865–75. A prolific writer, Waring wrote numerous books and hundreds of articles and pamphlets about scientific agricultural techniques and the sanitary drainage of houses and towns.[39] McHenry and Waring shared common interests in improving farming and drainage techniques; the two corresponded with each other over a period of years.

With the birth of a new baby in October 1871, the McHenrys apparently decided to spend that winter in town. McHenry kept only a partial journal that year and noted only one meeting regarding the railroad to Pikesville. He returned to his Sudbrook house at the end of March, driving out in his carriage while his helper took the omnibus. McHenry also remained in communication with Col. Waring.[40]

The McHenrys and their three youngest children remained at Sudbrook over the winter of 1872–73, while the three oldest stayed in town during the week with their grandmother. McHenry himself was extremely busy on a number of fronts during 1873. He was visited by Col. Waring, who seemed primarily interested in McHenry's stock and barns. He continued to meet with Western Maryland Railroad engineers regarding the station and the bridging of the railroad for the new county road.[41] He also purchased land in Pikesville, "hoping to get the passenger railroad company [the Baltimore, Pimlico & Pikesville horse-car line] to use it as a terminus." At a Directors' meeting of the Baltimore, Pimlico & Pikesville Railroad Company, McHenry "received much encouragement to hope that the road will soon be built to Pikesville" and he subsequently met with the directors again "to walk over the proposed extension of the line to Pikesville and endeavor to obtain the right of way."[42] This horse-car railroad was running "at irregular intervals" by 1873 along what became Park Heights Avenue between the present Park Circle and Rogers Avenue.[43] By 1875 the Directors of the railroad were discussing "the importance of the proposed [extension of the] road to those persons whose land it would pass through or near." They estimated that the cost of constructing the extension from Rogers Avenue to Pikesville, a distance of two and a half miles, would be about $16,000.[44]

By 1876 the Baltimore, Pimlico & Pikesville Railroad was not yet completed to Pikesville. A "Report to the Stockholders" in July pointed out that it was incumbent upon the company to find ways to lessen its indebtedness, since it was "competing with a parallel steam railway" (the Western Maryland

Railroad) and still had "an uncompleted road, without a proper terminus, and in these times of depression."[45] The horse-car line did not reach to Pikesville until about 1877.[46]

While the horse-car line struggled to extend its route to Pikesville, the Western Maryland Railroad had completed an addition to its line from Owings Mills to the city in December 1873.[47] By 1878, McHenry and members of his family were taking the train to town almost every day: the railroad had become an integral part of their lives. There were apparently five trains daily — 7:43 a.m., 8:10 a.m., 9:47 a.m., 2:16 p.m., and 4:00 p.m. McHenry regularly took the 9:47 a.m. train into town and the 4:00 p.m. train back to Sudbrook (spending the day at his office in the B&O Building). On occasion, McHenry or his son John would return by the "Pimlico cars" (the horse-car railway), which had by then completed its extension and had a terminus near the Pikesville Arsenal on the Reisterstown Turnpike Road. McHenry still had his coachman, Henry, who would take Sally McHenry and their children to and from the city for shopping, school and other activities. The family attended St. Mark's-on-the-Hill Episcopal Church in nearby Pikesville (and on occasion St. Thomas Episcopal Church, farther out in Garrison); McHenry attended monthly meetings of the Garrison Forest Farmers' Club; and the McHenrys and Blackfords still visited regularly and frequently dined together.[48]

Between 1873 and 1878, as transportation links between Sudbrook and the city materialized, McHenry made a series of attempts to initiate development of a suburban village on his estate. The initial overture came in the spring of 1873, when McHenry invited G.A. Roullier, "Civil Engineer & Surveyor" from Flushing, Long Island, to visit "for consultation about the subdivision improvement of Sudbrook."[49] McHenry and Roullier apparently reached some agreement between themselves, because Roullier returned to New York only long enough to bring his wife to Pikesville. Roullier worked for McHenry throughout much of 1873 and would continue to work for him, on occasion, over the next ten years.[50]

Double-decker omnibuses like this, about 1880, were drawn by horses. They were an early attempt to provide mass transportation. Hired help rode in the upper level. COURTESY OF THE BALTIMORE COUNTY PUBLIC LIBRARY COLLECTION.

McHenry's plans for turning his Sudbrook estate into a residential suburb suffered a setback almost immediately. No sooner had Roullier begun surveying when McHenry's resources unexpectedly had to be diverted to assist relatives in financial difficulty, possibly as a result of the Panic of 1873, a depression precipitated when several important Eastern banks failed. Heidleberg Farm in northern Baltimore County, mortgaged by McHenry's Aunt Read (whose note he had endorsed), was put up for sale after default in the payment of interest and sold for $5,000, "there being only one bid, that of Mr. Thos. Hill for me." McHenry recorded that he had "to make good some ten or eleven thousand dollars which I may be able to get out of the property by selling it in small lots." He took Roullier to see the Heidleberg property "with a view to subdivision."[51] The following year, McHenry's Aunt Sophia McHenry wrote him that her son Ramsey had been unable to get a loan and she would be forced to "look forward to financial ruin."[52] It appears that McHenry stepped in to assist.

Despite, or perhaps because of, these financial setbacks, McHenry continued to pursue his idea of developing a suburban village on his Sudbrook estate. An 1875 letter from Samuel Chew, a relative of McHenry's, lauded the idea:

> If I ever become a man of leisure I shall have great pleasure in visiting
> you at your Country place. I have heard that you have an admirably well
> devised plan for turning your farm into a Park for the common pleasure
> of several houses projected, and think that the idea is very clever.[53]

Prior to this time, McHenry had communicated his development plans to one F.W. Poppey, a landscape gardener in Poughkeepsie, New York, who had previously met Olmsted and worked on projects designed by him. In a letter to McHenry, Poppey informed him that he would soon be moving to San Francisco, having been named Chief Landscape Gardener "to lay out the extension Parks in contemplation." Poppey noted that he had been "especially recommended for this unique and interesting work on account of my experience in southern and arid countries" and thought that his appointment would reassure McHenry that he had, indeed, "thus far corresponded with perhaps the right man for your plans."[54] (Although Poppey's letter did not provide details, it was Olmsted who had recommended Poppey to the Park Commission of San Francisco and William Hammond Hall, the Park's Engineer and Superintendent. Upon learning who had been his benefactor, Poppey immediately wrote to thank Olmsted, calling him his "Guardian Angel.")[55]

During 1875 and 1876, McHenry intensified his inquiries and efforts toward developing a suburban village.[56] He studied the subject of macadam roads and "how to make such a road through districts in which no stone is to be found."[57] He was informed by his cousin, John Eager Howard, that the Western Maryland Railroad was "about to commence the erection of a big hotel" in Oakland, Garrett County, as part of a summer resort it was developing on its line.[58]

McHenry continued to correspond with Col. Waring, at one point apparently trying to interest Waring in being a partner or working on McHenry's plan to develop a suburban village. Waring politely turned him down:

> I have your letter of December 14. If I were situated as I was at
> the time we conversed about your property, I should be very glad
> to undertake to do something with it, but my time is now so fully

occupied with literary work and engineering, that I am obliged to let many necessary duties take their chances of being performed by others, and have decided not to branch out in any new directions.

It ought not to be difficult to raise funds for such an enterprise as yours after business revives, as it seems to me that it must do before long, but I doubt whether an effort to raise the necessary money now would result in success.[59]

Perhaps because Waring, the most prominent "sanitary engineer" of his day, was not available to help with drainage and sewerage systems for a suburban community, McHenry had to find another way to provide communal utilities. He wrote to Plymouth County in Massachusetts for information about their township system, possibly thinking that the implementation of a township system would be a way to assure necessary utility systems for his suburban village.[60]

On July 20, 1876, McHenry initiated what would prove to be a propitious connection: he wrote to Frederick Law Olmsted, Sr. about the possibility of developing his Sudbrook property with Olmsted's plans and assistance:

A Baltimore, Pimlico & Pikesville Railroad horse-car, about 1885, waits for passengers on Reisterstown Road at Walker Avenue. The Burnt House Tavern, which McHenry owned, can be seen behind the horse-drawn commercial cart.
COURTESY OF THE BALTIMORE COUNTY PUBLIC LIBRARY COLLECTION.

I have for some years had under consideration a project for the subdivision of a property of more than eight hundred acres in extent,
that I own at the distance of about six miles from the limits of
Baltimore City. I had once a short interview with you on this subject,
but found you very busy with other matters and I subsequently
employed for about a year a young surveyor [Roullier] who laid off
the entire property with great care and cross sectioned a portion of it.
The land is rolling and partly wooded and has a good stream of water
sufficient to turn a mill flowing through it. A turnpike road leading
to Baltimore touches it [on] one side; a railroad running in summer
five regular trains a day in each direction has a station upon it; the
neighbourhood is considered very healthy.

  I am not prepared however to make from my present income
extensive or expensive improvements, but I should be glad to make
arrangements with a capitalist to have the property subdivided and
improved under your direction upon terms, either of repayment of a loan
to be secured by mortgage at the end of a period of say five years, or of
an interest in the results, as might be agreed upon. Much capital is now
lying idle. An investment in real estate at a low valuation must be in all
probability safe if not likely to be immediately profitable and you may
know of persons who would be glad to make such an investment on
your recommendation and on condition that the money should be
expended on the land according to your plans.[61]

In response to McHenry's inquiry, Olmsted responded that he saw "no prospect of being able to
assist you in the manner suggested in your…[letter]. I shall be happy to advise you as to the laying out of
your property or to make plans for it whenever you shall be prepared to make use of my services."[62]

In September, McHenry wrote that he expected to be in New York in a week or two and hoped
to meet with Olmsted.[63] Olmsted responded, agreeing to meet McHenry when he came to New York.[64]
A letter to McHenry the following month stated that Olmsted had arranged with Jacob Weidenmann, a
noted landscape architect who often worked with Olmsted,[65] to visit McHenry "at any time you may
appoint within a month from this time."[66] It must have come as a surprise to Olmsted when, about a
week later, McHenry wrote:

I have given the question of the fitness of the time for commencing the
improvement of my property much thought — and have been unable
to feel warranted in undertaking even preliminary work at present.

  I understood you to say in New York that you would speak
of my project to a landscape gardener with whom you had frequently
worked and in whose capacity you had confidence, who would be able
to come on to see my property, on much lower terms than those that
you name for your own services. You did not name Mr. Weidenmann
but I presume from your note…that it was to him that you referred…

and I do not find that the conditions of his visit differ from those that govern similar visits by yourself, according to the printed statement sent to me not long ago.[67]

McHenry apparently had had second thoughts since first contacting Olmsted; these may have been related to his personal financial condition, given his concern about the cost of services. Whatever the reasons, McHenry concluded by saying: "I am convinced that my property has the elements with which to make a beautiful and in time profitable improvement and that such improvement should be planned by a master in the art — but I cannot feel assured that the present moment is propitious for a move in the enterprise."[68]

Olmsted wrote again to McHenry attempting to clarify any misunderstanding and to justify the proposed fee for the visit ($100 for a two day and two night trip from New York, plus traveling expenses):

> I find that you have not quite rightly understood me. For examining so large a property so far from New York and becoming responsible for advice upon which a large investment might turn, I should ordinarily charge fully double a number as the sum I named. For such advice, if worth having, surely that would not be a high charge —
>
> I thought that I had mentioned Mr. Weidenmann's name and described his position to you, which is not inferior to my own. I have often called him in consultation when my advice has been asked and in that case have divided fees equally with him. The charge named was much less than he would have made had you applied to him directly and in asking his assent to it, I told him that it must be a favor to me.[69]

There seem to be no subsequent letters between Olmsted and McHenry, making it appear that McHenry dropped the matter with Olmsted, at least for a time.

Who or what initially led McHenry to contact Olmsted is not known. Perhaps Waring recommended him. Or perhaps McHenry sought out Olmsted because he was the most distinguished landscape architect of the time. By 1876, Olmsted had a national reputation as a landscape designer. Not only had he designed Central Park, which McHenry visited on each of his trips to New York, but his work beginning in 1874 designing the newly expanded grounds of the U.S. Capitol in nearby Washington (and also planning the Capitol's West Front terrace as well as the terraces on the north and south sides)[70] was no doubt known to McHenry. It is also possible, given his social connections, that McHenry was aware that Olmsted was being approached to prepare designs for Baltimore's Mt. Vernon Place, on land that had belonged to McHenry's grandfather. And of course, Olmsted's 1869 design of the suburban village of Riverside, as well as his other parks, had received a good deal of attention. Regardless of what originally motivated McHenry to seek out Olmsted, he did not appear able to proceed with the project at that time.

McHenry apparently retained no correspondence or journals from 1877, but decided to keep a diary again in 1878. On March 19 he made the following entry: "Very fine day. Mr. Weidenmann, landscaping gardener of N.Y., came up by appointment to give advice about subdivision of Sudbrook. I drove him around the property in forenoon & he afterward went out on foot." On March 20 McHenry wrote: "Fine day. Mr. Weidenmann busy in morning. Went away by 12-noon Pimlico cars."[71]

These entries seemed to come out of the blue, there being no indication of any correspondence with Olmsted since October of 1876. In 1878 Weidenmann was still working with Olmsted. Olmsted himself was in Europe for part of that year, which may be why Weidenmann came down. Since there is a gap in McHenry's correspondence, it is difficult to ascertain exactly what happened during the intervening time. It seems there must have been continued or renewed correspondence with Olmsted, but just as suddenly as these new entries appeared, so did any mention of them disappear, without explanation. McHenry's surviving papers contain no subsequent letters or notes about Olmsted or Weidenmann, nor do we know if any plans emerged from the visit. Not long after Weidenmann's visit, McHenry and his family left for Ireland, remaining abroad about seven months.[72]

By December 1879, about a year after returning from Ireland, McHenry clearly had financial difficulties. His notes indicated that his anticipated income for a three month period was $2,000; his expenses were $2,550, leaving a deficiency of $550.[73] McHenry periodically kept financial notes and this was the first time that he had noted a deficiency. Shortly after, McHenry wrote out the pros and cons of renting his farm. Under the "pro" column, he cited the "urgent appeal of my wife to me to not again at this time undertake myself the management of the farm but to rent it, and her expression of a desire to spend the summers away from the place, believing it to be unhealthy from malarious influences, and to spend the winters in town to be with the children, some of whom may want to be 'in the world,' i.e. to be not buried in the country."[74] In other notes, he lamented: "Great are the troubles of any man owning a handsome place, a handsome family, fine horses, &c and not having money to meet all their demands upon him & a disagreeable wife who won't let him make the money at farming!!"[75]

McHenry's papers do not indicate whether or not the family moved to town, but he continued to pursue the development of his Sudbrook property after a brief hiatus. He again contacted Roullier, who agreed to come to Pikesville at "$6 per day and ¹/₂ expenses" (estimated at $5 each trip), with the time expended in traveling "not to count." Perhaps McHenry could no longer afford Olmsted given his strained financial situation and these reduced expenses were acceptable, because in notes a week or so later, additional details are provided about the number of helpers and axe men Roullier would need. The notes also described a personal interview with Roullier in March 1881 in Flushing, at which time he proposed to "make a complete topographical survey of Sudbrook at $2 per acre for say 700 acres." Roullier estimated that, with a double force, the project would take two months to complete.[76]

Although the project took longer than expected, Roullier stayed within his original estimate. McHenry paid him a total of $1,035 for services provided for five months (from July through November 1881), and an additional $15.80 was paid "for clearing woods under the superintendency of Mr. Mapes" (one of Roullier's assistants).[77]

In November and December 1881, Roullier wrote to McHenry three times regarding the project. Roullier agreed that he could meet an agent of McHenry's either in Flushing or Pikesville. Additional work toward a suburban plan must have been contemplated, because Roullier also stated that, while he did not have time to lay all the cornerstones himself, he could take Mr. Mapes onto the property and show him where to lay them. Roullier noted that "[w]hen we come to lay out drives, lots, etc., I shall have to visit Pikesville more or less frequently for the purpose of examining the work which will then be of a more difficult nature than that done during the past summer" and also that "the flat ground over the turnpike would be used to better advantage if subdivided into rectangular plats, as you suggest." Roullier's final letter of December 3, 1881, indicated that McHenry's agent (Thomas Hill) was expected to come to Flushing in a week or two "to examine the maps of Sudbrook."[78]

There was no further correspondence between Roullier and McHenry, but we know from letters written almost ten years later that Roullier did produce a topographical map of Sudbrook and that Olmsted used this map in preparing the 1889 design of the community.[79]

In an undated draft, which appears to pertain to this time period, McHenry picked up in mid-sentence and stated as follows:

> …until I could hear your views on these points and could also see the plat by which it is proposed to cut up the property — for I might not approve of it in part or in whole — and for this last reason I would not have clearings made immediately of roads or avenues laid out by Mr. Mapes. You do not say that in your offer you have stipulated for the conditions as to drainage and cesspools, etc., but I presume that you have as we have previously discussed that subject. It would be well on the map to show lines suitable for general drainage and to state that I shall be glad to unite with purchasers in organizing a company for draining, lighting and supplying with water. I don't feel disposed to lower my price in order to compete with Howard Villa and Mittnacht properties and shall feel very well pleased if the committee should select one of them, believing that when my plans come to be [known], I shall be able to offer advantages and to find customers. As for the employ-ment of Mr. Mapes permanently, I don't think that it would be right to draw him from Mr. Roullier's service, nor do I know that he has had experience in draining, road making, etc.....[80]

While we do not know for certain when the draft was written or to which "committee" McHenry refers, some inferences are possible. Given the topic and persons named, the draft most likely was written around 1881. It is likely that the "Mittnacht" referred to was a Mrs. Mittnacht who owned a fairly large piece of property in Pikesville next to the Arsenal and along the terminal block of the Baltimore, Pimlico & Pikesville horse-car line. The intended recipient is not stated, but given the reference to taking Mapes from Roullier's service, the letter clearly was not written to Roullier. The concluding portion of the draft encloses a notice of assessment McHenry received and a bill about which McHenry wanted an explanation. It thus appears that the letter was intended for someone who managed McHenry's properties and accounts — most probably Thomas Hill.

The "committee" may refer to a committee of the Board of Directors of the Baltimore, Pimlico & Pikesville Railroad Company, on which McHenry served and which he mentioned in his notes and journals. In a report dated July 1, 1881, the committee stated that the company faced a large unpaid indebtedness of $23,000 for which the stockholders had to provide more capital and expressed a belief that "with the extension of the road to Pikesville, and… with the gradual increase of population along the line, the road can eventually be made to pay."[81] (As it turned out, the company was sold at a trustee's sale in November 1881, and subsequently reorganized as the Pimlico and Pikesville Railroad Company).[82] Whether the Baltimore, Pimlico & Pikesville Railroad Company was planning to support a development along its route, and whether a community developed by McHenry might have been under consideration, are not known.

After multiple attempts, apparently McHenry completed some rudimentary plan for developing his estate. A brief announcement in the Towson *Maryland Journal* dated June 30, 1883, announced:

> *"Sudbrook Park," Pikesville.* We have received from Mr. Thomas Hill, the well known real estate broker, and the agent of Mr. J. Howard McHenry, residing near Pikesville…a map giving a view of a magnificent Park of 850 acres which he has just laid out which he styles "Sudbrook Park." It is laid out in a network of winding avenues, after the English and French park system. The land is from 400 to 500 feet above tide and is beautiful and rolling. Mr. McHenry's object is to induce persons in the city to build and reside in the Park, for the summer, at least, and thus gather together a community of sociable and agreeable people making country life the more desirable. As the Western Maryland Railroad runs through about the centre of the property, it would make a very desirable spot for a summer residence, affording very easy and rapid access with the city by means of that road, besides also being accessible by the Reisterstown Turnpike for driving purposes. Gwynns Falls, a beautiful stream, also runs through the upper portion of the Park. No one need to be restricted to acres, and can take as few or as many as he likes. Mr. Hill will furnish all the information desired.[83]

Unfortunately, the map of the proposed 850-acre Park was not furnished. The article implies that McHenry did not attempt to lay out a fully designed community with lots, but plotted only avenues amidst a park-like setting. But again, for reasons unknown, nothing seems to have come of this proposal.[84] Meanwhile, McHenry continued to live the life of a gentleman farmer at his Sudbrook estate.

It is interesting to speculate why McHenry first sought to develop his Sudbrook estate as a suburban village. At the time he first contacted Olmsted, planned suburban villages were rare in the nation as a whole and almost non-existent in the Baltimore area. Perhaps McHenry, an astute man of the times, foresaw that there would be an increasing trend toward suburban living, was aware of Olmsted's design of Riverside outside Chicago, and sought to be in the vanguard by developing a planned suburban community in the Baltimore area. Perhaps later, when his wife expressed dissatisfaction with the isolation of their country estate (which McHenry so loved), he hoped that by gathering "social and agreeable people" around them, at least for part of the year, she would find life at Sudbrook more to her liking. Perhaps, when his finances dwindled and the income from his farming estate was insufficient, developing his land seemed like an enterprising way both to retain it and to make money.

James Howard McHenry in his later years. Long interested in designing a suburban village on his estate, McHenry contacted Frederick Law Olmsted about the project in 1876, but died in 1888 without seeing his idea for a suburban village materialize. COURTESY OF THE MARYLAND HISTORICAL SOCIETY.

In addition to these possibilities, McHenry's notes and writings suggest that he had a strong personal interest in community planning quite apart from his personal plans for Sudbrook.[85]

Despite his various initiatives, McHenry's goal of developing a suburban village was not realized during his lifetime. James Howard McHenry died at his Sudbrook home on September 25, 1888, at the age of sixty-eight.[86]

We may never know exactly what combination of forces fueled McHenry's desire to develop his estate, but whatever the motivating forces, he clearly planted the seed that led to Sudbrook becoming a suburban village. Although this seed did not germinate until after McHenry's death, its eventual blossoming is attributable in large part to McHenry's personal vision and his efforts in 1876 to involve Olmsted in his plans.

Chapter 3

THE SUDBROOK COMPANY

Less than six months after James Howard McHenry's death, "The Sudbrook Company of Baltimore County" was formed for the purpose of "buying, selling, mortgaging, leasing, improving, disposing of, or otherwise dealing in Land."[1] The Company filed its Articles of Incorporation on March 16, 1889, providing for a board of seven directors with capitalization of $75,000.[2] The first directors were Hugh L. Bond, Jr. and John. H. Geigan of Baltimore City; Eugene Blackford and Charles G. Hill of Baltimore County; J. D. Winsor of Philadelphia, Pennsylvania; and Robert Winsor and Richard H. Weld of Boston, Massachusetts.[3] Bond became the Company's President and Blackford was hired as Manager of the planned development. While there is no definitive list of every stockholder, Eugene Blackford reported that the Company was owned by "Boston and Philadelphia capitalists."[4]

How did investors in Boston and Philadelphia link up with a group of Baltimoreans, quickly form a business venture to purchase land from the McHenry estate and less than a year after McHenry's death have a completed plan for a suburban village designed by F. L. Olmsted & Co.? This was, essentially, McHenry's 1876 vision realized, but what was the combination of factors that enabled it to materialize, finally, in 1889?[5]

Because definitive information either does not exist or has not been located, we must try to form a picture from the bits and pieces of information that we do have. While we do not know for certain how the stockholders and directors came together, there are curious links among them. In 1893 Blackford listed "the names of most of our stockholders residing in Boston": Robert Winsor of Kidder, Peabody & Co.; Robert Bacon of E. Rollins Morse & Co., Bankers; Henry B. Chapin, General Freight Agent, Boston & Albany Railroad; Richard H. Weld of Weld Bros.; and the heirs of the Brooks Estate.[6] All were prominent Bostonians.[7]

Hugh Bond, Robert Winsor, Robert Bacon and Henry B. Chapin all graduated from Harvard in the class of 1880, the same class that produced Theodore Roosevelt. All were hard-driving men who became quite successful in their chosen careers. In 1889, when the Sudbrook Company was formed, Bond and Chapin were working for railroad companies and Winsor and Bacon were with banking and brokerage houses. Although we do not know what specifically piqued their interest in a piece of property owned by the late James Howard McHenry in Pikesville, we do know that these four joined together as investors, at the relatively young age of thirty, to develop Sudbrook.

As for Weld and the Boston "heirs of the Brooks estate" who were stockholders, we again have possible links as to how they might have come to participate, but no definite knowledge. Weld is a Massachusetts name with a long history. Richard Harding Weld was born in 1835, graduated Phi Beta Kappa from Harvard in 1856, fought in the Civil War and was with the firm of Aaron D. Weld & Sons, Importers. In 1866, Weld married Laura Townsend Winsor, daughter of Alfred Winsor of Boston.[8]

Although it is pure conjecture, it is conceivable that Weld, who would have been fifty-four years old when the Company was incorporated, may have been related through marriage to either Robert or James Winsor, and in that way was drawn into the venture. A possible connection also exists between Robert Winsor and the "heirs of the Brooks estate." Winsor was the trustee of the Brooks Cubicle

Hospital, Boston Dwelling House Company. Quite possibly, it was through Winsor that the heirs of the Brooks estate ended up with an interest in the Sudbrook venture.[9]

James Davis Winsor of Philadelphia also appears to have been a stockholder.[10] Born in Boston, he was a second or third cousin of Robert Winsor.[11] Although surviving Company records do not mention the names of any Philadelphia stockholders, he is the only person from Philadelphia who seemed actively involved, and he was a director. Blackford intermittently wrote to Winsor with detailed information about the financial status of the Company and the future outlook for Sudbrook.

James Winsor was about the same age as Blackford and their wives were first cousins.[12] Judging from the content of Blackford's correspondence with him, the two families had a good deal of affection for each other and saw each other periodically. Winsor is one of the few people whom Blackford addressed by his first name, writing all letters to "My dear James" or "Dear Jim." Together with his brother William D. Winsor, James Winsor owned the Boston and Philadelphia Steamship Company known as the Winsor Line, which Robert Winsor had helped to organize.[13] James and William later owned the Merchant and Miners Line as well.[14]

Blackford himself owned one share of stock, possibly a complimentary share for his services as Superintendent of the Sudbrook Company (a title he soon changed to Manager). Blackford began receiving a salary of $41.66 per month in May 1889, and continued to receive this same monthly allotment until December 1893, at which time it was raised to $83.33 (approximately $1,000 annually), the level maintained throughout his employment.[15]

No records actually list Hugh L. Bond, Jr., the Company President, as a stockholder, but it is almost certain that he was, given his position and his subsequent investments in the development. Curiously, Bond seems never to have lived at Sudbrook, despite owning up to eight houses in the community and having a large financial interest in its success.

Even if we can tenuously link the various stockholders, it remains a mystery how they seized on the opportunity of purchasing a portion of the McHenry property and ended up retaining Olmsted. Again, we are left with conjecture.

It is likely that Hugh L. Bond, Jr. had known McHenry. Although McHenry was almost forty years older than Bond, both were from prominent Baltimore families and may have moved in the same social circles. Both were trained in law and had offices at the B&O Building in downtown Baltimore. McHenry had been pursuing his concept of developing his property as a suburban community for many years, and an article had appeared in a local paper describing this proposal in 1883. From a review of McHenry's papers over the years, it is evident that he discussed his vision and the potential for this project with friends and business associates. It is possible that McHenry had, at some point, approached Bond or others to go in with him on the venture; at the very least, Bond could have heard or read about McHenry's plans.

While we can only infer that Bond may have known McHenry, we know for a certainty that Eugene Blackford knew him and had been friends with him for many years. He saw him at monthly Garrison Forest Farmers' Club meetings, had served as an officer of the Farmers' Club with him and the two regularly visited each other on their almost adjoining estates. McHenry also involved Blackford in meetings he had with the Western Maryland Railroad regarding the location of the railroad line and station, and with the county regarding the relocation of county roads on McHenry's property. We can confidently assume that Blackford was well aware of McHenry's efforts to develop his Sudbrook estate given their long-standing friendship and their common interests as neighboring estate owners.[16]

How Bond and Blackford came together in their respective capacities as President of the Sudbrook Company and Manager of the fledging community is more difficult to surmise. It is possible that they, too, knew each other socially. It is also conceivable that, after McHenry's death, Blackford discussed McHenry's unfulfilled plan for a suburban village with James Winsor, who saw an investment possibility and brought in Robert Winsor, who recruited some of his Harvard classmates, including Hugh Bond, Jr., to carry out the project. Regardless of how Blackford and Bond initially came together, the two formed a variety of working and investment partnerships lasting from the Sudbrook Company's formation in 1889 until Blackford's death in 1908.

Based on Blackford's letters to Bond, which are preserved in Blackford's record books, the relationship appeared to be a cooperative but formal one, with Blackford's friendliest salutation being "My Dear Mr. Bond." Blackford, older than Bond by almost twenty years, consistently deferred to him in his capacity as President of the Sudbrook Company and always sought his advice when problems arose. In 1891, Bond became the owner of a cottage in Sudbrook Park and rented it out as an investment. Blackford managed this rental, as well as overseeing the construction and rental of three other houses in Sudbrook that Bond had built in 1892. In 1895, Bond and Blackford formed a partnership or "syndicate," which purchased land from the Sudbrook Company and built four houses intended for long-term lease.

Of the two men, Bond had by far the greater financial resources. He was the partner who invested the money, while Blackford's contribution was to oversee design, supervise construction and then provide the on-going management of Bond's and their joint properties. It is clear from Blackford's letters to his family and close friends that he was a man of limited financial means. While he appeared to live a comfortable life, owning both "Cleve," his 100-acre farm estate in Pikesville and a home he built in 1896 in Sudbrook Park, as well as an interest in the four syndicate properties with Bond, he also went through periods in which his resources appeared to be significantly depleted.

This, then, is the cast of players. But only a few would take on major roles in turning a portion of McHenry's Sudbrook estate into an Olmsted-designed suburban village.

Chapter 4

HUGH LENNOX BOND, JR.[1]
(1858–1922)

Hugh Lennox Bond, Jr. was one of three sons of Judge Hugh L. Bond (1826-1893), a Southerner by birth, and Annie Penniman Bond, whose family originally was from Boston. The Bond family home was the estate "Mount Royal" at Park and Reservoir Avenues near Druid Hill Park.

The best known member of the Bond family was Hugh's father, Judge Bond, a staunch supporter of President Lincoln and the Union cause. Although his abolitionist leanings caused him to be intensely unpopular with those Marylanders who sympathized with the South, he was a highly respected jurist who in 1861 was elected Judge of the Criminal Court, a position he held through the Civil War. In 1870 President Grant appointed him to the Fourth United States Circuit Court, where he was one of those chiefly responsible for breaking the power of the Ku Klux Klan. Esteemed as a man of genuine ability and high character, Judge Bond was also genial and mild-mannered, and refined and cultured in his tastes.

Interestingly, both Judge Bond and Frederick Law Olmsted had connections to the abolitionist movement. Olmsted had been offered the post of Secretary of the National Freedman's Aid Society, a group in which Judge Bond was active. Bond, Jr. might have heard of Olmsted through his father's abolitionist activities long before Sudbrook came on the horizon.

Hugh Bond, Jr. was born in Baltimore on December 23, 1858. He was well educated, graduating from Phillips Exeter Academy in 1876 and from Harvard College in 1880. He was admitted to the practice of law in 1882, continuing his studies with the law firm of Cowen & Cross. He soon entered the Law Department of the B&O Railroad Company and began a successful and prominent legal career. He was one of the lawyers who conducted the reorganization of the Seaboard Air Line Railway Company. He was also counsel for the Receivers of the Richmond and Danville Railroad Company and was a trustee of the Chesapeake and Ohio Canal Company.

When the B&O receivership occurred, Bond became counsel for the Receivers. In 1895, he was appointed the B&O's General Counsel. He held that position until his death in 1922. He was named second vice-president in 1903 and served dually as General Counsel and second vice-president until 1910 when, at his own request, he was relieved of the duties of second vice-president and succeeded by George M. Shriver (who lived at 607 Sudbrook Road in Sudbrook Park). In 1916, Bond was elected to the B&O's board of directors. An obituary noted that "his exceptional and minute knowledge of the road was considered invaluable in its upbuilding."

While not as politically active as his father, Bond was highly respected for his "philosophic grasp of legal principles" and his dedication to the B&O Railroad for forty years. His handling of the

Hugh L. Bond, Jr., 1880. Bond, a Baltimore attorney, was President of the Sudbrook Company and worked actively with Frederick Law Olmsted and his son John Olmsted during the design phase of Sudbrook. COURTESY OF HARVARD UNIVERSITY ARCHIVES.

B&O property through its receivership, and his ability to accomplish the reorganization of the B&O Railroad without any foreclosure of its mortgages or wiping out of its stock "has been regarded as a remarkable achievement only possible to a consummate lawyer and a resourceful genius."

Bond had wide-ranging interests outside of the law, even though he had limited time to pursue these interests, given the demands of his various positions. He read widely, with a particular interest in natural history and botany. He also enjoyed music and art. A man of multiple talents, he designed a portico for "Mt. Royal." In 1884, Bond married Jessie Van Renssalaer Beale of New York City, the sister of one of his classmates. They had five daughters. Although afflicted with heart trouble during the last year of his life, Bond attended to his professional duties until he suffered a stroke and died within twenty-four hours.

Hugh L. Bond, Jr. was only thirty years of age when he became President of the Sudbrook Company. He was actively involved with the Olmsted firm when it was designing Sudbrook in 1889. Once the community was functioning, he turned the day-to-day operations over to Eugene Blackford, the manager, but continued to make all major decisions. Bond owned or had an interest in eight houses in Sudbrook Park, but appears never to have lived in the community himself. Instead he inherited his family's Mt. Royal estate and lived there the latter part of his life, until his death on April 12, 1922 at the age of sixty-three.

Chapter 5

EUGENE BLACKFORD[1]
(1839–1908)

Eugene Blackford was born in Fredericksburg, Virginia in April 1839, the son of William Matthews and Mary Berkeley Blackford. William Blackford, a native of Frederick County, Maryland, had been trained as a lawyer but by about 1845, had moved to Lynchburg to become editor of the Whig newspaper, the Lynchburg Virginian. Subsequently, he was Cashier of the Exchange Bank of Virginia in Lynchburg. Mary Blackford, the daughter of General John Minor of Fredericksburg, had her hands full with five sons (of whom Eugene was the youngest) and two daughters. Little is known of Eugene's early life, except that he was raised in Lynchburg and attended the University of Virginia from about 1857 to about 1860.

Eugene Blackford was teaching in Barbour County, Alabama, at the start of the Civil War. While there, he was elected captain of Company K (the "Barbour Grays"), which became Company A of the Fifth Alabama Infantry Regiment, later commanding the sharpshooters of his Regiment, of his Brigade, and of Rodes' Division. He was present at first Manassas (Bull Run), Chancellorsville, Gettysburg and about seventeen other battles in Virginia and Maryland. In 1863 Blackford had four operations on varicose veins; in October 1864, after an all-night march, he was not able to keep pace with his regiment at the Battle of Cedar Creek. As a result, he was court-martialed, but reinstated after "a flood of petitions from peers, subordinates and superiors" attesting to his courage and integrity. A letter from Col. C. Forsythe, Commander of Battle's Brigade, and A. Bowie, Acting Brigade Surgeon, among other signatories, included the following praise:

> Distinguished for his constant devotion to his country, his valor on
> the field, his rigid discipline, his exemplary conduct on all occasions,
> [Major Eugene Blackford] stands forth a bright ornament to the
> military profession, illustrating in his person the chivalry of the South.

All five Blackford sons served in the Confederate army; two of the brothers wrote accounts of aspects of the Civil War which have been published. Mary Blackford kept almost all of her sons' letters, along with other family documents, preserving a rich account of that period. The Blackfords clearly were a literary family with a keen sense of history.

On June 27, 1867 Blackford married Rebecca Chapman Gordon, the only surviving child of John Montgomery Gordon. Because Blackford might never have met J. Howard McHenry or become involved in Sudbrook had he not been assisted early on by his father-in-law, some background on the Gordon family is pertinent.

Eugene Blackford, manager of Sudbrook Park from 1889 to 1908. Blackford, a long-time friend of James Howard McHenry, was hired to manage the development and day-to-day operations of Sudbrook and played a pivotal role in implementing Olmsted's design. COURTESY OF THE MARYLAND HISTORICAL SOCIETY.

Originally from Virginia, John Montgomery Gordon (1810–1884) met Emily Chapman, the nineteen-year-old daughter of Dr. Nathaniel Chapman of Philadelphia, on a trip to Niagara Falls in 1830. The two were married in Philadelphia three years later and came to Baltimore to live. Having studied law at Yale and Harvard, Gordon was admitted to the Bar in 1834 and prospered in business, assisted by family connections. The couple had five children, one of whom died shortly after birth. Except for his family, Gordon's deepest love was for the country, and he longed for a country home like his family's in Virginia.

In 1841, Gordon became President of the Union Bank of Maryland, which was Baltimore's second largest bank in size of capital. He was then able to acquire the country home which he had long desired. Soon after, he was elected President of the Frederickstown, Boonsborough and Cumberland Turnpike Road companies. His future looked promising until a series of tragedies struck. Between 1844 and 1852, his wife and two of his four children died. He carried on stoically — a widower with two daughters, Susan 14, and Rebecca, 10.

In 1857 Gordon was chosen to be one of the original trustees and treasurer of the Peabody Institute. In 1858, Union Bank moved into first place among Baltimore's financial institutions. That same year, Susan Gordon died. The weight of her death proved too much for Gordon. He abandoned all interest in the business world, left Baltimore and traveled in Europe. On his return in 1860, he withdrew from the Peabody, sold his home and moved to Virginia, living near Lynchburg and, later, Norfolk for several years. Rebecca remained in Baltimore with her aunt, Mrs. James S. Ryan, during the Civil War.

We do not know how Rebecca Gordon and Eugene Blackford met, but it appears that the Gordon and Blackford families may have known each other in Virginia. Following Eugene and Rebecca's marriage in 1867, Rebecca brought her father to live with them. In time, Gordon came out of his melancholy, revived by observing his daughter and son-in-law as a young married couple, which apparently reminded him of the early years of his own marriage. The birth of his first grandchild, Emily, on September 12, 1868 was a propitious event:

> When [Gordon's] first grandchild was born he gave his son-in-law the
> means to buy a house near Baltimore. Thus, "Cleve" came to be built, just
> west of Pikesville. [Gordon] probably helped choose its name, derived
> from the home of Major Blackford's great-grandfather, Landon Carter,
> near Fredericksburg, where [Gordon] had often hunted in his youth.

Cleve, while certainly ample for the Blackford family, was not an especially large farming estate compared to many of those in the area. Indeed, it appears that Eugene Blackford did much of the farm work himself, unlike his friend McHenry, who oversaw but remained removed from the actual work. An entry in Blackford's farm journal on December 25, 1869, revealed how a holiday turned into a normal workday for this man who could not afford to be merely a "gentleman farmer":

> Christmas Day. Unfortunately, I was obliged to work all day, thus
> spoiling my dinner, for which I had no time. The cows came out at
> noon, and my work was to get places for them, the cow house not being
> ready. Mr. Brown called while I was busy, thus making me lose time.

In addition to raising cows at Cleve, Blackford farmed his one hundred acres. Like McHenry, Blackford was an active member of the Garrison Forest Farmers' Club from its organization in 1874. Minutes of meetings indicate that these gentlemen farmers "expressed a preference for farming as a business and for the life of a farmer generally."

The Blackfords also had two sons, Eugene, Jr., and William Gordon. In 1871, the year Eugene was born, Blackford, along with Charles K. Harrison, George W. Evans and Charles Lyon Rogers, established the Pikesville Dairy Company on Argyle Avenue in Baltimore. The enterprise proved reasonably successful. The men, all owners of farming estates, used the Western Maryland Railroad (which then came as far as Owings Mills) to ship their milk to the dairy's downtown facility.

In 1889 Blackford was hired as manager of the Sudbrook Company, and in that capacity was the person most directly responsible for implementing the Olmsted plan in Sudbrook. It was he who directed the construction of the roads and sidewalks, the installation of the drainage systems, and the planting. Judging from his correspondence, Blackford was a conscientious, hard-working and gentlemanly manager with an eye for detail and a refined discernment regarding architectural styles appropriate to the community.

Blackford's generous intentions sometimes exceeded his own financial resources. He had at one point chosen two expensive lots in Sudbrook Park to purchase, intending one to be for himself and his wife, and the other to be a gift to his son-in-law, Arthur Poultney, but he never actually purchased either. Instead, he rented a cottage in Sudbrook for a number of years, as did his daughter and son-in-law, and later purchased a single, less costly lot on Winsor Road. Although he had wanted to assist his son-in-law, as he had once been assisted, his financial resources were insufficient to enable him to follow through on this purchase.

Blackford was active at St. Mark's-on-the-Hill, serving on various committees and later as warden and senior vestryman. This Episcopal church was built and paid for by Charles T. Cockey on three-quarters of an acre at the intersection of Old Court and Reisterstown Roads, on land that James Howard McHenry conveyed to Cockey in 1877. Blackford also served on a committee that oversaw the management of Mt. Wilson Sanitarium, located a few miles west of Pikesville off Reisterstown Road. Beginning in 1902, he acted as building supervisor for a prosperous landowner, Samuel Lyons, when Mr. Lyons built a house in Owings Mills. Blackford also served as rental and sales agent in connection with other properties that Lyons owned.

The Blackfords moved into their own home at 1008 Winsor Road in Sudbrook Park in 1896, retaining Cleve and renting it out for a number of years. Starting in 1902, Blackford and his wife began returning to Cleve for three months each summer, renting out their Sudbrook home. Blackford appeared both proud and protective of his Sudbrook home, describing it as elegantly furnished with a valuable library. He would not rent to families that had young boys unless their parents were "of the type that controlled their children."

Eugene Blackford died on February 4, 1908, at his Sudbrook home. He was sixty-eight years old. His wife Rebecca, sons Eugene and William, and daughter Emily Blackford Poultney continued to reside in Sudbrook for a number of years. While Blackford did not live to see Sudbrook completed, he was able to implement a significant portion of the Olmsted plan and thus had a profound influence on the early direction and development of the community.

Chapter 6

JOHN CHARLES OLMSTED[1]
(1852–1920)

When Frederick Law Olmsted married his brother's widow in 1859 and adopted her three children, the eldest, John Charles Olmsted, was seven years old. John thus spent some of his most formative years living with his newly constituted family in Central Park while his stepfather directed its construction. In 1863 the family journeyed to California and lived for two years amidst the splendors of the Sierra Nevada, where Olmsted managed the Mariposa Mining Company. Historian Arleyn Levee has noted that "this western experience was influential in teaching John to read natural land forms and to identify plant materials." John worked with the 40th Parallel survey teams in Nevada and Utah during the summers of 1869 and 1871, reinforcing his expertise in this area.

John graduated from Yale University's Sheffield Scientific School in 1875 and went to work in his stepfather's office. When the Olmsted firm moved from New York City to Brookline, Massachusetts in 1884, John became a full partner with the elder Olmsted and the firm became known as "F.L. & J.C. Olmsted." John's skills in art, architecture, engineering and photography enhanced the practice and his management expertise proved to be a much needed asset as the practice grew. In 1889 Henry Sargent Codman, who had apprenticed with Olmsted, also became a partner. From 1889 until Codman's untimely death in 1893, the firm was known as "F.L. Olmsted & Co." In 1893, with a substantial and ever-growing workload, both the elder and the younger Olmsted prevailed upon Charles Eliot to join them. The firm became known as "Olmsted, Olmsted and Eliot" until 1897, when Eliot died at the age of thirty-seven after contracting meningitis.

The elder Olmsted ended his active participation in the work of the firm in 1895 and John's stepbrother, Frederick Law Olmsted, Jr. (1870–1957) joined the firm after his graduation from Harvard University. With the death of Eliot, the firm was renamed in 1898 as "Olmsted Brothers," with John becoming the senior partner. He remained in that position until his death in 1920, presiding over a practice that grew from approximately 600 to more than 3,500 commissions. The two Olmsted brothers carried on their father's legacy and became founding members of the American Society of Landscape Architects. John was the Society's first president. In that capacity, he was responsible in large part for establishing membership standards and codes of practice for the profession. Before 1900, there were no

John Charles Olmsted. The nephew and adopted son of Olmsted, Sr., John was trained as a landscape architect by him and joined his firm in 1875. He assisted in the design of Sudbrook. COURTESY OF THE NATIONAL PARK SERVICE, FREDERICK LAW OLMSTED NATIONAL HISTORIC SITE..

formal accredited training programs for persons interested in the profession of landscape architecture.

Trained by the elder Olmsted, John C. Olmsted not only played an important role in various projects with his stepfather — including the planning of park systems in Boston, Rochester and Louisville — but went on to design comprehensive park systems for Seattle and Spokane, Dayton, Portland (Oregon), and Portland (Maine). He expanded the senior Olmsted's park and parkway designs in Atlanta, Buffalo, Hartford, Connecticut, and Brooklyn, New York, among others. The suburban community of Druid Hills, Atlanta, was developed under John's direction. He designed parks in Charleston, South Carolina, and New Orleans, as well as in numerous other cities, and worked on the playgrounds of Chicago's South Parks, introducing "an innovative approach to recreational planning as an extension of the settlement house concept." His institutional commissions included numerous schools and universities, among them Smith, Mount Holyoke, Amherst, Chicago, Washington, Iowa State and Ohio State. He also designed the grounds of asylums, libraries, hospitals and state capitols. His experience working on the World's Columbian Exposition of 1893 in Chicago led to commissions for exposition grounds in Seattle, Portland, Oregon, and Winnipeg, Manitoba. His proposals for the National Cash Register factory and its environs in Dayton expanded so much that he shaped much of the city's park system and some of its subdivisions. He also "urged controls over haphazard building to protect important vistas and areas of outstanding scenic beauty." As noted by Olmsted scholar Charles Beveridge, John did "an immense amount of work during his career of forty-five years, involving the whole range of design projects carried out by the Olmsted firm."[2]

John assisted the elder Olmsted in the design of Sudbrook and was the Olmsted firm's primary correspondent with the Sudbrook Company between 1889 and 1892. He also resumed work on his father's Druid Hills' design in 1902, after the project had lain dormant for almost ten years. Not only did John carry on the design legacy handed down by Olmsted, Sr., but he was a landscape architect of renown in his own right. His development of the Seattle park system, for example, featured particularly lush vegetation that "would have delighted Olmsted himself" according to Beveridge, as well as dramatic views, from the various parks, of Puget Sound, the Olympic range, the city skyline and the Cascades.[3]

It is difficult to follow in the footsteps of a legend such as Frederick Law Olmsted, Sr., and establish an individual identity. But, as Levee has observed: "In the Olmsted firm's remarkable history, John Olmsted maintained the continuity of the practice while expanding its professional growth. As a link between 19th-century romanticism and 20th-century pragmatism, he provided an interpretation of Frederick Law Olmsted's vision in the vocabulary of a new era."

Chapter 7

OLMSTED'S SUDBROOK

Compared to McHenry's aborted attempts, beginning in the 1870s, to turn his Sudbrook estate into a suburban village, events following his death moved forward swiftly. Shortly after the Sudbrook Company was formed in March 1889, principals of the Company corresponded with F. L. Olmsted & Co. regarding the design of the community.[1] Within six months the Olmsted firm had completed the "General Plan for Sudbrook" dated August 24, 1889.[2]

While questions about how or why the Company happened to choose Olmsted are left unanswered by the lack of documentation of any preliminary 1888 or 1889 contacts between principals of the Sudbrook Company and the Olmsted firm, by April 1889 work on the plan for Sudbrook clearly was in progress.[3] John Charles Olmsted, Frederick Law Olmsted's adopted son and partner, was the firm's correspondent with the Sudbrook Company on behalf of his father and himself.[4] John had been working with his father since 1875, and had become a partner in 1884. Due to multiple demands on the elder Olmsted at the time, John assisted in the design of Sudbrook.[5] Because Olmsted, Sr., continued to be involved with and directed the project, the design of Sudbrook is rightfully attributed to him.

John Olmsted's initial letter to Bond indicated that the project already was underway: "I received your telegram this morning asking when we would send a plan for the main road…."[6] While there must have been some prior communication, correspondence or contact, no earlier letters have survived.[7] Bond sent a plat which showed the proposed location of the station and road to Pikesville and the surveyor's choice of location for the overhead bridge that would be needed to take carriages over the Western Maryland Railroad tracks, stressing, however, that "of course, the location of the bridge is left to you."[8] He advised that the railroad required a nineteen foot clearance for overhead bridges and asked the Olmsteds to decide the "shape and location, with reference to the building, of the ground to be conveyed to the R.R. Co." The Sudbrook Company planned to convey to the railroad one acre of land, situated so as to extend westerly along the track to the intended grade crossing.[9] Bond noted that the Sudbrook Company's architects would prepare plans for the station[10] and expressed the hope that Robert Winsor had managed to see them by this time. Bond's letter indicated an urgency in getting the work started:

> We wish to be able to locate and clear the roads necessary to connect
> that corner which we selected as the best place to begin improvements,

Frederick Law Olmsted, Sr., the father of landscape architecture in America and designer of Sudbrook. This photograph probably dates from 1875–79, the period during which James Howard McHenry first contacted Olmsted about designing a suburban village on McHenry's Sudbrook estate. COURTESY OF THE NATIONAL PARK SERVICE, FREDERICK LAW OLMSTED NATIONAL HISTORIC SITE.

with the over-head bridge and the freight siding at the west end of the
cut. This is all we need at once but this much we must have, if we are
to do anything this year.[11]

Part of the reason for the urgency which Bond expressed may have come from agreements that
the Sudbrook Company had made with the executors of the McHenry estate about the development
of the property.[12] One of these required the Company to "guarantee the erection during the year 1889,
upon the land so purchased by it, of six houses or cottages to cost not less than $2,500 each without
the land, and a like number and style the following year."[13] Bond's letters indicated that the Company
originally may have intended to sell lots, expecting purchasers to build immediately, thus satisfying this
requirement. In order to be able to sell these first six lots, the Company needed a plan, or at least the
portion of the plan for the area where the first houses were to be erected. The Olmsteds did not like to
be rushed[14] or to provide portions of plans, but they complied and sent to Bond, at Winsor's request,
"a diagram showing six lots on the proposed main road, at a point where, if it be not desirable in order
to save important trees, there is not likely to be any material change of location."[15]

The Sudbrook Company either was unsuccessful in its attempts to sell lots quickly or for other
reasons abandoned that idea.[16] It decided, instead, that it would entice prospective purchasers by building
a boarding house and nine speculative "cottages," a term used to describe less formal but often sizable
houses of the period (those the Sudbrook Company initially built contained from six to twelve rooms).[17]

While the Olmsted firm tried to accommodate the Sudbrook developers, who pushed to have
the plan completed quickly, Bond's tardiness in providing information that the Olmsteds repeatedly
requested made the task more difficult. The Olmsteds wrote on April 19 requesting a map of the
Sudbrook property on a scale of one hundred feet to an inch. The map which they had, prepared on
a scale of two hundred feet to an inch, did not show the areas of the lots with sufficient precision.[18]
As they noted in a subsequent letter, the larger scale was necessary to limit errors on the final plan.[19]

On April 20 the Olmsteds sent Bond a preliminary study for the Sudbrook property, noting
that Bond "should not fix absolutely and unchangeably any more of the lines of roads and lots according
to this 'study' than your pressing exigencies necessitate."[20] The next step, they noted, would be a sketch
showing stakes which they wanted set, then an examination of the grounds and consultation with Bond
about any desired changes, after which the final plan could be prepared.

Two days later, the Olmsteds sent a sketch showing the location of stakes to be set "as soon as
possible." They proposed that one of them would visit as soon as the stakes were in the ground, and
that at that time, they could "settle everything and conclude upon a final plan."[21]

Even in 1889, nothing was as simple as it seemed at first glance. Obviously, the Olmsteds had
thought their instructions to Bond were quite straightforward and clear — stake out the roads and we
will come for a final review. But a ten-page letter sent to Bond by the Olmsteds three days later responded
to an impasse that Bond had reported. The formidable problem turned out to be none other than those
trademark Olmstedian curves.[22]

In 1889, the arrow-straight grid street was the norm and predominated everywhere. Olmsted's
then-revolutionary "curvilinear" roads presented very practical difficulties for the Sudbrook Company's
surveyor: he had no idea how to translate them from the preliminary plan to stakes on the ground.
Olmsted responded that "the curves we always draw 'freehand' in order to get them graceful."[23] Nevertheless, the firm agreed, at Bond's request, to prepare an additional plan showing the approximate radii

and tangents of the curves as a guide for the Company's surveyor.[24] For the third time, the Olmsteds asked to be supplied with a map on a scale of one-hundred feet to an inch, which they emphasized that they *had to have* in order to prepare their final plan.[25]

Another issue still "up in the air" and preventing completion of a plan was exactly how much land the Sudbrook Company would purchase from the McHenry estate. Although the deeds relating to the property had not yet been executed, the Sudbrook Company planned to purchase 204 acres, and had an option to purchase another adjoining one hundred acres. The Olmsteds suggested that the Company might want them to include the additional one hundred "bonded" acres in their final design, commenting "we expect that you will have the plan lithographed, and extensively circulated, and if so its effects as an advertisement would be much greater if it covered three hundred acres than if it were limited to two hundred acres. We would not mention it if Mr. Winsor had not remarked once, that he 'wished the company had bought more land while they were about it.'" This letter contained a concluding paragraph which the Olmsteds apparently inserted in an effort to stimulate action:

> We expect now to hear from you "stakes set," "100 foot scale map ready
> and forwarded," "I approve (or do not approve) of memoranda of sales,
> or approximate or lot number descriptions," "have already agreed on
> time of sale of lots (so & so 'wants them described accurately at once')."
> In the latter case, we can send you a tracing of the part of the plan in
> question much sooner than we could send you the whole plan.[26]

Two days later, Bond responded. He would provide them with a larger map on a scale of sixty feet to an inch and wished to show on this new map the actual lines of the Company's purchase. Bond planned to meet soon with a representative of the McHenry estate to resolve remaining issues about the boundary lines, and assured the Olmsteds that "we are not so pushed for time as to induce me to do anything that will embarrass us hereafter in carrying out your plan." As for the additional one hundred acres on which the Company held an option, Bond asked Winsor to decide after consulting the other Boston directors of the Company, and to communicate with Olmsted directly.[27] Bond acknowledged that the preliminary study "has pleased everyone who has seen it," but he voiced concerns about the proposed placement of the boarding house and the site shown for the station.[28]

From letters and the preliminary study, it is clear that the boarding house originally was proposed to be situated on the 2.5 acre Cliveden Road triangle that, on the General Plan of August 24, 1889, was marked "Reserved for Church or Other Public Building." The Olmsteds proposed this location for a number of reasons. The proposed Cliveden location was on "open land" that was not heavily treed. This portion of the property also was one of the highest spots of the 204 acres, providing an excellent view of the surrounding area. Between this proposed boarding house lot and Milford [Mill] Road, the preliminary plan shows an undeveloped area of 8.5 acres marked "Playground" (this became "Cliveden Green" on the 1889 General Plan). By placing the Playground next to the boarding house, the Olmsteds hoped to "keep the view open permanently, at least as far as the county road."[29] They expressed concern that many people would favor the lots nearer to the station because of the convenience and the fact that these lots were more wooded, thus leaving the land proposed to be occupied by the boarding house unused if that building were placed nearer the station.[30]

For his part, Bond had concerns about the proposed Cliveden location, which was one-third or more miles from the station and so "too great a distance in our summer climate."[31] To this latter reservation, the Olmsteds replied: "So far as walking in the sun is concerned, the *plan* is to plant trees along the road so that there need be little of the distance without shade."[32] They noted, however, that if it was decided to place the boarding house nearer the station, "that is all right and does not hurt the plan at all because the triangle would be appropriate for a church or other public building." At the same time, they suggested the possibility of planning for two boarding houses, "one on the hill top [Cliveden] — (breezes, view, playground, away from noise and smoke of R.R., &c.), the other near the station — (see more people passing, be more convenient, be in the woods, &c.)."[33]

As to Bond's concern that the station was located too far to the west on the preliminary study, the Olmsteds responded that they had used the diagram which Bond had provided. They commented, with some exasperation: "You will see, of course, how impossible it is to plan without knowing the facts, in a way definite enough for anything more than suggestions." The initial "study," from which the Olmsteds had reproduced the portion with six lots that they had forwarded earlier, had since been "completely altered, in every line" because of subsequent changes submitted by Bond showing the station further east, and "if now, we have to change again, because the station has been changed, more alterations may have to be made…"[34]

By mid-May of 1889, progress on the plan was slower than expected, primarily because the Company insisted upon having a "working drawing" showing radii and tangents of the curves, in addition to the customary general plan drawn with freehand curves. To accommodate this request, the Olmsteds had put a "first rate draughts man at work on the plan, solely" but this more detailed drawing could not be hurried because they "had to study the lines with the greatest care…making them with compounded radial curves and tangents."[35] John Olmsted wrote to Bond:

> We are very much disappointed that the plan is taking so long as
> we fear it may cause you inconvenience, but still the other causes of
> delay in getting your land on the market may make ours of minor
> consequence. We are extremely anxious to make this affair a success,
> so far as plans can ensure success, and are therefore taking every
> possible pains to get good lines.[36]

On May 21, Robert Winsor wrote Olmsted asking how soon he would be able to send the plans, because "my Baltimore friends are stirring me up about the drawings of the Sudbrook property, saying that it is very important for them to have them at once."[37] Winsor received a response the next day from John Olmsted, who explained some of the reasons for the delay, particularly the time it had taken "in rendering free hand curves into radial lines" to assist the Company's Baltimore surveyor. John stated that they had advised Bond to begin working on the lines already staked out, if it was a matter "of pressing importance." However, John Olmsted noted that when he had been in Baltimore recently, he was "surprised at how little had been done that might have been and as I supposed had been done. The road from Pikesville not only had not been contracted for but the material to be used in its construction had not been fully determined. The station had not been begun and the freight siding was only partly built." Olmsted concluded:

> No one, until they have had experience, ever supposes that much time

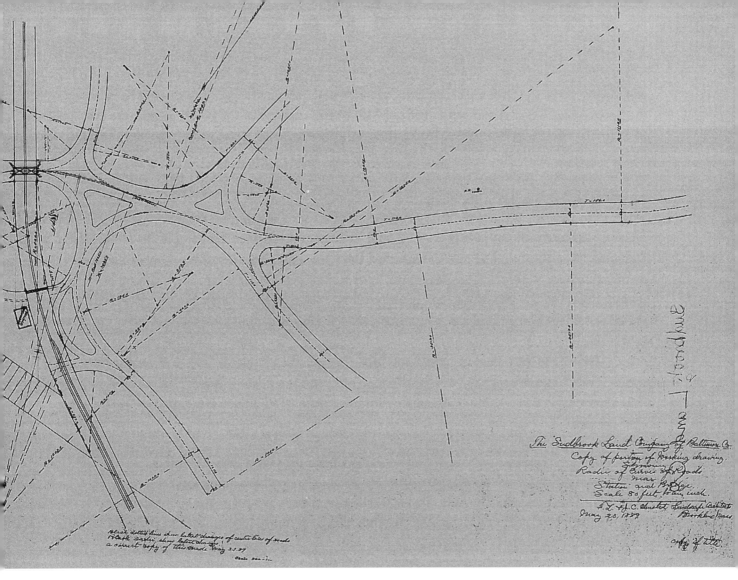

Working drawing by the Olmsted firm showing radii of curves of roads near the station and entranceway bridge to Sudbrook, May 23, 1889. COURTESY OF THE NATIONAL PARK SERVICE, FREDERICK LAW OLMSTED NATIONAL HISTORIC SITE.

is needed in negotiations, raising capital, discussing policies, studying out preliminary plans, adjusting conflicting requirements and interests, elaborating general and working drawings, surveying, calculating curves, quantities and cost of construction work, inviting specifications and contracts, getting bids & getting the work done in such an affair as this. We are always surprised at the time it takes in spite of our experience. It seems to be going as well as usual in this case.[38]

On May 24, 1889, the Olmsteds sent Bond a portion of the general working plan so that the Company could begin work. This portion covered the first area to be built — the roads near the station and bridge and "along the sites in the woods where the first houses are likely to be erected."[39] Next to come would be a cross-section for roads and a plan for the boundary of the purchase, which still remained to be resolved with the executors of the McHenry estate.

The boundary of the Sudbrook Company's purchase remained unresolved until early July 1889. The McHenry executors did not want to agree to the boundary line that the Olmsteds proposed, which would have given the Sudbrook Company more frontage along the upland area on what was then called the Seven Mile County Road (now, Milford Mill Road), and less of the low land near the Gwynns Falls (the current McHenry Road area). In the end, the parties reached a compromise giving the Sudbrook Company additional land in a southeasterly direction from and near the railroad station, as well as a smaller amount of additional frontage on the Seven Mile Road, in return for the Company also taking a part of the bottom, low-lying lands.[40]

On July 20, 1889, with "the numerous calculations and complex curves" in place, the working drawing was sent to Bond by express mail. Still to be completed were the approaches to the station from Sudbrook Avenue; Bond had not yet furnished the Olmsteds with a detailed survey of that area.[41] Also by that time, the Sudbrook Company must have made a decision to locate the boarding house near the station, since the Cliveden Road triangle originally set aside for it was now marked "Reserved for some public or semi-public purpose, as for a school, church, boarding house, club house, observation tower or the like."[42]

Before the final plan was inked and lithographed, the Company had to choose names for the streets. The Olmsteds suggested calling all the streets, except the lanes, "roads" because the word road "has a more suburban sound, or associates with informal curved lines better from association with country ideas."

> As for names, we dislike, as the result of experience, those sentimental
> & descriptive names which the cheapest land speculations most fondly
> indulge in, such as Glenwood, Idlewild, Riverside, Woodlawn, Oakdale
> & so on. They are only advisable if they are really appropriate and truly
> descriptive (which they seldom are), but even then they are disagreeably
> common place and hackneyed. It is safer to follow the custom of using
> the names of celebrated or notable men, for though they may be often
> used, they are associated with ideas that "wear well."[43]

Such names, the Olmsteds advised Bond, should be euphonious and ideally would be names "of purely local associations." The Olmsteds suggested the names of honorable families who had lived in the district, noting that they would have to rely on Bond to provide them with a list.[44] When Bond finally sent the list of names that had been chosen, he commented: "I followed your suggestion and adopted names connected with the property and neighborhood."[45] The list included McHenry, Howard, Winsor, Carysbrook, Sudbrook, Cliveden, Upland, Logsdon, Oxford, and Milford, as well as Monmouth and Belvidere, if additional names were needed.

The choice of "McHenry" and "Howard" as road names stemmed directly from James Howard McHenry. Sudbrook Road was derived from the original estate name, and its use was suggested by the Olmsteds:

> There is a certain advantage in sticking to one class of names, such as
> family names, but it is not essential to do so. For instance, the main…
> road from the bridge to the mill might be called "Sudbrook Road,"
> thus associating it in the mind with "Sudbrook Avenue," which you
> already have in use.[46]

Belvidere (spelled with an "i") was included on the Plan but never implemented; the origin of the name can be traced to John Eager Howard's Baltimore city estate of the same name, which also was McHenry's birthplace. Cliveden was the name of the country estate built by McHenry's maternal great grandfather in Germantown, Pennsylvania, where McHenry's grandmother (Peggy Chew Howard) was married.[47] Monmouth had associations with the McHenrys because McHenry's grandfather, James McHenry, had been present at the Battle of Monmouth.[48] Monmouth also was the name of an estate in Harford County owned by McHenry's Aunt Sophia McHenry and her son Ramsey. The origin of Logsdon Road (which was never implemented as shown but is replicated in part by the current Greenwood Road), may go back to the property before McHenry purchased it. In 1852, McHenry acquired a variety of parcels from Samuel and Mary Fletcher, including part of a tract known as Logsdon's Addition.[49] No other source for this name has been found. As for Carysbrook Road, the name may relate to McHenry's wife, Sarah Nicholas Cary; the McHenrys also had a son named Cary.[50] Most of the street names have a decidedly English flavor, as did the proposed Oxford Road, for which no specific connection with the McHenrys has been ascertained. Oxford was the only non-curvilinear road on the plan and would have run parallel to the Western Maryland Railroad tracks. The road exists today as Westover Road. The source of the name Winsor is not known, although there were two Winsors who were directors of the Sudbrook Company, at least one of whom also was a stockholder. Upland Road seems to have acquired its name because it traversed the highest elevation of the property. Glades Road was never implemented with that name (its equivalent is now Kingston Road), but may have been chosen as descriptive of that portion of the property in 1889.[51] Milford Road was pre-existing; it also was known as the Seven Mile County Road and is currently called Milford Mill Road. In addition to supplying names, Bond commented that the roads laid out by the Olmsteds, "have been found to fit the land admirably."[52]

Before completing the design, John Olmsted wrote to ask Bond whether the Company wanted to expand the right-of-way along the Milford Road boundary of the community so that there would be space "to put the path or sidewalk inside the trees and wall, [making it] as attractive as possible to your customers."[53] The question was repeated in a number of letters; eventually the Company decided not to include along Milford the six foot sidewalks that were to be installed throughout the rest of the community.[54] Subsequently, John Olmsted made one last suggestion to Bond — that the Company consider showing on the plan the houses already built (in shaded form) and those that they intended to build (in outline form only). This, he counseled, would "help to advertize the fact that there are houses and assist people holding the plan to locate themselves on the grounds."[55]

The "General Plan for Sudbrook" was dated August 24, 1889.[56] Although not lithographed until several months later, the working drawing was ready by August with enough detail to proceed. The Sudbrook Company began laying roads and building structures so that the development could attract purchasers immediately.

The design of Sudbrook embodied the classic features of an Olmsted community. As noted previously, modes of transportation were separated or made less visually intrusive — the train was below grade, the pedestrian and carriage bridges went over the tracks, and the topography of the roads was slightly recessed to minimize intrusion on the landscape. Situating the roads in a shallow cut helped emphasize the visual impact of the surrounding scenery. The bridge provided a distinct entranceway while the boundaries established a separate and self-contained neighborhood. The General Plan provided ample green spaces and common areas, although some of these were eventually filled in with houses or never realized at all. Smaller lots were included along Oxford (now Westover) and Logsdon Roads.

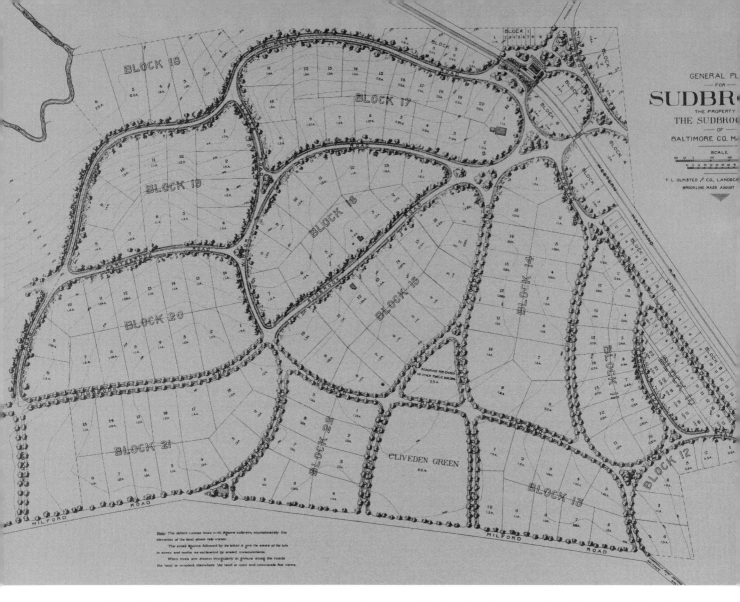

Olmsted's curvilinear road plan followed the natural contours of the land and was exceptional in an age when the straight grid pattern predominated. "GENERAL PLAN FOR SUDBROOK" BY F. L. OLMSTED & CO., AUG. 24, 1889. COURTESY OF THE NATIONAL PARK SERVICE, FREDERICK LAW OLMSTED NATIONAL HISTORIC SITE.

As in his other designs, Olmsted respected the natural contours of the land in his plan for Sudbrook. Five major roads fanned out from the entranceway bridge, connecting with other roads and weaving through the community in curves that ranged from subtle to serpentine. These five roads — Howard, Cliveden, Sudbrook, Winsor and McHenry — gently encircled the varying elevations of the property, with the highest points near Cliveden and Upland Roads, toward the center of the design. The Olmsteds had tried to obtain more upland property along Milford Road and less of the lowland property toward the Gwynns Falls, because the difference in the topography was substantial — going from 389 feet at the lowest point below McHenry to 497 feet at the highest points on Cliveden Road and Cliveden Road West. When the Company had to accept a compromise that gave them more of the lowland area, the Olmsteds carved deep lots below McHenry so that property owners would have access to higher ground for building.

As noted previously, road construction was of paramount importance in an Olmsted-designed community and Olmsted's 1868 Preliminary Report on Riverside had gone into some detail on this topic. No preliminary report was prepared for Sudbrook, but the Olmsteds sent an explanatory letter together with a diagram describing the cross-sections for roads that they recommended.[57] The cross section drawing displayed various topographical situations, showing roads in open land with little or no pitch, others with considerable pitch across the road, and some in wooded land. Diagrams showed a total right-of-way of either fifty or sixty feet, which included roadbeds of either eighteen or twenty-two feet, gutters which varied in size depending on the topography and roadbed, turf planting strips on both sides varying from five to eleven feet, and sidewalks of six to eight feet on both sides.

In open land, such as along Cliveden Road, the strip to be planted with trees was situated next to the road, followed by the sidewalk. Trees on the planting strips were to be set fifty or sixty feet apart in open land and "at regular intervals, so that they will come opposite each other on a curved street."[58] In wooded land, such as along Winsor Road, the sidewalk was to be situated next to the road, followed by the planted turf strip. The reason for locating the tree planting spaces on the house side of the side-walk in already wooded areas was "so that trees planted at irregular intervals in them may appear to be part of the forest."[59]

While ever cognizant of aesthetic considerations, the Olmsteds also took into account the practicalities of weather conditions and use:

> The turf strips between the sidewalks and roadways are of very great importance in a suburban street which has no curbs and should on no account be omitted…. In hard clay it will pay to under drain the streets with small agricultural tiles. It costs but little and is worth a great deal in wet weather, especially in spring.[60]

Well-made roads and sidewalks were essential in an Olmsted community, so that scenery could be savored during leisurely carriage rides or strolls along the shaded roads. From subsequent letters, we know that the Sudbrook Company paved its roads with macadam, or crushed stone, also called "metalling." The process was time-consuming. The Company would order carloads of various sizes of stone, which were delivered to the Sudbrook station under favorable freight rates, and then after grading the road beds and installing drains, it would unload the stone and transport it to the site, layer, oil, and roll it using a borrowed or rented steam roller, until an appropriately firm and smooth surface was attained. In the nineteenth century, these macadamized roads were considered "paved;" asphalt and concrete were not yet in widespread use.[61] A good macadamized road made year-round travel possible, drained quickly after rains and permitted reasonably smooth carriage rides.[62]

The Company's policy was that when someone purchased a lot, if the road had not yet been laid in front of the property, the Company would extend the water main pipes and drains and macadamize the road up to and in front of the property before construction began. After construction, the Company would grade the lot, put in a six-foot wide graveled sidewalk and prepare and plant the ten-foot wide planting strip between the road and the sidewalk.[63]

Even though much of Sudbrook was heavily wooded with oak, hickory and chestnut trees, Blackford's letters indicate that he planted numerous additional trees and shrubs in the ten-foot planting strips and in yards, as well as quite a few hedges and vines to cover fences that delineated side and rear property lines. Only three of his letters, however, actually named specific plant materials.[64] These letters indicate some of the species that Blackford ordered: Norway maples, American lindens, European ash,

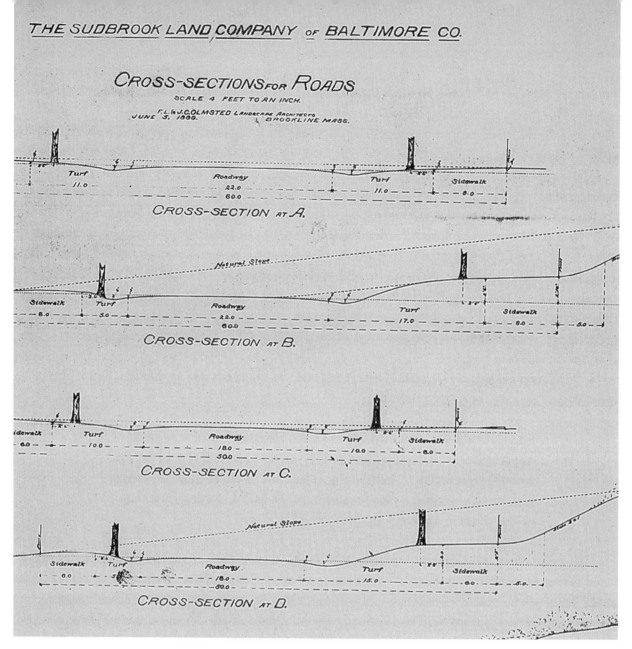

The Olmsted firm prepared six cross-sections for Sudbrook's varying road topographies, each with detailed accompanying instructions. DETAIL FROM "CROSS-SECTIONS FOR ROADS," JUNE 5, 1889. COURTESY OF THE NATIONAL PARK SERVICE, FREDERICK LAW OLMSTED NATIONAL HISTORIC SITE.

American elm and European larches, poplars, cut leaf weeping birch, black tartarian cherries, Windsor cherries, May Duke cherries, unspecified shrubs, California privet (probably for hedges), and prunus pisardi.[65]

As noted previously, the Olmsteds believed that deed restrictions were as much "a part of a plan for a suburb…as certain lines on paper."[66] An early letter to Bond raised the idea of restrictions and listed four which seemed to be derived from similar ones adopted at Riverside twenty years before. (Riverside's restrictions required purchasers to build, within one year from the time of purchase, a house costing at least $3,000, to be set back at least thirty feet, which thirty feet was required to be retained as an open court).[67] A follow-up letter to Bond set forth not four, but sixteen detailed restrictions "as seem to us desirable for giving full effect to our plan for a pleasant suburban village and for securing such sanitary conditions and customs as will in our opinion tend to greatly increase the value of your land after the settlement is well underway."[68] [See Appendix A]. The restrictions suggested for Sudbrook, which were to be incorporated into the deeds, appear to have been the most extensive that the Olmsted firm prepared.[69]

Many of the sixteen restrictions were intended to protect the master plan, moderate the impact of poor architectural design, and preserve the solely residential and non-speculative character of the neighborhood. Thus, specific provisions required that a house be erected on the lot within two years of purchase; that the completed house must not cost less than $3,000; that the house be set back at least forty feet from the street line to preserve a forecourt for the benefit of the neighborhood (except that porches with open sides could extend five feet into the forecourt); that side line setbacks be at least ten feet; that the house not be more than three stories above the ground; that only one house could be built if the lot were less than two acres; that houses be "distinctly in a rural and not in an urban style;" that fences and hedges not exceed four feet in height; that lots could not be subdivided; and that "no trade or manufacture nor business occupation of any kind shall be conducted from the said lot."[70]

In today's world, many of Olmsted's restrictions are effectively embodied in zoning regulations. But in 1889 these voluntary and contractually based land-use restrictions were significant, since they were essentially the first attempts at some form of "zoning" regulation, intended to sustain property values.[71] Because they embodied a new concept for buyers, the Sudbrook Company would have to educate its prospective purchasers on exactly how such restrictions would ultimately be to their benefit.[72]

Although the restrictions suggested by the Olmsteds did not provide for architectural review or control paint colors, Olmsted himself had strong opinions on how architecture should blend into the landscape. In this regard, his personal residence in Brookline, Massachusetts, is instructive. Early pictures show it buried "under a thick layer of vines and creepers….By means of this planting he achieved the goal that residences should 'seem to be a part of nature herself, rather than objects foreign to the general character of the place'."[73] This merging could be achieved in a number of ways. In addition to Olmsted's choice of permitting a profusion of vines to cover his home, one could use terraces to extend the building into its grounds, blurring the angular separation of structure and land. Another method was to use natural materials such as cedar shakes, or darker, more Victorian paint colors to create a continuum between densely planted outside grounds and the residence.

Olmsted did not favor white or brightly colored houses, since he wanted "no sharply defined lines mark[ing] the sudden transition from the formality of architecture to the irregularity of nature."[74] In early Sudbrook, most cottages either were brown shingle or painted darker colors than is the case in present-day Sudbrook. For example, 500 Sudbrook Lane originally had a very dark brown roof, reddish brown sides and olive green trim and shutters; the outside of the sashes and frame were cream colored. Number 503 Sudbrook, like 511 and 508, had darkly stained cedar shakes; sashes were cream colored and shutters olive green. Number 721 Cliveden Road had a sap-green roof, gray sides and a cream color for the trim.[75]

Protecting the overall design of Sudbrook from eccentric individual whim or tasteless development was a task that Eugene Blackford, the manager, considered his duty. It was a priority for Blackford to insure that anything built in Sudbrook was architecturally appropriate to the community. He participated in choosing architectural plans for, and personally oversaw the construction of, many of the early cottages. He was not shy about suggesting architectural changes if he felt any were necessary, and despite a willingness to please residents and renters, he found ways not to accommodate requests for additions or changes to cottages that he felt would not enhance their value or would be unsightly.[76]

Even plans for stables that were to be built in Sudbrook had to be submitted to Blackford and approved as architecturally appropriate.

Sudbrook's restrictions also extensively addressed sanitary issues, such as privy vaults, sewage and surface foul water and how many horses and cows could be kept (pigs were not permitted). Early in the planning process, the Olmsteds recommended that the Sudbrook Company install a "subsurface irrigation system of sewage disposal" which they had used successfully in others of their communities.[77] This system, developed by Col. George E. Waring, Jr., was implemented in Sudbrook; Blackford referred to it as the "Waring absorption system." It appears from later correspondence of the Company that it adopted Waring's system of total house drainage — for sinks, tubs, toilets, etc. The Sudbrook Company also installed some form of terra cotta tile and gutter system around the houses for rain water collection and disposal.

Providing for communal facilities such as water and sewer systems was particularly necessary in an area like Sudbrook that was not a part of any public utility system and had no township government to attend to these concerns. In addition to water, sewerage and general drainage systems, the Sudbrook Company provided roads and sidewalks (which it often extended around to back or side porches or doors), and piped houses to connect with a gas supply that either would be installed during construction or at a later time. There was a gas plant located near the boarding house which supplied it with gas; it is not known whether it supplied any other houses.[78] The Company did not provide centralized street or house lighting.[79]

After the design of Sudbrook was completed by the firm, John Olmsted sent Waring a copy of the restrictions and the General Plan for Sudbrook, commenting that the "most comprehensive thing we have done lately in the way of village organization is in the form of restrictions in the deeds of the Sudbrook Land Co."[80] In a later letter, he elaborated:

> Aside from greater particularity than is customary in restrictions against
> nuisances, occupation of lots by more than one family and the like,
> the chief novelty in this case is an attempt to provide for the public
> conveniences of water, sewerage, etc. by mutual agreement, without
> recourse to the laws for municipal government. There are no townships
> ....The district is governed by the county authorities and there is no
> regular way in which so small a community can get such public
> improvements.[81]

The Sudbrook Co. adopted and included in its deeds the restrictions suggested by Olmsted with only minor variations.[82] In some, but not all deeds, it changed the stated minimum cost of the house to be built from $3,000 to $2,500;[83] in actuality, only three houses — all constructed by the Company before the summer of 1890 — cost $2,500. All other houses cost over $3,000. In an early deed to Bond, the Company also added a provision within that same restriction stating that architectural plans had to be submitted and approved by the Sudbrook Company.[84] All of the restrictions in this deed to Bond were incorporated by reference in many subsequent deeds, extending the "architectural approval" requirement to a large number of other purchasers. But incorporation of the requirement did not seem to be uniform; in deeds in which the restrictions were written out in full, the provision — whether purposefully or by accident — was not included.

There were other inconsistencies also. Language stating that "within two years from the date hereof, a dwelling house shall be erected on the lot" can be found in some but not all early deeds.[85] While this language was not retained in all deeds, Blackford's letters repeatedly mentioned the requirement that purchasers of lots were required to build within two years. It seems that, while the Company may have removed this provision from deeds, it retained the requirement in a separate written agreement, as Olmsted suggested might be appropriate for some provisions.[86]

The most significant change from the suggested restrictions that the Sudbrook Company made was the deletion of the requirement that purchasers cooperate with the Company or its assigns, at any time before the establishment of a competent public authority, by contributing to the stock or bonds and sharing in the operating expenses to create public conveniences such as a public sewer system, public water supply, public light supply and the care and policing of streets.[87] The Company did bind itself so that "whenever a sufficient number of permanent residents will accept the charge, to convey to a corporation formed by such residents the title to all streets, ways, and public plots, and, for a nominal consideration, ample grounds for town or public hall, as well as absolute police and sanitary control of the property."[88]

Correspondence between the Olmsteds and the Sudbrook Company tapered off after February 1890. John Olmsted wrote to Bond a few more times to secure copies of the "blank form of deed showing the restrictions you finally concluded to adopt for the Sudbrook Co.," explaining they were wanted for a similar project near Denver.[89] After asking Bond what sales had been made and the prospects for more houses during the summer of 1890, Olmsted commented that the "progress you have made in developing the property seems to be very satisfactory and I have no doubt that the scheme will be a great success."[90]

The fledgling community, equipped with Olmsted's General Plan to guide its development, was on its way.

Chapter 8

Sudbrook's Beginning Years: 1889–1893

The Sudbrook Company seemed to know that Olmsted's General Plan, while "pleasing to all who had seen it," might not be sufficient to entice prospective purchasers to invest in property eight miles outside of Baltimore — a significant distance in the age of the horse and carriage — and far removed from the social, cultural and business activities of the city. Not that McHenry's property did not have many attractive natural features. It was five hundred feet above tidewater and much of the property was heavily wooded with oak, hickory and chestnut trees. Its "undulating surface" provided ample opportunity for Olmsted's landscaping genius. But what was needed to show purchasers more than the raw potential of the property was a community in miniature.

Between August 1889 and May 1890, the Sudbrook Company began to turn Olmsted's General Plan into what it hoped would become a suburban village of owner-occupied homes, with a few summer rentals. First of all, the community needed a connection with the small village of Pikesville, less than a mile away. Under agreement with the McHenry executors, the Company constructed, graveled and landscaped a road from Reisters Turnpike into its property (Sudbrook Lane today). Portions of Winsor and Cliveden Roads and Sudbrook Lane within the community were laid and graveled. The Company also built the two overhead bridges shown on the Plan, one close to the station for pedestrians and another for carriages about one hundred feet to the east, along Sudbrook Lane. In return for the Company's deeding over an acre of land for a dollar, the Western Maryland Railroad built a station designed by the Company's architects and equipped it with post office, telegraph and express services.[1]

To appeal to prospective buyers immediately, as well as to illustrate the type of community it envisioned, the Company also installed a waterworks system[2] and built nine cottages and a large boarding house — officially christened the "Woodland Inn" by the Sudbrook Company — with various outbuildings and a nearby livery stable. Remarkably, the nine initial cottages and the Inn were constructed between August 1889 and May 1890 and rented out during the summer of 1890[3] — all before the Sudbrook Company obtained title to 204 acres of the McHenry property on September 18, 1890. There is evidence, however, that the Company had entered into a contract of sale with the McHenry executors for the land (at a cost of $25,200) before executing the improvements.[4]

In accord with the deed restrictions, the buildings were all distinctly "in a rural style." While each cottage differed somewhat in design, size and accouterments, all had ample porches to catch the healthful breezes and all were fully furnished. Hoping to entice an upper middle-class clientele, the cottages also provided all the "modern conveniences" of the day. Except for three cottages that were built only for summer rental, the Company's cottages were suitable for year-round occupancy and were offered for sale. In a May 1890 letter to John Olmsted, Bond commented that "the place is much admired, and deservedly so, I think."[5]

Most of the cottages were referred to only by their number. Other cottages took on the name of an early occupant and retained that name long after the occupant departed. Cottage No. 1, on 1.4 acres of land at 511 Sudbrook Lane, was a two-story house covered with dark shingles, piped for gas, with eleven rooms, bath, range, pantries, "electric" bells,[6] an attic, a large cellar and a furnace. Cottage No. 2, across the street at 508 Sudbrook, was an eight room house on 1.04 acres, also shingled and similarly

Sudbrook bridge, about 1890. The original wooden bridge for carriages which Olmsted located to serve as the entrance to the heart of the community. Sudbrook's current one-lane bridge, built in 1907, is in the same location and serves the same purpose. FROM SUDBROOK COMPANY BROCHURE. COURTESY OF ROGER KATZENBERG.

Sudbrook Station, about 1890. Designed by the Boston firm of Cabot, Everett and Mead, this Western Maryland Railroad station was built by early 1890 to serve residents of Sudbrook and the surrounding area; it included post office, telegraph and express services. COURTESY OF WILLIAM AND ELIZABETH STELLMANN.

Sudbrook Park's water tower. Located at the highest point of the community near the corner of Cliveden West and Upland Roads, Sudbrook's waterworks system was fed by artesian wells. Although the water tower was not architecturally noteworthy, the water was said to be remarkably pure. COURTESY OF THE COX FAMILY.

Sudbrook's Woodland Inn, about 1890. The failure of lot sales to materialize as expected and the Inn's seasonal popularity — it opened in May and closed by November — contributed significantly to Sudbrook's early and unintended reputation as a "summer community." COURTESY OF THE COX FAMILY.

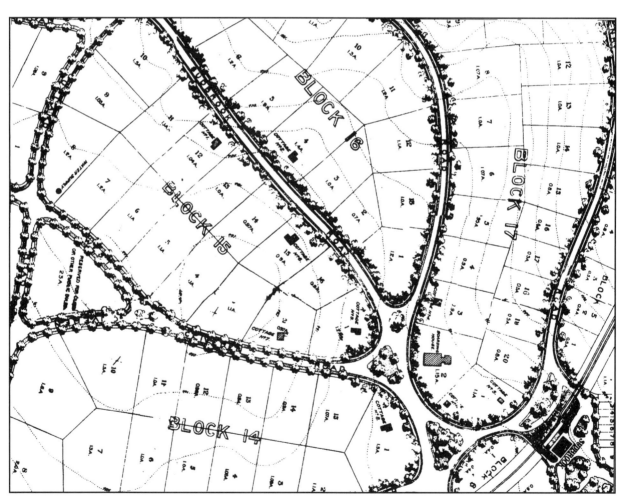

Detail from "General Plan for Sudbrook Park" by F.L. Olmsted & Co., 1890 lithograph, showing the actual location of the boarding house and the nine original "cottages" built by the Sudbrook Company. COLLECTION OF THE AUTHOR.

Cottage No. 1, about 1890. Located on 1.4 acres at 511 Sudbrook Lane, the selling price for this eleven room cottage designed by Cabot, Everett and Mead of Boston was $6,000. The six-foot wide graveled sidewalks are no longer visible today. FROM SUDBROOK COMPANY BROCHURE. COURTESY OF ROGER KATZENBERG.

Cottage No. 2, about 1890. This eight room cottage, also designed by Cabot, Everett and Mead of Boston, was located at 508 Sudbrook Lane and was available for $4,800. FROM SUDBROOK COMPANY BROCHURE. COURTESY OF ROGER KATZENBERG.

Cottage No. 4, about 1890. Located at 1020 Winsor Road next to the Inn, this six-room cottage was offered for sale or reproduction at $3,000. It had no kitchen and occupants were expected to take their meals at the Inn. FROM SUDBROOK COMPANY BROCHURE. COURTESY OF ROGER KATZENBERG.

Cottage No. 6, 505 Sudbrook Lane, about 1940. Originally an eight-room cottage, No. 6 was occupied year round by 1894 and purchased from the Sudbrook Company in 1895. COURTESY OF WILLIAM AND BETTY LOU TRABAND.

Cottage No. 10, about 1890. Similar in style to No. 4, this cottage was demolished by the State Highway Administration in the 1960s when it was preparing to build the six-lane Northwest Expressway through Sudbrook Park. (Part of the Inn can be seen to the left behind the cottage). FROM SUDBROOK COMPANY BROCHURE. COURTESY OF ROGER KATZENBERG.

A view of Sudbrook Lane looking toward the entranceway triangles and bridge, about 1890. The Woodland Inn is situated at the entrance to Winsor Road and Cottage No. 10 can be seen beyond and to the right of the Inn. FROM SUDBROOK COMPANY BROCHURE. COURTESY OF ROGER KATZENBERG.

Cottage No. 8, about 1890. Similar in design to Cottage No. 6, No. 8 originally was situated on the Cliveden Road side of lot 1, Block 14; it was moved in the 1960s to 505¹/2 Sudbrook Lane. FROM SUDBROOK COMPANY BROCHURE. COURTESY OF ROGER KATZENBERG.

Cottage No. 9, about 1890. Although part of the porch has been enclosed, this cottage still stands at 501 Sudbrook Lane. Note the wide graveled paths. FROM SUDBROOK COMPANY BROCHURE. COURTESY OF ROGER KATZENBERG.

equipped. The Boston architectural firm of Cabot, Everett and Mead designed both cottages.[7]

There was no Cottage No. 3. Its absence from an early map that listed by number the first cottages, showing a No. 10 but no No. 3, had long been a source of puzzlement. Blackford's letters and records indicate that No. 3 was the Inn property, not a cottage.[8]

The three cottages that were intended only for summer use as rentals were Nos. 4, 5 and 10. They were located very near the Inn and none had kitchens. Being the only cottages costing under $3,000, they were smaller than the other cottages and intended for " boarders" who would take all of their meals at the Inn. Cottage No. 4, at 1020 Winsor Road, is the only one of the three which survives. Cottage No. 5 was destroyed by fire in about 1927[9] and No. 10 was purchased by the State Highway Administration in the 1960s and torn down in anticipation of building a major expressway project, the Sudbrook portion of which later was abandoned. Although the Sudbrook Company's deed restrictions required that only one house could be built on lots of an acre, the Company disregarded its own rule by constructing both Cottages No. 5 and 10 on lot 1 in Block 17, containing 1.1 acres.[10]

The remaining four cottages constructed before the spring of 1890 were No. 6 at 505 Sudbrook Lane; No. 7 at 718 Cliveden Road; No. 8, originally situated on lot 1 of Block 14 of Olmsted's General Plan but moved to 505 1/2 Sudbrook Lane when the expressway project threatened; and No. 9 at 501 Sudbrook Lane. All four of these cottages were occupied during the early years by long-term tenants. Two of the cottages were purchased from the Company by 1895.[11]

The Woodland Inn, which no longer survives, was situated at the head of Winsor Road near the entranceway bridge adjacent to the intersection of Winsor, Sudbrook and Cliveden Roads. It was a two-story shingled building with forty-five rooms for guests, nine bathrooms, a parlor, sitting room, smoking room, kitchen, two pantries, two dining rooms, ample porches, a serving room, laundry, small confectioner's kitchen and ice houses.[12]

The Inn operated on a seasonal basis; it opened in May and initially closed by mid-October, although from about 1895 it remained open until November 1 each year. In 1892 the Inn acquired a furnace, permitting winter social events to be held there on occasion. Blackford asserted that the Inn could accommodate 250 guests, although how this was possible with forty-five rooms is a mystery.[13] The lessee of the Inn from 1890 through the season of 1906 was Mrs. Julia S. Thomson, about whom Blackford extolled "[she] keeps the best public table that I have ever seen."[14]

The Sudbrook Company financed its project, in part, through a $30,000 loan. Mercantile Trust & Deposit Company of Baltimore, as Trustee, held the mortgage deed of trust that secured the loan.[16] This deed of trust is significant not only because it confirms that the Inn and the nine original cottages were built before the McHenrys deeded over their property, but also because it provides important information about problems that would later impede the Company's development of Sudbrook.

The mortgage required the Company to make quarterly interest payments, with the full principal due in ten years. It also required pre-specified payments into a sinking fund whenever one of the Company's already improved lots was purchased, and required two hundred dollars an acre to be contributed to the sinking fund to release undeveloped portions of the property when they were sold. The intent was that money from the sale of lots and houses would accumulate in the sinking fund, to be used for further development and to pay the principal balance due in 1900. If the Company proved successful in selling its lots and existing cottages, it would have money to continue improvements and building, and also pay its debt to the bank. If sales lagged, the Company would not have funds available to finance further construction and might be hard pressed to pay back its loan.

Most of the information about the development of the early community comes from Eugene Blackford's letters; beginning in June 1891, they provide an almost day-by-day accounting of his activities as manager of the developing community. From that point, if not earlier, the community was called Sudbrook Park. The appellation "Park" had not been used during the design phase, when the suburban village-in-the-making had been christened "Sudbrook."[17]

The change to "Sudbrook Park" apparently was initiated by the Sudbrook Company. Although we do not know why the Company changed the name, one reason may have been to differentiate its property from the remaining portion of the Sudbrook estate that was still owned and occupied by the McHenrys. Another reason may have been a marketing attempt intended to convey the park-like environment being created. Based on Olmsted's writings about differences in the inherent nature and purposes of parks and suburban villages, he probably would not have approved of the change.[18]

We know little about the season of 1890 when the community first opened, since no records have survived.[19] Before the season of 1891 arrived, however, the Company prepared a twenty-seven page promotional brochure, with a map, photographs of the Inn, cottages and the station, a schedule of land and house prices and two pages of "references" listing Baltimore businessmen with their company affiliations. The lengthy advertising piece clearly pushed the *sale* of lots and houses; renting was not even mentioned. The brochure touted Sudbrook Park as being "seven miles from Union Station, Baltimore" on the Western Maryland Railroad, with "at present nine daily and four Sunday trains each way between Sudbrook Park and each of the four city stations, any one of which can be reached in from twenty to thirty minutes."[20]

Laden with heavy prose, the brochure reminisced about a half century before, when Baltimoreans "passed the summers in comfort under their own vines and fig trees…[and] the shaded seats and refreshing waters of the City Spring satisfied the requirements of nurses and children." Concluding that the times had changed and Baltimore was "no longer a dwelling-place, but a market and workshop," it presented another alternative:

> Other cities which have passed this stage give us the answer. The resident population of New York is said to consist only of millionaires and paupers. Years ago the intermediate classes seized upon Brooklyn as a dwelling place; and now not that city alone, but all the country within fifty miles of Trinity Church may be fairly called New York's lodging-house. Here live the business men of the great city, employers and employed; and in quiet villages, far from the sounds of traffic, have built them homes….
>
> Boston and Philadelphia boast of the beauty of suburban villages, to which their people escape after the burthen and heat of the day. Why should we not do likewise?… To those who have hitherto been compelled to undergo the evils incident to life in rented dwellings, and to that more fortunate class, who, owning city homes, can afford to add to their comfort by purchase of summer residences, we offer a property which combines all reasonable requirements.

Sudbrook Park was promoted for its high elevation, 500 feet above tidewater, its natural wooded

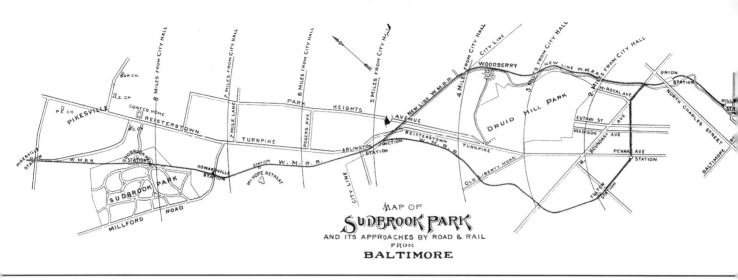

Map in a Sudbrook Company brochure, about 1890. The Company emphasized the community's rail connections with the city in an effort to attract year-round residents. The site marked "P.E. CH." was St. Mark's-on-the-Hill; the village of Pikesville was about a mile from the community. COURTESY OF ROGER KATZENBERG.

beauty and its "landscape effects which have been skillfully turned to account by the celebrated engineer, Frederick Law Olmsted, who has platted and laid out the ground." The promotional piece went on to describe the station, "a model of architectural skill" with its post office, express and telegraph offices, the Inn, the several miles of "substantially-built roads" that run through the park to connect with highways on either side, "affording pleasant drives and bicycle rambles," and the cottages "all of the most substantial construction, suited for summer or winter use."[21] Adding to the Park's appeal was that "pure water from a deep well on the highest part of the property" would be supplied to all buildings. "No expense has been spared to preserve the sanitary excellence of the park; the Waring system of subsurface drainage, approved by the best authorities on hygiene, and so successfully used at Newport, R.I., having been generally adopted."[22]

The deed restrictions which the Company feared could be a hindrance for some purchasers were explained to highlight their advantages:

> It too frequently happens that a single owner, while acting within the strict letter of the law, materially injures the value of adjoining property, either by construction of undesirable buildings or objectionable use of those already erected. To prevent the possibility of such a misfortune, the Company has adopted certain restrictions as to the character and location and occupancy of buildings. These, while interfering in no respect with use by purchasers of their property for residence purposes, being incorporated in the deeds given with the land, and guaranteeing the character of neighboring improvements, offer additional securities for the permanent value of their property.

Lots were listed from $800 to $1500, depending on size and location. Duplicates of cottages shown in the brochure started at $3,000 for a six-room model of Cottage No. 4 and went up to $6,000 for an expanded, twelve-room model of Cottage No. 2. Various payment plans could be arranged, with interest at six per cent for installment payments.

By May 1891 a tenth cottage, No. 11 at 1018 Winsor Road had been added. It was purchased by Hugh Bond as an investment and was quickly rented out for the 1891 season.[23] Notwithstanding the brochure, no additional sales had materialized. Yet, Blackford's letters for the time were optimistic. Writing in early August to his fellow director and friend James Winsor in Philadelphia, Blackford proclaimed:

> The season is now so far advanced, and everything has gone on so
> happily, and the outlook for the future is so bright, as to leave no doubt
> in my mind that any reasonable number of houses can be rented with
> no difficulty....I have applications now for two or more additional
> houses for next year, from most desirable tenants.[24]

While the rental outlook seemed strong, the Company could not survive long without sales. Unwilling to let sales hinge on stakes in the ground and drawings, it had built nine cottages and the Inn to attract potential purchasers immediately, expecting that they would be so enthralled with what they saw that they would want to buy lots and build for themselves. Yet, despite enthusiasm for Sudbrook Park, the summer crowd appeared quite content to return the following season as renters, not purchasers.

Perhaps feeling some desperation, the Company sent a proposition of sale to a "half-dozen or more" parties in late August, hoping to entice "influential & desirable gentlemen" either to purchase one of the existing cottages or to have one built "of substantially the same value" during the coming fall. Blackford stressed that the offer, which would terminate on October 1, was being made to a "very limited number."[25] A blatant emphasis on attracting only "the right people" to be residents of Sudbrook Park was a repeated theme in many of Blackford's letters.[26]

The offers which the Sudbrook Company made to a select few were intended to generate sales by making the purchase of a house in Sudbrook seem more like a no-lose investment than the purchase of a residence. The following "proposition" was typical:

> Proposition of the Sudbrook Co. in regard to the sale of Cottage No. 7, now occupied
> by Jos. Whyte, Esq.
> _____
>
> House, lot and furniture
> Estimated value today with lot @ $650 $4250.00
> *Proposition.* If he will pay $1000 cash down, the Sudbrook
> Company will lease to him for five years @ $250. per annum,
> and at the expiration of that time will convey to him, or his
> assigns, house, lot & furniture upon payment of $3250, at his
> option, the Company paying taxes, insurance & repairs during the term.
>
> Comparison of results under above proposition with results
> under present lease continued for five years.
> Present rental $450 x 5 yrs. = $2250.
> Add average int. @ 6% $337.00
> $2587.00
>
> _____
>
> Under Proposition $250 x 5 yrs. = $1250.00
> Add average int. @ 6%   187.50

Cash payment	1000.00	
Add int. on same for 5 yrs.	300.00	
		$2737.50

Amt. paid for option of purchase if money should be invested @ 6%	$150.50
If at the end of 5 years the property is worth $4250, then the gain is =	$849.50

If the property has depreciated $849.50, then there will be neither gain nor loss. The utmost possible loss is $150.50 int. on the $1000, in case the value of the property has fallen $1000.[27]

An "utmost possible loss" of only $150.50? What better way to convince Baltimoreans who could afford it that it made no sense to rent — that they could not lose if they purchased either a second, summer home in Sudbrook Park or sold their house in the city and moved year-round to the fledgling community? Or, as Blackford summarized in a subsequent letter, "I have been over the terms very carefully & cannot see any defect, nor any reason why it should not recommend itself very strongly to an intending purchaser. The risk remains entirely with us, which we are willing to take for the advantage to be gained by having men of influence & position identified with us."[28]

As autumn of 1891 approached, Blackford continued to be optimistic about the future. The Company had so far invested about $70,000 in buildings, furniture, the drainage system, the waterworks and plantings, and had brought in an income that season of about $6,200. Expenses had been heavy, but in the coming year the Company intended to begin charging for water and the care of lawns and walks.[29]

Blackford wrote again to James Winsor, saying that he knew of "no better paying investment" than building in Sudbrook Park:

Left: Cottage No. 11, 1018 Winsor Road. First occupied during the season of 1891, this house was one of eight rental properties in Sudbrook owned by Hugh L. Bond, Jr. COURTESY OF MARYLAND HISTORICAL TRUST.

Right: Cottage No. 12, 515 Sudbrook Lane. Designed and owned by George E. Coursen, this house originally had a large wrap-around porch and additional front detail similar to Cottages 11 and 14, both of which Coursen may also have designed. A fire in the 1920s destroyed the porch and front of the house. PHOTOGRAPH BY PEGGY FELDMAN-ESKEY.

The almost perfectly successful summer, the enthusiasm, I may say, of all who have lived at the Park or visited it, is already bearing fruit, as there are more applicants for cottages next year than can be accommodated, & four or five are very anxious for the Company to build for them as renters. This both Mr. Bond & I think unwise, as the money would of course have to be borrowed, and what funds we have are badly needed for opening and paving new roads, the finest part of the property being yet totally undeveloped. I think the people of Baltimore are now about to show appreciation of the enterprise & that sales will begin in earnest.[30]

To be ready when lot sales materialized, Blackford sought estimates for materials needed to open 6,600 feet of new roads and 13,200 feet of new sidewalks.[31] Work began in the fall of 1891 to extend Sudbrook Lane to Monmouth, spurred in part by the construction of Cottage No. 12, a large house at 515 Sudbrook Lane intended for year-round occupancy. George H. Coursen, who became the owner of Cottage No. 12, not only had designed his own house but also prepared and submitted plans for five additional architectural designs to Blackford, who set about getting estimates on the cost to build each. (These may have been requested because Bond was preparing to build three cottages).

As a beautiful autumn continued, guests at the Inn convinced Mrs. Thomson, its manager, not to close on October 1, but to remain open until the 15th. As a hopeful sign, discussions began about the sale of Cottage No. 7 (718 Cliveden Road) with Mrs. Decatur H. Miller, who was "charmed with the plans" but insisted on being allowed also to purchase the opposite lot, "to prevent anyone from building on it."[32] Blackford characterized the season of 1891 as "successful," with "a population of about 300" and "every room in every house & the Inn being full."[33] Sudbrook Park reveled in its summer popularity, even though it had made only one sale.[34]

When October 15 arrived, Blackford lamented "this has been a melancholy day at the Park; all of the summer residents moved out today."[35] A month later, he wrote to a summer renter, "I wish [Cottage No. 7] were sheltering you & yours at this time, as I am very lonesome now when at the Park.[36]

While convincing Baltimoreans to occupy Sudbrook's cottages year-round proved difficult, it was not because the cottages were unsuitable for year-round residence. Contrary to popular myth, except for a relatively few true "summer" cottages, most cottages in Sudbrook Park either were equipped for winter use or piped for heat and ready to have a furnace installed when needed. A number of Blackford's letters talk about how substantial the houses were, with Nos. 1 and 2 often used as examples, being "well built of specifications drawn by a Boston architect containing features not absolutely necessary in our climate. All the houses are paper lined & some have double floors."[37]

The initial difficulty in selling Sudbrook as a year-round suburban village may have stemmed in large part from the fact that the socially affluent of that period were expected to winter in the city (close to businesses, schools, social and cultural events), and to summer in the country (where high elevations, cool breezes, plentiful shade, pure water and improved sanitation systems promoted a more healthful environment). So prevalent was this pattern that the seasonal comings and goings of socially prominent Baltimoreans were dutifully reported in newspapers, which would announce such items as "Mr. & Mrs. Joseph White have returned to their home after a pleasant summer spent at a cottage in Sudbrook Park" or "Mr. & Mrs. Edward Simpson have returned to their city home, 6 Read Street east."[38] To live year-round in Sudbrook in the early 1890s — with no electricity, no local social activities and a somewhat limited train schedule into the city — seemed attractive to only the most hardy. Even Blackford, who had long lived at his Pikesville farm "Cleve," resided in the city during the coldest months.[39]

Blackford did what he could to make life comfortable for Sudbrook's few winter residents, a population that was sparse in contrast to the inflated summer habitation.[40] He wrote to John M. Hood, President of the Western Maryland Railroad, requesting four settees on the porch of the station for the winter, noting that there "were no seats last winter for passengers awaiting trains to their great discomfort." He also asked for the same train schedule as had been provided the prior winter, adding that it would be convenient to have the four o'clock train going west stop at the Sudbrook station.[41]

Despite what had been an apparently successful 1891 rental season, there were hints that the Company was operating with slim financial reserves. Blackford discovered negative balances in the Company's account when he went to make deposits. Bills submitted to George Slaughter, the treasurer of the Company, frequently went unpaid until Blackford submitted them a second or third time, while having to make some explanation to the annoyed creditor still waiting for a check. Even Blackford found it necessary to ask for speedy payment from a resident on a minor ice bill, "as I am at a loss for money at this time."[42] As 1892 dawned, sales still had not materialized as expected. By then, the Sudbrook Company had expended about $100,000.[43]

Blackford wrote to Bond suggesting that they advertise, changing the notices frequently to attract attention. He added: "I look for an awakening of our people with the disappearance of this snow, & think that we should keep the existence of Sudbrook Park before their eyes continuously." Blackford also reported to Bond that a recent ball held at the Inn was "a grand success, and I am amply repaid for some days of hard work by the notice it has brought upon the Park."[44] George Coursen, who was living in Cottage No. 1 while 515 Sudbrook was being built, provided Blackford with advertising copy. Blackford wrote back to Coursen that he had "mistaken his calling" and that the ads would run three times a week in the *American.* "Do let me have some more. You have the idea exactly, & if anything will attract the attention of our people, they will," Blackford exclaimed.[45]

While the Company, through Blackford, continued to market the community for year-round residents — "The place is by no means intended as a summer resort, but for permanent homes as well"[46] — it became apparent that the predominant rental pattern made the five month "season" from May to October, as Blackford realistically observed, "the sole season of profit…[and] the rent is for that period really."[47] Although all leases were drawn for a nine or twelve month period, the extension of leases until February (even when the cottage had been vacated in October) was primarily "to secure the tenant the refusal of the home for another year."[48] Each year on or before the first of February, "cottagers" were to let Blackford know if they wanted their cottage for the coming year. If the tenant gave notice in February that he or she did not plan to return, Blackford usually had a waiting list of persons seeking to rent cottages in Sudbrook for the season.

The winter of 1892 proved to be a severe and lengthy one, delaying the Company's road building. In March, Blackford commented that "this vile weather is throwing back the work very much, tho' I continued to load & empty two carloads of rotten rock last week."[49]

By spring 1892, there was welcome new activity. Three houses were going up — Nos. 13 and 14 at 500 and 503 Sudbrook Lane, respectively, and No. 15 at 721 Cliveden. Built by Hugh Bond, Jr. as investments, all were under lease before they were constructed. The occupants moved in during June 1892. These three cottages, situated in close proximity to the Inn, initially had no kitchens. In 1894, kitchens, dining rooms, pantries, and furnaces were added to Nos. 14 and 15, and these became residences occupied year-round by their tenants.[50]

Cottages No. 13, 14 and 15 were built by John Cowan, who had been McHenry's carpenter and who constructed most of Sudbrook's first thirty-five cottages. There is no information about who designed Bond's three cottages. Although Blackford had written in January 1892, to two companies in Grand Rapids, Michigan, D.H. Hopkins and F. P. Allen, requesting plan books of architectural designs for houses costing over $1,500, he received nothing from Hopkins and made no further mention of either company or their plans.

It is possible that Nos. 13, 14 and 15 were based on the plans that George Coursen had prepared and given to Blackford earlier. Nos. 11 (which Coursen also may have designed), 13 and 14 share certain stylistic similarities. As often happened with the early houses, Blackford took a basic plan, modified it and used it more than once.[51] Blackford's own house in Sudbrook Park, built in 1896 at 1008 Winsor Road, was redesigned by Cabot, Everett & Mead based on their plan for Cottage No. 2 (508 Sudbrook), with modifications suggested by Blackford. It is an exaggeration to say, as some residents do, that every old house in Sudbrook Park has a "twin," but some do, having been built from the same basic design and modified slightly the second or third time.[52] Plans for Cottage No. 6 clearly were modified and reused. When Blackford requested them back from John Cowan for a prospective purchaser, he was told that they had been used to build two houses and were "worn out."[53]

In addition to supervising the construction of Bond's three cottages and building a house behind the Inn to accommodate the eighteen servants who were employed there, Blackford was busy at Sudbrook Park with his annual spring preparations for returning cottagers — cleaning up from winter damage, overseeing repairs and the painting of the Company's cottages, ordering replacement furniture and matting for floors, handling rentals, responding to resident requests or complaints, and grading, seeding and planting.[54]

Fortunately for the Company, if not for Blackford's workload, sales began to materialize; Blackford added to his list of chores the surveying of lots for interested purchasers. As had been predicted by the Olmsteds, most of the early cottages were clustered in the more wooded area, near the station and the Inn. When Blackford thought that he had a prospective purchaser who would be willing to build farther away on Sudbrook Lane next to Coursen's No. 12, he wrote to Bond: "I am inclined to foster

Cottage No. 13, 500 Sudbrook Lane. Designed by Coursen and owned by Bond, this house was located near the Inn and was a popular rental until it was sold in 1907. PHOTOGRAPH BY BOOTS SHELTON.

Cottage No. 14, 503 Sudbrook Lane. Built as a rental by Bond in 1892, this house became a year-round residence by 1894.
PHOTOGRAPH BY PEGGY FELDMAN-ESKEY.

Cottage No. 15, 721 Cliveden Road. Also a rental owned by Bond, this cottage was first occupied in June 1892; it became a year-round residence in 1894. PHOTOGRAPH BY FRANCIS B. GAVIN, ABOUT 1940. COURTESY OF BETTY O'CONNELL ERWIN.

Western Maryland Railroad train and Sudbrook Station, as seen from the bridge, about 1890. The community's fate was closely linked to the access to the city that the railroad provided. FROM SUDBROOK COMPANY BROCHURE. COURTESY OF ROGER KATZENBERG.

any disposition to get away from that Hotel, where they are getting too thick."[55]

Once again, Blackford wrote to John Hood, President of the Western Maryland Railroad, asking for the same trains as were provided the previous year. Since the Inn was open already, and the summer crowd arriving, Blackford asked that the four o'clock train be scheduled to resume as soon as possible, noting: "Our future success is so intimately connected with the train facilities afforded by your Company, that I hope you will excuse me for being somewhat urgent in asking every indulgence in your power."[56] (Apparently, Blackford's request was granted, since he wrote no subsequent letters about this).

The year of 1892 seemed a good one for the Sudbrook Company. While sales still had not been as plentiful as hoped for, at least five lots were sold in 1892 to persons who intended to build for their own use and the new houses on Bond's three lots had been leased and occupied by June. The Company's requirement that houses had to be built within two years of purchasing a lot meant that houses would be constructed on the other five lots in the near future.[57]

By March 29 of that year, Blackford had to turn down requests to rent for the season, telling inquirers that "all cottages at Sudbrook Park have been sold, rented or leased."[58] A short time later, Blackford again reported that no cottages were available, but enclosed promotional literature and commented:

Left: Cottage No. 16, 717 Cliveden Road, was designed by Baltimore architect Thomas Buckler Ghequier for Horatio Armstrong and his family. The house was completed in April 1895. Right: Cottage No. 22, 726 Howard Road, was designed by Baltimore architect J. Appleton Wilson for R. W. Graves and his wife. The Graveses purchased the property in 1892 and it remained in their family until the 1960s. PHOTOGRAPHS BY PEGGY FELDMAN-ESKEY.

> There are 15 houses now…and all have been either leased or rented long since by a most desirable class of tenants. Lack of capital alone prevents us from building more, as there is a great demand for them, but it is wiser to develop the property with our money, & leave individuals to build for themselves in the future.[59]

During the summer of 1892, the Inn and all the houses were full and the Park was again a lively spot. Coursen had moved into Cottage No. 12. Houses for Edgar H. Bankard at 710 Cliveden Road and George Shriver at 607 Sudbrook Road were under construction. Blackford's family descended on Sudbrook *en masse* to pick out lots. Apparently, Blackford intended to purchase two lots on Cliveden Road, Nos. 10 and 11 in Block 14. He planned to keep No. 10 (709 Cliveden) for himself and build as soon as he could sell his farm "Cleve." No. 11 (711 Cliveden) he planned to give to his son-in-law to build a permanent residence.[60]

Inquiries on purchasing in Sudbrook continued to pepper Blackford's mail. In line with the then-prevalent thinking that the stench, water supply, unsanitary conditions and stagnant summer air in cities carried germs and promoted disease, Blackford's responses included information about the sanitary excellence of Sudbrook Park. He informed those who inquired that "the aim of this Company [is] to so develop its 204 acres as to offer a perfectly unobjectionable place of residence for those who wish to live in the country for the summer season or for the year round, by furnishing an abundant supply of the best water, enforcing the best system of drainage, and by so policing the whole tract as to ensure perfect sanitary results."[61]

Another advantage that Blackford trumpeted was the ability of purchasers to build to suit themselves or buy an existing cottage and "then leave it at any time in the care of the Co. officers — meanwhile having his lawn mowed & grounds tended for a small sum, thus doing away with the necessity of employing any male help."[62] (Female help, in the form of cooks and housekeepers, was *de rigeur* in those days, although Blackford touted proximity to the Inn and its dining facilities as an often overlooked advantage "in case of default of servants or a desire to have a rest from the cares of housekeeping.")[63]

In August Blackford wrote to Bond to congratulate him on his appointment as General Counsel for the Receivers of the Richmond & Danville Railroad System, adding that "I do hope that your presence will not be required in Washington, as stated in the papers." Blackford had been hoping to see Bond about increasing Sudbrook's water supply, since the "necessity of it is daily more apparent as the water in the well steadily declines, keeping me very uneasy." While Blackford had the plans and estimates ready, he apparently needed Bond's approval to proceed. But the letter continued on about a more personal matter.[64]

Blackford had been trying without success to sell his farm "Cleve" at the asking price of $15,000. Although he wanted to buy and build in Sudbrook Park and had chosen lots, these plans were dependent on the sale of his farm. Before he could reduce the asking price for his farm, he needed to know how much of an increase in salary he would be paid if he built and resided in the Park, "as this increase would be a factor in determining the sale, at a price which I otherwise could not afford. I feel a delicacy in making this proposition, but I am also aware of the advantages to be derived by my residence at the Park."

It seemed likely that having Blackford move to Sudbrook Park permanently and devote his full attention to daily operations and sales could only be beneficial to the Company. Moving beyond its summer-rental reputation was imperative if the Company was to succeed. Attracting purchasers and, ideally, permanent residents was a priority. As Blackford commented to Bond in a December 1892 letter: "We want young married people who will live [in Sudbrook Park] the year round & draw others near them."[65]

But a widespread financial depression was soon to impose unwelcome realities on the country. Neither the Sudbrook enterprise nor Blackford would be immune to the panic of 1893, a severe financial crisis that bankrupted more than two hundred railroads and gripped most of the industrialized world for months, with consequences that lasted for years in certain industries.[66]

Among those giants affected beyond the immediate crisis was Baltimore's B&O Railroad. Long term difficulties (that would later occupy much of Hugh Bond's time and distract his attention from

Edgar H. Bankard and his wife built this house (Cottage No. 18) at 710 Cliveden Road in 1892. The Bankards were long-time residents of Sudbrook Park. The stable (left rear) was built a few years later; like all stables in Sudbrook Park, it had to be architecturally appropriate. PHOTOGRAPH BY BOOTS SHELTON.

George M. Shriver, a B&O Railroad attorney, built this house at 607 Sudbrook Road in 1893. PHOTOGRAPH BY PEGGY FELDMAN-ESKEY.

Designed by Baltimore architect George Archer and one of many Sudbrook houses built by John Cowan, the Trego house at 600 Sudbrook Road was both sturdy and luxurious.
PHOTOGRAPH BY ROGER KATZENBERG.

Sudbrook) were precipitated when the house of Baring in London, which had been bankers to the B&O, failed during the 1893 depression. The railroad was severely affected: "[It] ceased to maintain its tracks and buildings and its efficiency declined, till it mortgaged even its magnificent Central Building at Charles and Baltimore streets. Finally, when a New York bank foreclosed on a loan in February, 1896, the New York courts appointed receivers."[67]

The mood in the country was not optimistic during the financially brutal winter of 1893. Personally, Blackford was not successful at selling his farm, and he eventually took it off the market. He rented it out for the summer for many years, although never at the price he thought it should command. He never bought the property on Cliveden Road that he had wanted for himself and his son-in-law.[68]

But in his letters to prospective purchasers, Blackford was ever the promoter. In a June 1893 letter to a businessman in Los Angeles who had seen an ad for a house in Sudbrook Park, Blackford sent a map of Sudbrook, noting the Sudbrook Company's investment to date and capitalizing on Sudbrook's Olmstedian lineage: "[It is] the result of a Boston enterprise & capital; about $150,000 has been expended here after the plans of F. Law Olmsted, the celebrated landscape engineer, he regarding it as his masterpiece."[69]

Blackford recited the litany of advantages of living in Sudbrook Park: "The roads are macadamized with 10 ft. strips of sod each side planted with trees & shrubs, then 5 ft. gravelled walks. There is a handsome R.R. station on the grounds with express, [postal] & telegraph offices & eleven trains each way….Also the electric line to Pikesville passes within a quarter of a mile of the property, with trains every 20 minutes."[70]

Blackford went on to describe the Trego house (600 Sudbrook Road) that was for sale, emphasizing those attributes that might appeal to an upper middle-class purchaser of that time:

> It is situated in a lot of two acres with beautiful shade trees, lofty elms, oak & poplar, contains hall 16' x 25', parlour, dining room, library, kitchen, pantry, cold room on first floor, seven bedrooms & bathrooms on 2d floor & billiard room 38' x 20' on 3d floor. All are trimmed with cypress finished in hand oil; the walls are coloured beautifully with plastico in various tints, and the floors are particularly fine, being doubled throughout. The house is plumbed in the best style known and has two water closets. The drainage is after the Waring system, the best now known, and the one adopted in all our buildings.[71]

Clearly important for those considering moving to a suburban village, and not forgotten by Blackford, was how to provide for the daily necessities of life:

> Every sort of supplies are brought to the door — ice, milk, vegetables
> & meat. The Company agrees, if desired, to keep the grounds of the
> cottages in order for a small sum, say $20 to $25 — thus doing away
> with the necessity of keeping a man servant. Water of the finest quality
> is furnished at $10 per annum. Each road has a water main laid.[72]

Despite a worthy sales effort, the California businessman did not purchase the Trego house. It was, however, sold in October 1893 to J. Hume Smith.[73]

While the panic of 1893 seemed to impact sales at Sudbrook (there were none), the community continued to attract an ample summer population of renters who appeared unaffected by the economic depression. A July 1893 article in the *Baltimore Sun* stated that "Sudbrook is unusually lively this summer, forming a centre for the festivity of the dwellers in the vicinity." Describing the social attractions of the community, the article noted that many families "meet three times a day in the large dining-room of the hotel" and that a "fourth reunion, of the young people only, occurs every evening in the ballroom, where a dance is enjoyed." Not only was there "much musical talent represented among the guests at the hotel and cottages," but dances were given by the "Sudbrookians" and the "Pikesvillians" on alternate Friday evenings, to which Green Spring Valley, Pikesville and "other places in the surrounding country send a large contingent." The tone of this article about "many a jolly time" at Sudbrook, with its happy families in their "cosy homes," contrasts rather starkly with an article immediately next to it which reported about the receivers, including Hugh Bond, appointed for the Richmond and Danville Railroad.[74]

In December 1893, the Sudbrook Company doubled Blackford's salary to $83.33, but the benefits of Blackford's moving to Sudbrook remained more intangible than apparent. Although sales would soon pick up, this may have been more related to the fact that the country began recovering from its financial reverses than to Blackford's having moved to the community. In addition, Sudbrook's sales were and would continue to be affected by the creation and growth of other new suburbs around Baltimore, some of which sought to attract the same clientele as Sudbrook Park.

Chapter 9

LOCATION IS EVERYTHING: 1892–1893

In order to understand some of the reasons why Sudbrook Park had difficulty selling lots when it seemed immensely popular and always had a waiting list of renters, it is necessary to place Sudbrook in the context of the entire metropolitan area. Although one of the earliest planned suburban developments near Baltimore, Sudbrook did not exist in isolation. Many external factors — including the availability and proliferation of other late nineteenth century suburban developments — would play a role in Sudbrook Park's ability to attract purchasers.

On February 18, 1892 the *Baltimore Daily News* ran a lengthy article titled "Suburban Developments...How Baltimore Is Forging to the Front." The title was misleading. The article was about only one suburb, Roland Park, which had hardly begun its development. Interestingly, this prominent piece of free advertising appeared only six weeks after Charles Grasty, one of the directors of the Roland Park Company, became publisher of the *Daily News*.[1]

The *Daily News* article sang accolades of both Roland Park and the new electric rapid transit that would soon link Roland Park with the city, proclaiming: "It ought to come at once." When the article appeared, Roland Park was still being readied for opening. The Roland Park Company, which had incorporated about two years after the Sudbrook Company, was hard at work putting in roads and improving one hundred twenty of its nearly eight hundred acres.[2] Nevertheless, the *Daily News* described it as "a suburban development...not equaled in character, if indeed, in magnitude, by any similar enterprise now in progress in this country." Even when Roland Park opened in June 1892, "there were no beautiful lawns, there were no set-back houses, and...lot sales were disappointing."[3] Despite the article's grandiose hyperbole, it provides some insight into the suburban movement in Baltimore in 1892 and the "selling points" of superiority claimed by almost every suburban development in the early 1890s.

Speaking about Baltimore generally, the article noted that "after having shown no suburban movement for many years, [Baltimore] will, in the near future, compare favorably with the cities in which suburban improvement has been notable." It continued:

> Not many years ago, and within the memory of the present generation, it was deemed necessary to have one's residence within a short walk of his place of business. One or two miles, at the outside, was the limit... The laying of rails, and the equipping of horse car lines was the first step...residences were then erected still more remote from the business centre.
>
> Americans are progressive...if anything, and the horse car is now being fast relegated to the curiosities of the past. The introduction of electricity and the construction of cable lines...has enabled the change and it is no longer considered either desirable or fashionable to live in the business section.[4]

According to the *Daily News,* Baltimore (population approximately 500,000) lagged behind

Electric and cable cars such as this Baltimore Traction Company car on the Baltimore, Pimlico & Pikesville line came into common usage in the 1890s and provided the necessary impetus for suburban development. COURTESY OF THE BALTIMORE COUNTY PUBLIC LIBRARY COLLECTION.

other large cities in developing suburban additions because it lacked rapid transit, "no electric or cable car lines having been in operation until 1891."[5] But now, "every line in the city is preparing to adopt the cable or electric system."[6] Roland Park did get a rapid transit electric line in May 1893. The *Daily News* was accurately prophetic when it concluded: "These improvements [rapid transit] mark a new era in Baltimore. They mean the beginning of great suburban developments which are now an absolute necessity to provide for the overflowing population."

Without doubt, availability and convenience of transportation was a key factor propelling the suburban movement, not only in Baltimore, but throughout the country. Before the installation in 1859 of Baltimore's first horse-car line (similar to the earlier horse-drawn omnibus except that it ran on rails), transportation choices were limited. As streetcar historian Michael Farrell has written:

To get around town the well-to-do had their own conveyances. Most others walked. It is true that there were hackney coaches which operated on a basis similar to the taxicabs of today; yet the fares charged by the hackneys were too high to make them readily available to the average person. Some idea of the rates is manifest from the fact that fifty cents was charged to carry one person to any of the railroad stations, with an additional charge of fifty cents when the coach was sent especially from the stables. (At that time, the wage of a laborer was only about one dollar a day.)....Like the hackneys, [the omnibus]... failed to offer a solution....[Introduced in 1844, it was] uncomfortable and slow, but, more important, it did not offer the comprehensive service which was urgently needed.[7]

While private carriages offered convenience to the affluent, comfort was not assured. Carriages traveled, at best, over cobblestone or paved (macadam) roads that had been rolled and packed firm by a steam roller; at worst, over gutted or poorly drained dirt roads. Train travel into the city, when available, could be far more comfortable for those who could afford it,[8] but early trains had their disadvantages also. They could be hot and dusty in the summer and alternately cold or overly hot in the winter, since heat was provided by wood or coal burning stoves. The horse-car rail lines that ran through the city and to a number of outlying areas by the 1880s were smoother than the old omnibuses and cheaper than train travel, but were still relatively slow modes of travel.

Introduced in Baltimore after 1890, electric and cable cars were a notable advance.[9] These new "streetcars" or "trolleys," as they were called, were smoother and faster than horse rail lines, cheaper and more frequent than trains, and in the case of the Lake Roland Elevated electric line, avoided some downtown street congestion to provide a faster commute.[10] The introduction of electrified streetcars provided a strong impetus for suburban development in Baltimore and contributed significantly to the apparent early success of suburbs like Roland Park.[11]

While convenient transportation was a necessity that was heavily touted as a selling point, early suburbs advertised an entire arsenal of advantages to lure prospective purchasers. According to the 1892 *Daily News* article, there was a veritable litany of reasons why Roland Park represented a suburb "unsurpassed for beauty and contrivances securing health and comfort by any in the United States." This litany very closely echoed Sudbrook Park's advantages. First was Roland Park's water — "its purity and the entire absence of disease-producing germs, and its fitness for drinking purposes." Next, its sanitary and sewerage system, developed by none other than George E. Waring, Jr. of Newport, R.I., the celebrated sanitary engineer whose system had already been implemented at Sudbrook Park. The article touted Roland Park's house setbacks, its graveled roads ("like the drives in Druid Hill Park"), its "paved" (graveled) sidewalks lined with rows of shade trees, its existing chestnut, oak, elm and beech trees, concluding that "the healthfulness of the place cannot be questioned."

Although Baltimore had been slow to catch the suburban fever that was spreading across the nation, it began to play catch-up by 1893, with developments springing up in every direction. On April 30, 1893 Baltimore's *Sunday Herald* carried an article titled "Monumental City Suburbs, They Cannot Be Eclipsed Anywhere in the Union."[62] The mere magnitude of the article was remarkable. Covering more than three standard newspaper pages, the article went into great detail about the

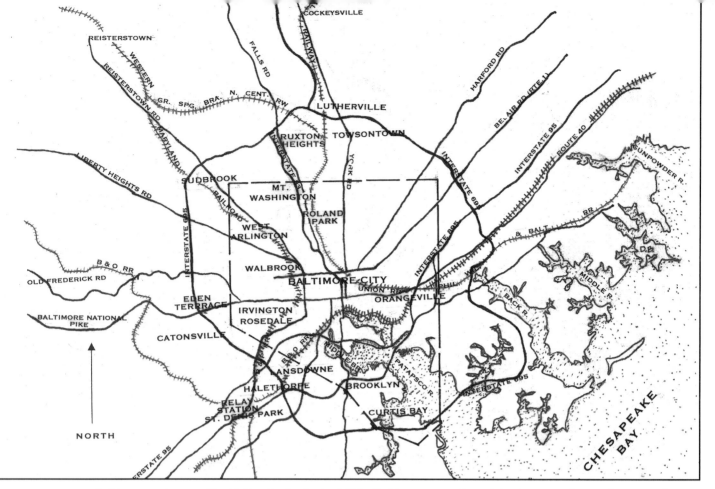

Baltimore and some of its 1893 suburbs. In the 1890s, Baltimoreans embraced developments close to the city and on convenient rail or electric trolley lines more quickly than they did suburbs like Sudbrook that were farther out. MAP BY DARRAGH BRADY, WITH CURRENT MAJOR INTERSECTING HIGHWAYS INDICATED.

multiple advantages (again, superlatives only) of thirteen city suburbs: Lansdowne, South Baltimore Harbor/Curtis Bay, West Arlington, Rosedale (in the Irvington section of West Baltimore, and not to be confused with the present day Rosedale area on the east side of Baltimore County), St. Denis Park, Cedar Heights, Ruxton Heights, Orangeville, Eden Terrace, Roland Park, Tuxedo Park, Halethorpe and Walbrook.

Some of the communities identified were located in areas already annexed to the city in 1888,[13] such as West Baltimore's Rosedale and Walbrook, or were close to the developed extensions pushing out from the city, like Roland Park and West Arlington. Others, like Lansdowne, St. Denis, Ruxton Heights and Halethorpe, were slightly farther from the city's limits. Interestingly, Sudbrook Park was not mentioned at all.[14]

One might gather from a quick perusal of the article's caption that all of these suburbs were well-established at the time, bustling with houses and residents. In fact, three of the named communities had no houses yet; one was in the process of building; and only nine had any existing homes. Given the total land to be developed in each subdivision, many were still sparsely built. With only a few exceptions, the closer to the city and the smaller and less expensive the individual lots, the more sales the developers had made.[15]

A number of standard themes have always appeared in advertisements promoting the suburban ideal.[16] In its review of new suburbs, the 1893 *Sunday Herald* article, for example, paraded a list of positive attributes in an effort to attract Baltimoreans to purchase both a residence and a way of life apart from the city: high elevations (from 200 to 600 feet above tidewater),[17] shade trees and green foliage, pure air, pure and wholesome water (some from artesian wells), good walks (either planked or graveled), macadamized roads, excellent natural drainage, accessibility to churches, stores and schools — and that key to all suburban development — convenient access to the city by either train or electric rail. Various subdivisions were declared free from "malarial and other deleterious influences."

Other inducements included monetary incentives to attract purchasers. Many of the more modest subdivisions offered terms of ten dollars down, five dollars a month. Most offered five to ten percent discounts for cash. Several suburbs offered extended payment terms with no interest and no taxes to pay until the land was deeded over. Several provided free transportation or had a special trolley to bring prospective purchasers to see the area. Certain communities boasted sizable house setbacks, electric street and residential lighting, sewerage systems, proximity to "some of Baltimore's most prominent families," and elegant, park-like surroundings.

The *Sunday Herald* article is instructive in many ways. In addition to highlighting the basic necessities and desired luxuries of late nineteenth century Baltimore suburbs, it conveys the influence that precipitating external events, particularly the introduction of streetcars, played in causing Baltimoreans to participate more actively in the suburban movement in 1893.[18] It also provides insight into the various styles of suburbs that grew up around Baltimore. As Waesche concluded in his study of Roland Park and environs, while all suburban house purchasers were by definition middle class (otherwise they could not have saved or earned enough money to buy or finance their home), "the middle class was not homogeneous," thus giving rise to as many types of suburbs "as there were different socioeconomic subgroups within the middle class."[19]

Baltimore's early suburbs can be classified into two principal types, the "industrial suburb" and the "commuter village."[20] Industrial suburbs had small to modest sized lots, were built around or situated in close proximity to industrial sites, and attracted laborers who worked nearby. While all commuter villages were located at some distance from industrial sites and commercial areas, the category encompassed a diversity of developments, ranging from more modest row house subdivisions like Rosedale on Frederick Avenue, which advertised that it was "lowest in price…twenty cents per day will pay for a nice lot in a short time," to more elite suburbs like Eden Terrace, near Catonsville, with no lot less than an acre and the minimum cost of a house set at $2,500.[21]

Of the suburbs described in the article, three were of the "industrial village" type: South Baltimore Harbor/Curtis Bay, Orangeville, and Lansdowne. Despite striking differences with Sudbrook Park and other suburbs far removed from the locus of industry and commerce, these three industrially-oriented suburbs advertised some of the same amenities. South Baltimore Harbor/Curtis Bay, with 1,500 acres to develop along Baltimore's waterfront, had constructed 200 brick houses and stores fronting on "streets graded and paved."[22] Orangeville, described as a natural town site for railroad men and mechanics "employed at Sparrows Point, Canton, Regester & Sons' Foundry…or anywhere in East Baltimore," boasted that "[e]very lot is well shaded with stately trees, so the purchaser is not required to wait 10 or 15 years for one of the grandest luxuries a country residence affords."[23]

Lansdowne, where adjoining property had been purchased for manufacturing purposes,[24] was described as "a model suburban village" with its broad avenues "lined with 75 cottages. A solid board-walk traverses the entire village, and at every 25 feet is placed a beautiful tree. Artesian wells furnish excellent water, while the drainage is all that could be desired."[25] Pure water, good drainage, trees, planked or paved sidewalks and streets — these were attributes that were important in all early suburbs.

As noted previously, there was a considerable range among commuter village suburbs. At the less expensive end of the spectrum were row house suburbs like Rosedale, a forty-acre tract adjoining Irvington.[26] Also appealing to persons of moderate income was Halethorpe. Located along the Baltimore and Washington turnpike road, it offered lots priced at $100 to $400. There already were thirty cottages on its 130 acres with twenty ready to build.[27] In addition to its graded, "handsome avenues" and the "large number of shade and ornamental trees" that had been planted, Halethorpe could boast that many of its side gutters had been paved and "its board walks and many beautiful Queen Anne cottages are models of neatness and elegance."

Certain of the other commuter villages discussed in the article vied to an even greater extent with each other, and with Sudbrook Park, for a more affluent clientele. Among this group were Walbrook, West Arlington and Roland Park — all described by later commentators as "large and stylish," while Sudbrook was "small and stylish."[28]

Walbrook, located above and at the end of North Avenue, east of what was then Tenth Street (now Ellamont Street), attracted a number of prominent Baltimoreans.[29] It also sported a "handsome Casino" with bowling alleys, billiard rooms and a hall for concerts and receptions. Although it had only sixteen houses situated on lots arranged in typical grid design, it had sold half of its 8,000-front feet of ground.[30] It would soon be served by two electric railway companies (the Lake Roland Elevated[31] with its state-of-the-art cars manufactured by the Pullman Palace Car Company[32], and the Edmondson Avenue branch of the Traction Company). Walbrook also offered advantageous tax benefits. As part of an area newly annexed to the city,[33] its tax assessment would not be increased until at least 1900, and then not until there were a certain number of dwellings, stores and streets open.

Curiously, in a time when many suburbs blatantly employed snob appeal to attract residents, West Arlington did just the opposite; it claimed that it was "not set up as a fashionable resort," but "took such precautions as to prevent the [introduction] of objectionable settlers."[34] Its lots of 50 by 150 feet or larger were priced at $300 to $750. It was served by the Western Maryland Railroad, and the Baltimore and Pikesville Electric Road was planned to run through the property. Water and gas works, as well as five hundred shade trees, were being installed.[35]

In discussing both Roland Park and nearby Tuxedo Park (also on Roland Avenue), the *Sunday Herald* article stressed that neither was a "separate" suburban town; rather, Roland Park was an "attractive residential extension to the city" and Tuxedo Park was "an addition to Baltimore itself."[36] Feeling connected with the city may have been important to purchasers in 1893, when few had experience yet with the phenomenon of "suburban living."

Tuxedo Park was "surrounded by the suburban homes of Baltimore's wealthy citizens and [located] directly across the street from the property of the Roland Park Company." It had sold some of its 400 lots, but had no houses yet and purchasers were under no obligation to build. Described as a "strictly first-class addition," there were restrictions governing the minimum cost of any house erected (a cost not stated but "not so high as to prevent the building of a modest little home"), and prohibitions against using any lot for "saloon purposes."

Roland Park was erecting twenty-five "villa cottages" on its first 120 acres and offered rebates, some as much as fifteen percent of the price paid.[37] It provided an excursion trolley for those who wanted a "look-see" and free trolley tokens to purchasers.[38] Many of the lots in Roland Park's Plat One were of modest size, and one of its first houses sold for a moderate $1,500. In 1892 the Roland Park Co. sought plans for constructing more expensive houses (from $2,000 to $4,000), and Roland Park's manager, Edward Bouton, began building a $7,000 house for himself.[39]

Although Roland Park (particularly Plats Two and Three, designed by the Olmsted firm) and Sudbrook shared similar design elements such as graveled streets and sidewalks, profusely planted spaces along the road, restrictions regarding house setbacks, a drainage system developed by Waring, and an Olmsted design tradition, Roland Park sold lots at a much faster pace than did Sudbrook. One reason was Sudbrook's location: conservative Baltimoreans took a long time to accept year-round suburban living, and suburbs closer to the city (like Roland Park) were settled more quickly.[40] Another reason may have been Sudbrook's refusal to sell to land speculators. The *Herald* article specifically stated that neither Roland Park nor Tuxedo Park required purchasers to build within any specified time, although Roland Park offered "liberal inducements" for construction. This was a major difference from Sudbrook, where lots had to be built on within two years of purchase.[41] It is impossible to know to what extent the two-year building requirement dampened the sale of lots in Sudbrook Park, but it undoubtedly had some impact — evident when comparing Sudbrook to the developing Ruxton Heights, which was almost as far from Baltimore, but sold its lots more quickly.

Overlooking Lake Roland, Ruxton Heights was situated seven miles from Baltimore and had been open about a year at the time of the 1893 *Herald* article.[42] Over half of its 204 building lots had been sold already and it had about seventy-five residences within a half mile radius of the Ruxton train station (on the Northern Central line); by comparison, Sudbrook had fourteen cottages in 1893. While the sale of lots in Ruxton Heights was no doubt spurred by its lower lot prices ($200 to $350 for lots 50' to 100' wide by 115' to 205' deep), and other advantages (its trains ran more frequently and it was about to get electricity), the difference in sales volume between it and Sudbrook Park was telling. Ruxton Heights did not prohibit sales to investors, and offered a bonus of five percent of a house costing at least $2,000 if completed within a certain time limit.[43] It also charged no interest on deferred payments. This package of inducements combined with a lack of restrictions had a positive impact on sales.

St. Denis Park near the "historic and picturesque" Relay train station in southwestern Baltimore County also resembled Sudbrook Park in some ways. "The vicinity abounds in scenic views of sublime grandeur," the *Herald* rhapsodized, and "St. Denis Park is in the midst of this beautiful scenery…on the line of one of the best managed railroads in the world."[44] St. Denis was described as having stately trees, plank walks along its main avenues and roads, lamps, and free pure water piped from Catonsville.[45] There was also "a handsomely appointed park" near the Relay station for the use of the community's residents. The Viaduct Hotel was located in close proximity. While only eighteen "rural homes of architectural beauty and neat design" had been built, all 200 of St. Denis' town lots had been sold.

Also near Catonsville, about six miles due west of City Hall, was the new suburb of Eden Terrace, developed by Victor Bloede.[46] Eden Terrace sought to attract an elite clientele of "business men, professional men or men of leisure." The *Sunday Herald* waxed enthusiastic about the development:

> The peculiar value of Eden Terrace as a suburban residence site is not
> alone due to its close proximity to the City of Baltimore, giving it
> practically all the comforts and advantages of city life, but to the fact that
> while heavily wooded with the undisturbed growth of half a century, it
> is flanked on all sides by costly and artistic improvements. Thus,
> instead of pioneers in a new locality, with all the inconveniences and
> discomforts that this usually implies, those who select a home here will
> find themselves surrounded by all the city conveniences and advantages,

and superb villas and country residences occupied by persons of wealth and refinement — a community second to none in the state.[47]

With seventy acres to develop, Eden Terrace had only three or four houses at the time; lots could not be less than an acre and the few houses that had been built cost at least $5,000 each.[48]

Sudbrook Park's main competition for the more affluent buyer would come from communities like Eden Terrace, St. Denis Park and Roland Park.[49] At the time of the article in 1893, Sudbrook Park with fourteen cottages was eight miles from City Hall. Its lots of an acre, more or less, were selling for $800 to $1,500 per acre. Its houses at that time were selling for $4,000 to $6,000. The Sudbrook Company professed to be agreeable to any reasonable terms of purchase, but charged six percent interest on deferred payments. Sudbrook Park did offer some inducements to purchasers. By arrangement with the Western Maryland Railroad every person who purchased or built a house in Sudbrook received one annual pass for each thousand dollars (up to five) spent, and was entitled to free transportation of all packages that might be carried in baggage cars.[50] The railroad reduced freight rates on building materials for persons building in Sudbrook. The Sudbrook Company did not appear to be in a position financially to offer more extensive inducements. Had it been able to, perhaps its sales would have been greater, particularly in the early years.

A common social consideration offered by the early suburbs was the assurance that "undesirable" aspects would not intrude. Often this meant no saloons or liquor stores, to keep out the "rough element." Suburbs appealing to a more elite clientele, however, not only wanted to keep out the baser members of society, but tried to entice purchasers based on quality-by-association. "Many wealthy families among the Maryland aristocracy own estates adjoining Roland Park," the *Sunday Herald* announced. The *Herald* also printed a long list of prominent men who had estates near Eden Terrace, including Ernest Knabe, "the piano manufacturer of national fame," and it asserted that "many of Baltimore's best citizens have purchased lots" in Ruxton Heights. And so on for Tuxedo Park, St. Denis Park, West Arlington, Halethorpe and Walbrook. Place of residence was a strong indicator of social status, and status was such an important component of advancement and place in society at that time that books like the *Social Register* and the *Society Visiting List* were bibles to those with enough lineage and affluence to care.[51]

Almost all of the suburbs named in the article, even the most modest ones, had one advantage over Sudbrook Park: electricity for street and residential illumination. It would be years before Sudbrook exchanged its interior gas and oil lamps for electric lights.[52] This may have had some impact on the sale of year-round residences, particularly when an affluent purchaser could build at the same cost in another community, such as Roland Park, that offered many of the same attributes along with the advantage of electricity. The lure of "lamps sufficient to turn night into day" must have been a powerful one in 1893.[53]

Finally, the article reported in detail on that most significant key to prosperity for a suburb in 1893 — its transportation links with the city. Here, Sudbrook Park with its nine to twelve trains each day could not compete as effectively. Both the industrial suburb of Lansdowne and the commuter suburb of Ruxton Heights had thirty-five daily trains each way; Halethorpe had fifty trains; St. Denis Park had fifty-six trains daily. In addition, most of the named suburbs were already served by electric rail lines, or were soon to be. These ran every five to ten minutes, at a fare usually half that of a train trip of the same distance.[54]

While Sudbrook's Eugene Blackford looked with disdain upon electric lines, considering them inferior to travel by train, they were unquestionably the wave of the future. The *Herald* article noted that the cars of the Lake Roland Elevated (which would serve Roland Park, Tuxedo Park and Walbrook, among others) were being built by the Pullman Palace Car Company and would be "models of beauty, luxury and ease" that would be "brilliantly lighted at night with electricity" and warmed in the winter with a heating apparatus.[55] While Sudbrook Park's residents had access to the Pimlico & Pikesville Electric Line, the cars were not as luxurious and the line's terminus was a mile away on Reisterstown Road. Suburbs with an electric line going through or immediately adjacent to their property would reap the benefits many times over.

No late-nineteenth-century suburb operated in a vacuum, immune from the impact of others. Each suburb competed head-on with others that appealed to people of the same income levels, and all were engaged in a race to succeed. Whether catering to a working-class or elite clientele, the difference between profit and loss for all suburbs "depended on the rapidity with which lots could be sold off to home owners."[56]

Eventually there would prove to be more than enough people desiring the advantages that suburbs offered to fill them all, but some suburbs of the early 1890s would reach this goal more quickly and directly than others. As 1894 began, all of Baltimore's early suburbs would struggle to attract purchasers and to regain ground that had been lost during the financial panic of 1893.

Chapter 10

A YEAR OF RENEWED VIGOR: 1894

There were signs by December 1893 that the country's financial crisis might be abating.[1] Beginning then and carrying over into January 1894, Eugene Blackford, manager of Sudbrook Park, had a bidding war on his hands among three people who wanted to buy Cottage No. 7 (718 Cliveden Road). Had the tide turned for the Company? The answer, as time would reveal, was both yes *and* no. For the short term, however, there were positive signs.

As early as October 1893, Blackford had a boarder from the Inn who wanted to rent Cottage No. 7 through the winter; the Company willingly agreed to put in a furnace.[2] Next, W.A. James, who had rented Cottage No. 2 (508 Sudbrook Lane) before Blackford moved into it, began inquiring about purchasing No. 7. L.R. Meekins also wrote to Blackford about purchasing No. 7. Blackford felt obligated to notify Mrs. Decatur H. Miller, who had leased No. 7 and previously indicated that she might want to buy it. To his delight, all three were interested.

Blackford was in an excellent bargaining position. James was trying to get the house at less than the asking price of $4,540. Blackford responded that he had named the lowest price, reminding James that "it is of doubtful advantage to the Sudbrook Co. to dispose of this property. There is probably no piece on the plat in such demand, for renting at least…. Anxious as I am to effect sales, I greatly prefer that they should be of unimproved lots, and not of such as deprive the Company of income."[3]

Before the end of January, Mrs. Miller had beaten out her competitors for No. 7.[4] The recently widowed Mrs. Decatur H. Miller was precisely the type of purchaser the Sudbrook Company wanted — she and her son, Decatur H. Miller, Jr. (who rented Cottage No. 8) were listed in both the *Social Register* and the *Society Visiting List* (also called the *"Blue Book"*). Moreover, as Blackford wrote to Meekins: "A friend in town… told me last summer that if ever Mr. Decatur H. Miller consented to buy here that the fortune of the Park would be made, such is the general appreciation of his business…[and his] well known aversion to put out money where it cannot be easily reconverted into cash."[5] Apparently, Miller, Jr.'s blessing on his mother's purchase was tantamount to his having bought the house himself, at least in Blackford's mind.[6]

Knowing that Meekins still presented a possibility for a sale, Blackford agreed to provide ample assistance if Meekins bought a lot and built. Blackford would provide plans, make alterations, draw the specifications and contracts, furnish estimates of grading, drainage, walks, etc. and "superintend the building of the house." Best of all "my services shall not cost you a cent" since these services are, "let us say, for the good of the Sudbrook Co." And if that were not incentive enough, Blackford added that "Mr. Cowan tells me that the times are singularly suitable for building. Large stocks of lumber have accumulated & hence seasoned stuff can be had, labour is abundant, & he will be able to finish up in ninety days, unless very rainy weather prevents."[7]

By early February, Meekins had bought a lot "at the edge of the woods" and Cowan began work on Meekins' house, No. 23, at 719 Cliveden Road.[8] Blackford then corresponded with Horatio Armstrong, who had bought a lot in 1892, about his plans to build. In a short time, the Armstrong house (No. 16)[9] was under construction at 717 Cliveden Road.

Development at Sudbrook Park seemed to be stirring again and the Company made

Cottage No. 7, 718 Cliveden Road, was one of the original cottages built before May 1890 by the Sudbrook Company. A popular rental, it was purchased in 1894, the first Company-owned cottage to be sold.
PHOTOGRAPH BY PEGGY FELDMAN-ESKEY.

Cottage No. 23, 719 Cliveden Road, was built in 1894 by Kate and Lynn. R. Meekins, who called it "Lyndhurst." Subsequent owners, the Alexander Earlys, renamed it "Chudleigh" about 1912. This photo dates from about 1937. SUDBROOK PARK, INC. ARCHIVES.

Waiting for the train at Sudbrook, about 1890. These hillside stairs were across from the station's original location. There was also a pedestrian bridge east of the station that provided access for residents. FROM SUDBROOK COMPANY BROCHURE.
COURTESY OF ROGER KATZENBERG.

improvements in the appearance of the community. Blackford obtained permission to replace with a twelve foot platform the existing narrow one at the foot of the steps leading from the railroad track into Sudbrook Park. He had steps eleven feet wide built and politely asked the railroad to attend to broken masonry around the station's cellar windows, noting "I am anxious to have the surroundings of the station very attractive & shall do all I can to keep them so."[10]

With better times also came more mundane yet elemental matters to which Blackford had to attend. To Armstrong, he wrote: "The men who are at the work of priming, persist in putting on red, and as they speak no English, I cannot understand whether they have received orders to that effect or not. Please let me hear from you."[11] To a renter and parent, he wrote: "I am doing all in my power to preserve the birds in the Park [but your son was here yesterday with his rifle] and four victims were the result. I appeal to you, as I do not care to make myself a bugbear to the children."[12]

As a continuing sign that times were improving, Blackford wrote to a New York architectural firm requesting plans for houses costing no more than $4,000, commenting that the area he managed had about twenty cottages and "good prospects of building many more, now that times have improved, or seem about to improve."[13] In other correspondence, Blackford commented that of these twenty cottages, only seven ("all of which were built for summer use") will be vacant for the winter.[14] (Within the next few months, two more of these seven cottages would be equipped for year-round residency).[15]

As was customary, Blackford wrote Hugh Bond in early September about the soon-to-end season: "Everything has gone on prosperously, far more so than in any former season, and it would seem from all I can hear that there are several who intend to build; at any rate, there are universal expressions of enthusiastic admiration for the place."[16]

Also astir in Sudbrook was a move to add a casino, or neighborhood clubhouse, to be funded with stock subscriptions. Such casinos were popular in elite suburbs of the time.[17] Sudbrook's casino proposal got off to an enthusiastic but tumultuous start. At the initial meeting on the proposal, $1,100 was subscribed to the casino by Sudbrook residents, with sufficient promises to ensure the $1,500 needed.[18] But Bond's non-appearance at the initial meeting provoked residents, who claimed that the

The Trippe Cottage at 706 Cliveden Road West was designed by Baltimore architect George Archer and built the end of 1894. PHOTOGRAPH BY PEGGY FELDMAN-ESKEY.

The Sudbrook Company required property owners who wanted to build stables to submit their plans in advance for approval. Blackford insisted on designs that were architecturally appropriate. This stable, at 709 Cliveden, had a porch, gabled ends and windows. PHOTOGRAPH BY BOOTS SHELTON

Sudbrook Company had waived the right to vote its stock, thus allowing the holders of the $1,500 worth of outside shares to control matters. As related later by Blackford, while the Company wanted residents to manage affairs without interference, it did not want them, "to gain control of the whole business…and manage it in their own interests entirely."[19]

Blackford feared, correctly, that the casino had "come to grief temporarily."[20] But he talked as if the implementation of the casino was a *fait accompli* when it suited his purpose. In his reply to an inquiry by J.E. Trippe about the advantages offered at Sudbrook Park, Blackford added as a post script, "I should say that a very handsome Casino containing ball, billiard, card, supper & reading rooms, with bowling alleys is underway."[21] Actually, it was not until a few months later that John Cowan began building the casino addition to the Inn, which included a bowling alley and new wing for the billiard table.

In addition to touting the casino, Blackford's letter to Trippe emphasized that Sudbrook "was laid out by Mr. Fred. L. Olmsted of Mass., and is one of his finest pieces of work." Next he mentioned the lots of not less than one acre, roads beautifully graded and macadamized with a ten-foot planting strip on each side, planted with trees and shrubs, a six-foot graveled walk, a four-inch water main "fed from a reservoir, which in turn is filled from deep wells of *absolutely* pure water, as shown by analysis," no subsequent subdivision allowed, and last but not least, the various fare passes and inducements offered by the Western Maryland Railroad, "making it the most desirable road to live on out of the City.…The Sudbrook Co. will build any kind of house desired on any terms that are reasonable. It will no longer build to rent, tho' I have 50 applications for such houses."[22] Trippe must have liked what he heard, because he bought a lot at 706 Cliveden Road West and built Cottage No. 28. The house was designed by George Archer, who had also designed the Trego cottage at 600 Sudbrook Road.[23]

Whereas Blackford had pushed advertising to promote Sudbrook in 1892, by October of 1894 he boasted that "no advertizing is done. We are able & willing to wait for the type of people we want, knowing that they will not be hurried." In the same letter, he proclaimed that Sudbrook Park had adopted "all the features of the best managed & most successful places of the kind about Phila. & Boston," and pointed with pride to the Waring system: "the drainage is a fad of mine & is about as perfect as it can be…we trust to good water, good roads, good drainage, & the consequent good health to build us up."[24]

Blackford began writing for more house plans to erect four new cottages, commenting to architects in Philadelphia and New York that he had had "great difficulty in getting plans for houses costing from $3,500 to $4,000, since 25% to 30% must be added to your estimates to build here in a substantial manner" and "I have tried our architects, but their houses have always cost $5,000." He wanted plans that included a parlour, dining room, library, kitchen and water closet (w.c.) for servants on the first floor, and at least four bedrooms and baths upstairs, plus one or more bedrooms for servants on the second or third floor. And of course, "as much porch room as possible." His letters insisted on plans which would ensure that heat from the kitchen "cannot enter the house" and suggested separating the kitchen from the dining room by a "corridor ventilated by windows at each end," explaining, "I have been forced to reject every plan without this arrangement, having ignorantly built some without it & having them on my hand in consequence." Since the lots were an acre or more, he cautioned that, "the elevations must be attractive all around." He managed to insert that the premises were "beautifully laid off by Fred. Law Olmsted. There are probably no grounds so handsome around any City."[25]

The four cottages which Blackford intended to start building that fall were to be owned by a syndicate of Hugh Bond, who was financing the project, and Blackford, who would oversee construction and manage the properties. Before undertaking the investment, the partners had occupants under lease

Hugh Bond and Eugene Blackford formed a partnership to build these four cottages in 1895. Clockwise from top left: No. 24, 1017 Winsor Road; No. 25, 1016 Winsor Road; No. 26, 724 Howard Road and No. 27, 708 Cliveden Road. PHOTOGRAPHS OF NOS. 24, 26 AND 27 BY PEGGY FELDMAN-ESKEY. PHOTOGRAPH OF NO. 25 BY LEN FRANK.

for each cottage for a minimum term of three years. Nos. 24 and 25, at 1017 and 1016 Winsor Road (in the "wood land") were to be occupied by the families of Charles A. Webb and George Cator. Nos. 26 and 27, at 724 Howard Road and 708 Cliveden Road ("on upland open ground") were leased by the families of Alexander Early and William B. Rayner. Blackford's correspondence suggests that he used the New York architectural firm of Child & deGoll, working particularly with E.S. Child, although Child appears to have designed only No. 26 (724 Howard Road), not all four of the houses.[26]

Blackford sent Cowan the house plans from the New York architect, asking for an estimate to build. As usual, Blackford had "overhauled the specifications" and added a kitchen porch since it would "not do to build without it." He also wanted "the style of finish…as in Meekins' house" (clapboard).[27]

It was a very busy time not only for Blackford, but also for John Cowan, who was working on the four new houses and the casino addition when the Sudbrook Company agreed to build a private stable to be leased by Charles Webb and George Cator. Cowan designed and constructed it, with two distinct parts "built together for the sake of economy." Blackford insisted on seeing any changes to the plans before work was begun, "as the architectural features should be kept constantly in mind, the building being quite conspicuous."[28] The design had to be appropriate to the community; even stables in Sudbrook Park were built with porches, windows and gables — often resembling smaller versions of the larger homes with which they were associated.

At the end of 1894 there were twenty cottages in Sudbrook Park, with five more under construction.[29] The good news was that Sudbrook seemed to have renewed vigor in 1894. The bad news was that by this fifth year after Sudbrook's founding, only nine individuals not connected with the Company had purchased or built homes in the Park.

While Sudbrook's cottages and the Inn continued to fill to capacity each May through October, and there was always a waiting list of persons to rent (as well as a list of fifty or more who wished to rent if the Company would build for them), sales had never matched expectations. Even with its growing year-round population (nineteen of the twenty-five cottages were, or soon would be, equipped for year-round residency and at least sixteen were occupied year-round), the influx of a hundred or more summer guests at the Inn largely sustained Sudbrook's reputation as a summer community. The Company continued to struggle with its inability to sell a great number of lots and to promote large-scale permanent residency.

A continuing puzzle to Blackford, and one that he never did understand, was Sudbrook Park's popularity during "the season" as a place to rent or "board" at the Inn, but its lack of appeal to these renters as a place to purchase lots and build. If Blackford needed any additional confirmation that Sudbrook's renewed vigor might be short-lived or that the outlook for turning the tide on sales was dim, he was soon to get it.

Chapter 11

HIGH HOPES: 1895–1907

The increase in sales that began in the mid-1890s did not, as it turned out, portend a permanent trend for Sudbrook Park. Nevertheless, 1895 continued to stir the Company's hopes. Not only were five houses under construction (the Trippe cottage and the four owned by the Bond/Blackford syndicate), but Blackford was turning down prospective renters for the coming summer unusually early, by January 14, explaining that "the demand for [cottages is] so active that they are engaged far ahead." As always, he added that the Company did have lots to sell.[1]

As January got underway, Blackford responded to Dr. Samuel Kemp Merrick, who would become one of the Park's long-time residents,[2] with information about Sudbrook Park. He enlarged on his usual recitals about the community's advantages. Now, in addition to Olmsted's grades and curves and the high elevation, he claimed that the pure water "has worked some very remarkable cures, or is said to have done so."[3] Lest Sudbrook Park still be thought too far out in the country, he remarked that based on his own experience of two years, housekeeping was "actually easier than in town" because "marketing, washing & ice [are] hauled free. Grocers from town deliver goods here, and green groceries, fish, oysters &c are brought in abundance to the door."

In March John A. Barker, a real estate agent, purchased Cottage No. 6 at 505 Sudbrook Lane. The Company had thus sold the second of its nine original cottages and could add another family to its list of year-round residents.

Also in the spring of 1895, perhaps heartened by sales that began in 1894, the Sudbrook Company set out to build a house that it would offer "for sale only." Blackford decided to use an architectural design (the "Westin house") from a plan book, which had also been used for Cottage No. 25 at 1016 Winsor Road. He wrote to Bond:

> It is not the handsomest; No. 24 [1017 Winsor] or my house [508 Sudbrook] is that clearly, I think, but it has the great advantage of a library, which the other lacks. Some defects were naturally apparent when built, & these Cowan agrees to remedy — change the plain to turned balusters; carry the porch around the other side (the shady one); make the kitchen & room over it two feet larger, &c., &c. for $3,900.[4]

The new cottage, No. 29, would be located at 610 Upland Road. The house was planned to have a total of thirteen rooms, including seven bedrooms, four open fireplaces, two bathrooms, two water closets, a large and airy cellar, and a furnace (this was to be a year-round residence from the start!). It would be sided with white Maine cedar shingles, sit on an acre of land, have ample porches and a southwestern exposure. The selling price, with the lot, was to be $6,000.

While construction got underway on No. 29, the four syndicate houses and the Trippe house (No. 28 at 706 Cliveden West) were being completed. Bond and Blackford had intended for Cottages Nos. 26 (724 Howard) and 27 (708 Cliveden) to have furnaces from the beginning. Nos. 24 (1017 Winsor) and 25 (1016 Winsor) were to be piped for heat but not have furnaces, since they would only be occupied by their lessees during the season. However, when the lessees of Nos. 24 and 25 insisted that furnaces be added, the Company gave in, making all of the syndicate houses fully equipped for winter use.[5]

Just as the new construction was beginning to rejuvenate Blackford's outlook about the future of the community, the Western Maryland Railroad made a surprise announcement. Blackford was informed in May 1895 that the railroad wanted to move the Sudbrook station.[6] Blackford's letters do not indicate why the railroad wanted a new location, but neither Bond nor Blackford was happy about it. Because of the community's total dependence on the railroad, however, it was vital to maintain a good working relationship.

One account guessed that "long flights of wooden steps at each end of [the pedestrian] bridge made it very inconvenient for the elderly residents to cross,[7] and doubtless was the reason the Railroad Company moved the station."[8] But this rationale does not seem likely in light of Blackford's efforts to accommodate residents and insure their comfort. Had there been cumbersome stairs and had residents complained about them, Blackford almost certainly would have raised the issue with the railroad or at the very least discussed it in his letters to Bond. His complete silence coupled with Bond and Blackford's resistance to the move, leads to the conclusion that moving the station must have served some railroad purpose,[9] and was not done to accommodate residents.[10]

As was often the case, Blackford played the diplomat and Bond was the "heavy." Blackford replied to John Hood, President of the Western Maryland Railroad: "[Bond] thinks that as all the roads & paths are laid off so as to radiate from the present Station as a center, that it would be most disastrous to put it elsewhere.…We think it best for our interests to leave it where it is."[11]

Apparently, the railroad was not dissuaded. After an eight-month lull with no further correspondence recorded, Blackford sent Hood an outline of the proposed new station lot and approaches.[12] Obviously, the railroad must have been moving the discussions forward. The Sudbrook Company, however, raised additional objections.

Bond insisted that the matter be put before the Company's stockholders. In addition, the McHenry heirs had to be consulted, since "they regard the present position of the station as of great importance to the value of their land adjoining on the Northeast." There was also the question of rights to the abandoned land if the station was moved, since the Company had not had to pay for the acre on which the station was located. Although Blackford feared that the McHenrys might require payment for the land or take back their reversion in it, he placated Hood: "No unnecessary delay will be thrown in your way, but some correspondence with the Boston & Phila. directors will be requisite."[13]

Blackford wrote eight more letters about this matter before May 1896, when the station was moved from its original location on the north side of the train tracks and about a hundred feet west of the carriage bridge, to its new location on the south side of the tracks east of the carriage bridge on Howard Road — approximately lot 3, Block 7 of Olmsted's Plan. In one of these letters, he expounded on his concerns regarding the reversion of the old station lot to the McHenrys:

> If such a reversion took place, they would enter into possession without
> the restrictions, which are attached to a transfer of any lot by the
> Sudbrook Co., and could sell or use it for any purpose, and prohibit, if
> they chose, any passage over it of the travel, which must seek that outlet
> towards Pikesville. I would greatly fear that a store or some nuisance

would be set up there…The idea of this lot passing untrammelled into their hands fills me with apprehension.[14]

The actual moving of the station must have been a remarkable operation. Blackford did not describe it but wrote to Hood about the arrangements: "Knowing the habit of contractors like Mr. Spicknall, I have told him that I must be assured beforehand of the [planned] route, & of reparation of all damage to roads, &c."[15]

There is also an account that William T. Cox and his son, Thornton, moved the station using "only workhorses and the ingenious rigging of rollers, skids, drums, etc., to get the building up the grade and across the tracks to its new location. This took all of ten days!"[16] It is possible that both Spicknall and Cox were involved in moving the Sudbrook station. Spicknall might have engineered and overseen the move, with Cox doing the actual work.[17]

Moving the station was a major change to the Olmsted Plan for Sudbrook. Despite the Company's reservations, it had little choice but to yield to the railroad's wishes on this matter. Once the station had been relocated, Blackford began grading and paving the passenger approach roads and sidewalks, and planting to make the new location as attractive as possible.[18]

By November 1895, there were twenty-six cottages in Sudbrook Park; twenty-one of these were equipped for winter use.[19] In response to an inquiry for winter lodging, Blackford wrote: "All the houses here, fitted for winter occupancy, are rented, or are occupied by their owners….The hotel closes on Nov. 1st in each year, so that there is no board to be had."[20] Although the majority (over eighty percent) of Sudbrook Park's cottages were occupied year-round by 1895, the community was still thought of by many as primarily a summer resort, probably because the total number of homes was relatively small.[21]

Scattered but on-going construction activity continued in 1896. Bond's tenant in Cottage No. 11 (1018 Winsor) wanted to rent the cottage year-round, if Bond would add a kitchen, pantry, furnace and cellar. Bond did not accommodate the request, claiming the house and lot were not "worth the considerable outlay required to put it in a condition to be a comfortable residence throughout the year." He did, however, raise the house twenty-five inches, put dormer windows in each of the two large rooms on the second floor and paint the entire house in return for a year's lease. The work was completed in March.[22]

Soon after, excavations began on another cottage being built by the Sudbrook Company, No. 30 at 722 Howard Road. By June, it was occupied by Mifflin Coulter[23] and family, under a lease arrangement of at least three years.[24]

Meanwhile Cottage No. 29 (610 Upland), completed in the fall of 1895, remained empty. The Sudbrook Company was adamant that it would not rent the cottage, hoping to turn the tide from rentals to sales. In April Blackford wrote to a realty company saying, "I have had 49 [rental] offers for it, but it is for sale only. Last week, there was an average of two a day in person, tho' the sign on the house says 'for sale only'….I think that a purchaser will turn up yet. Some of those who find they cannot rent will return to buy. I have just sold the lot adjoining for $1150 per acre." Despite the fact that No. 29 was "first class," the house sat empty for months.[25]

In March, after renting Cottage No. 2 (508 Sudbrook Lane) since 1893, Blackford decided on a lot in Sudbrook for his own residence. He bought ten pounds of dynamite in May to begin digging a cellar. Located at 1008 Winsor Road, it would be Cottage No. 31. John Cowan was to be the builder, using plans modeled on Cottage No. 2 —with additions and modifications suggested by Blackford and implemented by the architectural firm of Cabot, Everett and Mead of Boston. Blackford continued to rent out "Cleve" as he had done each summer since he had lived at Sudbrook Park, still unable to find a buyer for it.[26] Dr. Samuel K. Merrick decided to purchase a lot in Sudbrook Park rather than in the St. Denis area near Relay,[27] and began to build immediately. Grading and drainage system work began on the Merrick cottage (No. 32) at 517 Sudbrook Lane.

Spring meant that it was painting time again in Sudbrook Park. Blackford complained to his supplier about the frequent complaints he had received "as to differences between the colors on your sample cards, and the results when those colors are applied…I chose your No. 57 as the color for the hotel — an olive green — & used large quantities of it. The result is a pumpkin yellow, and furnishes the subject for many gibes against me. In defense, I carry the sample in my pocket to show when taunted about it."[28]

It may be hard to imagine a building the size of the Sudbrook hotel being pumpkin yellow, but at least Blackford developed a sense of humor about it. A few years later, when Bond agreed to paint Cottage No. 13 (500 Sudbrook Lane) for Reuben Foster, Blackford wrote Foster saying: "As no small part of my unwillingness to repaint the cottages arises from the hostile criticisms passed upon the results, [Bond and I] agreed that you should choose the colours, and that as in the case of all works of art, 'Foster painted it' shall be put in some corner, so that the critics may know the artist." [29]

The Sudbrook Company gave up finding a purchaser for Cottage No. 29 (610 Upland) and in July rented it to Dr. Merrick and his family while their house was being completed. With No. 29 rented, all of Sudbrook's houses and the hotel were occupied for the summer of 1896. An article in the

The relocated railroad station on Howard Road in Sudbrook Park, about 1917. To the left of the stairs was a baggage trolley to transport heavy parcels up the steep incline. The station remained at this location until the Western Maryland Railroad ceased running passenger trains into the city in 1957. COURTESY OF WILLIAM AND ELIZABETH STELLMANN.

Cottage No. 29, 610 Upland Road, was built "for sale only" by the Sudbrook Company in 1895. While the Company immediately had a long waiting list of people eager to rent it, the cottage sat vacant for a year before the Company agreed to accept a lease. PHOTOGRAPH BY PEGGY FELDMAN-ESKEY.

Cottage No. 30, 722 Howard Road, about 1940. Built by the Sudbrook Company in 1896 and first leased to Mifflin Coulter, this cottage was purchased in 1910 by long-time Sudbrook residents, Dr. and Mrs. Herbert Harlan. COURTESY OF THE COX FAMILY.

Cottage No. 31, 1008 Winsor Road, about 1901. Eugene Blackford built this house for his family in 1896. An expanded version of Cottage No. 2 at 508 Sudbrook Lane, the house was designed by the Boston firm of Cabot, Everett and Mead. COURTESY OF WILLIAM AND ELIZABETH STELLMANN.

The Merrick cottage, 517 Sudbrook Lane, about 1897. Pictured with Dr. Samuel K. Merrick and his wife, Mary Charlton Graff, were their daughter Charlton and their sons William (far left), Robert (seated) and Seymour. The family's kitten, Beauty, played in the foreground, while their coachman, James, waited with their carriage and horse, Stranger, under the porte-cochere. COURTESY OF STEWART McLEAN.

Next page: Cottage No. 34 at 709 Cliveden Road was built in 1897-98 by long-time Sudbrook resident Oscar Webb and his family. The house was designed by Baltimore architect George Archer. PHOTOGRAPH BY BOOTS SHELTON.

Baltimore Sun observed that "this season Sudbrook Park is well populated, though not to an extent unpleasantly reminiful of the discomforts and inconveniences of the city," and pointed out that "the tall forest trees, cultivated shrubbery, long, rambling walks, fragrant flower beds and smooth, cool lawns of Sudbrook suggest a repose and refreshment that make the park one of the most attractive of the many suburban communities."[30]

Damaging weather battered Sudbrook that autumn. Blackford informed Bond that the "destruction here by the storm was very great, tho' chiefly in trees. The Co. came off very well in all their houses. You lost a little in glass….Our No. 26 lost its chimney, which in falling knocked a hole in the roof….It will take a good while to clean up."[31] Later that same month, Blackford moved into his new house on Winsor Road and requested a railroad pass for Mrs. Blackford for the year.[32]

Sales continued. In December two long-time renters purchased lots. C. W. Linthicum, who had been renting 500 Sudbrook Lane (Cottage No. 13) since 1892, bought an acre lot at 713 Cliveden Road. He began building Cottage No. 33 at once, and moved in when it was completed in 1897. Oscar Webb, who had rented 501 Sudbrook (Cottage No. 9) since 1890, bought one and a half acres, also on Cliveden Road — the lot that Blackford had originally wanted for himself. Webb continued to reside in No. 9 through 1897 and into 1898 while he was building Cottage No. 34 at 709 Cliveden Road. He moved into his new house, designed by the architect George Archer, before the spring of 1898.

By December 1896 the Sudbrook Company apparently decided that it would be better to rent No. 29 (the "for sale only" house at 610 Upland) than to let it remain empty and not produce income. Blackford wrote to James McEvoy, who had previously rented No. 5 for the summer, to see if he would

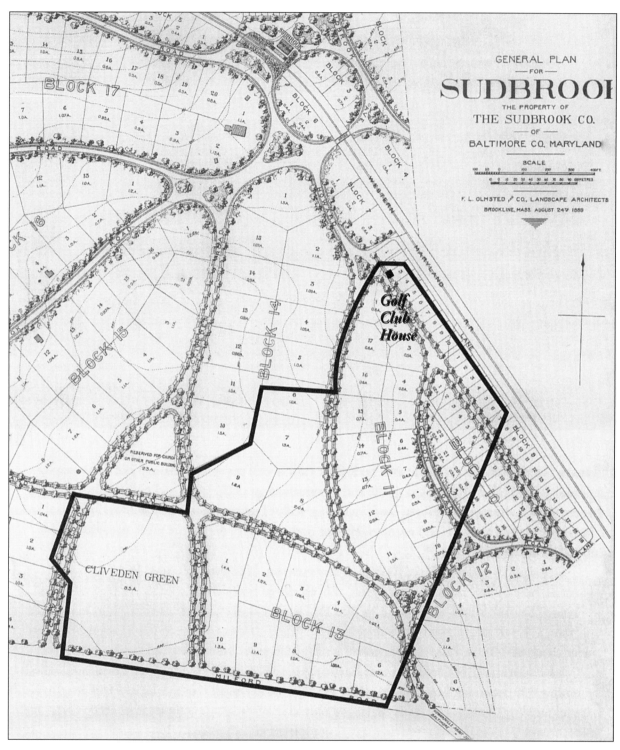

Outline shows approximate area of the Sudbrook golf course, a change to the Olmsted Plan that was added by the Sudbrook Company in 1898. PREPARED BY ELLEN KAHAN ZAGER.

like No. 29 when the Merricks moved out. He added: "You will be glad to hear that we have just sold two lots for immediate improvement; also that the new well has proved a great success, yielding about 30,000 gals. a day at this time of drought."[33]

Sales had grown between 1894 and the end of 1896:[34] the Sudbrook Company had sold twelve properties. It also had built one cottage for sale (No. 29, still unsold) and one cottage for lease (No. 30). From twenty-six cottages at the end of 1895, Sudbrook could now look forward to having thirty-one cottages — based on the sale of lots in 1896. Of the soon-to-be thirty-one cottages, the Company owned eight; Bond owned four and the Bond/Blackford syndicate owned four. Only five of the first thirty-one cottages were strictly for summer use. These numbers were hardly spectacular, but there was no denying a hint of optimism in the air. It was soon to be dashed.

The year 1897 was a total bust in terms of sales. Not a single new house or lot was sold. The year was especially devastating for the Company after it had finally begun to make progress selling lots to permanent residents. Even nature was unkind — Blackford wrote that the winter of 1897–98 was "the coldest & most protracted winter...since the Park opened."[35]

Anxious to regain sales momentum in 1898, the Sudbrook Company began working on improvements in November 1897. Blackford requested bids for the construction of five thousand feet of road in Sudbrook, to be "8 inches thick in center tapering to 6 inches at edges." The road bed was to be prepared by the Company. Stones were to be in three sizes "in layers, each to be rolled with a fifteen ton roller and the last to be screened material, free of dust." Bids were to include two and a half inches of No. 1, dust-free fine stone to cover 4,600 feet of old road.[36]

As road work continued into 1898, Blackford sent out routine letters asking the prior year's tenants if they wanted their cottages again. He mentioned the many improvements that would greet those returning, including a fine pool table in the hotel, the macadamizing of all the roads with fine limestone and a new water supply.[37]

He also sent out letters soliciting new residents — sales proposition letters similar to those he had written when the community had first opened. In one letter, he added: "If you have never seen the place I should be glad to have you see it, as there is no equal to it as far as grounds are concerned in this Country."[38] As he had done years before, he presented the purchase of a house in Sudbrook as a "no-lose" proposition. Lots in Sudbrook Park were selling "at the low rate of from $800 to $1200 per acre, a sum about half of that charged for that of other suburban properties by the lot of 40'x150', where the improvements consist only of sticks put up with the information that this is such & such an avenue — no water, no drainage, no nothing." Referring to what is now the Ralston community, northeast of the bridge from Sudbrook, he added: "Just across the R.R. from us, Wood Harmon & Co. bought last fall 60 acres, & staking it out in this way, are said to have sold every lot, 40'x150', as from $190 to $250 apiece, thus making about $2,000 an acre."[39]

Ralston seemed to prove again that the smaller and cheaper the individual lots, the quicker they sold (even though the per acre price was actually higher than in Sudbrook Park). With no requirement to build within a certain period of time, land speculators often grabbed up cheap lots on the chance they would ultimately make money. It must have been particularly disheartening for Blackford to watch as this neighboring developer sold lots so quickly, after having made no improvements, when Blackford was still having such difficulty securing purchasers after working so diligently, for so many years, to make Sudbrook a desirable community.[40]

An important amenity added in 1898 to improve Sudbrook Park's competitive position was a

Top and next page: J. Appleton Wilson's architectural drawings for 507 Sudbrook Lane, about 1900, showing front and side elevations, floor plans and mechanical systems. COURTESY OF CHRIS AND DEANA KARRAS.

Bottom: Cottage No. 37 at 507 Sudbrook Lane was built for Frederick and Mary Robbins Hoffman in 1900, from architect J. Appleton Wilson's design. PHOTOGRAPH BY PEGGY FELDMAN-ESKEY.

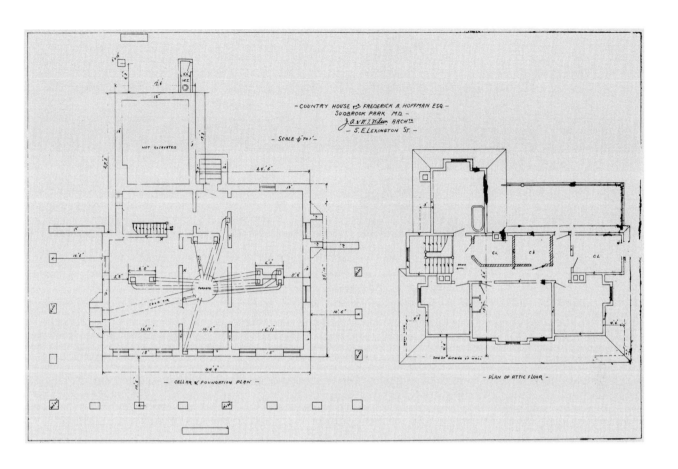

- COUNTRY HOUSE ᵒᶠ FREDERICK A. HOFFMAN ESQ. -
SUDBROOK PARK MD. -
J. A. & W. J. Wilson ARCHTS -
- S. E. LEXINGTON ST. -

- SCALE ⅛" TO 1' -

NOT EXCAVATED

- CELLAR & FOUNDATION PLAN -

- PLAN OF ATTIC FLOOR -

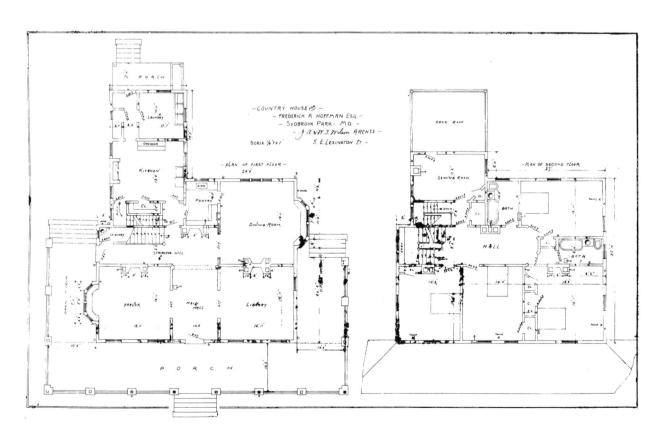

- COUNTRY HOUSE ᵒᶠ -
- FREDERICK A. HOFFMAN ESQ -
- SUDBROOK PARK - MD. -
J. A. & W. J. Wilson ARCHTS -
SCALE ⅛" TO 1'   S. E. LEXINGTON ST. -

PORCH

LAUNDRY

DRESSER

KITCHEN

PANTRY

CL

DINING ROOM

STAIRCASE HALL

PARLOR

MAIN HALL

LIBRARY

PORCH

- PLAN OF FIRST FLOOR -

DECK ROOM

SEWING ROOM

BATH

HALL

BATH

- PLAN OF SECOND FLOOR -

Left: Cottage No. 38, 605 Upland Road, was built in 1901-02 by the Sudbrook Company under a lease arrangement with Senator Isidor Rayner. Elevations for this large home, which was subsequently divided into several apartments, were designed by the Baltimore firm of Wyatt and Nolting. COURTESY OF THE MARYLAND HISTORICAL TRUST. *Right: Cottage No. 39, 711 Cliveden Road, was the last house built in Sudbrook while Eugene Blackford kept records. Sold to F. C. Tyson in 1904, the property was developed by 1905.* SUDBROOK PARK, INC. ARCHIVES.

Club House and golf club "to make this place more attractive & induce persons to reside here."[41] The Club House was situated on Howard Road, across from 724 Howard Road (Cottage No. 26). The nine-hole golf course encompassed land from the station along and to the east of Howard Road (the area encompassing the current Greenwood Road), then in a southerly direction to the current Milford Mill Road, taking in the upper part of Cliveden along Upland to the water tower.[42] "As this improvement promises to do more than any thing yet attempted to attract buyers here," Blackford asked for the railroad's "favourable consideration" to drain the Club House bathroom into the railroad's pit, at the edge of its right-of-way.[43] It took five more letters to Hood to obtain the needed permission so that work on the Club House could proceed.

The structure itself, designed by Sudbrook homeowner and architect George Coursen, was to be a large room attractively furnished with numerous lockers and a large fireplace, from which would open two dressing rooms and a small kitchen with the stove vented into a single chimney. The cost was not to exceed $1,500. Blackford thought that the Club House would "undoubtedly become the nucleus of a Casino" and wanted Coursen to design it with that in mind.[44] Although Blackford never mentioned Roland Park in connection with Sudbrook's golf club, it seems probable that the fact that Roland Park had established a golf club in 1896 might well have contributed to Sudbrook Park's desire to add one.[45] Not only were the two suburban areas competing for the same clientele, but golf was a novel and very popular sport and a golf club was a significant amenity. [46]

Despite the improvements made by the Sudbrook Company in early 1898 (including newly resurfaced roads, a pool table in the hotel, a new water supply and the Club House with adjoining nine-hole golf course), in retrospect it is clear that Sudbrook's building boom was over. In the nine year period between 1898 and 1907, only four more cottages would be built.

The first of these was Cottage No. 36, which the Sudbrook Company constructed in 1898 at 520 Sudbrook Lane. It was the first house to have electric lights and the grandest in the Park at the time — with thirteen rooms, three bathrooms, six fireplaces, a furnace and a cemented cellar with laundry — intended, of course, for year-round residency. Built for a very demanding lessee, Frank B. Hooper, the house had a dumb-waiter and other conveniences he insisted upon. But No. 36 presented a series of problems from the start. The Company chose Robert Coit of Boston to design the house, but Hooper insisted on using his own architect, George F. Barber & Co., and builder, Louis Duncan. Before the house was completed, Duncan reneged on his agreement and "threw up the contract," leaving the Sudbrook Company to finish constructing the house at a loss.[47] Hooper was only in the house about a year when he began to be in arrears on his rental payments. The Company was forced to dun him almost continuously from 1900 through 1907, when the Company's records end.[48]

In 1900 Frederick A. Hoffman purchased 1.9 acres and built a house at 507 Sudbrook Lane designed by architect J. Appleton Wilson. Blackford prepared the floor plans and supervised the building. The process went smoothly, except that Blackford initially was "much disturbed" that the elevation of the house had been "increased above ground by one foot" since it had been laid off. Blackford wrote Hoffman: "This will necessitate the spreading of much clay over the soil to give the house a decent appearance, & even then will not look well in my judgment. It is too late to change it now, but I think it right to note it here."[49]

In 1901–02, only one new house went up in Sudbrook. The Sudbrook Company built it for U.S. Senator Isidor Rayner,[50] under a five-year lease agreement with an option to buy. Rayner had advanced most of the construction costs to the Company; his loan was secured by a mortgage on the property.[51] The house contained fifteen rooms and was the largest in Sudbrook Park, situated on two

By 1907, eighteen years after the community's inception, there were only thirty-five cottages in Sudbrook Park.
PREPARED BY ELLEN KAHAN ZAGER.

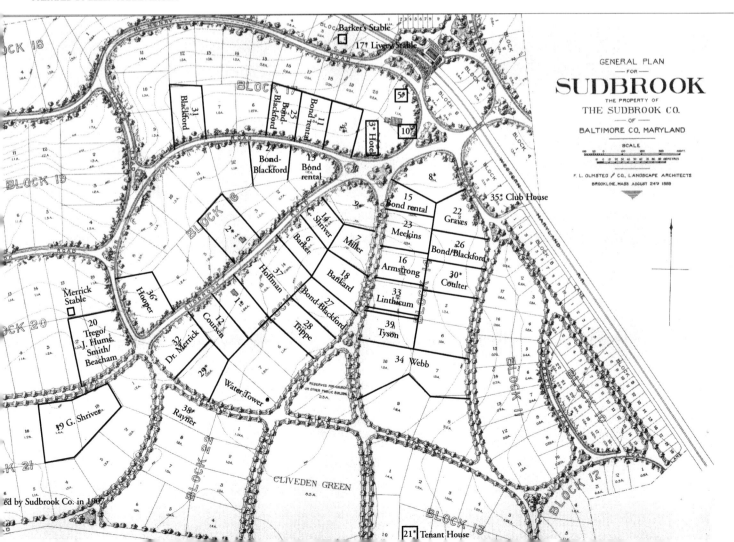

acres of land at 605 Upland Road (across from No. 29). Blackford described it as "a very large showy house…I think of Colonial style, [so] there is much more show for the money than is the case in other styles." It was also the most expensive that the Company had built — $7,000 with land valued at $2,200, for a total of $9,200. House elevations were drawn by McKenzie of the Baltimore firm of Wyatt and Nolting;[52] Blackford again did the floor plans and details. The builder was Benjamin F. Grove, who defaulted on his contract before the house was completed. The Sudbrook Company once again had to finish construction at a loss. Senator Rayner and his family began occupying the house in 1902.[53]

No houses were built or bought in Sudbrook in 1903. In 1904, F. C. Tyson bought lot 11, Block 15 on Olmsted's General Plan. He proceeded to construct a house at 711 Cliveden Road, between C.W. Linthicum and Oscar Webb. His was Cottage No. 39, the last to be constructed while Blackford kept records.[54]

For the three-year period from 1894 through 1896, Sudbrook Park had experienced a small surge in sales, having sold one of the Company's existing cottages and eleven lots for building. This trend ended abruptly in 1897. Over the next ten years, a mere four houses were added, and only two of these were outright sales — the other two houses were owned by the Company and constructed under lease arrangements.

The decline in sales was so dramatic and protracted that we are bound to wonder: what could have caused it?

Chapter 12

The Promise Fades: 1907–1910

We may never know for certain exactly what caused Sudbrook's sales to pick up for a period in the mid-1890s and then to fall off precipitously, culminating in the Company's figurative, if not literal, demise in 1910.[1] There were five factors, however, that hindered the development of Sudbrook Park from its inception into 1907: (1) Sudbrook's location far from the center of town, together with the reluctance of Baltimoreans to embrace permanent suburbs, (2) transportation problems, (3) Sudbrook's lack of amenities, (4) random external events, and (5) management, capital and financing issues.[2] No single issue was decisive, but the cumulative effect of all of these factors played a part in dampening sales and in dissipating the positive sales momentum that had emerged.

Eugene Blackford was often exasperated with the slowness of Baltimoreans to embrace suburban living, bemoaning the fact that if only Sudbrook Park had been near Boston or Philadelphia, its lots would have sold in a few weeks. Regardless of whether Blackford was personally familiar with other cities' suburbs or whether he based his comments on what the stockholders and directors of the Sudbrook Company told him, his observations were accurate. Baltimore did lag behind other large east coast cities in accepting permanent suburbs.[3] As historian Harry G. Schalck has observed: "The concept of year-round suburban living for the middle class seems to have taken hold in Baltimore relatively late. Before 1900 well-to-do families left city row houses for Catonsville, Mt. Washington and Towson only during the summer months."[4]

Although closer to the city and settled at a much faster pace than Sudbrook, even Roland Park had to cope with the reluctance of Baltimoreans to give up their winter homes in the city. In spite of company advertisements "that touted [Roland] Park as an ideal place for year-round residence, there were mad semiannual migrations when the seasons changed. A number of [Roland] Park families left every summer….On the other hand, an entirely different contingent of city dwellers bought places in [Roland] Park strictly as summer houses."[5] As one of Roland Park's earliest residents observed: "In 1891, Baltimoreans, conservative as always, listened politely to Edward H. Bouton explain the plans of his syndicate for developing the land to the north of the city [Roland Park]. They listened politely, and…they stayed away in droves….At the very outset, the Roland Park Company had to combat the Baltimore tradition that the 'country' was habitable only in summertime."[6]

Given the resistance of many Baltimoreans to year-round suburban living until after 1910, an additional hurdle facing Sudbrook's developers was the stipulation suggested by Olmsted to prevent speculative buying. Of Baltimore's early suburbs, Sudbrook appeared to stand alone in requiring purchasers to build within two years. Lot sales in many other suburbs far exceeded the number of homes built.[7] Clearly, investors and speculators were willing to take a chance on lots in still-novel areas. Sudbrook's requirement that purchasers build within two years guaranteed that it would not appeal to these investors, thus eliminating a significant part of the market.

While all early Baltimore suburbs had to contend with the local mind-set against permanent suburban living, not all were located as remotely as Sudbrook. Transportation problems, over which the Sudbrook Company had little or no control, had an almost immediate impact on development in

Sudbrook. Convenient electric transit lines and steam railroad links with the city were key factors in promoting and sustaining suburban growth in Baltimore.

By 1893 the conversion of horse car lines to electrical power provided the impetus for new developments outside the city limits. Electric street rail travel became the single most important force in promoting the growth of permanent suburbs in Baltimore. The fact that electric streetcars were cheaper than steam railroads and ran much more frequently was an enticing drawing card to persons who were willing to relocate to the suburbs only if they could maintain ready access, not only to their businesses, but to the social and cultural attractions in the city. Pikesville had the Baltimore, Pimlico & Pikesville Railroad, launched in 1872 as a horse-drawn car on tracks.[8] In 1881 it was purchased at a foreclosure sale and reorganized as the Pimlico & Pikesville Railroad Company. The line was electrified in July 1892 — one of the earliest electrified lines in the Baltimore area.[9] Its route ran alongside the Reisterstown Turnpike (now Reisterstown Road), from near Fulton Avenue to what is now Park Circle, then cross-country over what became Park Heights Avenue (then a private right-of-way) to the Confederate Soldiers' Home in Pikesville (the present State Police headquarters).

By January 1895, Blackford was aware that electric lines were a factor to be reckoned with in the competition for suburban buyers, even if streetcars were too pedestrian for his taste:[10]

> I am convinced from the result of my observations that Electric roads
> do not fulfill the requirements of 1st class suburban travel — for several
> reasons. Their cheap rates to all attract…[persons] with whom it is
> unpleasant to travel. One cannot smoke or read his paper, which the
> comfortable smoker on a R.R. train permits & in these days the
> reading of the daily paper is part of any man's duty. One cannot ride
> undisturbed, but must "move up, sit close" or finally stand up, nor
> can he reach the centre of the City without changes of cars. Marketing,
> baggage & washing cannot be taken by Electric cars, all of which items,
> in my judgment, place the Electric road far behind the Steam.[11]

At the time he wrote this, Blackford was fifty-six years old. His opinion of electric street rail travel reflected not only the fact that such travel was less comfortable, but perhaps also a longing to preserve the lifestyle to which he had become accustomed — a kind of privileged cocoon, separated from the lower working classes that were getting a larger foothold in Baltimore.[12] Because railroad travel was more expensive, Blackford could be assured that he probably would not be sitting next to laborers, riff-raff or others he might deem undesirable.

One of the disadvantages of Pikesville's electric line was that it ended at Fulton Avenue:

> I am confident that a connection with the lines of City [electric street
> rail] roads which terminate about the terminus of the Balto. &
> Pikesville Electric line is absolutely necessary for a successful line in this
> direction. The City lines to which I allude will convey passengers to any
> part of the [town], whereas if a connection is made [in only] the red
> line of cable cars out Baltimore St., the connections would be very
> limited. This is a point to which I attach great importance, having often
> heard residents of the Park comment on the great inconvenience of it…[13]

The Baltimore, Pimlico & Pikesville Railroad, electrified in 1892, was one of the earliest electrified lines in the region. Its influence on the development of Sudbrook Park was limited because its terminus on Reisterstown Road was a mile or more from the community. (The building to the right of the streetcar is the Burnt House Tavern). COURTESY OF THE BALTIMORE COUNTY PUBLIC LIBRARY COLLECTION.

Despite Blackford's claims in his letters to potential buyers that the electric line was only a quarter mile from Sudbrook, it actually was seven-tenths of a mile from Sudbrook's entranceway bridge to the line's Pikesville terminus.[14] For most residents of Sudbrook Park, it would have been a walk of a mile or more. This distance, coupled with the fact that riders had to change lines at Fulton Avenue to get downtown, made the Pikesville electric line a less attractive mode of transportation for residents of Sudbrook.[15]

Had the electric line run closer to Sudbrook and gone all the way into the city, it would have given a tremendous boost to the development of Sudbrook Park. By 1895 Sudbrook was competing with other suburban developments that had electric lines situated in their midst or on their border. Some communities had the added advantage of being located on two electric lines. Walbrook, for example, was served by both the Lake Roland Elevated Railway Company (which also served Roland Park) and the

Edmondson Avenue Branch of the Traction Company. Once fully operational, these electric street car lines ran cars as often as every five minutes. In an 1893 article, Baltimore's *Sunday Herald* pointed out that "electric cars run to and from Walbrook from 5:30 in the morning to midnight, making it perfectly convenient to reach one's business at any reasonable hour in the morning, and enabling residents at Walbrook to attend places of amusement, &c., in the evening, with as much facility as if residing in the heart of the city." [16]

Compared to schedules like the one serving Walbrook, the Western Maryland Railroad's limit of twelve daily trains each way in 1895 proved a drawback to persons seeking a place of permanent residence, presenting a problem that would plague the Sudbrook Company and Blackford throughout the period. Unlike the Northern Central Railway (with thirty-five daily trains serving Ruxton Heights, for example), the Western Maryland Railroad was not primarily a passenger carrier. Its major business was as a freight hauler, and its passenger trains were started as a service to scattered settlements along its route in the hope that they would increase in size, creating a more substantial ridership. It is doubtful that the Western Maryland Railroad made money on its passenger lines in the 1890s, which may be why it would curtail the schedule and cancel various trains serving Sudbrook without advance notice.[17]

Not long after it moved the Sudbrook station in May 1896, the Western Maryland Railroad issued staffing and scheduling decisions that created serious problems for Sudbrook Park. In February 1897 Blackford wrote to John Hood, the President of the Western Maryland Railroad, after learning that Sudbrook's train service would be reduced and that the railroad had plans to remove the station master, who also functioned as postmaster — meaning Sudbrook would lose its post office. Blackford lamented that "this, together with a lessened train service, will check development with us, I fear, just as it appears to be starting up."[18]

The railroad acquiesced and did not remove the station master, but after six weeks of the reduced train schedule, Blackford wrote to ask Hood for "relief…from what appears a complete paralysis of [the Sudbrook Company's] business," explaining:

> Two recent purchasers, & one other, who had just begun building at the time of the change, all declared that nothing would have induced them to do so had they known that the train service would be as much curtailed. This I might have ascribed to temporary annoyance had it not been followed by a complete cessation of all inquiry after lots or houses, the latter a thing quite unknown since the opening of the Park.
>
> Though the trains in the past have not of course been as frequent as on the N.C.R.R. [Northern Central Railroad], yet the hours were so well chosen, and the accommodation as to bundles, marketing, &c. so liberal, that residence on your line was as agreeable as on the other….Under this system we were here steadily building up, in spite of long continued depression of business among the very classes whom we wish to attract here.[19]

Among the railroad's changes were an "annoying requirement as to stamps upon packages" (requiring Sudbrook residents to pay the full charge for their accompanying packages and bundles, a charge that until that time had been waived) and the withdrawal of the 11:25 p.m. train. Blackford

Waiting for a train at the Sudbrook Station, about 1890. The Western Maryland Railroad's sparse schedule of daily trains when compared to other passenger railroads of the time, along with its sporadic and sudden scheduling changes, put a damper on development in Sudbrook Park. COURTESY OF THE COX FAMILY.

noted that, already, three families had reluctantly given notice that they would leave Sudbrook because of these changes. Blackford posited that the Sudbrook Park population was "more influential & intelligent" than that from the railroad's other stations, "being drawn entirely from business & social life in town, with which they remain closely connected, & do not wish in any way to sever their interest." He explained:

> I cannot go to such people & urge them to buy & build here when it
> must be confessed that when the trains passing between six & seven
> o'clock p.m. have gone by, they are cut off from all intercourse with
> Baltimore until the next day. I am simply laughed at. Such people wish
> to go into town to visit, to dine & to the theatre, which they cannot do
> [now] unless confronted on their return with a half mile walk from
> the electric car & all the annoyances besides of that mode of travel in
> winter.[20]

Blackford asked that the railroad restore the old schedule, especially the 11:25 p.m. train during the winter. That alone would "do more for the interests of the Co. & of your suburban business generally than anything I can do towards making known the attractions of this place." He also expressed confidence that if the railroad restored the train service it had provided in the past, "there will be within 5 years a summer population of 500 people & half as many in the winter, all solely dependent on your road for travel."[21]

The reduced train schedule definitely appeared to put a damper on inquiries and sales during 1897 — the year in which the Sudbrook Company made no new sales. In September of that year, Blackford wrote Hood, saying that residents were asking whether the railroad would run the theater train that winter. "As the train is regarded by all as indispensable to winter life here, I write to ask if you will allow one to assure applicants for houses that this service will be maintained throughout the winter."[22]

Since there was no further correspondence about the late train, it is likely (though not certain) that Hood acquiesced. In a few months, Blackford again wrote to Hood, begging for the continuation of the "cheap freight rate" that the railroad gave the Sudbrook Company in 1890. Blackford noted that he was continuing the development of the Sudbrook property, needed fifty cars of furnace slag from Thurmont for the roads, and had to be assured of the cheap rate. Apparently, Hood granted the request. Lower officials of the railroad made Blackford's life less than pleasant, however, harassing him about which cars qualified for the cheaper rate and fining him if cars sat too long at the siding.[23]

In September 1898 the railroad made a sudden change in station masters. The new appointee displeased a large number of residents, prompting Blackford to complain:

> You may not be aware of how much the comfort of a resident here
> depends upon the willingness of the Agent to oblige, a disposition
> which all claim to be wanting in Mr. Geary.... [H]e seems very capable,
> but simply lacks that quality which is absolutely required in the master
> of a suburban station. I therefore respectfully request that some other
> provision be made for him, if possible, & some one else sent here.[24]

The following September, Blackford requested that Hood add "a train this fall & winter leaving town at some time after the departure of [the train] at 6:10 p.m., say at 7:30. I am constantly confronted with this by those who contemplate buying & building here, or by renters.... The absence of such a train has undoubtedly militated against settlements at this point & elsewhere along your line."[25] In October 1900, Blackford asked Hood to change the time of the last train going into the city from Sudbrook. The 9:00 p.m. time "suits nobody" but a later train would permit "all those who come into the country to spend the evening" to return "at a convenient hour."[26]

In February 1903, hearing that the railroad would no longer issue special passes to mechanics and laborers employed by the Sudbrook Company, Blackford issued a pointed protest. He noted that the employees could not afford to pay the regular rates, and "I should be at a great loss to supply their places, they having been with me for 15 years." This time, the railroad would not bend and as a result, Blackford lost the services of his long-time engineer who ran the water works and performed numerous other jobs for the young community.[27]

Each year the Sudbrook Company wrote at least one letter to the Western Maryland Railroad about some scheduling or rate problem. In 1904 when the railroad changed the morning train, Blackford wrote: "As the Blue Mountain will no longer stop here, our people will be forced to take the electric cars, which will be very inconvenient. I do not think a greater blow could have been given to the development of suburban traffic, which is altogether dependent on the convenience of the trains."[28]

In December 1905, the papers authorizing the postmaster to assume his duties had not come through, and Blackford again sought immediate consideration, since Sudbrook's "prosperity" was at stake. About this time, the railroad was laying a double track and Blackford hoped this would resolve most of the problems. In a formal letter to Bond, he summarized his observations as manager:

> I find it difficult to reconcile the eagerness with which the cottages are sought at fair rentals, with the slow demand for the land for building, especially as those who have bought are most enthusiastic admirers of the place, and as to its healthfulness and the excellence of the water all are agreed.
>
> No doubt some of it is due to the high price of building material, and the present condition of labour, but in my opinion, it is chiefly due to the irregularity & infrequency of the train service, and to the comparative poverty of our people, who are unwilling to tie up their capital.
>
> The first obstacle will soon be removed by the double tracking of the railroad, now in progress; the last is disappearing, accelerated by the rapidly growing disposition to live in the country, owing partly to the rise of rents in the City.[29]

The railroad did double-track its line and in 1906-07 it replaced the original slightly bow-shaped, wooden carriage bridge going over the tracks with the timber deck structure that is still there.[30] Since Blackford's letters end in early 1907, we have no information on the impact of the double tracking on the community after that time. It is clear, however, that Sudbrook's early development was integrally intertwined with and dependent on the Western Maryland Railroad. Whenever it reduced service, there was a corresponding dampening of sales. Moreover, since the reductions were unpredictable, the impact was probably broader than realized, discouraging potential purchasers who did not want to be surprised the next month or the next year by an erratic change of train schedule.

A lack of certain amenities that were available elsewhere also contributed to the sluggish development of Sudbrook Park. As noted in Chapter 9, most of the communities being developed around Baltimore in 1892 or later had electricity from the start. In contrast, Sudbrook did not have a single house with electric lights until January 1899, when the house at 520 Sudbrook was completed.

Mrs. Thomson considered getting electric lights for the hotel early in 1897, but according to Blackford, seemed "unwilling to pay the additional cost of electric lighting over that by gas." Soon after, Blackford appeared interested in electric lighting for Sudbrook's houses and agreed to look into it further.[31] In September 1900 Blackford wrote that the matter of increased light had to be solved before the opening of the next season.[32] In 1901 Blackford was still investigating lighting for Sudbrook Park. To one company he wrote: "Under present circumstances my Company could not go to such expense in installing a lighting plant, but I shall use your letter for reference in talking up the matter with property owners, without whose assistance in the business we cannot proceed." [33]

In 1902, *ten years* after many other suburbs had electricity, Blackford wrote that Sudbrook's houses "of course have very modern conveniences, *some* with electric lights." By June 1903 the hotel had electricity on the first floor, but the bedroom floors, kitchen, pantries and basement still were lit by a "Kemp gasoline gas generator."[34]

Sudbrook's lack of electricity was a strong negative factor in attracting year-round residents, and it affected summer occupancy as well. As late as 1904, when Blackford was trying to rent out his Sudbrook house for the summer, he had to report that it had no electric lights. Electric lighting in Sudbrook became available in 1899 only at an increased charge, while in Roland Park, which was closer to the city but still part of Baltimore County until 1918, this luxury actually was less expensive than within the city limits and no more expensive than the cost of gas in town.[35] This differential in cost undoubtedly had an impact.

Another amenity that purchasers expected was telephone service. Again, Sudbrook lagged behind and this could have affected sales. In 1898 Blackford asked John Hood for permission to put a phone in the station, saying: "The Chesapeake Telephone Co. has at last consented to put a slot telephone at some point in the Park. This has long been regarded as indispensable by those who live or contemplate living here, and we are very anxious to meet their view." Telephone poles were installed in Sudbrook in April 1899. Blackford tried to keep them "on the rear & divisional lines, so as to avoid the unsightly appearance along the roads."[36]

Although not a part of the original Olmsted Plan, the Sudbrook Company's addition of a nine-hole golf course with Club House in 1898 was intended to attract purchasers who wanted special amenities. It was installed at a time when sales had begun to lag, and most likely was an attempt to remain competitive with Roland Park, which had added a golf course and large club house in 1896. Sudbrook's Club House, which cost about $1,500 to build, was not on a scale with Roland Park's large shingle-style structure, which became the Baltimore Country Club. Moreover, when Roland Park initiated the Baltimore Country Club in 1898, it provided that community not only with "exclusivity" (a social commodity in great demand among many Baltimoreans of that time), but also year-round opportunities for social events. In contrast, Sudbrook's hotel (more comparable in size to the Baltimore Country Club) did not require membership, a major component of exclusivity, and it closed from November to May.[37]

A number of external events also affected the willingness of Baltimoreans to purchase in Sudbrook Park. In the 1890s, when suburban living was an entirely novel concept, suburbs strove mightily to maintain sterling reputations to ensure a clientele. Unfortunately, Sudbrook had the bad luck to be on the receiving end of some unfavorable publicity.

In March of 1900, Blackford wrote to Bond to inform him, after the fact, that he had subscribed $25 on behalf of the Company toward a fund "to employ detectives to work upon the case of the robberies & assault here." Although no details were provided, it seemed that John Barker, owner of Cottage No. 6, had "worked himself & others…to a state of great excitement" about it and Blackford hoped that the effort "would do something to counteract any ill results, which [Barker] says will follow the reports going abroad."[38]

There were also problems with Sudbrook Park's water supply. As Sudbrook's roster of residents increased after 1894, there were periodic episodes of insufficient water pressure. The Company addressed this problem by digging additional wells, adding another pump, raising the water tower and eventually installing water meters. But residents were not happy when they did not have the desired water pressure, and many complained for months on end when water meters were installed. Sudbrook also received some adverse publicity in the summer of 1901, when its water supply was contaminated for a brief period after a heavy rain. Blackford thought the likely cause was a nearby stable. Given the importance attached to the purity and quality of water in the 1890s, anything less than perfection was intolerable. While this event may not have reached the papers, it no doubt circulated by word of mouth.

Another incident occurred soon after. Sudbrook resident Charles Linthicum, who had complained to Blackford about the contamination the year before, wrote an article about a temporary lack of water in June 1902 that was published in the newspapers. Blackford replied that while he accepted the blame, he "regretted that anything should have been in the public prints, as well calculated to injure the value of property here."[39]

Other events affected Sudbrook's development generally. The financial panic of 1893 began a depression from which various industries did not recover for several years. In 1898, fearing "the [Spanish-American] war scare" Blackford reduced rent on Cleve and a number of Sudbrook cottages as a result. Mrs. Thomson's rent for the hotel, which always had been $2,000 for the season, was reduced to $1,600 and there were no sales of lots or houses in 1897 or 1898.

In 1896 a mortgage tax law took effect in Maryland. Blackford wrote to an elected official in 1900 to urge that it be repealed, exhorting: "Prior to the passage of the present law I could borrow money for building here at 5%, at which figure operations could be profitably undertaken; the effect of the law was to raise the rate to 6% which has effectively stopped operations in the building line."[40] The tax was still an issue several years later, when Blackford replied to a Sudbrook renter who wanted Bond to construct an addition to his house: "There are no difficulties but those of money in the way.... There is already a mortgage of $3000 upon the house, and it is doubtful whether it could be increased, especially as our idiotic legislature is hesitating about repealing the mortgage tax law."[41]

In February 1904 the great Baltimore fire devastated a good portion of the city. Although there were no deaths, few injuries and few homeless, fifteen hundred buildings were destroyed. The one hundred forty acre area that was destroyed was almost entirely commercial, creating losses of equipment and inventory for many small business owners.[42]

The effect of the fire on Sudbrook was mixed. One renter would "in consequence of the fire" not be able to occupy his house that summer. Blackford encouraged Mrs. Thomson to lease the hotel again, noting that there was a "prevailing idea" that the city would be unhealthy that summer and "the demand for quarters nearby is active." But in his very next letter to a realtor, Blackford stated: "Being somewhat apprehensive as to the effect of the fire upon the demand for country houses, I propose to reduce the rent."[43] In the summer of 1904 Cottage No. 4 was vacant for the first and only time and Cottage No. 10, rented at a greatly reduced price, was vacant by August 9.

A major problem for Sudbrook Park — not apparent for years but ultimately crucial — involved weaknesses in the Sudbrook Company's dual management structure, the limited capital it had available for development and the manner in which its mechanism for financing constrained development. It is of interest to compare and contrast Sudbrook with Roland Park because Roland Park was one of the few communities from that time with extensive documentation about many of these issues and also because the two communities shared many similarities.[44]

Sudbrook Park's management structure was two-pronged: Hugh L. Bond, Jr. was the President of the Sudbrook Company, the ultimate decision maker and the personal financier for eight of the houses; Eugene Blackford was the on-site manager who handled all aspects of the day-to-day construction and operation of the community. Except for Bond's letters to the Olmsteds during the design phase, we know him only through Blackford's letters to him. He never lived in Sudbrook Park and visited only on occasion. He functioned as an absentee landlord, leaving Blackford to care for all of his rental properties. Bond's position as general counsel and head of the B&O Railroad's legal department, and his involvement as counsel to railroads (including the B&O) that went into receivership, occupied most of his time. As a result, he did not seem to take an avid personal interest in the community except as an investor. Because he was seldom on site, he had to depend on Blackford's account of a situation in making decisions. Blackford, in turn, clearly deferred all major decisions to Bond.

Blackford comes across in his letters as a very politic, gentlemanly man. Except for a few letters evincing exasperation or anger, he was very careful not to offend and usually went out of his way to keep residents happy and to resolve complaints. His personal work habits reflect a man who took on whatever jobs had to be done and devoted whatever time was necessary to see them through — a jack-of-all-trades in many ways. When the water pump broke and he needed his engineer to do something else, Blackford himself worked the pump for three weeks. While he often took on menial jobs, he also had a patrician attitude. His feeling about Sudbrook seemed to be: If we build it, they — "our people" — will come. Thus, Blackford was perplexed when the enthusiasm for permanent suburbs that had become a pattern around Boston and Philadelphia did not materialize among Baltimoreans. In Baltimore, different rules seemed to apply. And Blackford was at a loss to know how to promote Sudbrook Park when its beauty and Olmstedian lineage were not enough. While Blackford was a diligent manager, with an engineer's mind for detail, he was neither a visionary nor a salesman.[45]

Roland Park's Edward Bouton seemed to be both. In addition, he was dynamic and entrepreneurial in manner. Initially Secretary and later President of the Roland Park Company, as well as its resident manager, he was a decision maker.[46] Not only did he work directly with Roland Park's designers (George E. Kessler of Kansas City who planned the original plat and later Frederick Law Olmsted, Jr.), but he had a grand vision of what he wanted to create and a single-minded tenacity that enabled him to do most of what he set out to accomplish. As a salesman and promoter, he did not wait for people to come, but brought them to Roland Park. Whether using an open coach tally-ho for Roland Park's grand opening or providing free trolley tokens, he actively brought prospective purchasers to see the area. He also had far more capital at his disposal than did the Sudbrook Company. The Roland Park Company was initially capitalized with $1,000,000, while the Sudbrook Company was capitalized with a mere $75,000. That alone made a big difference in what each could afford to do. Bouton also had the savvy to promote his new development in a way that he knew would appeal to status-conscious Baltimoreans, and he left nothing to chance. Whereas Blackford at times considered advertising to be beneath him, Bouton had a sizable advertising allowance and spent it all while getting Roland Park established.

Sudbrook pre-dated Roland Park by two years, yet by October 1893 (two years after the Roland Park Company had incorporated), Roland Park had sold lots worth $122,635 and houses worth $185,000. By contrast, Sudbrook Park had sold only nine lots (averaging about $1,000 an acre) and none of its existing cottages. By 1895, Roland Park had over 250 houses, when Sudbrook Park had only twenty-six cottages. Roland Park was much larger (an original 800 acres to Sudbrook's 204), but the sales numbers are so disparate that factors such as the managerial styles must have played a role, together with such other factors as distance from the city, transportation links, availability of electricity and investment capital.

By about 1910, when Roland Park became identified as one of Baltimore's "premiere" suburbs, it drew a number of residents away from Sudbrook Park. People like the Charles Slagles, who had rented Cottage No. 9 (501 Sudbrook Lane) from 1899 through at least 1907, moved to Roland Park.

In earlier years, it often appeared to be just the opposite. Charles Grasty, a director of the Roland Park Co., tried to rent a cottage in Sudbrook during 1901, but none was available.[47] Hiram Woods, also a director of the Roland Park Co., similarly inquired about renting.[48] Others with Roland Park addresses wrote to Blackford during the 1890s about buying land and building in Sudbrook Park.[49]

Thus, while Sudbrook Park and Roland Park had similarities, the driving personalities behind each of the two communities were quite different and the capital at the disposal of the two companies was in no way comparable. In addition, the Sudbrook Company's method of financing future growth and development contributed heavily to its undoing, although the financing mechanism might have been quite successful had the Company sold all its lots and the original cottages as well.

The Sudbrook Company started out with an outstanding loan of $30,000 dating from 1890. Until the $30,000 note came due in ten years, the Company made quarterly payments of interest at six percent. As long as rentals were good, the Company could meet its quarterly payments and handle ordinary maintenance expenses on the properties.

The full principal amount was due at maturity. The mechanism for accumulating the principal was a sinking fund, established as part of the mortgage deed of trust securing the note. Each time a lot sold, at least $200 had to be deposited into the sinking fund in order to release the property from the lien of the first mortgage. Since there were about 229 lots on Olmsted's General Plan, the sinking fund would have amounted to $45,800 had all the lots sold. The mortgage also stipulated that specified sums be deposited in the sinking fund upon the sale of each of the nine original cottages and the hotel. The sales of these buildings would have enriched the sinking fund by another $28,000 for the nine cottages ($43,000 for the cottages *and* the hotel property). Had these sales materialized, the Sudbrook Company would have had ample money to pay off its $30,000 debt and to continue to improve all of the roads, build more houses for sale and eventually turn management over to the residents when they constituted a sufficient number to manage their own affairs. Because sales were so dismal, this process was cut short. Moreover, the Company added to its debt by borrowing another $10,000 in 1892 to extend the water supply so that purchasers of lots could connect easily to the system when they constructed their homes.[50]

Some of the difficulties that would later cause the dismantling of the Sudbrook Company were evident by 1898. Blackford, summarizing the Company's operating and financing policies, sadly but optimistically described the situation in which the Company found itself:

> The policy of the Sudbrook Co. has been to use the income, accruing from rents, to pay fixed charges and for development. The capital stock issued is about $63,000, & the bonded debt $40,000, against which there is a sinking fund of from $12,000 to $15,000. It was of course anticipated that the sales of land would have been far greater than they have been, but continued depression in business ever since the inauguration of the Co. has been the cause of this. Of the 205 acres, only about 21 have been sold. Handsome improvements have been put upon each acre of these by the owners. On its own property, the Company has built & owns 8 cottages, an hotel, 2 private stables, a livery stable, two servants houses attached to the hotel & a complete water system with about two miles of water mains lain.
>
> From these improvements its income is derived. There is great

& active demand for the houses for rent, and it is not doubted that the time has arrived, barring a war with Spain, when there will be a more active demand for lots. We have a magnificent piece of property, with R.R. Station on the grounds, beautifully laid out, with macadamized roads & sidewalks. It cannot fail to commend itself to our people finally. The same property, at a similar distance from Phila. or Boston, would be sold in a week at prices 3 or 4 times greater than we are asking.[51]

Under the terms of its notes, the Company's bonded debt of $40,000 came due beginning in 1900. Yet in 1898, having $15,000 at most in its sinking fund to apply against this debt, the Company borrowed another $4,000 to construct Cottage No. 36 (520 Sudbrook Lane) for Hooper.[52] Unless sales escalated astronomically, or unless the stockholders put in more of their own money, the Company — in less than two years — would be at least $25,000 short of what it needed to pay off its outstanding $40,000 debt. Its $4,000 loan would fall due (but not be paid) in 1901. And in 1901, it borrowed another $6,000 to construct a house for Senator Rayner at 605 Upland.[53] Viewed in retrospect, it is easy to see how the Company's financing policies, combined with low sales, contributed to its ultimate collapse.

Either the Company did not notice the black clouds gathering, or if it did, like a gambler convinced that the next roll will be a winner, its response was to deplete the sinking fund further in the hope of stimulating future sales. The decision to construct the Hooper house (520 Sudbrook) in 1898 proved to be a loss from the start, increasing the drain on the sinking fund. That same year, the Company made major expenditures to increase the water supply, resurface roads and build the golf course and Club House. In 1901, after borrowing $6,000 from Senator Rayner to build a house to his specifications, the Company again was forced to dip into the sinking fund to cover construction overruns. Between 1898 and 1907 the Company sold only two lots, adding a mere $400 to the sinking fund. Based on letters written by Blackford after 1900 referring to the $30,000 note as still outstanding, we can only assume that the Sudbrook Company re-negotiated that loan with the bank, since it did not pay it off and yet managed somehow to stay afloat.

In 1904 Blackford wrote his friend James Winsor in Philadelphia that the Company had paid off its second mortgage of $10,000 but that the $30,000 first mortgage was still in existence. In addition, Bond had advanced more than $5,000 to the Company, backed by a stock note. Blackford summarized the situation:

> The truth being that the income from rentals is not sufficient to conduct the business and the sales are too slow to rely upon. [Having] but this small income with which to pay taxes, insurance, expenses of water supply, repairs, &c and it being insufficient, I [have] simply become a mechanic for a larger part of the year & do an immense amount [of work] which would otherwise require skilled repairs.
>
> We are all the while hoping that we will be able to make sales, and that the already built [cottages] can be sold. I manage the property in good repair, and in an attractive shape, and it steadily increases in popularity. Compared with land prices & rentals about you, ours are

trifling, but the houses were built when materials and labour were much cheaper, and in themselves they earn a fair return, but cannot carry, being so few, the cost of maintenance of the whole property including interest....I have been much disappointed by the financial outcome of the business, which has been no success. Tho' paradoxical as it may seem, it has otherwise been eminently so.[54]

Blackford's concluding sentences summed up the contradictions of Sudbrook's early years. It was popular among seasonal guests, always had waiting lists of renters, and its permanent residents quickly developed a strong sense of camaraderie and community spirit. Many members of the same extended family rented cottages or purchased homes. They enjoyed leisurely strolls around Sudbrook Park and special events, like the Fourth of July, with its parade and full day of festivities. Blackford often commented that Sudbrook Park was a wonderful place to bring up children, especially boys.[55] The spirit that Olmsted wanted to pervade his communities took root early. But the Sudbrook Company was unable to make a financial success of Sudbrook Park.

An inventory of the Sudbrook Company's property in November 1905 is instructive. At that time, 32.75 acres had been sold and improved and there were 174.25 acres remaining, of which 140 acres or more were adaptable to building sites "after deducting roads and lowland."[56] All of the Company's property could be valued at $152,600.00. In addition, there were one and one half miles of four-inch and three-inch water mains and a water tower, the value of which could not be estimated, "but their cost formed the chief part of the item of $9,130.72 for water supply." Also, there were about one and a quarter miles of macadamized roads and a quarter mile each of gravel and dirt roads "all with gravelled side walks." A formal accounting accompanying the inventory summarized the Sudbrook Company's status as follows:

There has been expended, during the 16 years of the corporate life of the Company, for purchase, development, water supply & buildings, the sum of $155,792.33, of which amount $71,700.00 was from Stockholders, and $31,945.75 from sales, leaving a balance of $52,146.58 to be met by loans.

The income has not been sufficient to maintain the property, and pay the interest on these, hence the deficit & the cessation of development...[57]

To this dismal report Blackford added a positive conclusion, blindly refusing to recognize the irreconcilable problems that faced the Company: "In closing, I can confidently say that at no time has the outlook been so encouraging." Despite this professed optimism, the outlook was anything *but* encouraging for the Sudbrook Company.[58]

Blackford last wrote to Bond on January 24, 1907, enclosing an interest payment. By that time, Blackford's handwriting had become faint and difficult to read. A year later, on the morning of February 4, 1908 he died at his home at 1008 Winsor Road at age sixty-nine. His funeral was held at St. Mark's-on-the-Hill Episcopal Church in Pikesville, where he had been a warden and senior vestryman. An obituary in the *Baltimore News* read:

Major Blackford was a native of Lynchburg, Va. and a graduate of the University of Virginia. He had a gallant war record in the Confederate Army and commanded a battalion in the Fourth Alabama Regiment [sic]....He had been a resident of Maryland since 1875 and had a fine place near Pikesville. He was interested with Mr. Chas. K. Harrison and Mr. C. Lyon Rogers in the formation and conduct of the Pikesville Dairy, and was also one of the promoters in organizing Sudbrook Park, which has now become one of Baltimore's most attractive suburbs....[59]

With Blackford's death, the Sudbrook Company lost not only a tireless worker, but its primary link to the community it was developing. Whatever his shortcomings as a visionary and promoter, he had dealt diligently with the myriad day-to-day problems of a developing community at a time when suburban living was still in the experimental stages. Without Blackford, there was no one with the requisite interest and ability to attend to the administrative and managerial needs of Sudbrook Park and the Sudbrook Company.

If another manager was hired, we have no record of it. Although public records show that the Sudbrook Company relinquished its interest in Sudbrook Park in 1910, in the absence of Company records we do not know with certainty the series of events that led to this. We can assume, however, that the depression caused by the Panic of 1907 did not have a salutary effect on the Company's fortunes.[60] Moreover, without Blackford's care and passion, the community must have languished.

Residents formed the Sudbrook Park Improvement Association in 1908.[61] Although we know nothing about its initial purposes, perhaps the formation of this association was a response, at least in part, to Blackford's death and a desire among property owners that there be continuing oversight and an organized way to deal with issues affecting the community.

As for the Sudbrook Company, assuming that it had the same stockholders and directors listed in its 1889–1893 records, the period between 1908 and 1910 saw the loss of a number of them. A month after Blackford's death in February 1908, Richard Harding Weld died and Henry Chapin, deeply saddened by the death of his son in 1908, died two years later. It is unlikely that Robert Bacon, Hugh Bond or Robert Winsor had much time to devote to Sudbrook affairs after Blackford died. Bacon had been appointed Assistant U.S. Secretary of State in 1905 and was in France serving as U.S. Ambassador from 1909-1912. Bond, who had been the B&O Railroad's general counsel and head of the legal department since 1895, was additionally appointed Second Vice President in 1903. By 1910 he had requested to be relieved of these duties, the combined positions being too much for him to handle. Robert Winsor was by 1908 a nationally recognized financier, director of more than twenty-seven large corporations and a trustee of at least five. It is unlikely that Sudbrook Park was one of his main priorities.

With the Sudbrook Company's sales still lagging in 1910, its outstanding loans must have come due. After transferring its remaining interest in Sudbrook's land and improvements — either at its own initiative or because the bank threatened to exercise its lien over the property — the Sudbrook Company withdrew as an active player in the development of Sudbrook Park. The loss of Blackford as manager and the Sudbrook Company's subsequent relinquishment of its controlling interest were events whose ripple effects would be felt for years to come.

Chapter 13

THE CHANGES BEGIN: 1910–1939

The loss of Eugene Blackford as manager and the demise of the Sudbrook Company as the dominant force in developing Sudbrook Park not only affected those most immediately involved, but had consequences for the Olmsted design that have reverberated through the years. In large part, Sudbrook had become popular as a place in which to reside or spend "the season" because it was so attractive — a result of Olmsted's Plan and the restrictions which he had insisted were as much a part of a plan as lines on paper. Blackford had implemented the Plan and enforced the restrictions, but Blackford's ever-present vigilance was a service not easily replaced.[1] Blackford's death early in 1908 brought to an end almost nineteen years of focused control and direction. The formation of the Sudbrook Park Improvement Association in 1908 may have been one way in which the community responded, but because the Association left no records of its activities during this period, it is not known how extensive a role it assumed in maintaining the community.[2]

Between early 1907, when Blackford's records ended, and 1910 when the Sudbrook Company gave up its role as the developer of Sudbrook Park, sales of the Company's undeveloped lots and houses were sparse,[3] although Bond sold some of the cottages that he owned in the Park.[4] The financial Panic of 1907 could not have helped the Company's fortunes. Given Blackford's description of the Company's shaky financial condition in 1907, and the scarcity of its sales after that time, it is almost certain that the Company was in default on its loans by 1910. A major upheaval was imminent.

On November 1, 1910 the curtains closed on the first phase of Sudbrook Park's development, as the Sudbrook Company relinquished its ownership and control by transferring all of its Sudbrook Park land and improvements to one Patrick Casey.[5] The next day, Casey transferred the same Sudbrook Company land and improvements to Charles F. Stein and Joseph Berman.[6] Stein, an attorney, and Berman, in real estate, both had offices at 231 Courtland Street in the city; together, they were involved in countless real estate transactions throughout Baltimore city and county.[7]

Casey was also named as the mortgagor in a mortgage to the Sudbrook Company made simultaneously with its transfer of land to him.[8] Under the terms of this mortgage, Casey agreed that at the end of five years he would pay the Company the sum of $39,000 as the balance of the purchase money for the property, with interest at five percent per annum due semi-annually. Upon payment of specified amounts — for the hotel and for the eleven cottages — to Mercantile Trust & Deposit Company, which still held the first mortgages on all of the land owned by the Company, these properties would be released from the bank's lien and the lien of the second (Sudbrook Company) mortgage.

Since Casey faded into oblivion after the transactions of November 1 and 2, while Berman and Stein remained connected for many years with the sale of property in Sudbrook,[9] it is probable that Casey was a form of "straw-man,"[10] a mere pass-through for the real parties in interest, Berman and Stein. Although identified as the mortgagor and thus ostensibly liable on the mortgage, if Casey (a widower) had no land or money that could be attached, he himself would have remained essentially judgment-proof, while insulating Berman and Stein — to whom he had transferred title to the land — from any liability on the mortgage.[11]

Although exactly what precipitated the dual November 1910 transfers of all of the property

About a dozen houses, such as this one at 510 Sudbrook Lane, were built between 1910 and 1915, after the Sudbrook Company ceased to operate. PHOTOGRAPH BY PEGGY FELDMAN-ESKEY.

owned by the Sudbrook Company remains unknown, the structure of the transactions along with subsequent events suggests that they were part of an arrangement between the Sudbrook Company and the Mercantile Trust & Deposit Company to work out the sale of the property and repayment to the bank, to which the Company was heavily indebted. By 1910 the Sudbrook Company appears to have owed Mercantile, as Trustee, at least $34,000 in principal.[12] Mercantile apparently elected not to foreclose, but allowed the Company to secure a purchaser — on terms agreed to by the bank and with the bank retaining a first lien on all property — in the hope that the land would be sold and the outstanding debt would ultimately be paid. An arrangement of that nature might have been in the best interests of both the bank and the Sudbrook Company.[13] Moreover, Bond was well-known and admired for having accomplished the reorganization of the B&O Railroad without any foreclosure of the railroad's mortgages;[14] he no doubt would have been equally skilled in protecting his own and the Sudbrook Company's interests from foreclosure.

From November 1910 forward, the Sudbrook Company no longer exercised any apparent influence over the course of events in Sudbrook Park. Instead, between 1910 and 1923, the Sudbrook Company's property was transferred several times among investors and realty companies in a fashion comparable to a game of musical chairs. Berman and Stein initially took control of the Sudbrook Company's property, but in 1911 Stein conveyed to Berman all of his interest in the Sudbrook Park

Several houses were built on lots smaller than those Olmsted had envisioned when speculative investors gained control of Sudbrook Park. This quaint example on Upland Road is typical of that era. PHOTOGRAPH BY PEGGY FELDMAN-ESKEY.

property to which both had held title.[15] In 1913 Berman conveyed all unsold property in Sudbrook Park to Jennie Miller Hysan and her husband, of Prince Georges County, Maryland.[16] After holding the property about two and a half years, the Hysans in 1916 conveyed it to the Milburn Realty Company, of which Berman was President.[17] In 1918 the Milburn Realty Co. transferred the property to the newly formed Sudbrook Development Company of Maryland, which five years later transferred the same property to the Jones Herman Realty Company.[18] By 1923 when the Jones Herman Realty Company bought the property, there were about fifty houses in Sudbrook Park; there had been no large scale development despite multiple transfers of the property.[19] More than half of the original 204 acres remained undeveloped and there would be no further development until the late 1930s.

Viewed in retrospect, two aspects of the period from 1910 to 1923 stand out. First, the role that land speculators played in setting in motion changes to the Olmsted Plan, the full effects of which would not be realized for several decades. Second, the stark contrast between the outwardly tranquil tone of life that former Sudbrook Park residents almost uniformly recalled, and the chaotic behind-the-scenes picture that emerges from tracing the multiple and often confusing transfers of property.

The changes to the Olmsted Plan that began when the Sudbrook Company relinquished control of Sudbrook Park in 1910 were not glaring at first, but would become so as the years went by. The first noticeable one involved the deed restrictions. While deeds that conveyed existing houses in

Sudbrook which were purchased between 1910 and 1913 still incorporated the Olmsted restrictions by reference,[20] deeds for undeveloped land fell into one of two categories. In the first category were deeds transferring undeveloped property that conformed to the lot sizes shown on the 1889 Olmsted plat. These continued to bind the purchaser to the Olmsted restrictions, but inserted new language permitting the restrictions to be waived "at any time" by a writing signed by all of the parties to the deed.[21] This was not what Olmsted had intended. His provisions bound all property owners and required the Sudbrook Company to enforce them without exceptions.[22] As a practical matter, houses built during this period continued to comply with the original restrictions, but the groundwork was being laid for future changes of a larger magnitude.

In a second category were deeds conveying undeveloped property that did not conform to the 1889 plat. By June 1912, Edward V. Coonan & Co., Surveyors & Civil Engineers (also with offices at 231 Courtland Street) had surveyed and subdivided the land.[23] Many of Olmsted's sizable lots were whittled down to parcels measuring fifty feet by one hundred fifty feet. These were offered for sale on an installment plan. The selling price was $375, payable ten dollars down and five dollars a month.[24] No longer was Sudbrook Park being marketed in acre lots to purchasers who had to build within two years; land now was available in small parcels to speculators and investors. Although a few small lots and groups of these lots were sold in 1912 and 1913, there was only sparse development in the area that had been subdivided into new fifty foot lots. The houses that were built on these smaller lots were located on or near Upland Road, perhaps because from this location the community's existing water system could be readily accessed.[25]

The installment agreements attached to the sale of the small parcels contained ten restrictions, several modeled on Olmsted's in the Sudbrook Company deeds. For example, these revised restrictions included a thirty (rather than forty) foot setback, a five (rather than ten) foot side yard, and allowed a house to be built on a lot only fifty feet wide (rather than an acre). In accordance with Olmsted's provisions, no more than two horses and one cow were permitted, the ground could not be stripped of its topsoil, and the ground floor of any house had to be higher than the center of the street. The restrictions reserved the right to lay sewer or water pipes but did not include Olmsted's provisions to insure proper sanitary practices. In addition, two new restrictions were inserted. One was a racial restriction that prohibited transfer of the property to any "negro or person of negro descent."[26] The other required that no trees be removed — except those necessary for building — until the property was paid for and title had vested in the purchaser.[27] These modified restrictions ran with the land until terminated by mutual consent of the seller and purchaser.

The principal players following in the footsteps of the Sudbrook Company never lived in or had any emotional investment in Sudbrook Park or its Olmsted legacy.[28] With Blackford and the Sudbrook Company out of the picture, there seemed to be no one with a personal interest in following Olmsted's Plan and maintaining the restrictions that insured the Plan's proper implementation and long-term survival. It appeared that Sudbrook's new owners had gotten involved, as might be expected, for the sole purpose of selling the land as quickly as possible, and whatever methods they used, they initially managed to revive sales.

Between 1910 and 1913, there was a marked increase, compared to the prior ten year period, in sales of existing houses and undeveloped acre lots in the area that the Sudbrook Company already had improved with roads, sidewalks and water connections. In the eight months between November 1910 and July 1911, at least eleven properties were sold. Dr. and Mrs. Herbert Harlan, who had rented

Cottage No. 11 (1018 Winsor Road) since 1898 bought Cottage No. 30 at 722 Howard Road on November 7, 1910.[29] That same day two and a half acres on Upland Road, including the Rayner cottage at 605 Upland, was conveyed to Ella M. Emery (who was never known to have lived in Sudbrook).[30] In addition, Mary R. Hoffman purchased an additional 1.06 acres near her home at 507 Sudbrook Lane.[31] In December, Cottage No. 5 near the livery stable was conveyed to Thomas Ross, a handyman who had assumed some of Blackford's maintenance duties.[32] The property at 610 Upland (the "for sale only" house) was briefly held by an investor named Willoughby Hall, who soon after transferred it to long-time Sudbrook resident, Judge H. Arthur Stump.[33] The Arthur Poultneys, after living in the Park since 1893, bought 508 Sudbrook Lane (Cottage No. 2) in December 1910.[34] The William E.R. Duvalls purchased Cottage No. 8, at the intersection of Cliveden and Howard Roads.[35] The Ezra Whitmans purchased 501 Sudbrook Lane (Cottage No. 9) the following month.[36]

In April 1911 Clarence Tucker, a lawyer from Centreville, Maryland[37] bought an acre of land on the 2.3 acre triangle on Cliveden Road that had been marked "Reserved for Church or Other Public Building" on the 1889 Olmsted Plan.[38] Tucker and his wife built a house on the property. The failure to maintain this lot for its designated purpose was a major deviation from Olmsted's comprehensive design for a suburban village.

Jesse Cassard (the brother of Oscar Webb's wife, Grace Cassard Webb) and his wife had moved into 504 Sudbrook Lane. The Cassards had long summered in Sudbrook Park, either renting a house or living at the hotel. A new resident whose name will be seen again, Clarence Reynolds, built a house next to the Poultneys at 506 Sudbrook Lane in June 1911.[39] Reynolds was the Secretary of the Mercantile Trust & Deposit Co.[40] That same month, Emma Middleton bought property at 1007 Windsor Road (now being spelled with a "d"); architect Laurence Hall Fowler designed the house.[41] Nathan Pendleton purchased 520 Sudbrook Lane (the old Hooper house).[42] William R. Howard, Jr.,[43] who also had rented in Sudbrook for a number of years, bought the house previously owned by George Shriver at 607 Sudbrook. In March 1913, the Trippes sold 706 Cliveden Road West to Francis D. Hamilton. Between 1911 and 1915, houses went up at Nos. 1010, 1013, 1014 and 1015 Windsor Road, and at 510 Sudbrook Lane.[44] All of these homes were built in compliance with the deed restrictions adopted by the Sudbrook Company.

Although many parcels of undeveloped property in Sudbrook Park were transferred several times between 1910 and 1923, the primary mode of development remained individuals who built lot by lot in the area where the Sudbrook Company had installed roads and water pipes. There was no widespread development of large areas — in part because some of the problems that had hindered sales by the Sudbrook Company still remained unresolved.

A May 3, 1913, *Baltimore News* article, "New Trolley Line To Tap Northwest," for example, confirmed that streetcar transportation was still an issue for Sudbrook Park. Apparently, "private interests" were looking into a line connecting suburbs on the Liberty Pike with the United Railways and Electric Company, beginning at the Gwynn Oak junction, going out Liberty Heights Avenue, turning into Rockridge Road, traversing Villa Nova, "touching Sudbrook Park" and continuing toward Randallstown. The article noted that this section had long been in need of electric line service. After pointing out how rapidly the northwest area had developed despite this deficiency in transportation services, the article observed:

> The great expansion of this territory, which is at present reached either
> by railroad or after a walk of appreciable extent to the Emory Grove

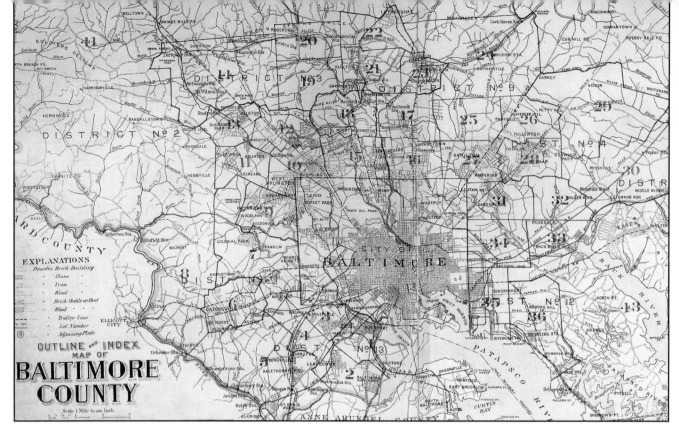

By 1915, the number of suburban developments had grown, but Sudbrook Park was still at the outer edge of the developed area. THE BROMLEY ATLAS OF BALTIMORE COUNTY, 1915. COURTESY OF THE BALTIMORE COUNTY PUBLIC LIBRARY COLLECTION.

electric line, has been little short of astonishing to those who have observed and who know how vital to any suburban development is a convenient and adequate car service. Sudbrook Park has had, of course, a residence colony for years, composed of people who had been accustomed to using the Western Maryland railroad twice daily to and from town. But new developments have sprung up, their residents being people who look upon the 5-cent electric car service as the only means of transportation between suburb and city…[45]

Despite the article's optimism about this suggested line, it never materialized.

After 1913 sales seemed to stagnate and renewed efforts were made to attract purchasers. A small inconspicuous newspaper advertisement proclaimed Sudbrook Park "The Garden Spot of Maryland" and enumerated: "Some of the Good Features: The best class of people live there. Macadamized roads. Beautiful shade trees. High elevations. Artesian water. Swimming pool, 50' x 109'. Golf links and tennis court and a large hotel. Lots $375 and Up. Cottages $3,900 and Up. Terms To Suit You. Apply to: The Sudbrook Park Office, 231 Courtland Street."[46] This was the address of Charles Stein, Joseph Berman, and the civil engineering and surveying firm that had prepared the 1910 plat proposing to subdivide Sudbrook Park.

The advertisement previewed changes that were just beginning. Now there was a swimming pool located across and near the railroad tracks on the way to Pikesville, close to the area where the station originally had been. From photographs, bathhouses at the pool resembled shoddily made garden sheds. They were neither tasteful nor attractive, and there was no landscaping. Blackford would have been dismayed, since under his more able direction, even plans for stables had to be approved to insure that the structures would be architecturally appropriate.

The swimming pool presented problems from the start: "As the long freight trains went by, the pool was showered with cinders from the smoke stacks of the powerful locomotives. Most of the time the pool had a skim of cinders and/or algae."[47] The pool "was fed by a spring of cold, *cold* water. There were rumors that the overflow was undermining the tracks of the railroad. Be that as it may, the pool was closed after only a few years use, and remained closed for many, many years until the buildings finally collapsed and the big hole was filled in with dirt."[48]

The residents of Sudbrook in 1913 were a mix of newcomers[49] and long-time residents.[50] High society was moving elsewhere and the changes were being noticed. The hotel, long a popular social hub, was only sparsely populated in June 1913, as recounted by long-time resident William H. Stellmann:

> I am temporarily fixed at the Hotel, but I do not like it at all; there are very few people there and I don't know any of them very well and a great many not at all….The room which I have in the Hotel is on the second floor…I pay Miss Bowerman $12.00 per week for my room & board which I think is really very high….I can get a room and private bath in town for $3.00 per week and my meals certainly will not cost me as much as $9.00 per week, for I really only eat two meals a day and at 50 cents per meal it would only be $7.00 per week. [Yesterday I] took the 8 o'clock car on the electric to town. The ride in was delightful and if I move to town, I know I shall miss the country very much, but I hate to be…surrounded by people I do not care for. There are [a] different sort of people at the hotel now than there were when I first started going there when Mrs. Thompson [sic] kept it.[51]

Possibly hoping to revitalize Sudbrook's hotel, a group of Sudbrook residents joined together to form the Sudbrook Park Hotel Co. in December 1913. The incorporators were William E.R. Duvall (Cottage No. 8), Clarence I. Reynolds (506 Sudbrook Lane), and James McEvoy (in the old Coursen cottage at 515 Sudbrook Lane). The new corporation's capital stock was $15,000.[52] Sudbrook's hotel, however, never reached its prior apex and, like several other parcels in Sudbrook Park, ended up being transferred repeatedly.[53]

Joseph Berman had transferred all remaining Sudbrook Company property, including the hotel, to Jennie Miller Hysan in June 1913.[54] Hysan conveyed the hotel property (about two and a half acres, including the improvements) to the Sudbrook Park Hotel Co. the following December, subject to a mortgage debt of $9,500 which the Hotel Co. assumed.[55] In 1919 the Sudbrook Park Hotel Co. transferred the hotel to Milburn Realty Company, of which Berman was President, subject to two outstanding mortgages: a $5,000 mortgage from Eugene Blackford, the late manager's son, and a $4,500 mortgage from Max Cohen.[56] The following year, Milburn Realty Company sold the hotel to Wilsie Adams and his wife, who became mortgagors on a mortgage from Berman that was assigned back to Max Cohen.[57] The Adams defaulted three years later; Oregon R. Benson, Jr. bought the hotel for $15,000 at a public sale on April 24, 1923.[58] Benson received title to the property in May, and that same day transferred title to George M. Henderson, a widower, who owned the 2.51 acre property until 1931.[59]

This 1915 map shows the location of the swimming pool, the railroad station on Howard Road and tennis courts to the left of the station. Large areas of undeveloped land still surrounded Sudbrook Park. Although not yet implemented, the subdivision plan prepared by Coogan in 1912 is shown. PLATE 13, THE BROMLEY ATLAS OF BALTIMORE COUNTY, 1915. COURTESY OF THE BALTIMORE COUNTY PUBLIC LIBRARY COLLECTION.

Even in 1913, and increasingly after that, permanent suburbs had finally become fashionable and the summer resort era was on the wane. Despite a variety of owners and efforts, the popularity of the hotel never returned to its late nineteenth century level. An advertisement on May 15, 1924, announced the opening of "Sudbrook Inn."[60] But it never opened for the summer of 1925 and on a cold and blustery day in March 1926, the hotel burned to the ground.[61]

Symbolically, the loss of the hotel represented the passing of the early era of Sudbrook Park. Built in 1889-1890 and first occupied in the summer of 1890, the boarding house, as it was initially called, had been intended as an adjunct to the permanent residential suburb, not as the hub of a summer resort. It was not unusual for suburban developments located in areas without a sizable town nearby to have boarding accommodations for visitors and single men and women. What Sudbrook's Boston and Philadelphia developers did not anticipate was that the Baltimore market would not immediately replicate the pattern of suburbs around Boston and Philadelphia, where the concept of suburban residency had caught on earlier and more quickly. Therefore, rather than being peripheral to the developing community, Sudbrook's hotel became its center. Even the evolution of its name — from boarding house to Woodland

Inn to the Sudbrook hotel — provides some insight into how its status and image changed in the early years of the community. When the original houses — built as models intended to sell quickly — languished as rental properties, and sales never came anywhere near meeting expectations, Sudbrook's reputation as a summer community with the hotel as its social nucleus seemed sealed.

While this configuration had consequences for Sudbrook because the venture was not financially successful and thus development of the Olmsted Plan was never fully implemented, it is also possible that the hotel provided an impetus without which Sudbrook's development would have been even more delayed. After all, in the late nineteenth and early twentieth centuries, Baltimoreans still considered Sudbrook remote and very much "in the country." It had minimal train service to the city and was late getting crucial amenities like electricity and telephone service. Had there not been a hotel to serve as a social magnet for the people the Company wanted to attract, it seems likely that the development would have been less successful.

Buttressed by the hotel, the lifestyle in Sudbrook Park for at least its first twenty-five years was one associated with persons of social position and wealth. It was a way of life far removed from that of the general population. Most of Sudbrook's cottages included accommodations for servants. The professions of Sudbrook's men (none of the women in these families was employed outside the home) were uniformly of high status. There were doctors, stockbrokers, lawyers, judges, entrepreneurs, men in their family's businesses, officials of banks, railroad and steamship lines, an architect and a U.S. Senator. These were prominent people, many of whom had lengthy family pedigrees.

A high percentage of Sudbrook Park's seasonal and permanent population was listed in the *Social Register*, the *Society Visiting List*, or both. For example, in the 1898 *Social Register*, twenty-nine listings were persons who resided in Sudbrook all or part of the year, although only five used a Sudbrook Park address; in the 1913 *Social Register*, thirty-one listings were Sudbrook residents, fourteen of whom listed Sudbrook as their permanent address; and in the 1915 *Social Register*, twenty-two listings were of Sudbrook residents, with thirteen claiming Sudbrook as their permanent address. Since Sudbrook only had between thirty to forty houses in these years, a large portion of its total population was included in elite society.

Sudbrook Inn, Sudbrook Park
Pikesville, Maryland
WILL OPEN MAY 15, 1924
The Best Summer Hotel in Maryland. All Kinds of Amusements—Tennis, Dancing, Croquette, Quoits, Swings, Baseball. Room and Board Within the Reach of All. Make Reservations Early. Call Vernon 3181.
ELIZABETH G. DURM,

Flyer advertising the Sudbrook Park Inn, about 1924. As living year-round in a suburban community became commonplace in the twentieth century, the Sudbrook Inn struggled to attract a clientele. The Inn was destroyed by fire in 1926. COURTESY OF THE MARYLAND HISTORICAL SOCIETY.

A similarly high percentage of residents were listed in the slightly less exclusive *Society Visiting List*. As early as 1889-90, when Sudbrook only had nine cottages, six seasonal occupants were listed. By 1893–94 this number had increased to fourteen; by 1895–96 it was twenty-three (thirteen of whom listed Sudbrook Park as their permanent address); in 1898 and 1907 the number had jumped to twenty-eight (with fourteen listing Sudbrook as their address in 1898, but only nine in 1907); and in 1916, twenty-nine of Sudbrook's residents were listed, twenty as permanent residents.

Not surprisingly, everyone seemed to know or be related to each other, or be associated by business. Oscar Webb (who lived at 501 Sudbrook Lane from 1890 until he moved to a house he built at 709 Cliveden) was related to Charles Webb (who leased 1017 Windsor from 1895 to 1898) and B. Deford Webb (who leased Cottage No. 8 beginning in 1901 and later purchased 721 Cliveden). Oscar's wife, Grace Cassard Webb, was the sister of Jesse Cassard, who with his wife Sophie Reese Cassard, had summered in Sudbrook from its early years; they built the house at 504 Sudbrook Lane (their son, Reese Cassard, played the piano at the Sudbrook hotel). Charles Webb's wife was Mary Cator; she was related to the George Cators who lived at 1016 Windsor, and to Carrie Cator, wife of Dr. Herbert Harlan (they leased 1018 Windsor from 1898 to 1910 and then purchased 722 Howard). Eugene Blackford's daughter, Mrs. Arthur Poultney, first lived at 511 Sudbrook Lane and then at 508 Sudbrook, which she and her husband purchased. The families of long-time renters John Littig and Ed Norris (whose wife was Mary Murdoch) were related through marriage to Hugh Bond, Jr. (Bond's sister-in-law was a Murdoch). Mrs. Eliza Miller and her son, D.H. Miller, Jr., both were long-time seasonal residents (Mrs. Miller owned 718 Cliveden; her son and his wife rented Cottage No. 8 from 1890 to 1900). Mrs. William Ross Howard, Jr. (607 Sudbrook Road) was Louisa Thomson, daughter of the long-time proprietress of the Sudbrook hotel. Mifflin Coulter's daughter Nannie (722 Howard) married Albert Gambrill (the Gambrills had been seasonal renters in Sudbrook since it opened), and Margaret Coulter married William B. Rayner (708 Cliveden), the son of Senator Isidor Rayner (605 Upland). After 1913 there were several marriages among the children of various Sudbrook families. These included the Emorys who lived at 500 Sudbrook Lane for several years — one child married Proctor Brady (713 Cliveden), another married Katherine Linthicum (715 Cliveden) — and the Herbert Stitts (604 Upland, she was Mary Pendleton, whose family lived at 520 Sudbrook Lane).[62]

Dr. Herbert Harlan and Judge Henry Harlan were brothers, as were James Shriver and George M. Shriver. Dr. and Mrs. Harlan leased 1018 Windsor from 1898 to 1910, when they purchased 722 Howard. Judge Harlan's family leased 708 Cliveden from 1900 to about 1920. The James Shrivers leased 610 Upland from 1899 to 1903. The George Shriver family built 607 Sudbrook in 1893 and lived there until around 1910.

Business associations were common. George Shriver was employed by the B&O Railroad, as was Hugh Bond; Shriver took over for Bond as 2nd Vice President when Bond asked to be relieved of that position in 1910. Judges Henry Harlan, H. Arthur Stump and James P. Gorter (whose wife was Anne Poultney) had been in practice together before being appointed judges. The Stumps began renting 610 Upland in 1903 and later purchased it. The Gorters rented 511 Sudbrook for several years. And the list goes on.

As a further measure of social status, several residents of Sudbrook Park were listed in Eleanor Stephens Bruchey's *The Business Elite in Baltimore 1880–1914:* Reuben Foster (500 Sudbrook Lane) — President of the Baltimore, Chesapeake and Richmond Steamboat Co. (later the Chesapeake Steamship Co.) and a receiver for the Richmond and Danville Railroad (as was Hugh Bond, Jr.); Eugene Blackford (the manager's son, at 1008 Windsor), partner in Gill and Fisher; Charles W. Slagle (501 Sudbrook Lane) — a senior partner in Chas. W. Slagle & Co., who also established the Seacoast Packing Co., organized the Baltimore & Hanover Railroad and was an organizer of the American Fire Insurance Co.; John R. Bland (1020 Windsor) — founder and president of the United States Fidelity and Guaranty Co.; and George Cator (1016 Windsor) — a director of Armstrong, Cator & Co., an organizer of the Fidelity and Deposit Co. and organizer and president of the American Bonding Co.[63] In addition, Charles Slagle was featured in Thomas Scharf's *History of Baltimore City and County*.[64]

Indeed, Sudbrook in its early years consisted of a very homogeneous and socially well-connected population. Blackford had written to a prospective buyer from Roland Park that in Sudbrook, "merit & not wealth command influence," but clearly Sudbrook's residents had enough wealth to buy into a materially comfortable upper middle-class lifestyle.[65] Until about 1913, almost everyone in Sudbrook except the hired help was from a white, Anglo-Saxon Protestant background. Many from Sudbrook attended St. Mark's-on-the-Hill, the Episcopal church in Pikesville. Although Olmsted's restrictions were not of a racial or religious nature, Blackford carefully screened applicants and made it clear that he did not want to rent or sell to Jews.[66] Blacks were not even mentioned. Society was so definitively segregated along racial lines that it probably was not even an issue. These abhorrent prejudices, of course, were quite common in that era.[67]

While immigrants were crowding into Baltimore and laborers by the thousands were striking to demand subsistence wages and decent working conditions, life in Sudbrook Park both before and after the turn of the century moved in patterns typical of an upper middle-class gentility.[68] Thanks to Olmsted's design and Blackford's implementation, Sudbrook Lane from Sudbrook Park to Pikesville "was a very pretty road lined on both sides with maple trees."[69] After 1898, Sudbrook Park had its own golf course, frequented by many of the men and some of the women, along with members from outside the community. Tournaments were often held with the Maryland Country Club, Green Spring Valley and the Suburban Club. The Fourth of July was a day of parades, games, contests and festivities. The hotel was the gossip and social center of the community, with its "fifty or more rocking chairs lined-up like soldiers" on the porch.[70] During the day, children gathered to play baseball. In the evenings, residents strolled to the hotel to hear Reese Cassard at the piano, to dance to local bands, or to see a Paint and Powder Club performance. Unless tutored privately or by Mrs. Thomson's daughter, the children of most Sudbrook families attended private schools in the city or farther out toward Reisterstown.[71] The 8:06 train was the one that school children took to Baltimore for their 9:00 a.m. classes.[72]

Even as a parade of absentee investors and speculators in turn took title to the land relinquished by the Sudbrook Company, daily life in the community retained much of its affluent, intimate cachet. There was a horse and carriage — called Brown's Air Line by locals — to take patrons to and from the hotel and the electric line about a mile away in Pikesville. The fare was ten cents, not cheap considering that one could ride the electric line from Pikesville to the city for only five cents. There were regular workers around the Park whom everyone knew, like the station master (who was also the postmaster). Norman, known only by his first name, was a porter, baggage carrier and coachman, and did other odd jobs. Thomas Ross was a "capable jack-of-all-trades."[73] From 1904 on, he was in charge of the Sudbrook Company's livery stable. After Blackford's death, he assumed some of Blackford's duties.

Technological innovations also made their appearance; slowly but surely they would affect the community. Before about 1910 there were very few automobiles in Sudbrook Park. Senator Rayner's son, Will, had the first car, which residents called the Red Devil. Before long, William Stellmann had a

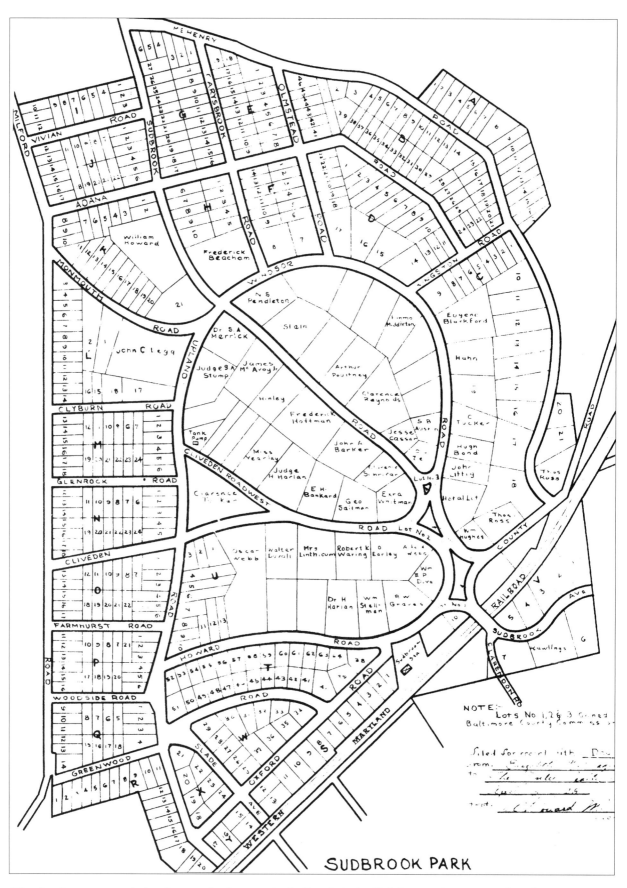

Plat showing a proposed plan for new development in Sudbrook Park, filed for record in 1928. This plan was never implemented exactly as shown, but approximates the new development that began in 1939 and continued until 1954.
BALTIMORE COUNTY LAND RECORDS OFFICE.

Cholmers-Detroit with a hum that announced its approach from a distance.[74] The Frederick Beachums (600 Sudbrook Road) had a Kissel and the Merricks got a hand cranked Ford Touring car in 1911. Gas was about eight cents a gallon, but because there were not yet gas stations dotting the road, drivers had to have their own supply. The Merricks had a 100-gallon tank installed for this purpose. The speed limit in the Park was six m.p.h. Even at that pace, the graveled roads were quite dusty when cars drove over them. The solution was to oil them, then cover the oil with sand — helping to alleviate some of the mess.[75]

Sudbrook had always been connected to the mercantile village of Pikesville, which was growing at this time. Field's Drugstore sold medicines, as well as milkshakes and ice cream soda for five cents. Corbett's and Foley's provided groceries, Coughan's supplied meats and Tony's stand was the place for fresh fruits in the summer. Before telephones, orders would be placed one day and delivered the next. In addition, hucksters came around the Park with fresh vegetables, fruits and other seasonal items. Provisions could also be sent out on the train and delivered. Residents even ordered liquor and ice cream for delivery to their home. During this period, when many parcels of property in Sudbrook were transferred from party to party, and some sold at public auction, the day-to-day life of Sudbrook's residents retained an outward tranquillity that may have belied some of the larger issues facing the community.[76]

While the future of Sudbrook Park remained uncertain after the Sudbrook Company withdrew, the development of Guilford in 1913 and Homeland in 1922 gave new impetus to what was being called the "Roland Park-Guilford-Homeland District." Frederick Law Olmsted, Jr., and the Olmsted firm designed both Guilford and Homeland. Edward Bouton oversaw their development. The fact that this competing "district" also acquired an "institutional infrastructure" of churches and private schools contributed to its stability and popularity.[77] By then, Bouton clearly was attracting high income buyers, a market that he mined expertly. As Sudbrook settled into a sleepy period with little movement — the ruins of the hotel and the swimming pool in daily view — the new vibrancy of these areas that bore an Olmsted imprimatur drew a number of Sudbrook Park residents away. By around 1920 a number of long-time residents, including the Harlans and the Stumps, decided to move to the Roland Park area.

While Sudbrook once had rivaled and perhaps even exceeded Roland Park's ability to attract a high percentage of socially elite Baltimoreans, those days were on the wane. Quite probably people left Sudbrook Park or chose not to purchase because there were no longer the controls that could insure a retention of property values. By 1920 the Sudbrook Company and Blackford were long gone, and all of the Olmsted restrictions expired. Development was at a standstill and the community's long term fate was unsettled. Property sales were now in the hands of the Sudbrook Development Company, whose Articles of Incorporation had been filed on April 16, 1917. The incorporators were Louis Croner, Harry Israelson and Joseph C. Smith. They, together with a Max Covalerchek were the directors — none of whom were heard from before or after. The office was in the city at 545 Calvert Building. The company was capitalized with a mere $5,000.[78]

Very little in the way of new development occurred in Sudbrook during the 1920s and 1930s. By this time, there were about fifty houses. Although Sudbrook had become the year-round residence of many families, it still lacked a winter social life and trains never exceeded twelve a day. Some families, like the Benjamin Reads (who in 1913 inherited Emma Middleton's house at 1007 Windsor Road) lived in Sudbrook ten months a year, taking an apartment in the city during December and January.[79]

Yet even with the loss of the hotel in 1926 and the reversion of the golf course to fields, many

Sudbrook Park residents chose not to move but settled into a simpler lifestyle that no longer revolved around the hotel. Some joined the Baltimore Country Club or other country clubs and continued to play golf with their former Sudbrook friends and neighbors who had moved away. For many in Sudbrook, tennis became the local sport. In addition to the courts near the train station, there were at least six private tennis courts put in by residents.[80]

Beginning as early as 1913, new residents introduced some diversity in Sudbrook Park. Not much at first, but a little. A family named Jelenko lived at 1014 Windsor from 1913 to 1934. The Whelan family moved into the Armstrong home at 717 Cliveden. They were Catholic, and one of the sons later became Monsignor Thomas Whelan.[81] While many socially well-connected residents remained, there would be a growing displacement of this group by persons of comfortable but not affluent means.

In April 1928 a plat was filed for record with a deed from Elizabeth Slagle to the Onlee Realty Company. This plat, similar to the one prepared by Coogan in 1912, proposed several new roads and divided all of the then-undeveloped portion of Sudbrook into many small lots. For whatever reason, no immediate action was taken to develop this particular plat. Perhaps the Great Depression of 1929 intervened.

Until almost 1940, Sudbrook Park consisted of about fifty homes, mostly the cottages built between 1889 and 1923. But a new construction boom would soon hit the country, and Sudbrook's undeveloped land would not remain fields of wildflowers or dense woods much longer.

Chapter 14

NEW DEVELOPMENT: 1939–1954

Sudbrook Park remained virtually unchanged in size and configuration until 1939, when it began to be transformed from a community of about fifty homes to one of almost five hundred — a process that took about fifteen years to complete. Because of the unifying strength of Olmsted's 1889 design, the enlarged area did not take long to be assimilated into the existing community, despite some major changes to the Olmsted Plan as a result of the new development. An improving economy and the automobile were the impetuses driving development both locally and nationally.

As the economy revived toward the end of the decade following the 1929 Stock Market Crash, the building of suburban houses had resumed. It was a trend that would mushroom after World War II as developers in the Baltimore area, as elsewhere, hastened to meet the increased demand for houses. Builders were now constructing smaller homes on smaller lots to accommodate the young middle class families who were beginning to flock to suburbs — spurred in large part by the widespread mobility that resulted from increased automobile ownership.[1] Clearly, times had changed over the fifty years that had elapsed since Sudbrook was designed. Suburbs had evolved — from being a novel experiment, to being accepted, to being mass-produced.

After lying dormant for years, Sudbrook Park's undeveloped land — approximately a hundred acres surrounding the already built community — would be developed primarily by two builders, Foster Fenton[2] and William Chew. Both Fenton and Chew inserted new roads, subdividing Olmsted's original large blocks to create a larger number of smaller blocks. The developers also multiplied the total number of lots by carving Olmsted's one-acre lots into parcels measuring fifty by one hundred fifty feet, a process which began in 1912 but was not implemented to any appreciable degree in that earlier period. Altogether, about half of Sudbrook Park's acreage was developed with lot sizes greatly reduced from the sizes shown on the 1889 Plan.[3]

Fenton launched the new development in the late 1930s[4] by constructing about sixteen one-and-a-half and two-story Cape Cods on Monmouth Road. Had the houses been developed in accordance with lot sizes on the 1889 plan, there would have been six rather than sixteen houses.[5] While lot sizes were being drastically reduced, much of the ambiance envisioned by Olmsted — including substantial setbacks and an emulation of the landscaping of the older area — was perpetuated. Since Monmouth to the current Milford Mill Road had been constructed years before by the Sudbrook Company, it followed the curvilinear design shown on Olmsted's Plan.[6] (Monmouth was being referred to as Sudbrook Avenue or Sudbrook Road by the late 1940s; today, it is part of Sudbrook Lane).[7]

Immediately to the west of Monmouth, Fenton developed Adana Road,[8] a street newly carved out and not on the Olmsted Plan. To entice purchasers, Fenton furnished two model homes at what is now the corner of Adana at Windsor. A 1940s sales brochure described the homes as "substantial modern six room cottages of solid masonry on large beautiful wooded lots" and noted that they could "be purchased on the Federal Housing Administration plan with payments less than prevailing rentals for apartments or houses."[9] Three basic house plans — the Chase, the Belvedere and the Franklin — were offered.[10] Both the Franklin and the Chase were priced at $4,380; the Belvedere cost $4,850. All three had annual ground rent of $84. The purchase plan for the Franklin and the Chase required $100

down, $100 when the roof was on and $380 at completion for a total down payment of $580. Monthly payments on these two models were $36.50.[11] The Belvedere cost slightly more, requiring a $650 down payment and monthly payments of $38.74.

The deeds to properties sold by Foster Fenton enumerated fifteen covenants which were to run with the land.[12] These restrictions emulated the intent but not the specifics of certain of the Olmsted and Sudbrook Company restrictions, prohibiting the erection of any dwelling costing less than $3,000; mandating a thirty-five foot setback from the lot line; insisting on residential uses; prohibiting live poultry, hogs, cattle or other livestock; and requiring approval of house plans by a committee from the area. In addition, the Fenton covenants contained a provision that prohibited occupancy of any building by anyone of "negro, oriental or Hebrew extraction," unless they were "employed in or about the premises by the owner or occupant of said land."[13] As noted previously, such repulsive covenants were not confined to Sudbrook Park. A number of communities, including Roland Park, Guilford and Homeland in the city, and Dumbarton in Pikesville, also had restrictions of a similar nature for a time during the first half of the twentieth century.[14] Restrictions such as these persisted until they were declared unconstitutional in 1948; thereafter, they could not be enforced.[15]

After Adana Road, Fenton developed the 900 block of Windsor Road (whose layout was in accordance with the Olmsted Plan although the lot sizes were smaller) and then houses on Carysbrook Road. Carysbrook Road was on the Olmsted Plan but not in its current location. Its configuration, however, carried out Olmsted's intent, although it curved toward the south rather than in a northerly bow as platted in 1889. For a number of years, Adana Road ended at Carysbrook.

As the community grew, steps were taken to formalize the residents' association that had originated in 1908. The "Sudbrook Park Improvement Association, Inc." was formally incorporated on September 29, 1941. Although most of the all-male original board of directors was made up of residents from houses in the older section of Sudbrook, within a few years its officers and committees included representatives from the newer area of Sudbrook as well.[16] The Association's purpose was to "organize and operate a community organization for community improvement and protection, better fellowship and a stimulation of interest in a higher development and improvement of the living conditions of the community known as 'Sudbrook Park'." Membership was open to all residents or property owners in Sudbrook Park. Dues were $2.50 for those with a fifty-foot frontage and $5.00 for those with larger frontages. The community was kept informed through *The Sudbrook News,* a newsletter issued about four times a year under the auspices of the Improvement Association.[17]

There seem to be no surviving community newsletters from 1942, the year that the *Baltimore Sun* focused attention on an unsightly dump that Sudbrook residents wanted to abolish. It was located "above Sudbrook Park and below the Old Court road," along Greenwood Road (then called Greenwood Avenue).[18] Trash and large-scale dumping of garbage reportedly had been allowed to accumulate over the previous fifteen years, ruining "the natural beauty of the spot" and killing "many fine trees." One nearby resident remarked: "Years ago, that particular stretch of road was one of the prettiest in this section. The heavily wooded glen was an ideal picnic spot and there was a lovely little stream winding down the hill where the children could wade. But look at it now."[19] As a result of the *Sun* articles, the Board of County Commissioners agreed to clear the dump, post "no dumping signs," and issued instructions to arrest anyone found dumping refuse in the area.[20]

While the new development was beginning to take root, the November 1943 edition of *The Sudbrook News* provided evidence that, even as Sudbrook moved into more modern times, it retained

ORGANIZED IN 1908
INCORPORATED 1941

SUDBROOK PARK IMPROVEMENT ASSOCIATION
INCORPORATED
PIKESVILLE, MARYLAND

April 5, 1948

Dear Neighbor:

Work on clearing and grading the recreation area on Greenwood Road is scheduled to begin within the next week or so. Once that is done, planning for the development of the area as a community center will get underway. We will not be able to do too much this year, but it is important that we make a beginning now. The community's families are young, most of the children are in the "small fry" stage, but within the next ten years we will have more than 500 teen-agers living within the boundaries of the Park.

What we should have, and what we hope to provide eventually, is recreation for every family; for every member of the family. That will need organization; it will take a lot of work; and it will cost money. Perhaps, our hopes, our goal, will not be realized in full but we must, at least, provide for our young people. That is the primary responsibility of the community.

We need a fund in order to get going on the project. The ladies of the Sudbrook Club are doing their part and their initial contribution of two hundred dollars is more than generous. But we need more than that and we are appealing directly to you for a contribution. It need not be large; make it anything you like but remember, this is one donation that will be spent directly to help you and yours.

There will be no solicitation of contributions. Attached you will find a list of neighbors to whom your contribution may be made. A report on progress will be printed in the next issue of the Sudbrook News. Many thanks.

Very truly yours,

SUDBROOK PARK IMPROVEMENT ASSOCIATION

Andrew MacDonald Secretary

Note: Next meeting of the Association - 8:00 P.M., Monday, April 12, in St. Marks Church, Reisterstown Road.

Letterhead of the Sudbrook Park Improvement Association, 1940s. From 1908 on, Sudbrook had a community association, first called the Sudbrook Improvement Association, then the Sudbrook Club, Inc., and recently renamed Sudbrook Park, Inc. SUDBROOK PARK, INC. ARCHIVES.

aspects of its early past. Among the items was a note that the Clarence Tuckers (at 705 Cliveden Road) had "closed their house and gone to the city for the winter." The Western Maryland train still provided access to and from the city. *The News* remarked that the 7:26 a.m. train to town and the 4:35 and 5:25 p.m. trains back to Sudbrook were well patronized, "but the 9:12 a.m. train to the city isn't picking up enough customers. Why not try that train when you have some shopping to do downtown? The one-way fare to or from the city is 22 cents." *The News* also contained the following appreciation of Sudbrook Park's resistance to the conventional grid layout, perhaps an unknowing tribute to Olmsted:

> The post office people evidently did the best they could numbering the homes in the Park and if you should find the 400 block of one road paralleling the 1000 block on another remember our roads have a tendency to wander off vaguely in any direction that strikes their fancy. Sudbrook Road, for example, leaves Sudbrook Avenue at the Bridge, waves good-bye to Windsor at Doctor Nichols' [500 Sudbrook Lane], curves slightly…for a little ways and finds itself running smack into Sudbrook Ave. and Windsor again up by Bill Foley's place [520 Sudbrook Lane]. That kind of thing would upset any well-bred city street but not old Sudbrook Road; gracefully yielding the right of way it makes a right turn into the woods and on beyond the Howard home [607 Sudbrook Road]…until it blends gently with Olmstead [Road].… While causing strangers and salesmen to go quietly mad, [this] has a marked effect on Park residents and even in the new development it is not unusual to find different numbered blocks on each side of the street, and a rugged individualist with a house in the 100 block firmly entrenched between two neighbors who live in the 900 block.[21]

The Sudbrook Improvement Association had eighty-four dues-paying members by January 1944. That month, *The News* expressed the hope that every resident would be a member by the end of the war, "when the problems of adequate public transportation and a school bus service for the community will have to be tackled." All of the officers of the Association were men, although they expressed pleasure at having a "one hundred percent increase in the number of ladies attending the [last] meeting." (Apparently, two women joined them). Meeting topics included issues such as house numbering, snow removal, a playground for the children of the community, victory gardens, water pressure and a community club room. There was also a committee to have "street direction signs erected at the entrance to the Park" because visitors "still have trouble locating us back here in the woods."

World War II had an impact on Sudbrook Park, as it did on other communities. Since most home construction was suspended during the wartime emergency, lots were not selling. In 1944 lots in the 900 block of Olmstead Road were offered at $50 each and there were no buyers. As housing became scarce, however, real estate prices climbed: one of Foster Fenton's houses on Carysbrook Road, offered at no more than $4,850 in 1940, sold for $7,200.[22]

Community cohesiveness, which had been a hallmark of the early years of Sudbrook, continued to be encouraged. *The News* noted that "with the father draft just beginning, one block in the Park has six neighbors whose husbands are off at the wars." Residents were asked to lend a helping hand to these families. Plans were being made to erect a Roll of Honor to acknowledge the men and women of the community in the service of their country. Blackouts were discussed; each block had a warden to assist and monitor blackout response time. Men ages seventeen to fifty-five were asked to volunteer one night a week to the 600th Company Maryland Minute Men (a Civilian Defense unit), for training on how to protect "vital points in your neighborhood."[23] A few months later, *The News* reminded residents that civilian defense activities were "at a low ebb" but "it is important that the framework of the organization is maintained, just in case."[24]

During the war, residents used the still undeveloped land beyond Adana and Carysbrook (toward Milford Mill Road)[25] to plant victory gardens. Victory gardens also were planted by residents on vacant land that is now occupied by the Milford Mill United Methodist Church (915 Milford Mill Road).[26] *The News* noted that "[a]ccording to the President, the nation's victory gardeners accounted for 42 percent of the fresh vegetables produced last year and their output is badly needed again this year."[27]

After the war ended in 1945, there was a nationwide building boom. Now, in addition to Foster Fenton, other builders participated in constructing houses in Sudbrook. Some built only a few houses; others operated on a larger scale. In about 1946, a builder named Vanik constructed some very substantial brick homes on Cliveden Road between Upland and Milford Mill Road.[28] Vernon Finney also built a few houses on that section of Cliveden Road. William Chew constructed homes along Westover and Greenwood Roads, in the area that once was the Sudbrook golf course.

While Olmsted had included some relatively small lots in his 1889 Plan (e.g., along the current Westover Road), postwar development typically involved considerably smaller lots than the original Plan had envisioned. By the time the new development was completed, a number of new streets had been added or reconfigured. Some — like Carysbrook, Olmstead, McHenry and Greenwood — retained a curvilinear style, imitating Olmsted's curves without duplicating exactly the lyrical gracefulness of his Plan.[29] Others follow Olmsted's original layout exactly (Cliveden from Upland to Milford Mill Road) or in large part (Westover). A few, like Cylburn, Glenrock, Farmhurst and Woodside, were added using the straight grid pattern.

The difference between a very subtle Olmsted-designed curve and these 1940s grid-style additions is quite noticeable when looking at the new roads added from Upland to Milford Mill Road. Cylburn, Farmhurst, Woodside and Glenrock are arrow-straight. Standing at any point where each of these four streets intersects with Upland, one can see easily down to Milford Mill running perpendicular at the far end of the block. But at Cliveden and Upland, one must be at a particular spot in the intersection to see through to Milford Mill. There is an almost imperceptible curve. Cliveden Road, for its full length, is laid out exactly as Olmsted designed it.

None of the builders of the new houses implemented Olmsted's triangular greenspaces with clusters of trees at intersections, such as exist at the entranceway to the community, and at the intersections of Windsor/Sudbrook, Howard/Sudbrook, Upland/Sudbrook and Cliveden/West Cliveden. This was a major deviation from the Olmsted Plan. The newer houses were, however, constructed with attractive setbacks, and many of the newer areas emulated the planting in the older areas of Sudbrook. Today, with the exception of a few streets, most of Sudbrook (both the older and the newer sections) is under a canopy of majestic oaks, towering tulip poplars and other magnificent shade trees. Azaleas, rhododendrons, dogwoods and lilac trees abound.

As the community grew and men and women returned home after the war, residents began funneling a tremendous amount of volunteer energy and time into activities that contributed significantly

View of entranceway after crossing the bridge into Sudbrook Park, about 1947. The landscaping on the triangles near the bridge was dense, creating the type of intimately enclosed spaces that Olmsted had intended for his suburban villages. A small directional sign was erected because visitors frequently got lost amidst Sudbrook's looping and curving roads. SUDBROOK PARK, INC. ARCHIVES.

toward making Sudbrook a cohesive and socially active community. Pre-war concerns also were addressed. In 1948, the Sudbrook Park Improvement Association had a drive to collect funds for the Geilfuss Motor Coach Company, which operated small buses that came through Sudbrook and went to both Pikesville and Liberty Road. In inclement weather, or on days when residents did not want to walk to Pikesville, the Geilfuss bus was a welcome adjunct.[30] It also took children who lived in Sudbrook to and from St. Charles, the parochial school on Church Lane in Pikesville.

The Sudbrook Park Improvement Association had never been successful at involving women and had remained a men's organization. After some time, it convinced the women of the community to start their own group to raise funds for Association projects and to assist in worthwhile social, recreational and cultural endeavors.[31] The Sudbrook Club was organized January 29, 1946 to fill this role.[32] According

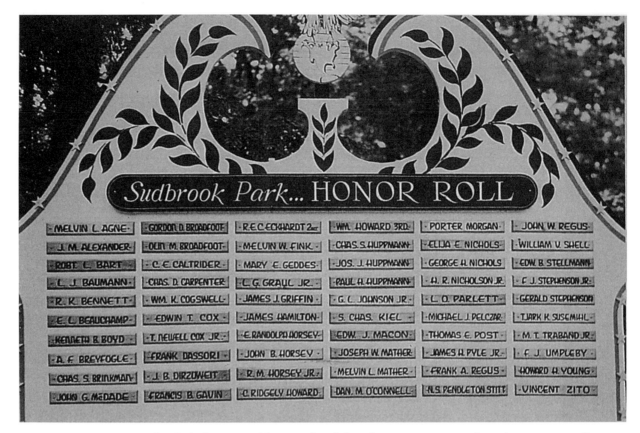

Sudbrook Park Honor Roll, which during World War II listed those "serving our nation from this community:"
Melvin L. Agne, J.M. Alexander, Robt. L. Bart, L.J. Baumann, R.K. Bennett, E.L. Beauchamp, Kenneth B. Boyd,
A.F. Breyfogle, Chas. S. Brinkman, John G. McDade, Gordon D. Broadfoot, Olin M. Broadfoot, C.E. Caltrider,
Chas. D. Carpenter, Wm. K. Cogswell, Edwin T. Cox, T. Newell Cox, Jr., Frank Dassori, J.B. Dirzuweit, Francis B.
Gavin, R.E.C. Eckhardt, 2nd., Melvin W. Fink, Mary E. Geddes, L.G. Graul, Jr., James Hamilton, E. Randolph
Horsey, John B. Horsey, R.M. Horsey, Jr., C. Ridgely Howard, Wm. Howard, 3rd, Chas. S. Huppmann, Jos. J.
Huppmann, Paul H. Huppmann, G.L. Johnson, Jr., S. Chas. Kiel, Edw. J. Macon, Joseph W. Mather, Melvin L.
Mather, Dan. M. O'Connell, Porter Morgan, Elija E. Nichols, George H. Nichols, H.R. Nicholson, Jr., L.O. Parlett,
Michael J. Pelczar, Thomas E. Post, James H. Pyle, Jr., Frank A. Regus, N.S. Pendleton Stitt, John W. Regus, William
V. Shell, Edw. B. Stellmann, F.J. Stephenson, Jr., Gerald Stephenson, Tjark K. Susemihl, M.T. Traband, Jr., F.J.
Umpleby, Howard H. Young, Vincent Zito. SUDBROOK PARK, INC. ARCHIVES.

to a local newspaper article:

> Among its first activities were obtaining stop signs, sidewalks and school
> crossing guards in the Park. The women also determined to encourage
> residents to take proper care of their grounds and see that the triangle
> areas in the community were well kept....
>
> The members of the club [also] are ever vigilant to carry out
> what has become their most important job: to keep Sudbrook Park a
> strictly residential community. The women declare with pride that "we
> have no beauty parlors here, no drugstores, no small shops. We insist
> on only one family to a house and discourage anyone who wants to

operate a private business from his home." Large trucks are prohibited from traveling through the area…. As for the physical care of the Park, [the] president of the club credits both the builders and residents who have always tried to avoid cutting down trees or shrubs, thus helping Sudbrook to remain the "lovely wooded area" which so delighted its original residents.[33]

For twenty-five years, the Sudbrook Club was a women's organization that was extremely active and effective in raising funds for community projects, encouraging neighborly cooperation and providing a social nexus for the women of Sudbrook.[34] The Club maintained a committee to act as liaison to the Improvement Association. Before long, the women's group was sponsoring all of the holiday events that have added a special charm to life in Sudbrook Park — the Fourth of July parade (with antecedents back to early Sudbrook), the Halloween parade with trick or treat night, the annual community Christmas tree lighting,[35] the judging of the best holiday decorations, and the Twelfth Night tree burning. Later, the Sudbrook Club added an annual May flower and bake sale to its calendar of events. All but the holiday decorations contest and the tree burning are still an integral part of life in Sudbrook, using Sudbrook's open greenspaces and playground area as gathering places where residents can share in the "harmonious association" that Olmsted envisioned.

In addition to bringing residents together, several of Sudbrook Park's traditional events were noted by the local press and one in particular, the Twelfth Night burning-of-the-greens, was apparently responsible for introducing the custom in other communities in Maryland.[36] Initially held at the intersection of Windsor, Adana and Kingston Roads, and later at the McHenry Road playground (now called the Sudbrook Stream Valley Park), the January 6 evening event was supervised by the fire department and included a holiday ceremony and songs around the fifty-foot blazing fire. Residents from all over the community could be seen for days before dragging their Christmas trees to the bonfire site.[37] Sudbrook's event reportedly had been inspired by a similar practice in Lansdowne, Pennsylvania. After Sudbrook began its annual ritual in 1946, other Maryland communities — including Rockville in Montgomery County and Easton in Talbot County — adopted the custom, which Sudbrook Park had to discontinue in the 1970s for environmental reasons.

For many years the Sudbrook Club also sponsored a Fall Dance, a Yuletide Dance, a Valentine's Day Dance and a Spring Dance as fund raisers and for the sheer enjoyment of getting together. At least one dance a year as well as a December holiday dinner for residents celebrating both Hanukkah and Christmas was still being held through the mid-1970s. All of these events were well attended.

Members of the newly formed Sudbrook Club, the women's group that was ever vigilant to maintain Sudbrook as an attractive and purely residential community, while also sponsoring holiday parades and events that fostered cohesiveness among residents. SUDBROOK PARK, INC. ARCHIVES.

Holiday traditions in Sudbrook Park. The July Fourth parade is a tradition that dates back to the earliest days of the community. Other events, such as Halloween and Christmas festivities, began in the 1940s and are still a popular and integral part of the community's life. COURTESY OF THE COX FAMILY AND SUDBROOK PARK, INC. ARCHIVES.

In the 1950s, these four brick Cape Cod style houses were built at the front of the large lot where Sudbrook's Woodland Inn once stood. At right, those houses in 1997. SUDBROOK PARK, INC. ARCHIVES.

Throughout the 1950s and 1960s, the Sudbrook Club held numerous luncheons, dinners, card parties and fashion shows. It also raised money and collected canned goods to give to charitable organizations at the holiday season. The Club annually gave a small ($100 to $300) scholarship to a graduating senior from the community. High school seniors who lived in Sudbrook Park and attended the local public high school could apply. Awards were made on the basis of merit, with some consideration given to need. For many years, the Sudbrook Club held eight board meetings as well as eight general meetings a year — the latter with programs, guest speakers, appointed hostesses and refreshments. The year's schedule of activities was printed in a small booklet that was distributed to all members. Later, a roster of members was added to the booklet; a similar directory is still compiled and distributed by the community association.

In 1947 the women of the Sudbrook Club sought land in the community to provide their children with a safe place to play in the summer.[38] As a result of their efforts, a little more than one acre on the Sudbrook Park side of the existing Greenwood Road "S-curve" was conveyed to the Sudbrook Park Improvement Association by William R. MacCallum and John O. White, to be used for playground recreational facilities and/or a recreational center. The grantors and their heirs reserved the right to take possession of the property if it was not used for the designated purpose. The Sudbrook Club equipped the area with swings, see-saws, picnic tables and other recreational equipment. Called "the old playground" by residents who remember it, this area was long the site for community activities, including an organized summer Parks and Recreation Program for children, community picnics and Fourth of July festivities. In 1971 the Greenwood Road area was abandoned as a playground site when a new playground was opened on McHenry Road with outdoor swings, climbing equipment and a basketball court provided by the county.[39] The area is known today as the Sudbrook Stream Valley Park.

Although the time commitment by volunteers was enormous, the many activities of the Sudbrook Club not only made Sudbrook Park a special place to live, but energetically promoted a cohesive spirit among residents. When former residents talk about Sudbrook Park as having been a "magical place" to live, grow up or raise their children, they are referring to both the Olmstedian ambiance and the neighborhood closeness — enhanced by shared community activities — that have long been part of Sudbrook's special mystique. It is the same spirit of harmonious association and "communicativeness" that Olmsted intentionally cultivated through his design. It pervaded the early community and has continued through the years. None of the communities surrounding Sudbrook Park can claim the same degree or history of cohesiveness. Although intangible, this aspect of the community is real. Its existence is not by accident, but the natural and intended outgrowth of Olmsted's artful design — a design powerful enough to absorb the modifications that were made and weave into one a community of various architectural styles, built in several stages.

The last major phase of development in Sudbrook Park began and concluded in the 1950s. The site of the old hotel, long vacant, was filled in by the construction of four brick story-and-a-half Cape Cod style houses that became 1022-1026 Windsor Road and 400 Sudbrook Lane. William Chew, the developer, continued to develop similar brick Cape Cod houses along Olmstead, Kingston and McHenry Roads.[40] The October 1954 *Sudbrook News* commented that about "160 new cottages went up between Olmstead Road and the falls this summer. Some of them are so close to the [Gwynns Falls] stream a tobacco-chewing housewife could hit a floating bullfrog smack between the eyes from her living room window." The *News* added that with the completion of these additions, for the "first time in 15 years, not a single new home is under construction within the boundaries of the Park... [and] generally speaking, home development in Sudbrook Park is at an end."[41]

The transportation revolution created by the automobile was about to affect Sudbrook as well. Between 1920 and 1940, automobiles in Maryland tripled from 100,000 to 300,000, more than half of them in the Baltimore region.[42] To handle this increasing automobile traffic, Maryland constructed three-lane highways and bridges, installed traffic lights in the city and built high-capacity roads on major corridors.

The second surge in automobile traffic came in the 1950s, when the secondary road system was rebuilt in its entirety to reduce curves and grades, and major projects such as Baltimore's Harbor Tunnel, the Bay Bridge and the Baltimore-Washington Parkway were implemented. The third phase of projects was the interstate highway system, which included the Baltimore Beltway. The six-lane Beltway, covering a distance of thirty-three miles, opened in 1962.[43]

The Beltway was far enough from Sudbrook not to have a negative impact on the community. But the October 1954 *Sudbrook News* contained a single sentence about another interstate that was to pose a serious and potentially devastating threat to Sudbrook Park — the Northwest Expressway. The project was little more than a rumor, one *The News* could not even corroborate: "Checking up, also, on the oft repeated rumor or report that there are plans to run a highway cityward directly parallel to and on [the Sudbrook Park] side of the Western Maryland Railroad tracks, we were unable to uncover anything definite one way or the other."[44]

With only this hint of a threat, Sudbrook residents in 1954 had no idea what was in store for them over the next thirty years, or the series of battles that they would, before long, begin fighting to preserve Olmsted's Sudbrook.

Chapter 15

SAVED BY PRESERVATION: 1955–PRESENT

From the 1850s, when James Howard McHenry amassed his 850-acre Sudbrook estate, to the 1950s, when the community was completed, Sudbrook's journey to full development had followed a path with many twists and turns. McHenry's intent to turn Sudbrook into one of the first planned suburban villages in the region — preferably one designed by Frederick Law Olmsted — had been repeatedly frustrated and was realized only after his death, when several Boston and Philadelphia investors purchased 204 acres from his estate and hired Olmsted to design the community. Early Sudbrook Park, managed by McHenry's friend Eugene Blackford, was immediately popular with affluent and socially-pedigreed Baltimoreans. But to the Sudbrook Company's surprise and detriment, the majority were content simply to rent for the summer. When lot sales failed to materialize, the Company could not meet its mortgage obligations and in 1910 transferred all remaining property to speculative developers. High society began moving away and the sale of lots once again stagnated, but the small community continued to nurture long-standing traditions and a harmonious lifestyle. The new development which began in 1939 and ended in 1954, while ushering in major changes, finally completed the original intent for the 204-acre parcel: Sudbrook became a community with multi-sized lots woven together by Olmsted's tree-lined curvilinear roads and the cohesiveness his design fostered. With the full community finally in place, life in Sudbrook Park in the mid-1950s settled into a pleasant tranquillity. Yet Sudbrook was on a collision course with a planning mind-set that would become entrenched in the 1960s and 1970s: the almighty primacy of the automobile and the perceived imperative by state and county planners to build major new highways to accommodate increased vehicular traffic.

The northwest corridor where Sudbrook Park was located was growing after World War II, with new suburbs dotting the landscape in every direction. Reisterstown Road, the primary northwest artery, was becoming congested. Widening it as a major highway would dislocate businesses that had sprouted up along its entire length. The Baltimore County Department of Public Works devised a solution: build a new highway to the south of Reisterstown Road to handle the projected increase in traffic. In June 1948 the county suggested that Maryland's State Roads Commission, predecessor to the State Highway Administration (SHA), extend Wabash Avenue from the city all the way to Reisterstown, following a route along the Gwynns Falls Valley "to bypass communities along Reisterstown Road (U.S. Route 140)."[1]

The proposed project, known as the Northwest Expressway,[2] was routed through the northern section of Sudbrook Park,[3] even though at the time most of the land along the Western Maryland Railroad tracks from Sudbrook Park past Old Court Road was undeveloped. Rather than reserve this land for the project, Baltimore County made a decision to permit businesses to develop along it from just past Sudbrook to just past Old Court Road. Once these businesses were in place (and some arrived as late as the 1970s), the only path that state and county planners seriously considered for the expressway project was through Sudbrook Park.[4] To planners, Olmsted's picturesque triangles and greenspaces were nothing more than undeveloped and underutilized land — an ideal spot to locate a six-lane expressway. Despite sporadic rumors in the 1950s that the SHA intended to build a major highway through the northwest corridor, its plans were not well publicized. Very few Sudbrook residents knew, or could

Left: Cottage No. 8, one of the original nine built by the Sudbrook Company in 1889-90, in its original location north of and adjacent to 721 Cliveden Road. SUDBROOK PARK, INC. ARCHIVES. *Above: After being purchased by the Traband family, Cottage No. 8 was moved to 505½ Sudbrook Lane in March 1960 to escape demolition by the State Highway Administration.* COURTESY OF WILLIAM AND BETTY LOU TRABAND.

discover, specifics about the project.[5] Moreover, a combination of funding problems, a 1965 recommendation to add a rapid transit component, and proposed new safety standards for highways all contributed to further delay the project during the 1960s.[6] During this time, the SHA was quietly purchasing property along the intended right-of-way, which included Sudbrook Park.[7]

Between the late 1950s and early 1960s, the SHA acquired and demolished Cottage No. 10 — one of the original houses built by the Sudbrook Company — with absolutely no regard for its historic value. The SHA also tore down the house that had been rebuilt on the site of Cottage No. 5, which had been destroyed by fire in 1927.[8] Cottage No. 8, also built by the Sudbrook Company in 1889–90, was slated for demolition but saved when a resident of Sudbrook purchased and moved it to its current location at 505½ Sudbrook Road around 1960. The SHA purchased but did not immediately raze the Graves Cottage (No. 22) at 726 Howard Road; 753 Howard Road, built by Oregon Randolf Benson, Jr. in about 1920; nineteen houses along the northern side of Westover Road closest to the railroad tracks, and five houses on the east side of Howard Road nearest the tracks. While some residents continued to rent their own houses from the state, many moved out of the community. No other community along the proposed route was as heavily affected as was Sudbrook Park: not only did the SHA demolish two homes (one of which dated from 1889) and predicate the salvage of another historic home on its being moved from its original location on the Olmsted Plan, but it also purchased twenty-six homes and various open space areas in Sudbrook Park, with up to fifteen more homes on the south side of Westover Road slated for possible future demolition.

Although residents of Sudbrook Park were uniformly opposed to the expressway project, they took no steps to actively resist or fight the plans during the 1960s.[9] In today's more active civic environment, it is almost incomprehensible that there was not organized opposition to a proposal which would wreak such devastation, but the lack of publicity about the project combined with a naiveté and feelings of powerlessness against the state bureaucracy resulted in community passivity and resignation during this decade.[10] In choosing the route for the expressway project, the state either was not aware of or ignored the fact that Sudbrook had an historic legacy of national significance. Even Sudbrook's residents were not fully aware of the community's importance as one of only a few intact Olmsted designs or the leverage that Sudbrook's history could provide.[11] It would take several more years and a more immediate threat of devastation to force the community to look at and value its past as more than just a nostalgic pleasantry.

Meanwhile, the state continued to expand its plans. In 1968 state planners decided to add a rapid transit rail line to the Northwest Corridor Project, to be located in the median strip of the six-lane expressway. Ironically, the Western Maryland Railroad had only stopped running passenger trains in about 1957 along essentially the same route. The railroad had demolished the Sudbrook Park station shortly after it terminated passenger service.[12]

By the early 1970s, several Baltimore suburbs were in the news for their efforts to fight highway proposals, such as the Interstate 70 project through Leakin Park in west Baltimore and an expressway slated to go through the historic districts of Federal Hill and Fells Point in the city.[13] After almost twenty years of community passivity, several residents in Sudbrook Park began to voice opposition to the proposed expressway/transit project.[14] They also began to realize that if Sudbrook Park wanted to fight this threat effectively, it needed to mobilize and speak officially through its community association.[15] The Sudbrook Improvement Association, the de facto men's civic group, had dissolved in the mid-1950s and been supplanted by the extremely active Sudbrook Club, the de facto women's social group.[16] Those convinced that the community could fight the SHA wanted to convert the Sudbrook Club to a civic organization composed of both women and men.[17] Despite strongly divided feelings, this change was adopted by 1974.[18]

Until 1973 very little, if any, official notice was paid to Sudbrook's historic character. But as required by federal law, the SHA consulted the Maryland Historical Trust (MHT) about whether there were any existing or potential historic sites along the proposed expressway route and set in motion a discovery process. A Goucher College student volunteer gathered information about historic sites along the route and her report was used by the MHT to nominate about eighty acres of Sudbrook for the National Register of Historic Sites and Places.[19]

By necessity, the eight-page nomination form was hurriedly put together. In three single-spaced typed pages about the architecture of various houses, it contained only one short paragraph mentioning Olmsted. There was no discussion (or evidence of understanding) of Olmsted's design principles, no mention of Olmsted's 1889 Plan (which no one even seemed to be aware of), no mention of landscape design elements, and no mention of streets outside the "old house" section that were true to the Plan, or closely evocative of it. The designated historic area was chosen with little or no reference to Olmsted, but rather simply by drawing a line around the old houses.[20]

On June 19, 1973, this portion of Sudbrook Park was entered on the National Register. Once Sudbrook was officially recognized as a National Historic District, the SHA had to reconsider its plans to make a 200-to-300-foot "open cut" through Sudbrook for a six-lane expressway and transit line.[21] The open cut would involve replacing the existing bridge with a significantly longer and wider one, adding a second bridge to span Greenwood Road, and demolishing most of the entranceway triangles with their majestic oaks and other plantings — and residents saw that it would do irreparable damage to the historic fabric of the community.

Whenever federal funds are used for a project that will affect a National Register property, government agencies must hold public hearings and prepare an Environmental Impact Statement (EIS). They must show, among other things, that they have examined various alternatives and that the chosen alternative will not adversely affect the historic site, or if it will, what steps will be taken to mitigate the negative impact. The SHA had completed a draft EIS in February 1973, before Sudbrook was listed as a National Register District.[22] Now, however, Sudbrook Park's historic status presented problems for the SHA. How would it mitigate the adverse impact of a 200-to-300-foot "open cut" through an historic district?[23]

Although the SHA had promised the community a final answer by January 1974, more than two years went by before it was forthcoming. During this period, developed communities inside the Beltway realized that they would bear the brunt of the adverse impact. Sudbrook Park and a number of these communities voiced strident opposition to the proposed expressway and rapid transit.[24] A neighboring community, Gwynnvale, opposed the expressway's proposed alignment because it went right through a flood plain — McHenry's "lowland area" that Olmsted had voiced concerns about in 1889.[25] But not all groups along the alignment were opposed. Outside the Beltway, the route would traverse primarily undeveloped land. Many developers, businesses and residents in the Westminster, Reisterstown, and Owings Mills areas, expecting to benefit greatly from the proposed project, supported it.[26]

Meanwhile, the Sudbrook Club continued to meet with representatives of the SHA and Baltimore County, as part of a larger Northwest Transportation Corridor Task Force, hoping to work out a compromise. Sudbrook's representatives had been told by the agencies involved and by elected officials that if the community wanted to be spared the expressway, it would have to accept the transit line. Moreover, there was a good deal of political support state-wide in the early 1970s for a rapid transit system. When compared with the combined expressway/transit project, which required a 200 to 300 foot right-of-way, the transit line alone, requiring about a sixty foot right-of-way, was clearly the lesser of the two evils.

Believing it necessary to compromise, and feeling pressure from officials to accept the rapid transit line, Sudbrook's leadership in June 1975 shifted its position from that of opposing *both* the expressway and the transit line to that of agreeing not to oppose the transit line. At a public meeting, Sudbrook Club representatives presented their compromise position, called Alternate 9, to the community. Alternate 9 stipulated that (1) the expressway be deleted inside the Beltway, (2) the Milford Mill transit station be greatly reduced in size and (3) the transit line run along the railroad right-of-way to the Beltway.[27] After heated discussion, Sudbrook residents were asked to vote on the proposals so that community leaders could take a consensus back to county officials. An overwhelming majority voted to oppose both the expressway and the transit line.[28]

Community leaders, fearful that a failure to compromise might jeopardize any SHA concessions and not fully aware at the time of the basis for Sudbrook's historic significance or the protections afforded an historic district under federal law, sought to change residents' minds. The meeting dragged on late into the night. After some urging, those still present voted to accept Alternate 9, with certain conditions. This compromise, later adopted by members of the Northwest Transportation Corridor Task Force, stipulated that:

*The expressway should not be constructed south of the Beltway.

*The rapid transit system should be constructed adjacent to the Western Maryland Railway from the city line to Owings Mills.

*The Maryland Department of Transportation, the Baltimore Regional Planning Council, and Baltimore County must study the need for, the impact of, and modifications of the transit stations at Old Court Road and Milford Mill Road.[29]

Another year went by. It was June 1976 before the Maryland Department of Transportation filed its final EIS requesting federal funding for the project, confirming that it was dropping plans to build the expressway through Sudbrook Park. Local newspapers announced Sudbrook's victory. Lost in the excitement was the statement that the rapid transit line would be continued from Patterson Avenue to Painters Mill Road, running parallel to the Western Maryland Railroad tracks only "to Sudbrook Lane."[30] Few residents were aware that the transit line would be *within* Sudbrook Park or that, as proposed, its impact on the Sudbrook Historic District would be devastating. As word gradually circulated about the expressway victory, Sudbrook residents assumed that their battles were over. The next couple of years were quiet — the calm before a new storm.

Plans were underway during the spring and summer of 1978 to celebrate the dedication of Sudbrook's new historical marker. A house tour and receptions at several of the old houses were planned, along with a formal dedication ceremony. The community was enjoying its historical status and new-found tranquillity.[31]

In July 1978 at least one Sudbrook Park resident was jolted by an article in the *Baltimore Sun* announcing that the transit line would come through Sudbrook Park. The article noted that six Sudbrook Park homes "within" the historic district (five on Howard Road and one on the current Sudbrook Lane) and fourteen homes "outside" the district (on Westover Road) would be affected. The fate of these homes was uncertain because final design plans were still incomplete, but the "vagueness of the homes' status…characterizes a continuing situation that community residents have complained of since the early 1950s…when the State first announced plans for the Northwest expressway." The article went on:

> Somewhat typical of the lengthy controversy is the lack of coordination and communication among officials in the highway and rail bureaucracies, due in large part to the fact that few who started the project are still working on it. One planner, noting the confusion, commented, "I was still in grammar school when they started talking about this."
>
> Several highway administration officials, for example, did not know [that] the portion of the right-of-way between the city line and the Beltway would be used for rail transit, even though it was their agency that acquired the property years ago.[32]

By this time, three of the four key community leaders who had fought to delete the expressway had moved from Sudbrook. There were two kinds of reactions among residents. Either they thought that

Unveiling of Sudbrook Park's historic marker at formal ceremonies on September 24, 1978. The community did not realize it at the time, but there were several factual inaccuracies on the marker, which still stands on the Cliveden Road triangle. COLLECTION OF THE AUTHOR.

nothing would ever actually be built, since it had already been almost thirty years and no project had materialized, or they had an attitude of resignation — that the plans were now a "done deal" and it was too late to effect any changes. It took the naiveté of a relatively new resident who had not been actively involved in earlier battles to stir a small group of residents into action. In a short time, the full community rallied again in support of efforts to gain concessions from the MTA and effect new changes.

The first step was to contact the MTA and ascertain what the plans were for the transit line and how Sudbrook Park was affected. As proposed, the plans called for the transit alignment to be adjacent to the Western Maryland Railroad until just before it approached Sudbrook's bridge, at which point it would veer off in a southwesterly direction, going in front of the bridge, crossing Greenwood Road, going behind Windsor Road, proceeding to the Old Court Station and then traveling along the median strip of the Northwest Expressway outside of the Beltway. This alignment was to be in an "open cut" through Sudbrook, necessitating the removal of the existing Sudbrook entranceway bridge and its replacement by a much wider and longer bridge that would traverse both the Western Maryland Railroad tracks and the new transit line, as well as a second bridge to reconnect Sudbrook and Windsor Roads with relocated Greenwood Road (slated to have its "S-curve" straightened). All trees in or near the line of construction were to be felled. A large station at Milford Mill Road, with parking for 800 cars, was to be adjacent to Sudbrook Park on the east. Another station would be about a mile away from Sudbrook at Old Court Road. Up to nineteen houses already owned by the MTA on the north side of Westover Road were slated for demolition.

Next, Sudbrook Club representatives contacted the Maryland Historical Trust, expecting to hear outrage about this proposal and eliciting that agency's support. Instead, the MHT confirmed that, indeed, it had signed a Memorandum of Agreement in 1976 governing the moving of one house (753 Howard Road) and raising no objections to the state's proposed plans. The 1976 Agreement ignored the fact that the proposed alignment would (1) destroy Olmsted's gateway entrance, including the purposefully narrow bridge and significant greenspaces; (2) result in the loss within the historic district of ninety mature trees, the taking of historic district land and the building of two new bridges in the district with no effective mitigation; and, (3) replace Sudbrook's densely landscaped greenspaces and majestic oaks with a retaining wall topped by a security fence along the open cut. The 1976 Memorandum of Agreement indicated that even the MHT did not understand or appreciate the elements of Olmsted's landscape design plan and considered the old houses to be the only historic feature "at risk."[33]

Sudbrook representatives were told that it was too late for the MHT to reopen the matter or insist upon more protective changes since it had signed the Memorandum of Agreement, but that the agency would support any preservation concessions that the Sudbrook Club could gain from the SHA or MTA.[34]

The Sudbrook Club next contacted state Delegate Paula Hollinger, who set up a meeting

Proclaiming "Finally, an answer for Sudbrook Park," a July 30, 1978 Baltimore Sun *article announced that a rapid transit line would cut a swath through Sudbrook Park, requiring this house at 753 Howard Road to be moved.*
REPRINTED WITH PERMISSION OF THE BALTIMORE SUN.

among elected officials, the MTA and Sudbrook Club representatives in January of 1979. The MTA took the position that the only area it had to be concerned about by law was the "historic district," even though the Sudbrook Club was concerned with the entire community. It quickly became obvious that any leverage that the community as a whole had was based on the protections afforded under federal law to properties on the National Register of Historic Sites and Places.[35]

Between January 1979 and June 1980 the Sudbrook Club tried to work informally with the MTA to mitigate adverse impact. At one of the meetings held in Sudbrook Park, a resident expressed the community's desire to preserve its bridge and entranceway greenspaces as they had been designed by Olmsted. She then drew on a napkin a sketch of a tunnel-like configuration and asked if the MTA would consider such an alignment instead of the "open cut" and two new bridges which would so devastate the historic district.[36] Ironically, this casually drawn request set in motion changes that would prove instrumental in preserving Olmsted's original entranceway design. The MTA agreed to consider a tunnel, provided the Sudbrook Club confirmed that the community was in agreement with retaining the existing narrow bridge. A survey was taken and the results were overwhelmingly in favor of retaining the bridge.[37]

In early January 1980 the MTA contacted Sudbrook representatives to tell them that the agency

Sudbrook's entranceway bridge, an integral component of the Olmsted design. The bridge was saved from destruction when the MTA agreed to a cut and cover tunnel rather than an open cut for the portion of the line near the bridge.
PHOTOGRAPH BY EDWARD STRAKA.

was considering constructing a 1,000 foot or longer "cut and cover" tunnel through the historic district and preserving the existing bridge, and that they had released information about their plans to the newspapers. Shortly after, an article appeared in the *Baltimore Evening Sun* proclaiming "Maryland May Build Rail Tunnel as Help to Historic District." The article contained graphics of a 1,000 foot tunnel being proposed to replace the planned "open cut." While the article noted that no final decision would be made for three months, it quoted the MTA's representative as saying that "based on preliminary studies, we feel it is a feasible alternative and is cost-effective" because the tunnel proposal "would mean two bridges — one at Greenwood road, the other a rebuilding of one at Sudbrook Lane needed to cross the open cut — would not have to be built."[38]

When Sudbrook Club and MTA representatives met later that month, the MTA was considering a 1,200 foot tunnel and Sudbrook Club representatives asked that it be at least 2,000 feet. Again, the MTA agreed to look into it. Present at the meeting was a new person whom no one seemed to know, who had come to speak against retaining the existing bridge. The group discovered that he was from the Baltimore County Department of Public Works. The county very much favored the proposal for an open cut and a new bridge to be built with primarily federal funds, thus relieving the county of having to pay for a new bridge. Before leaving, the county representative issued dire warnings about the safety of the existing bridge.[39]

Following this meeting, Sudbrook representatives retained an engineering firm that had

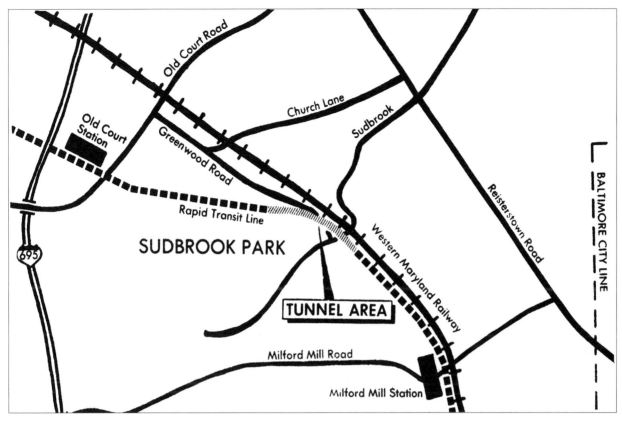

Drawing shows the alignment of a 1000-foot tunnel through Sudbrook Park, proposed by the MTA in January 1980 but later reduced to half that length. REPRINTED WITH PERMISSION OF THE BALTIMORE SUN.

experience with historic bridges to evaluate the bridge and ascertain if there were any significant safety issues. The consultant studied the county's own bridge reports, met with the county, and examined the bridge himself. He determined that it was structurally sound and could be preserved at significantly less cost than constructing a new bridge.[40]

At each meeting with the MTA, Sudbrook representatives insisted that the Milford Mill station be eliminated or downsized. As it was, the Milford Mill Station was to be the costliest (more than $13 million) in Phase B of the transit line.[41] (Phase A of the line, mostly tunneled through the city, was to run eight miles from Charles Center to Reisterstown Plaza. Phase B, almost all above ground, would go six miles from Reisterstown Plaza through Sudbrook Park to the Owings Mill Station). Originally proposed for 800 cars, the Milford Mill station was by then being designed for 1,200 cars. Its construction would require clear-cutting more than thirteen acres of wooded land that bordered Sudbrook Park on the east and replacing the trees with concrete. Although Sudbrook ideally wanted the station eliminated, it was willing to accept a "kiss and ride" or greatly downsized station, and suggested on many occasions that the MTA design it to replicate the old Sudbrook Park railroad station.

Simultaneously with these MTA discussions, Sudbrook also had to battle (1) plans to widen Milford Mill Road to four lanes (thus eliminating most of the trees) and (2) proposals to have MTA "feeder" buses, forty-five feet long, coming through Sudbrook Park's narrow curvilinear roads. Both of these proposals arose out of concerns raised by the Transit Station Area Development and Access Study (TSADAS) under the auspices of the Baltimore County Office of Planning and Zoning. TSADAS was formed in 1974 to address the impact that rapid transit would have on the area, including potential issues when only Phase A of the line was operational, as well as access issues when both Phases A and B were operational. Both the widening of Milford Mill Road and the proposal to send MTA buses through Sudbrook Park eventually were defeated. But TSADAS, the feeder bus study and Milford Mill Road widening issues involved countless meetings over many years, requiring considerable time and energy on the part of Sudbrook (and other communities') representatives.[42]

After the January 1980 meeting between representatives of the Sudbrook Club and the MTA, MTA officials agreed to study Sudbrook's request for a longer tunnel and greater mitigation of adverse visual and noise impact. By this time, the MTA had agreed to preserve Sudbrook's bridge. The agency said that it would contact Sudbrook's representatives again when it reached the "thirty percent design phase."

In May, while discussing the transit line with one of the MTA's on-site engineers, a Sudbrook representative saw plans that showed the tunnel had been reduced to 500 feet. The Sudbrook Club requested a meeting with the MTA, and the two groups met in June 1980. At this meeting, L.A. Kimball, the Administrator of the MTA, told the community that the alignment and tunnel were finalized, that funding had been applied for, and that "You will see and hear the trains — make no mistake about that."[43] This stance directly contradicted statements made by other MTA officials and engineers to the Sudbrook community over the previous two years of meetings, when the community was reassured repeatedly that the MTA would so effectively mitigate any adverse impact that the community "would not see or hear the trains…in fact, in five years, we will come back and you won't even know the system is there."

Realizing that the MTA had applied for federal funding without any concern for the unresolved issues and without even informing the community that the "final design" had been substantially altered from what the MTA had proposed only four months before, the Sudbrook Club consulted legal counsel. In August 1980 it retained the law firm of Semmes, Bowen & Semmes. Residents were strongly committed to preserving Sudbrook Park, and began funding the legal effort through individual contributions. In the fall of 1980 the community received a $1,200 grant from the National Trust for Historic Preservation to help defray legal expenses in its effort to preserve the Sudbrook Park National Historic District.[44]

During the next two years, the Sudbrook Club worked with its legal counsel to promote its interests on various fronts. Meetings and communications with the MTA took on an adversarial tone, but continued. The community also elicited the support of its elected officials in Washington, who still had to fund Phase B of the line. (Phase A was funded and opened in November 1983). Representatives of Senators Charles Mathias and Paul Sarbanes and of Congressman Clarence Long participated with Sudbrook representatives in meetings with the MTA and the federal Urban Mass Transit Administration (UMTA).

In addition, the Sudbrook Club contacted the editors of the Frederick Law Olmsted Papers project in Washington, D.C., and a Sudbrook resident began to research the Olmsted history of Sudbrook at the Library of Congress. The Sudbrook Club also sought input from and began to work with a representative of the Maryland Historical Trust to prepare a request for an expansion of the historic district boundaries to the full 204 acres designed by Olmsted in 1889. Through this process, many Sudbrook residents began to understand that the essence of the historic significance of the community was that it incorporated and exemplified elements that Olmsted deemed vital to creating a suburban village — which to him was more than just "a place." It was a way of life that he designed, a "respite for the spirit" that would encourage "harmonious association" among residents. This was an entirely different emphasis than that reflected by the 1973 historic district nomination, which described Sudbrook's significance as primarily architectural — a collection of nineteenth century houses typifying certain styles that, by the way, were located in an area that happened to have been designed by someone named Olmsted.

By February 1981 funding for Phase B of the rapid transit line was in doubt. President Ronald Reagan's budget cutbacks and policy changes threatened the extension. In April, UMTA "denied Maryland funding that would have permitted construction to begin on the six-mile segment running from Reisterstown Road to Owings Mills."[45] News articles reported that, while the denial applied only to the current fiscal year (ending Oct. 1), "the project is officially deferred and will remain in that status until there is an upturn in the economy."[46]

For Sudbrook Park, this lack of funding was good news because it bought time. To mount a full scale legal action and bring suit against the MTA would have been extremely costly. Moreover, the politics of the project were an issue. The transit project had been strongly supported by Harry Hughes when he was Maryland's Secretary of Transportation. By 1981 Hughes was Governor and he very much wanted to see the project completed. Among the general public, there was a good deal of support for the transit line, even though some thought it was a waste of money and dubbed it "the line that went nowhere."[47]

Later in April, news reports indicated that Governor Hughes had met with U.S. Transportation Secretary Drew Lewis, and the Governor was "optimistic" about getting funding for the second leg of the subway. Despite his optimism, the Governor "received no indication when federal money for the $190 million project might be forthcoming." There was also discussion on "possibly shifting some federal highway funds into the rapid rail project [but]…such funding shifts, called interstate transfers, require federal approval."[48]

Another event created devastation in Sudbrook in June 1981, taking precedence over MTA matters. On Sunday, June 21 an extremely violent thunderstorm (believed by some to have been accompanied by a tornado) ripped through a portion of Sudbrook's historic district. Cottages Nos. 4 and 9 (1020 Windsor and 501 Sudbrook) were the most severely damaged. Huge oak trees, ripped up by the storm, were thrown into the two houses. Cottage No. 11 (1018 Windsor) also sustained damage in the storm. Elsewhere in Sudbrook, trees were felled and streets were closed. The community was without electricity, telephone service and potable water for three days. Neighbors helped each other, but it took a good deal of time to clean up from the storm's damage.[49]

Life eventually returned to normal in Sudbrook and rapid transit once again loomed as an issue. In September 1981 news reports trumpeted that "more than $200 million in federal money formerly earmarked for completion of Interstate 70 in West Baltimore may now be used for extension of the Baltimore subway to Owings Mills if Congress approves."[50] The U. S. Department of Transportation had approved the transfer, the paper reported, and work could move forward if Congress appropriated sufficient money in the fall to get the project started.

An article in November 1981 announced that "Metro Gets $7 Million for 2nd Leg." The article went on to explain that a House-Senate conference committee in Washington had approved the money and "barring a presidential veto, yesterday's agreement by conferees 'virtually assures' the $180 million six-mile extension of the city's new subway system, according to elated state and city officials." David Wagner, then Administrator of the MTA, noted that the funds still had to survive Reagan's budget cuts, but Wagner expected construction "to begin 'within three months' with completion [of Phase B] by 1986."[51]

Although still in a potentially adversarial position with the MTA, the community's relationship improved when David Wagner took over as Administrator. The two sides continued to correspond and communicate. The Sudbrook Club worked with the MHT to prepare its boundary expansion request, well aware that if the expanded area were to be entered on the National Register it would greatly increase Sudbrook Park's leverage, since the entire 204 acres could then claim the protections of federal law applicable to historic districts. An expanded historic district most probably would require an amended or new EIS and additional mitigating steps to protect the enlarged area. Since funding for Phase B of the line had secured approval, this expansion would be Sudbrook's last hope to obtain more protections.

In June 1982 counsel for Sudbrook met with David Wagner and learned that Phase B was going forward, but because funds were needed immediately for use north of the Beltway, construction of the area inside the Beltway was being delayed. Design drawings were at that time seventy to eighty percent complete, and it was not too late to affect them. Wagner indicated that Sudbrook would have to address design issues with the MTA no later than the coming winter.

Sudbrook submitted its boundary expansion request to the MHT in August 1982. The Governor's Consulting Committee was scheduled to consider the request at a meeting in October. Sudbrook had worked on this project for two years. A resident had done the historical research and

A storm with high winds wreaked havoc on this house at 501 Sudbrook Lane (Cottage No. 9), uprooting a large oak tree and throwing it into the house. Several other houses were damaged by the storm, which left the community without electricity, telephone service and potable water for three days. REPRINTED WITH PERMISSION OF THE BALTIMORE SUN.

In a crowded meeting room, Sudbrook residents listen intently to an update on the route of the rapid transit line through the community. Hundreds of residents attended the meetings held in the late 1970s and early 1980s to protest the MTA's original plans. COLLECTION OF THE AUTHOR.

written the request. Working with the association's attorneys, a formal presentation binder complete with maps, overlays and photographs had been prepared at considerable expense. Throughout this time, Sudbrook representatives had kept the MHT representative apprised, and he had indicated that he felt that the expansion had an excellent chance of being approved. Thus, it came as a complete shock and deep disappointment when shortly before the Consulting Committee was to meet, he informed a Sudbrook representative that the MHT had voted not to recommend approval of the proposed expansion.

Sudbrook Club representatives and legal counsel attended the Governor's Consulting Committee meeting, still hoping that the request would be approved. Some members of the Committee were in favor of the expansion, but the weight of the MHT's negative recommendation, combined with the view that without "period" houses even areas true to or closely modeled after the Olmsted design could not be deemed "historic," appeared to prevail. When it was clear that the proposal would not garner the necessary votes to be approved, Sudbrook withdrew its request in order to preserve its opportunity to return at a later time without prejudice.[52]

Meetings with the MTA and the community continued. Throughout the years that the rapid transit was an issue, 150 to 200 or more residents attended each status and informational meeting of the Sudbrook Club. These meetings were held periodically throughout these years, most at the nearby St. Charles School or at Ames Methodist Church in Pikesville. Residents were also kept informed of progress and new developments through the community newsletter. These were years of tremendous activity, as residents joined together to work for the common goal of preserving Sudbrook and mitigating the adverse impact of the transit line and stations.

Sudbrook's leverage to effect additional changes for anything but the narrowly drawn historic district dissipated when the boundary expansion request failed. By this time, Sudbrook's relationship with the MTA was less adversarial, and the community continued to work to gain whatever relief was possible. The bridge was being saved, roads were to be returned to their original alignments (Greenwood would retain its S-curve), the transit line would be tunneled for about 550 feet, and retaining walls would be erected along Westover Road and behind Windsor Road where the transit line would not be tunneled. In addition, the MTA agreed to work cooperatively with Sudbrook to re-landscape all areas in the community that were being affected, and the MHT took an active role in assisting Sudbrook by requiring that it approve the landscaping plans.

Prior to construction, the MTA intended to clear-cut all areas in which it would be working — still a problematic issue. In 1984 Sudbrook asked the MTA to bring to Sudbrook an urban forester, at the time one of only three in the country, for consultation about retaining as many trees and other vegetation as possible during construction. The MTA acceded to this request. Steve Clark & Associates established a tree preservation program before construction began so that a number of existing large trees as well as other vegetation (along Howard Road, the bridge and entranceway triangle area, and both sides of Greenwood Road outside of the immediate area of construction) were saved.

Construction of Phase B of the transit line was underway in 1983 and "pre-construction surveys" were slated to begin in Sudbrook by the end of that year.[53] Construction within Sudbrook did not commence until 1984. It was wrenching to watch as Sudbrook's towering, stately trees were felled and the entire area was invaded and torn apart by bulldozers, chain saws and work crews. The bright orange "Tree Preservation Program" fencing was a small reminder to residents that, while the community may have lost the war, it had won a few battles.

Throughout 1986 and 1987 representatives of the Sudbrook Club worked extensively with the MTA and its consulting landscape architects on re-landscaping plans for Westover Road (where fourteen houses were demolished along the line), Howard Road near the bridge, the entranceway greenspaces, the area behind Windsor Road and the S-curve section along Greenwood Road.

Phase B of the rapid transit line opened in July 1987. Sudbrook's entranceway had been shorn of its previously lush plantings and large oak canopy, giving it the cropped look of a new Army recruit. The trees and other vegetation that were spared the chain saw and bulldozer at least contributed to re-establishing a semblance of the pre-construction ambiance of the area.[54]

With the transit line built and operating, Sudbrook no longer had that major project to address, but other issues remained. One of the most persistent carry-over problems from the expressway/transit project involved nine state-owned houses in Sudbrook. These houses, originally purchased as part of the right-of-way for the expressway but not needed when that project was abandoned inside the Beltway, had been the subject of countless letters and meetings for more than sixteen years. For as long as it owned them, the SHA/MTA rented these houses in Sudbrook at prices significantly below market rates, supposedly expecting the renters to repair and maintain the homes. Instead, a number of the homes deteriorated to such a degree that they were eyesores and a blight on the community. A number of them were vacant for extended periods of time.

Starting in 1979 and continuing into 1995 the Sudbrook Club wrote, called and met with the SHA and the MTA asking that the houses which the SHA originally purchased in Sudbrook for the expressway, and which later were turned over to the MTA, be returned to private ownership. Sudbrook also involved the MHT and its elected officials as needed. Particular emphasis initially was put on the historic house at 726 Howard Road, which even in 1979 had been allowed to deteriorate to such a degree that it was almost beyond rehabilitation. While the MTA agreed that the house was not needed for the project, the agency dragged its feet about releasing it.

The SHA had purchased 726 Howard Road (the old Graves house) in 1965 for $16,000. In the early 1980s the SHA still was renting it for $160 a month and permitting the occupant to turn the second floor into an apartment that he or she could sublet in turn. In 1981 the Sudbrook Club involved the MHT, which inspected the house and agreed to insist on historic easements to assure appropriate restoration. By 1982 the house was declared "no longer habitable" and was boarded up. While the house was vacant, vandals set fire to it. The back portion was burned but the house was not destroyed. After that the MTA moved quickly, obtaining appraisals and proceeding through the State Clearinghouse process for the disposal of excess property. The house was auctioned in a sealed bid; the State accepted the high bid of $50,100. The new owner, a resident of Sudbrook with a strong interest in historic preservation, restored it to good condition at considerable personal expense.[55] After continuing efforts

Sudbrook Park's tranquil bridge and entranceway triangles (below) were invaded by bulldozers, chain saws and construction crews while the rapid transit line cut its way through the community. Although a tree preservation program saved some mature trees, Sudbrook lost many towering oaks in the transit line's path. PRE-CONSTRUCTION BRIDGE PHOTOGRAPH COURTESY OF THE COX FAMILY. PHOTOGRAPHS OF CONSTRUCTION BY BAYARD HOCHBERG.

Sudbrook's entranceway area after construction of the rapid transit line, with the cropped look of a new army recruit.
COLLECTION OF THE AUTHOR.

by the community and despite innumerable delays over many years, all but one of the remaining MTA-owned houses were finally returned to private ownership in 1995.[56]

Sudbrook Park found itself addressing other issues connected directly or tangentially to the subway's presence — such as zoning issues, speeding and increased traffic (on Olmsted's curvilinear roads designed to promote "leisurely contemplation" and never intended as major thoroughfares) and pressures for development, including the impact should the MTA ever sell air rights over adjacent transit stations.[57] While Sudbrook Park still does not look the same as before the construction of the rapid transit, the new landscaping now has a strong foothold and the community has adapted to its intruder.

But Sudbrook's battles to preserve its historic design and Olmstedian lineage have not ended and probably never will. In 1990 a Baltimore County Councilman introduced a proposal to amend the Master Plan to study reviving the possibility of extending I-795 (the Northwest Expressway) inside the Beltway to connect with Wabash Avenue, i.e., through Sudbrook Park.[58] Sudbrook Club representatives quickly and strenuously objected. Although the specific provision about extending I-795 inside the Beltway was removed, the Council did approve a general study to examine alternatives for relieving Beltway traffic, which could still revive extending Wabash.[59] There is no doubt that Sudbrook will need to remain vigilant, because the old Northwest Expressway idea is far from dead and will probably be resurrected in many shapes and forms in years to come. Sudbrook also faces preservation issues regarding the retention or replacement of its entranceway bridge. Presently, the community is working with Baltimore County to reach a solution that preserves Sudbrook's constricted gateway entrance while satisfying historic, aesthetic and safety needs. Frustrated by the difficulties of trying to deal in piecemeal fashion with each problem that arises, the community has also begun work on a comprehensive plan for Sudbrook Park.[60] When finalized by the community, it will be presented to the Baltimore County Council for adoption; if adopted, the plan will become part of the county's Master Plan to provide guidance and direction for the future.

Sudbrook's efforts over the past twenty-five years to resist public works projects that would eviscerate the community's historic fabric have taught a valuable lesson: preservation requires active stewardship. In 1993 Sudbrook gained additional protection in preserving its historic design and attributes when it was entered on the Baltimore County Landmarks List. The 600 block of Cliveden Road was added to the district in 1995. In the future, perhaps even more of the community will be added. To replenish its trees, the community has enthusiastically participated in the Tree-mendous Maryland program, which provides trees for public areas at reasonable prices.

Sudbrook celebrated its centennial year in 1989 with several community activities and a good deal of fanfare. The Sudbrook Club sponsored a house tour and an old-fashioned ice cream social at the playground. A formal commemorative program, held on October 15 at one of Sudbrook's entrance-way triangles, was the culmination of the centennial festivities. In addition to political dignitaries, guest speakers, members of both the Maryland Historical Trust and Friends of Maryland's Olmsted Parks and Landscapes, and past and current residents, many of the MTA representatives who had worked on the rapid transit project came. It turned out to be a beautiful and profoundly satisfying autumn day.

The prior sixteen years had been tumultuous ones for the community. Yet there was much to celebrate. Despite many unwelcome changes, despite having had to compromise, despite losing far too many majestic trees, despite having to re-landscape areas made barren by construction, despite a large ugly feature impinging on the historic community — much had been restored and saved. By tenacious hard work and luck, the community had more than once narrowly escaped even more extensive damage from proposals for the six-lane expressway and the open-cut rapid transit line. The integrity of Olmsted's design had not been irreparably destroyed. And once again, the artistry and skill of Olmsted's Plan had prevailed despite the changes that had been imposed on Sudbrook.

As old friends, and even old enemies, joined together in celebrating one hundred years of Sudbrook's history, words of Eugene Blackford almost a century before rang as true as when he wrote them: "If you would like at any time to see Sudbrook in its autumn days, we would be very glad to have you…. To us permanent residents, the most beautiful [time] but now begins."[61]

Keynote speaker Arleyn Levee, a landscape historian and designer, addresses those gathered to celebrate Sudbrook's Centennial on October 15, 1989. PHOTOGRAPH BY SALLY GRACIE. SUDBROOK PARK, INC. ARCHIVES.

Sudbrook's Olmstedian curves and landscape are especially inviting in the autumn. PHOTOGRAPH BY THE AUTHOR.

Epilogue

Creating cities and suburbs that are visually inviting, spiritually refreshing and psychologically energizing has long been a challenge. Beginning with Central Park in 1858, Frederick Law Olmsted fashioned his first and most famous statement about the importance of nature and the power of tranquil scenery in answering this challenge. Olmsted believed that his landscaping principles could be used to improve the physical, mental and social well-being of all citizens — wherever they lived. The parks, suburban villages, campuses, and public and private grounds that he designed are evidence of the soundness of his thesis — a thesis subsequently verified by scientific studies confirming nature's ameliorating effects.

Over the past several years, numerous books and articles in the popular press have focused on the problems of our cities, the continuing flight of citizens to the suburbs, and the resulting ugliness created by haphazard suburban sprawl. Sprawl is the antithesis of the Olmsted approach. Interestingly, just about everyone — from politicians to planners to home buyers —claims to abhor it. Yet it proliferates. Why do we keep repeating the same mistakes? It is not that we have no models or that we do not know what works.[1] Nor is the issue really money. While tasteful comprehensive planning and the preservation and landscaping of open spaces is initially more expensive, it more than pays for itself in the long run. Despite this knowledge, our landscape is littered from city to suburb with the now costly blight that has resulted from short-sighted and inept planning. Such mistakes carry a high long-term price tag for taxpayers and municipalities alike.[2]

In *The American City, What Works, What Doesn't*, architect and urban scholar Alexander Garvin quotes the late James Rouse, developer of Columbia, Maryland, who denounced the kind of random suburbanization that creates endless eyesores:

> Relentlessly, the bits and pieces of a city are splattered across the
> landscape. By this irrational process, non-communities are born —
> formless places without order, beauty, or reason; with no visible
> respect for people or the land.[3]

Garvin argues that we can solve the problems of our cities and suburbs if we just study the past. In commenting on suburbs that work, he says: "Some residential suburbs are designed in a manner that makes one's stay there a rich experience. The landscaping of an Olmsted subdivision, for example, enhances the experience of traveling home, spending the day on one's property, and mixing with the neighbors." The successful marketing of residential subdivisions, Garvin notes, "requires more than a nice house at an affordable price."[4]

Successful suburbs, like successful city neighborhoods, give residents more than a place to live: they impart a sense of belonging, a sense of community. It takes no particular genius to simply buy land and build houses, as so many suburban developers have proved repeatedly — to the detriment of us all. Creating a community that truly *functions* as one is a rare accomplishment, but one at which Olmsted excelled. Riverside, Sudbrook and Druid Hills remain thriving communities, thanks to Olmsted's vision, artistry and skill. They are all communities where residents regularly walk, bike or jog along the gently curving roads; gather on the inviting triangles and green spaces; and share a cohesiveness unusual in today's world.

Well before suburban living became an ensconced phenomenon of American life, Olmsted foresaw the need to plan suburban villages "the end of which must be, not a sacrifice of urban conveniences, but their combination with the special charms and substantial advantages of rural conditions of life." Even in Olmsted's time, desultory and haphazard development was a problem, and he bemoaned that the "misfortune of most existing suburbs is, that…no intelligent design has been pursued to secure any distinctly rural attractiveness, the only aim apparently being to have a plan…." In what was to become a prophetic statement, Olmsted opined that "no great city can long exist without great suburbs."[5]

In discussing Olmsted's Riverside and similar "garden city developments," historian Christopher Tunnard commented:

> These rare examples of residential parks may be regarded as among
> the most important American contributions to nineteenth century
> planning….Above all, as Riverside shows so clearly, they proved that
> suburbia need not be universal, that a suburb could be planned as a
> unit, and thereby promoted the idea of self-contained neighborhoods
> within the urban pattern. Those of us who are confronted with the
> problems of suburban planning today may have been able to
> modernize these principles, but not to improve on them.[6]

Similarly, Lewis Mumford, in summarizing the contribution of Olmsted and Charles Eliot, Jr., noted:

> Between them, they contributed more to the improvement of
> town and country than any dozen contemporaries. One may, indeed,
> seriously question if anything like their work has been relatively
> accomplished by later schemes of civic improvement — however
> elaborate their technique, however systematic their propaganda.[7]

Olmsted's innovative principles of planning and design have formed the foundation for the practice of landscape architecture in the United States. While Americans today take for granted existing urban parks, curvilinear streets and those suburbs that are picturesque and nourishing, these seemingly "natural" touches of lasting beauty might never have become an integral part of the American landscape without the influence of Frederick Law Olmsted.

Where the existing topography possessed natural features of beauty, Olmsted's designs worked to enhance them. In designing Sudbrook, Olmsted used five main curvilinear roads that followed the topography of the hills in the area. Where nature had not been so kind and the landscape was barren, Olmsted employed his artistic talents to outline, paint and color-in with trees and other vegetation what would, in time, become a scene so naturalistic that it seemed impossible that it had not been there forever.

Today we recognize that Olmsted's design principles — carried on by his stepson John Charles

Olmsted and his son Frederick Law Olmsted, Jr. in the firm their father founded — "comprise the history in the United States of environmental design, a concept not even named until our own generation." Without question, Olmsted and his firm contributed to the American landscape a "continuum of professional creativity unmatched in America."[8]

Olmsted's legacy remains important and vital as we move into the twenty-first century. Today, perhaps more than ever, we need the healing tonic of nature that Olmsted prescribed as an antidote for the ills of urban stress. While Olmsted did not scorn or retreat from the growth of commerce or industry, he believed it imperative that the soothing balm of naturalistic scenery be woven into the fabric of cities. He designed his suburbs in conformity with nature to provide "respites for the spirit" and to actively encourage the "harmonious association" of residents.

Perhaps the ultimate test of the soundness of Olmsted's designs is whether they can survive the onslaughts of time and change and still remain true to their planner's vision. Certainly Sudbrook Park meets this test. From its beginnings over a century ago, through many decades and changes, it has endured as a living tribute to Olmsted's vision — still a vital and cohesive community in every sense.

Having lived in Sudbrook Park for twenty-seven years, I share with many other residents, both past and current, the sense that there is something uncommonly rare about Sudbrook, something intangible that stays with those who have had roots here, long after they have moved away. Olmsted's landscape, and the feeling of community that he created, have exerted a profound and lasting influence on countless people who have called Sudbrook Park their home over the past century. My own affectionate feelings about Sudbrook are mirrored in the words of a resident of Riverside, who reportedly said: "I am saddened by those who have never lived anywhere in particular. Perhaps those who have never loved a place are as deprived as those who have never loved a person."[9]

Appendix A

Suggested Restrictions[1]

With a view to establishing certain conditions and customs in the neighborhood favorable to the growth of a pleasant suburban village, the parties to this agreement do hereby mutually agree to the following restrictions:

The party of the second part [any purchaser of property in Sudbrook Park] hereby agrees:

Value of house.

1st. that within two years from the date hereof a dwelling house shall be erected on the lot hereby conveyed which shall cost when ready for occupancy not less than $3000.

Forecourt.

2nd. that in order to preserve a forecourt for the benefit of the neighborhood, the main front wall of said dwelling house shall be placed at least 40 feet back from the street line, but usual porches with open sides or cornices or eaves may extend 5 feet into the forecourt, and bay windows may also extend 5 feet into the forecourt provided they shall be distinctly bays opening from wider rooms and distinctly faced on both sides by the main wall of the house and provided that they shall be included within a trapezoid whose base along the front wall of the house does not exceed 18 feet and whose sides form an angle of 45 degrees with the base, and provided they shall be no more than one story in height inside whether attached to the ground floor or to the second or third stories, but such bays may have porches or verandas under or over them if permanently open at the sides and front. No steps or uncovered piazza terrace, ramps, vases or other structures shall be placed in the forecourt beyond five feet from the main front wall of the house, which shall exceed four feet in height above an imaginary straight plane connecting the intersection of the ground floor of the house and its main front wall with the edge of the sidewalk at the street line.

Side spaces.

3rd. that no portion of the dwelling house shall be nearer to the side lines of the lot than ten feet.

Number of stories.

4th. that said dwelling house shall not be more than three stories high above the ground.

Elevation of house.

5th. that the ground floor of the house shall be higher than the centre of the street opposite the centre of the house in order that a connection can at some future time be made with a public sewer in the street.

Style of house.

6th. that the dwelling house and other structures placed on the lot shall be distinctly in a rural and not in an urban style.

One dwelling only.

7th. that one dwelling only shall be erected on the lot if the lot is less than two acres in extent, exclusive of the street but if larger than two acres one dwelling may be erected in each full acre, but this restriction shall not be deemed to prevent the erection and use of a tenement for a servant whose whole time is employed by the occupants of the dwelling house.

Stable.

8th. no other buildings, except a stable and usual outhouses for domestic purposes only shall be erected in said lot, and no part of said stable and outbuildings shall be nearer the street-line than sixty feet, nor nearer the side line of the lot than five feet — and said stable or outbuildings, including roof and any other part — shall not be higher than thirty feet above the surrounding ground.

Fence.

9th. that no fence shall be erected or hedge grown of a greater height than four feet above the ground.

No trade.

10th. that no trade or manufacture nor business occupation of any kind shall be conducted from the said lot.

Animals.

11th. that not more than four horses and two cows shall be kept upon the said lot, and no horse or cow shall be allowed to run at large unless securely picketed or fenced in; that no horse or cow shall be allowed upon the streets or upon any unfenced vacant land in the vicinity unless led by a halter or securely picketed; that no pigs shall be kept on said lot under any circumstances and that no fowls or any other domesticated or wild animals except said four horses and two cows shall be kept or raised on said lot after notice in writing from any two residents living within one thousand feet of the said lot has been served upon him stating that such animals or animal are objectionable to them.

Privy.

12th. that no privy vault shall be built or used on said lot unless said privy vault is absolutely water tight and unless it is daily disinfected with dry earth and that the use of said privy vault shall be immediately discontinued if and when objected to in writing by any two neighbors living within one thousand feet from the said lot.

Manure & offal.

13th. that no manure or offal shall be accumulated on the lot except in a water tight covered pail or in a close building so that the smell may not annoy the neighbors.

Sewage disposal.

14th. that no sewage or foul water shall be allowed to stand or flow upon the surface of the lot nor to flow onto any adjoining lot or street. Until a public sewer is provided all sewage produced on the lot shall be disposed of by a leaching cesspool or by subsurface irrigation or shall be removed to a safe distance. No leaching cesspool shall be constructed within sixty feet of an existing well and no well shall be sunk within sixty feet of a leaching cesspool and connection shall be made for all house sewage with a public sewer within one year after such sewer has been constructed.

No stripping.

15th. that the said lot shall not be stripped of its topsoil nor allowed to go to waste by wasting away nor made disorderly in appearance by being excavated for gravel or other materials or by having rubbish dumped upon it.

Single residence.

16th. that the said lot shall not be subdivided or sold in parcels but shall be held as a single residence.

And the said party of the second part in order to facilitate the creation of those public conveniences connected with streets such as a public sewerage system, public water supply, public light supply and the care and policing of the streets, hereby agrees to cooperate at any time before the establishment of a competent public authority, with the said parties of the first part [the Sudbrook Company of Baltimore County] or any corporation which may be assigned the right by them, either by contributing to the capital stock or bonds of said supply or sewerage company and sharing in the running expenses or by agreeing with them to pay a sufficient neutral or annual assessment to reimburse said company for the use of its capital and for running expenses, which assessment shall be in proportion to the length of the frontage of the said lot.

And the said party of the second part hereby expressly agrees to assume said liability in one or other of the two above mentioned ways within one year after receiving notice in writing from said company that the owners of a majority of the frontage along the street or streets in which said supply or sewerage system shall have been proposed to be extended have agreed with the said company as to terms; provided, however, that the charter of said supply or sewerage company shall expressly provide that a duly constituted and competent public authority shall at any time have the right to buy out all the rights and property of the said supply or sewerage company at a valuation to be determined by three arbitrators, one to be appointed by the chief executive of the local government having competent jurisdiction, one by the said company and the third by the other two.

And the said party of the second part hereby agrees to pay to the said parties of the first part and to their successors and assigns the sum of two dollars for each and every day which shall elapse between the serving of a notice by the said parties of the first part or by any two residents living within one thousand feet of the lot hereby conveyed to the effect that any one of the agreements herein contained are being violated and until such violation shall cease and said sum or sums shall be collected by process of law if not otherwise paid.

And the said parties of the first part do hereby agree that they will not sell any land abutting upon either side the lot hereby conveyed or directly facing it on the opposite side of the same street without embodying in the deeds all of the above restrictions and agreements but this shall not be held to apply to land adjoining the land hereby conveyed and lying in the rear of the same, nor to prevent the addition of other restrictions not incompatible with any of the above. That the said parties of the first part hereby agree that so long as they maintain their corporate existence they will continue to enforce all of the said restrictions upon the adjoining land and if necessary by actions at law, at their own sole expense.

And the said parties of the first part do hereby reserve to themselves the fees and title and all rights upon the streets laid out upon land now or hereafter belonging to them except the simple right of passage on foot or in vehicles between the said lot hereby conveyed and the proposed railroad station to be called Sudbrook, by such course or courses as they shall from time to time determine, and thence by way of Sudbrook Avenue so called to Reisters Turnpike, but the said parties of the first part shall grant the right to a duly chartered company to lay pipes under or to suspend electric wires over all streets which shall have been graded and shaped and which shall have been in use by the public over one year, whenever such company has obtained the assent in writing from the owners of a majority of the frontage on said street or streets to bear their share of the expense of maintenance.

And the said parties of the first [part] do hereby agree and expressly bind themselves to transfer in fee simple without cost to a duly constituted and competent public local government all the land in the streets which they shall have permitted the public to use uninterruptedly for one year and to the triangles and other spaces not exceeding one acre each in area which may lie between the streets or at their junctions, and further that they will at any time sell to any local government or to trustees, with proper guarantees as to free use by the public for all time, under reasonable regulations, one or more play-ground and public school lots at a rate not exceeding two hundred dollars an acre, to which shall be added all taxes and all assessments, or charges in the nature of assessments, for public improvements which shall have been paid or charged off in book accounts to the said land in proportion to its frontage by the said parties of the first part together with interest at five per centum per annum.

And the said parties of the first part hereby agree to sell to any duly organized church corporations or to the trustees of any church society for religious and charitable purposes exclusively, a lot or lots of land which said church society or societies may select out of any land belonging to the said parties of the first part to an amount not exceeding one acre to any one church society, at a rate not exceeding two hundred dollars an acre, to which shall be added all taxes and assessments and charges for public improvements, as above specified, which shall have been paid by the said parties of the first part together with interest at five per centum per annum.

And all the above agreements and restrictions shall extend in full force to and terminate at the 1st of January in the year 1920 unless sooner terminated or modified by mutual agreement in writing and duly recorded by the parties to this covenant or their successors, heirs or assigns and at and after the said 1st day of January, the land hereby conveyed shall rest and remain with the said party of the second part or his heirs or assigns absolutely and in fee simple, without conditions or limitations so far as the agreements herein contained are concerned.

APPENDIX B

The First Thirty-Five Cottages: 1889–1907

No.	Address	Year Built	
1	511 Sudbrook Lane	1889–90	Designed by Cabot, Everett & Mead of Boston
2	508 Sudbrook Lane	1889–90	Designed by Cabot, Everett & Mead of Boston
3	Woodland Inn	1889–90	Burned 1926
4	1020 Winsor Road	1889–90	Summer cottage
5	Lot 1, Block 17	1889–90	Summer cottage; burned in 1927
6	505 Sudbrook Lane	1889–90	Purchased by John Barker in 1896
7	718 Cliveden Road	1889–90	Purchased by Eliza C. Miller in 1894
8	Lot 1, Block 14	1889–90	Moved to 505½ Sudbrook Lane in 1961
9	501 Sudbrook Lane	1889–90	Rented to Oscar Webb 1890–97
10	Lot 1, Block 17	1889–90	Summer cottage – demolished for expressway project

Nos. 1 through 10 originally owned by the Sudbrook Company.

No.	Address	Year Built	
11	1018 Winsor Road	1890–91	Originally a rental owned by Hugh L. Bond, Jr.
12	515 Sudbrook Lane	1891–92	Apparently designed by purchaser, George Coursen
13	500 Sudbrook Lane	1892	Originally a rental owned by Hugh L. Bond, Jr.
14	503 Sudbrook Lane	1892	Originally a rental owned by Hugh L. Bond, Jr.
15	721 Cliveden Road	1892	Originally a rental owned by Hugh L. Bond, Jr.
16	717 Cliveden Road	1894	Designed by Thomas Buckler Ghequier for Horatio Armstrong and family
17	Livery stable	1889–90	Gone
18	710 Cliveden Road	1892–93	Initially the home of Edgar H. Bankard and family
19	607 Sudbrook Road	1893	Initially the home of George M. Shriver and family
20	600 Sudbrook Road	1892–93	Designed by George Archer for William and Isabel Trego
21	Lot 9, Block 13		Tenant house rented to Sudbrook Co. workmen
22	726 Howard Road	1892–93	Designed by J. Appleton Wilson for Roswell and Sophie Graves
23	719 Cliveden Road	1894	Initially the home of Lynn R. Meekins and family
24	1017 Winsor Road	1895	Originally a rental owned by Bond and Blackford
25	1016 Winsor Road	1895	Originally a rental owned by Bond and Blackford
26	724 Howard Road	1895	Originally a rental owned by Bond and Blackford
27	708 Cliveden Road	1895	Originally a rental owned by Bond and Blackford
28	706 Cliveden Road West	1894	Designed by George Archer for the Jos. Trippe family
29	610 Upland Road	1895	Built by the Sudbrook Co. "for sale only"
30	722 Howard Road	1896	Built by the Sudbrook Co.; leased to Mifflin Coulter

No.	Address	Year Built	
31	1008 Winsor Road	1896	Designed by Cabot, Everett & Mead of Boston for Eugene Blackford and family
32	517 Sudbrook Lane	1896–97	Initially the home of Dr. and Mrs. Samuel K. Merrick
33	713 Cliveden Road	1897	Initially the home of C.W. Linthicum and family
34	709 Cliveden Road	1897–98	Designed by George Archer for Oscar Webb and family
35	Club house-golf course	1898	Gone; designed by George Coursen, Sudbrook resident
36	520 Sudbrook Lane	1898	Built by the Sudbrook Co.; leased to Frank Hooper (house destroyed by fire in 1920s)
37	507 Sudbrook Lane	1900	Designed by J. Appleton Wilson for Frederick and Mary Robbins Hoffman
38	605 Upland Road	1901–02	Designed by McKenzie of Wyatt and Nolting; built by the Sudbrook Co. for lease to Senator Isidor Rayner and family
39	711 Cliveden Road	1904	Initially the home of F. C. Tyson and family

Source: Compiled from information in the Blackford Record and Account Books, Manuscript Division, Maryland Historical Society, Ms. No. 131, Vols. 1–5, 1891–1907.

NOTES

Guide To Frequently Used and Abbreviated Citations

A. Correspondents' Names:

FLO   Frederick Law Olmsted, Sr.
JCO   John Charles Olmsted
FLO, Jr.   Frederick Law Olmsted, Jr.
JHM   James Howard McHenry
HLB   Hugh Lennox Bond, Jr.
EB   Eugene Blackford
RW   Robert Winsor
JDW   James D. Winsor

B. Unpublished Sources:

PFLO/LC Papers of Frederick Law Olmsted, Library of Congress, Washington, D.C.
             Citations give reel or box number, followed by frame number or folder, if applicable.

OAR/LC Olmsted Associates Records, Library of Congress, Washington, D.C.
             Citations give volume or container number, followed by page or reel number.

             (i.e., A1:123 for volume A1, page 123, or B2: R54 for container B2, reel 54. The folder number is the same as the job number assigned a given project by the Olmsted firm—job 1054 is the Sudbrook Land Company. Series A are the letterpress books. Series B are the job files).

JHMP/MD-MHS James Howard McHenry Papers/ Manuscript Division — Maryland Historical Society
                   Citations give manuscript number: box

JHMJ/MD-MHS James Howard McHenry Journals/Manuscript Division — Maryland Historical Society
                   Citations give manuscript number: box

JHMAB/MD-MHS James Howard McHenry Account Books/Manuscript Division — Maryland Historical Society
                   Citations give manuscript number: box

BR&AB/MD-MHS Blackford Record & Account Books/Manuscript Division — Maryland Historical Society
                   Citations give manuscript number: box: volume and page

                   The volume numbers are my own notations, not the MHS's.
                   Vol. 1   1891–1894
                   Vol. 2   1892–1902
                     Vol. 3   1894–1899
                     Vol. 4   1899–1906
                     Vol. 5   1902–1907

BCLR   Baltimore County Land Records, New Courthouse Building, Towson, Maryland

BCMR   Baltimore County Mortgage Records, New Courthouse Building, Towson, Maryland.

Chapter 1: Frederick Law Olmsted and the American Suburb

1. Kenneth T. Jackson, *Crabgrass Frontier, the Suburbanization of the United States* (New York and Oxford: Oxford University Press, 1985), p. 45. See also p. 25. Jackson notes that writings as early as 539 B.C. describe the "suburban ideal" of combining the best of both country and city. While "suburbs" even today are not entirely uniform, Jackson identifies "essential similarities in American suburbanization... that can be summed up in the following sentence: affluent and middle-class Americans live in suburban areas that are far from their work places, in homes that they own, and in the center of yards that by urban standards elsewhere are enormous." (p. 6). It is important, however, to distinguish nineteenth century planned suburbs, which were "historical settlement forms with specific characteristics" from the modern concepts of "suburbia" ("a sociological term used to describe a lifestyle or attitude as much as it describes a place") and "suburban sprawl" (a colloquial term describing unplanned and random development that has devastated the natural landscape). See Michael Robinson, "The Suburban Ideal: 19th Century Planned Communities," *Historic Preservation,* Vol. 30, No. 2, (April–June 1978), p. 24.
2. Jackson, pp. 46–47.
3. David Schuyler, *The New Urban Landscape* (Baltimore: The Johns Hopkins University Press, 1986), pp. 11–13.
4. Until the development of New York City's Central Park in the late 1850s, there were no public parks in America. Growing out of the use of rural cemeteries for recreational purposes, the public parks movement in this country was led by Andrew Jackson Downing, author, nurseryman, designer of houses and grounds, and editor of *The Horticulturist,* and William Cullen Bryant, poet, naturalist and editor of the *New York Evening Post.* Their writings in the 1840s gave impetus to the concept of a large public park in New York City. Robinson, "The Suburban Ideal," p. 26.
5. Charles E. Beveridge, "Frederick Law Olmsted's Theory of Landscape Design," *Nineteenth Century* (Summer 1977), p. 38 (hereafter cited as "Olmsted's Theory of Landscape Design").
6. Beveridge, "Olmsted's Theory of Landscape Design," p. 38.

7. Charles E. Beveridge and Paul Rocheleau, *Frederick Law Olmsted, Designing the American Landscape* (New York: Rizzoli International Publications, Inc., 1995), p. 10. Olmsted's mother died when he was four. His father remarried and had four more children. As the only children of their father's first marriage, Frederick and his younger brother, John, had a special bond.

8. Charles Capen McLaughlin, "The Environment: Olmsted's Odyssey," *Wilson Quarterly*, Vol. VI, No. 3 (Summer 1982), p. 80.

9. Beveridge and Rocheleau, p. 11.

10. Beveridge and Rocheleau, pp. 11–12.

11. Beveridge and Rocheleau, pp. 13–16.

12. McLaughlin, p. 82.

13. Beveridge and Rocheleau, p. 21 (noting also that Olmsted's "critique of slavery contributed significantly to the ideology of the Republican party, which was taking form in these years.")

14. Beveridge and Rocheleau, p. 21.

15. McLaughlin, p. 83.

16. McLaughlin, p. 84.

17. The oldest of his brother's three children, John Charles Olmsted (1852–1920), would later follow in his stepfather's footsteps as a landscape architect renowned in his own right, trained by Olmsted, Sr., and the senior partner of the Olmsted firm from 1898 until his death in 1920. In addition, Frederick and Mary went on to have two children of their own. One of these two, Frederick Law Olmsted, Jr. (1870–1957), also was trained by his father and followed in his footsteps as a landscape architect of renown, active in the firm and senior partner from John's death in 1920 until 1950, when he retired. Olmsted, Jr., designed plats 2 and 3 of Baltimore's Roland Park (after 1897), as well as being active in other Olmsted firm designs in the Baltimore area.

18. Behind-the-scenes political maneuverings and Olmsted's lack of budgetary control to carry out his artistic plans prompted him to submit his resignation as superintendent of Central Park in 1861. Although he subsequently withdrew the resignation, his acceptance of the directorship of the Sanitary Commission precluded his active involvement with Park business during the Civil War. Olmsted and Vaux retained their titles as landscape architects to the park board, but their positions were of a consulting nature. After resigning from the Sanitary Commission, Olmsted thus needed to find full-time employment. Beveridge and Rocheleau, p. 70; and Laura Wood Roper, *FLO, A Biography of Frederick Law Olmsted* (Baltimore: The Johns Hopkins University Press, 1973; Johns Hopkins Paperbacks edition, 1983), pp. 154–55.

19. Beveridge and Rocheleau, p. 27.

20. The three commissions were for a park system in San Francisco, for what is today known as the University of California Berkeley campus, and for a cemetery in Oakland. The park system he designed for San Francisco was deemed too expensive and never carried out. He did, however, design Mountain View Cemetery in Oakland (1864–65) and the Berkeley campus (beginning in 1865). *The Master List of Design Projects of the Olmsted Firm 1857–1950*, compiled by Charles E. Beveridge and Carolyn F. Hoffman (Boston: National Association for Olmsted Parks in conjunction with the Massachusetts Association for Olmsted Parks, 1987), pp. 2, 51 and 135. In addition, while in California Olmsted was appointed chairman of the commission in charge of managing Yosemite Valley, which the federal government had ceded to the state. Olmsted's plan for preserving Yosemite as a scenic reservation was not adopted at the time, but fifty years later his son, Frederick, Jr., borrowed many of his father's ideas from the report when he wrote part of the legislation creating the National Park Service. Beveridge and Rocheleau, pp. 201–207.

21. Beveridge and Rocheleau, p. 116.

22. Beveridge, "Olmsted's Theory of Landscape Design," p. 42. When Governor Leland Stanford wanted Olmsted to recreate a New England style campus on the grounds of Stanford University, Olmsted convinced him that such a style was inappropriate to the semi-arid West. Beveridge and Rocheleau, pp. 132–33 and 221–222.

23. Beveridge, "Olmsted's Theory of Landscape Design," pp. 41–42.

24. Beveridge and Rocheleau, p. 38. Beveridge notes that "the superficial nature of purely decorative gardening and its lack of relation to its natural surroundings heightened Olmsted's perception of such work as 'artificial'. On the other hand, he viewed his own landscape designing as a process of working with and enhancing nature and therefore natural." Beveridge and Rocheleau, p. 42. At the same time, some of Olmsted's clients wanted flower gardens. Olmsted made provisions for gardens, but separated them, placing them out of sight from the spaces that he designed for broad landscape effect. To one of his clients, Olmsted remarked (perhaps only partly in jest): "If the gardener shows himself outside the [garden] walls, off with his head." Beveridge and Rocheleau, p. 164.

25. Olmsted, Vaux & Co., "Preliminary Report upon the Proposed Suburban Village at Riverside, Near Chicago" (New York: Sutton, Bowne & Co., Printers, 1868), p. 7 (referred to hereafter as "Preliminary Report").

26. Although there also were some suburbs removed from cities, vital to the formation of suburbs separated from cities would be the development of convenient transportation links to the city. The growth of railroads contributed enormously to the growth of early suburbs along their routes. By the end of the nineteenth century, with the advent of the electric trolley, the number of suburbs increased at an even faster pace. But year-round suburban living, as a concept and lifestyle rather than merely an escape from the heat of the city in the summer, was an idea that would take time to develop, with some cities and regions being slower than others to catch "suburban fever."

27. "Preliminary Report," pp. 6–7.

28. As early as 1857, an article in *The Crayon* identified Llewellyn Park as "the first development… of an idea which may mark a new era in Country Life and Landscape Gardening in this country." Almost one hundred years later (1947), in a study of "The Romantic Suburb in America," Christopher Tunnard called Llewellyn Park "the first [American] romantic suburban community" developed on picturesque principles of gardening established by Andrew Jackson Downing and Alexander Jackson Davis. The term "romantic" referred to "an informal, naturalistic, and above all picturesque manner of laying out grounds." John Archer, "Country and City in the American Romantic Suburb," *Journal of the Society of Architectural Historians*, Vol. 42, No. 2 (May 1983), p. 139.

29. Beveridge and Rocheleau, p. 117.

30. During his career, Olmsted was involved in planning some forty-five additional communities and subdivisions. Beveridge and Rocheleau, p. 124.

31. Changes to Olmsted's plans, whether of Central Park or his communities, have been inevitable over the more than a hundred years that most have existed in active use. Riverside, Sudbrook and Druid Hills each underwent changes — some precipitated by their development companies not being able to afford full implementation or going out of business. Only about 1,000 of Riverside's 1,600 acres were developed; the roadways and public spaces were true to Olmsted's design even though a majority of the half-acre lots planned by Olmsted were divided into two lots. Just over half of Sudbrook's roads were laid out according to Olmsted's plan, and the central core of about 100 acres was developed with the plan's lot sizes, but as had happened in Riverside, later developers further subdivided the remaining lots; they also built on the area reserved as a village green. Olmsted again provided ample public spaces in his plan for Druid Hills; these were retained when John C. Olmsted resumed work on the project in 1902. However, the ponds in Olmsted's Druid Hills plan were never constructed and again, some of its lots were further subdivided. Beveridge and Rocheleau, pp. 123–125.

32. James F. Waesche, *Crowning the Gravelly Hill, A History of the Roland Park-Guilford-Homeland District* (Baltimore: Maclay & Associates, 1987), p. 41.

33. BR&AB, MD-MHS, 131: 3: 1, p. 92, EB to JDW, October 28, 1891.

34. From having walked along Sudbrook's roads for years, I was aware and had written that there were major perceptual differences between an

Olmsted-designed curvilinear road and the typical road that has a curve. I would like to thank Catherine Mahan, ASLA, for explaining the difference from a design aspect when we worked on a symposium ("Sudbrook and the Olmsted Legacy of Design in the Baltimore Area," November 10, 1996, at the Maryland Historical Society). The difference is apparent when comparing Sudbrook's Olmsted-designed roads with roads meant to emulate his design but not added until the 1940s.

35. "Preliminary Report," p. 17.

36. Beveridge and Rocheleau, p. 117.

37. "Preliminary Report," p. 20.

38. "Preliminary Report," p. 21.

39. Thanks to Sudbrook residents Mike Sotir and John Leith-Tetrault who found and showed me the remnants of these long-ago graveled sidewalks at each of their residences on Cliveden Road.

40. "Preliminary Report," pp. 28, 12 and 13, respectively.

41. Edward Everett Hale (1822–1909) was an author and Unitarian minister with whom Olmsted had been associated in free-labor colonization activities during the mid-1850s. Hale's 1869 book, *Sybaris and Other Homes,* "described living conditions among Boston's poor and attempted to persuade readers of the viability of creating suburban communities for laboring men and their families." When Hale became editor of the *New Examiner,* he asked Olmsted to write an article on "the Subject of Laborers' homes." Both Hale and Olmsted were interested in creating suburban residential communities to counteract the isolation of rural life. David Schuyler and Jane Turner Censer, eds., *The Papers of Frederick Law Olmsted,* Vol. VI, *The Years of Olmsted, Vaux & Company 1865–1874* (Baltimore: The Johns Hopkins University Press, 1992), p. 348.

42. Schuyler and Censer, p. 347 (FLO to Edward Everett Hale, October 21, 1869).

43. Beveridge and Rocheleau, p. 121. See, also, Schuyler and Censer, pp. 472–477.

44. Beveridge, "Olmsted's Theory of Landscape Design," p. 42.

45. Walter Karp, "The Central Park," *American Heritage,* Vol. 32 (April–May 1981), p. 86.

46. Beveridge and Rocheleau, p. 116.

47. While Olmsted had idealistic goals of bringing various income levels together within a community, an idea well before its time, the Sudbrook Company apparently felt otherwise. In various letters, the manager of the Company commented that, while the Plan showed smaller lots, the Company was not planning to develop them. Present day Sudbrook does contain a mixture of larger and smaller lots.

48. "Preliminary Report," p. 24.

49. *Riverside in 1871, With a Description of its Improvements, Together with some Engravings of Views and Buildings,* Office of the Riverside Improvement Company (Chicago: D. & C. H. Blakely, Printers, n.d.), p. 13.

50. OAR/LC, A: 4: 498, JCO to HLB, April 16, 1889. See Appendix A for the full text of the suggested restrictions, which were to apply to all but the small lots sold by the Company.

51. In Wilber Harvey Hunter's preface to John Dorsey and James D. Dilts' *A Guide to Baltimore Architecture,* 2d. ed. (Centreville, Maryland: Tidewater Publishers, 1981), p. XLIV, Hunter credits Baltimore's Roland Park with being the first Maryland community to incorporate land-use restrictions, stating that the "first three categories [of Roland Park's deed restrictions] are no less than land-use zoning, the first such effective restrictions to be applied in Maryland…" Sudbrook's deed restrictions unquestionably preceded Roland Park's and were more extensive than Roland Park's as to land-use requirements. Thus, Sudbrook, not Roland Park, would be the first to have adopted land-use planning in Maryland.

52. John W. McGrain, *Master Plan History — Modern Planning* (Towson, MD: Baltimore County Office of Planning and Zoning, January 1989), pp. 6–9. In 1939, Baltimore County's administration introduced a county-wide zoning bill in the General Assembly, but the Assembly restricted its coverage. Clark S. Hobbs in an article in the *Baltimore Evening Sun* on April 22, 1940, commented on the state of zoning at that time: "[The Baltimore County Metropolitan District] sprawls helter-skelter without benefit of plan, without effective control of land use… you can build a cow stable or a mansion pretty much where you choose, dump your garbage and trash in the nearest gully, establish an automobile graveyard where it suits your convenience…." Zoning was extended to all of Baltimore County by an act passed during the 1941 General Assembly.

53. Beveridge and Rocheleau, p. 116.

54. See Beveridge and Rocheleau, p. 116 and Robinson, p. 26.

55. Schuyler and Censer, p. 555. Waring also was an inventor. Among other things, he developed an "earth closet" that he claimed was more healthful than the then-prevalent "water closet."

56. George E. Waring, Jr., *The Sanitary Drainage of Houses and Towns* (New York: Hurd and Houghton, 1876), p. 73.

57. Waring, p. 71, and see Waring, generally.

58. Correspondence of Eugene Blackford, manager of the Sudbrook Company, indicates that all of these systems were installed at Sudbrook Park. Blackford repeatedly referred to using Waring's systems, although the intricacies of each system were not discussed.

59. While working on Biltmore, Olmsted's health and memory began to fail. In 1895, he abruptly withdrew from his practice, hoping for improvement. Despite rest and European travel, he lapsed into senility. In 1898, his family committed him to McLean Hospital, whose grounds he had designed. He died there in 1903. Beveridge and Rocheleau, p. 257; and Charles Capen McLaughlin and Charles E. Beveridge, eds., *The Papers of Frederick Law Olmsted,* Vol. 1, *The Formative Years 1822–1852* (Baltimore: The Johns Hopkins University Press, 1977), p. 45.

Chapter 2: James Howard McHenry's "Sudbrook"

1. *Atlas of Baltimore County, Maryland,* Surveyed & Published under the Direction of G. M. Hopkins, C.E., reproduced from 1877 originals; repr. (Baltimore: Baltimore County Records Management Division, 1971).

2. "James McHenry, Soldier-Statesman of the Constitution," A Bicentennial Series Pamphlet (CMH Pub. 71–4, n.d., available from Baltimore's Fort McHenry), pp. 2–5.

3. "The Re-Creation of Grey Rock, Baltimore County," *Maryland Historical Magazine,* Vol. 50, No. 2 (June 1955), pp. 88–90.

4. "The Charms of Mt. Vernon," pamphlet, Downtown Partnership of Baltimore, Inc., n.d. The four park squares and Monument commonly are referred to as Mt. Vernon Place. The parks have been designated a National Historic Landmark, having been recognized as "one of the finest remaining examples of nineteenth century urban planning in the United States." [For further information see Frank R. Shivers, Jr., *Walking in Baltimore: An Intimate Guide to the Old City* (Baltimore: The Johns Hopkins University Press, 1995).] Frederick Law Olmsted, Sr. prepared plans for an 1880 re-landscaping. Olmsted corresponded with Robert Garrett, John M. Lanahan and John Bogard about the designs for the four squares between December 1876 and December 1879. See PFLO/LC, 16: 095–103, 16: 376–379 and 26: 417–537. (Thanks to Charles Beveridge who brought this information to my attention.) Mt. Vernon Place was re-landscaped in 1916 by Thomas Hastings of New York; it is doubtful that anything remains of Olmsted's earlier design. Other than Sudbrook, Mt. Vernon Place was the only Maryland design with which Olmsted, Sr. was involved.

5. Robert Barnes, *The Green Spring Valley, Its History and Heritage,* Vol. Two, *Genealogies* (Baltimore: Maryland Historical Society, 1978), pp. 61–62. Barnes does not state a cause of death, but it is thought that Juliana McHenry died after an illness. Telephone interview with Mrs. Joan McHenry Hoblitzell on June 27, 1996.

6. JHMP/MD-MHS, 544: 4, undated notes of James Howard McHenry, recounting information on the McHenry family. McHenry states that John McHenry (his father) "died at the age of 31 years of bilious fever leaving one child, J. Howard McHenry, now living, aged 53." Since McHenry was born in 1820, we can ascertain that the notes were written around 1873. McHenry makes no mention of his mother in these notes. See also Barnes, p. 61. Mrs. Juliana Watts, a descendant of McHenry, has notes prepared by her mother which indicate that John McHenry took ill with typhoid fever when returning from a visit to the mountains of Western Maryland. Nursed by the Sisters of Charity in Emmitsburg, he died and was buried there. Telephone interview with Mrs. Watts on August 30, 1996.

7. Unless otherwise noted, information about McHenry's life was provided courtesy of Mrs. Joan McHenry Hoblitzell, from writings of Julia McHenry France (daughter of John McHenry and Priscilla Stewart) that are contained in an unpublished 1959 McHenry/Stewart family album by Marjorie Ober Keyser McHenry (hereafter referred to as "The McHenry Family History").

8. JHMP/MD-MHS, 544: 4, passport issued to McHenry on Sept. 13, 1845. The passport describes McHenry's nose, mouth, chin and forehead as "ordinary." Another passport issued in 1851 gives his height as 5' 11".

9. JHMJ/MD-MHS, 544.1: 3 (journals dating 1845–1852, recounting McHenry's trips abroad).

10. Katherine Dehler, "Mt. Vernon Place at the Turn of the Century: A Vignette of the Garrett Family," *Maryland Historical Magazine,* Vol. 69, No. 3, (Fall 1974), p. 282. As Dehler points out, John Work Garrett, President of the B&O Railroad, later bought the property for his son Robert. Robert and Mary (Frick) Garrett turned it into "the most magnificent and interesting private residence in Baltimore."

11. I have not been able to ascertain with certainty the exact acreage of the Pikesville estate owned by McHenry, who seemed to be buying and selling real estate from the 1850s well into the 1870s. In November 1852, McHenry purchased parts of various tracts of land near Pikesville from Samuel James Fletcher and his wife Mary. (Barnes, p. 62). In 1855, McHenry paid $2,531.25 to purchase "a large number of acres" lying south of what was then Pomona, a Pikesville estate owned by Alexander Riddell, who perhaps agreed to sell some of his land because he had no children. (Dawn F. Thomas, *The Green Spring Valley, Its History and Heritage,* Vol. One, *A History, Historic Houses* (Baltimore: Maryland Historical Society), pp. 322–323). The grantor-grantee indexes in the Baltimore County Land Records office show 27 transactions between 1852 and 1873 in which James Howard McHenry was the grantee; 15 are deeds and the others are mortgages, assignments and releases. The 1877 *Atlas of Baltimore County, Maryland* in its "List of Patrons — Third District" states that McHenry owned 846 acres; this would appear to have been a number provided by McHenry. The McHenry Family History states that he bought 1,000 acres near Pikesville. McHenry's estate papers, in one listing, indicate that his estate owned and offered for sale or other disposition 853.459 acres; another list among the estate papers tabulates "unsold" property totaling about 136.75 acres. (JHMAB/MD-MHS, 544.2: 3, Will and Estate Ledger). It is unclear whether the "unsold" property is a part of or separate from the 853 acres. Whether 850 or 1,000 acres, McHenry had a substantial estate in the Pikesville area.

12. Although the origin of the name "Sudbrook" is uncertain, it is said to have been the name of a village or town in England that McHenry visited and liked. Telephone interviews with Mrs. Juliana Watts and Mrs. Marjorie McHenry Bride, Aug. 15 and 22, 1996, respectively. A long-time Sudbrook resident, the late Mr. Edward Stellmann, told me that in his travels through England many years ago, he came upon a small town called Sudbrook. John McGrain, who has done extensive research on the history of Baltimore County, shared with me that the name "Sudbrook Park" is identified as the former seat of the Duke of Argyle, "now headquarters of the Richmond Golf Club" in the county of Surrey, due south of London. J.G. Bartholomew, *Gazetteer of the British Isles,* 9th ed. (Edinburg: J. Bartholomew, Publisher, 1963) p. 653. Nov. 20, 1996, letter from John McGrain. The *Gazateer* also identifies a village and a hamlet called "Sudbrook."

13. The McHenry Family History.

14. Receipts for furniture and various other purchases indicate that the McHenrys were in Paris from at least October 1855 to April 1856. JHMP/MD-MHS, 544:1, receipts folders.

15. No architectural plans can be found in McHenry's papers, but it appears that his architect was Edmund G. Lind and that McHenry became displeased with cost overruns. In personal notes, he ruminated on the relationship between architect and client, "fearing from an estimate of the amount already spent or due upon my new house that the ultimate cost will far exceed the sum named by the architect and accepted by me as a basis upon which my consent was given to the execution of the plan submitted...." The original estimate was $11,000, exclusive of mantels, heating and either lighting or plumbing (McHenry cannot recall which). (JHMP/MD-MHS, 544: 1, McHenry's notes dated November 17, 1860). McHenry complained in a letter to Lind that the actual costs had exceeded the estimate and he declined to pay any more. Quite a few years later, there were two letters from Lind to McHenry. In the latter one, Lind stated that he was leaving the country for a year or two, and "if there are any of your plans you would like to retain from my collection they are at your service." JHMP/MD-MHS, 544: 3, McHenry to Lind, undated; Lind to McHenry, Jan 5, 1882 and March 17, 1882, respectively. (Architect Edmund G. Lind (1829–1909) designed Baltimore's Peabody Institute and was an organizer of the American Institute of Architects. For more on Lind, see Dorsey and Dilts, pp. 278–79).

16. The McHenry Family History.

17. Barnes, p. 62. Barnes lists Charles Howard McHenry as the third child and states that C. Howard died in infancy. C. Howard was, however, the youngest of the McHenrys' children; records of St. Thomas Church in Garrison, where Charles Howard McHenry is buried, confirm that he was born Oct. 17, 1871 and died June 19, 1874. I have listed the children in the order that McHenry did in his notes. (In an 1873 journal entry, McHenry stated that he was spending the winter at Sudbrook with his wife "and three youngest children, viz. John, Sophy and C. Howard. The elder three, Julia, Cary and Nelly board with their grandmother at 97 N. Charles Street [to be closer to their schools]." (JHMJ/MD-MHS, 544.1: 2, entry of Feb. 1, 1873).

18. Judging from the following, McHenry did not spend the period of the Civil War (1861–65) abroad: (1) An account in his handwriting with Mason Brown, who apparently was doing work on Sudbrook, is dated 1861–62. (2) A member of the First Maryland Calvary C.S.A. recounted an incident in September 1862, when the writer found McHenry, his wife and child being held up by Confederate pickets on their return from visiting Mrs. McHenry's brothers at the Confederate camp and "straightened things out to the satisfaction of the pickets and bade Mr. and Mrs. McHenry good night and goodbye." Samuel H. Miller, ed., "Civil War Memoirs of the First Maryland Calvary, C.S.A.," *Maryland Historical Magazine,* Vol. 58 (June 1963), p. 157. [Note: Sally McHenry's two brothers, "grandnephews of Thomas Jefferson, both served with distinction in the Confederate Army" and "were widely known in Maryland and Virginia following the war." Miller, p. 157, fn. 28.] (3) On Sept. 4, 1864, McHenry signed a note of exchange to purchase property in Pikesville. (4) In March 1865, McHenry made a "Calculation of contents of haystack," which is with his farm receipts. (JHMP/MD-MHS, 544: 1). (5) Also in 1865, McHenry was elected a director of the Gwynns Falls Railroad, chartered that year. J. Thomas Scharf, *History of Baltimore City and County,* Part I (Philadelphia: Louis H. Everts, 1881; repr. Baltimore: Regional Publishing Company, 1971), p. 356, fn. 1. The combination of these local events seems to confirm McHenry's presence in the Baltimore area during most of the period of the Civil War.

19. McHenry's notes show that he was in Baltimore in May 1867, but in Nice, France by November 1867. Correspondence to and from McHenry, as well as purchase receipts and bills for "medical attendance" for Sally McHenry (whose sixth child, Sophia, was born in London on October 13, 1868), indicate that they spent time in Nice, France as well as Brighton, London and Mayfair, England during that time. See JHMP/MD-MHS, 544:1 and JHMJ/MD-MHS, 544.1: 2, JHM's 1871 Journal, entry of Feb. 18, 1871.

20. Two of Sally McHenry's sisters, Jennie and Hetty Cary, were highly publicized Confederate supporters. They made the first battle flag used by the Southern forces and were members of the "Monument Street Girls," a group which defied Federal edicts by waving the forbidden Stars and Bars flag at Union soldiers stationed at Federal Hill. A warrant was issued for Hetty's arrest; she and Jennie escaped to Virginia, carrying supplies and drugs badly needed by Confederate soldiers. Altogether, Hetty made six trips through the battle lines and blockades, often under fire. Hetty's reputed beauty (Gen.

Beauregard pronounced her "the most beautiful in that city of lovely women — Baltimore") kept her from being arrested on at least one occasion. The two sisters became "crown princesses of Richmond's wartime society," socializing with the Jefferson Davises, high government officials and generals. (Elizabeth H. Moberly, "Baltimore's Barbara Fritchie," newspaper clipping [source unidentified and n.d.] in The McHenry Family History, sent to me by Joan McHenry Hoblitzell).

21. JHMP/MD-MHS, 544: 2, JHM (Brighton, England) to Dr. Hilbers, April 19, 1869.

22. JHMP/MD-MHS, 544: 1, list of "Periodicals to be sent to JHM, Pikesville, Maryland," 1872. McHenry later compiled a list of "Possible Periodicals for 1881" that contained forty-nine periodicals and newspapers. McHenry meticulously compared in columns the cost of each if purchased through three different sources. JHMP/MD-MHS, 544: 1. (As other of his notes indicate, McHenry seemed to have limited surplus funds by 1881).

23. One of McHenry's notes was an "Estimate of Property" which listed "ground rents and 14 houses and farm." In addition, he appeared to own the Burnt Tavern in Pikesville; a printed notice among his papers shows him offering it "for sale or rent" and one of his many "lists" contained this item: "Build new hotel in rear of present Brick tavern or Burnt House and pull down this building." JHMP/MD-MHS, 544: 1, 4 and 1, respectively, undated notes of JHM and printed notice.

24. The relatives with whom McHenry seemed closest were his Uncle Benjamin Chew Howard, who died on March 6, 1872, at the age of 80 and was the last son of Col. John Eager Howard (at his death, McHenry wrote: "He was truly a nobleman — one whose character was unblemished in either his public or his private life." JHMJ/MD-MHS, 544.1: 2, Vol. 14, 1872 diary); his Aunt Sophia C. Read (whom he often visited and with whom he frequently stayed when he attended to business in the city); and his Aunt Sophia McHenry (she lived at an estate called Monmouth in Harford County and corresponded with McHenry, who visited on a regular basis). The friends with whom McHenry maintained the closest connections were Eugene Blackford and Alexander Riddell. Blackford lived on a nearby farm and was active in the Garrison Forest Farmers' Club with McHenry. The two families regularly visited each other and frequently dined together; in addition, McHenry involved Blackford in many of his meetings and discussions regarding efforts to secure transportation from Pikesville to the city. Riddell owned Pomona, the estate adjoining Sudbrook. McHenry would often walk over to visit him. (See, JHMJ/MD-MHS, 544.1: 1 and 2, journals and diaries dated 1870, '71, '72, '73 and '78). McHenry also maintained extensive "visiting lists" for New Year's Day. On pleasant days, he and Sally would go for a ride in their rockaway (carriage) and visit friends.

25. McHenry's journals and diaries recounted rather matter-of-factly his and his family's daily comings and goings, the weather, issues of importance to him and the not infrequent deaths of relatives and friends, but occasional traces of feelings are evident. He clearly was deeply saddened by the death of his Uncle Ben (Benjamin Chew Howard). He also seemed to delight in his children's joy at Christmas and on their birthdays. His children's letters to him reveal both deep affection and respect for his authority.

26. Among his extensive written discourses, McHenry included "Habits and Practices [the] adoption or imitation of which I hope my children to avoid," and lengthy notes on "Education" (which stressed the importance of "improving oneself," the need for "descendants of a good family to cultivate the talents and virtue that distinguished their ancestors," and "the importance of the **immediate interest** taken and shown by the parent in the pursuits and feelings of the child." [Emphasis in original]). He also sent a number of admonishing letters to his son Cary, when he went away to school, regarding thriftiness. Cary often seemed on the edge of trouble as an adolescent. He was suspended from Yale for lighting a bonfire to celebrate a victory over Harvard and received numerous "marks" for irregularity of attendance at classes. McHenry seemed quite concerned that Cary was doing nothing constructive with his life after graduating from law school, and wrote him a lengthy letter urging him not to rest on the laurels of his past family history but to continue his education, improve himself and do something worthwhile with his life. JHMP/MD-MHS, 544: 4 and 1 (undated notes of JHM on undesirable habits and education) and 3 (correspondence of May 31, 1878 and December, 1879 from Yale; the May letter about the suspension is addressed to W. M. Cary, Jr., McHenry's brother-in-law, because McHenry was in Europe from May to November 1878.)

27. Thomas, p. 90 (noting that several such agricultural societies were formed around this time to address issues relevant to the owners of large farming estates). Minutes of the Garrison Forest Farmers' Club, 1874–1879 and 1885–1907 (MD-MHS, Ms. No. 381), provide an interesting glimpse into the concerns of gentleman farmers of that period.

28. JHMP/MD-MHS, 544: 2, Hill to JHM (London), May 31, 1869. (In 1881 the Union Railroad and tunnel connected together "the Baltimore and Potomac, Western Maryland, Northern Central, Philadelphia, Wilmington and Baltimore, and Baltimore and Delta Railroads" at Canton. Apparently there was some idea of constructing a line to Pikesville, but that seems not to have materialized by 1881, when the route of the railroad was described as beginning near Charles Street at a junction with the North Central Railroad, going through the city, with one branch heading north toward the Philadelphia turnpike and the other south to Canton. Scharf, Part I, p. 354.

29. The Western Maryland Railroad, according to information prepared by C. Stewart Rhine of the Western Maryland Railway Historical Society ("A Backward Glance" by C.S. Rhine; unpublished manuscript), was chartered in 1852 to be a "farmers' railroad." It started in Owings Mills, at the end of the Northern Central Railway's Greenspring Branch (this line came west from the Northern Central line at Lake Roland). The track reached Westminster in 1861. In 1873 the Western Maryland Railroad built a new line from Owings Mills into Baltimore. It was this new segment that was under discussion in 1870 and which, when constructed, went through Pikesville, traversing McHenry's land. (I thank Mr. Rhine for his assistance in providing information and consultation about the Western Maryland Railroad).

30. JHMJ/MD-MHS, 544.1: 1 (Vol. 12), 1870 diary of JHM (March 22 — W.M.R.R.'s Gen. Trimble came to discuss railroad matters; April 8 — Gen. Trimble and Mr. Osborn discussed location of the railroad; May 25 — visit to McHenry by Mr. George Bokee, elected President of the W.M.R.R. on May 17 (see Scharf, Part I, p. 357) and later the McHenrys visited the Blackfords; June 7, 8, 9 and 10 — surveyors at work on the line; Dec. 19, 20 and 21 — surveyors back at Sudbrook doing location work.)

31. JHMJ/MD-MHS, 544.1: 1 (Vol. 12), 1870 diary of JHM, Dec. 2 — visit to Central Park; Dec. 3 — visit to Llewellyn Park.

32. Andrew Jackson Downing (1815–1852) in his short lifetime achieved international recognition as a landscape gardener, architect, writer and horticulturist who promoted the art of "rural improvement." He was the editor of The Horticulturist, a popular magazine that McHenry subscribed to, and it was Downing who brought Calvert Vaux from England in 1850 to be his partner. Downing's writings influenced Olmsted and had a lasting influence on suburban residential design. Catherine M. Howett, "Andrew Jackson Downing," in William H. Tishler, ed., American Landscape Architecture, Designers and Places (Washington, D.C.: The Preservation Press, 1989), pp. 31–33.

33. David Schuyler, The New Urban Landscape (Baltimore: The Johns Hopkins University Press, 1986), pp. 156–159.

34. Michael R. Farrell, The History of Baltimore's Streetcars (Sykesville, Maryland: Greenberg Publishing Company, Inc., 1992), p. 13. But when the omnibus lines were introduced to Baltimore in 1844, they were described as "quite handsome affairs, well fitted up, richly decorated, and drawn by good horses." Their arrival was heralded by the Baltimore Sun, May 1, 1844: "In other cities,…these lines have tended to enhance the value of property in the outskirts of the city, enabling persons to reside at a distance from their places of business, in more healthy localities." Scharf, Part I, p. 361.

35. JHMJ/MD-MHS, 544.1: 2 (Vol. 13), 1871 diary of JHM (entries April 17–May 13, 1871). McHenry also journeyed to New York City and again "drove through the Central Park."

36. Entry of June 17, 1871. JHMJ/MD-MHS, 544.1: 2 (Vol. 13), 1871 diary of JHM (entry June 17, 1871). It appears that this agreement was implemented; the station became known as Pikesville or Roslyn Station and today would be situated along the railroad's right-of-way, west of Old Court Road near the beltway. (This was **not** the same location as the Sudbrook Park station, built years later).

37. In a Sept. 6, 1871 entry, McHenry stated: "I went today to Boonton, N. Jersey to see Mr. Rossi, C.E., with whom I have been in correspondence." Although no additional information is provided, it is interesting to note that McHenry seemed to be in correspondence with a

number of civil engineers and landscape gardeners during the 1870s, apparently in connection with his idea of developing a suburban village. JHMJ/MD-MHS, 544.1: 2 (Vol. 13), 1871 diary of JHM (entry of Sept. 6, 1871).

38. JHMJ/MD-MHS, 544.1: 2 (Vol. 13), 1871 diary of JHM (entry of Sept. 11, 1871). McHenry's daughter Julia accompanied him on this trip.

39. George E. Waring, Jr. (1833–1898) went on to attain considerable success and international renown as a professional expert in the sanitary drainage of houses and towns. Dumas Malone, ed., *Dictionary of American Biography*, Vol. X, Part I (New York: Charles Scribner's Sons, 1936), pp. 456–57. (Drainage systems developed by Waring were later used in developing Sudbrook Park and also in Baltimore's Roland Park).

40. JHMJ/MD-MHS, 544.1: 2 (Vol. 14), 1872 diary of JHM (entry of April 22, 1872).

41. The bridge referenced was not the current bridge into Sudbrook Park, but may have been on Old Court Road. In 1873 the current Sudbrook Lane road and bridge did not exist. See *1877 Atlas of Baltimore County*, Third District map.

42. JHMJ/MD-MHS, 544.1: 2 (Vol. 15) 1873 diary of JHM (entries March 31, April 7 and 22, 1873). Although the Baltimore and Pikesville Railroad Company had been authorized to receive subscriptions by an act in 1866, nothing came of it. In 1870 another act authorized the Baltimore and Reisterstown Turnpike Company (of which McHenry was a director) to construct a passenger railway between Baltimore and Pikesville, which was commenced in 1872, with a branch road to the agricultural grounds at Pimlico. Scharf, Part I, p. 370.

43. Farrell, p. 37 (noting: "This line was long plagued by the bottleneck of a single track along that portion of its route adjoining Druid Hill Park. Some idea of the unsophisticated way of running a suburban line in those unhurried days is evident in the following item from the *Baltimore Sun:* 'Mr. Chenowith, the overseer of the farm, also had the duty of going to Pikesville at 5 a.m. to see that the (horse car) service got started.' ")

44. JHMP/MD-MHS, 544: 2, memo of JHM, Nov. 21, 1875.

45. JHMP/MD-MHS, 544: 2, Report to Stockholders of Baltimore, Pimlico and Pikesville Railway Co. dated July 1, 1876. The depression that is referred to most probably was the aftermath of the Panic of 1873, a major financial crisis.

46. Extrapolation from McHenry's letters (the line did not go to Pikesville in 1876, but was extended by 1878) and Farrell, map, p. 34.

47. Scharf, Part I, p. 356.

48. JHMJ/MD-MHS, 544.1: 2 (Vol. 16), 1878 diary of JHM.

49. Apparently, McHenry had talked with Frederick Law Olmsted prior to this time about preparing a plan for a residential subdivision on the property, but McHenry found Olmsted very busy and so hired Roullier. PFLO/LC, 15: 622–23, JHM to FLO, July 20, 1876 (recounting this earlier interview).

50. JHMJ/MD-MHS, 544.1: 2 (Vol. 15) 1873 diary of JHM (entries April 28 and 29, May 13, July 9, 10, 15 and 19, Aug. 23, 29 and 30, Dec. 9 and 11). Roullier also surveyed the premises of St. Thomas Church in Garrison on Aug. 29, 1873. (McHenry's journals of this time also mentioned John Cowan, McHenry's carpenter. Years later, Cowan built many of the first thirty-five houses in Sudbrook Park).

51. JHMJ/MD-MHS, 544.1: 2 (Vol. 15) 1873 diary of JHM (entries May 13 and Dec. 9 and 11). McHenry does not state an exact location of Heidleberg Farm, but it was most likely near or beyond Towson, since journal entries talk about going there by way of Towsontown.

52. JHMP/MD-MHS, 544: 2, letters from Sophia McHenry to JHM (1874).

53. JHMP/MD-MHS, 544: 2, S. Chew to JHM, March 6, 1875.

54. JHMP/MD-MHS, 544: 2, F.W. Poppey to JHM, March 8, 1875. (Interestingly, it was Olmsted who tried to convince William Hammond Hall, the designer of San Francisco's Golden Gate Park, to devise a plan for San Francisco parks in keeping with the climatic conditions of the semi-arid West. Beveridge and Rocheleau, p. 216–17.)

55. William Hammond Hall wrote Olmsted that "there is not a competent landscape gardener on this coast that I can hear of" and asked Olmsted to recommend someone. (PFLO/LC, 14: 60–62, Wm. Hammond Hall to FLO, Feb., 13, 1874). Olmsted recommended Poppey because of his experience in Western Texas, in arid country, and his "disposition to travel out of beaten tracks and find new methods for new conditions." PFLO/LC, 14: 556–558, FLO to F.W. Poppey, Jan. 21, 1875. (Olmsted may have met Poppey in Texas during his tour in 1854, or perhaps later in Texas through Olmsted's German émigré friends). The connection between Poppey and Olmsted was brought to my attention by Charles Beveridge, Series Editor of the Frederick Law Olmsted Papers.

56. By 1876 it seemed to be common knowledge that McHenry was hoping to develop some sort of suburban village on his Sudbrook estate. One Pikesville landowner whom McHenry had solicited about selling his property along the route of the proposed horse-car line to Pikesville responded that he was in favor of steam, but not a horse-car railroad, adding: "I agree with you that no one takes more interest than you do in the improvement of the whole neighborhood…. If at any time you wish to lay out avenues through your place and afterwards to close up the old road, for **one** you will not find me putting any hindrance in your way." JHMP/MD-MHS, 544:3, E.L.J. Waldron to JHM, Oct., 1876 (emphasis in original).

57. JHMP/MD-MHS, 544: 2, JHM to Jacob Tome, April 6, 1875.

58. JHMP/MD-MHS, 544: 2, Jno. E. Howard to JHM, Sept. 5, 1875.

59. JHMP/MD-MHS, 544: 2, Geo. E. Waring to JHM, Dec. 18, 1875 (and an earlier letter, April 13, 1875).

60. JHMP/MD-MHS, 544: 2, JHM to County Commissioners of Plymouth Co., Mass., Feb. 1 and 2, 1876. (In a subsequent discourse on which he noted "handed to Mr. Gittings of Balt. Co. delegation in Legislature who promised to show it to his colleagues. 6 February [18]82," McHenry raised the question of "the expediency of subdividing any one that may desire to make the experiment, or all of the counties of the state into townships." JHMP/MD-MHS, 544: 3. Feb. 6, 1882).

61. PFLO/LC, 15: 622–23, JHM to FLO, July 20, 1876.

62. JHMP/MD-MHS, 544: 3, FLO to JHM, July 28, 1876. (After an unpleasant experience with Riverside's developer, E. E. Childs, Olmsted may have wanted to avoid recommending a project or getting involved in any way beyond an arms-length fee-for-service arrangement. Childs had agreed to pay Olmsted and Vaux either a percentage commission or its value in Riverside lots, to which they agreed. Childs defaulted on his payments to the landscape architects, leaving them with lots as payment. Several years later, the land was worth half its original valuation and had to be sold at a loss. Roper, pp. 322–324. See also Schuyler and Censer, pp. 291–293 (FLO to Edwin Channing Larned, Nov. 10, 1868).

63. PFLO/LC, 16: 003, JHM to FLO, Sept. 5, 1876.

64. JHMP/MD-MHS, 544: 3, FLO to JHM, Sept. 6, 1876.

65. Jacob Weidenmann (1829–93), originally from Switzerland, was a European trained architect and engineer who had studied the writings of Andrew Jackson Downing and moved to America in 1856 to take advantage of opportunities for landscape gardening. He became associated with Olmsted and Vaux, supervising the execution of their plan for the Hartford Retreat for the Insane and also designing Bushnell Park, Cedar Hill Cemetery and various private residences in Hartford, CT. He wrote *Beautifying Country Homes* (1870), went to Europe to study, and resumed his association with Olmsted and Vaux in 1871, when he moved to New York to work on the firm's design of Prospect Park. In 1874, he became Olmsted's partner and the two designed Congress Park in Saratoga Springs, N.Y. Weidenmann also helped Olmsted prepare plans for Mount Royal Park in Montreal, the United States Capitol grounds and other important projects. Weidenmann worked independently on some projects as his reputation grew, and received a medal and diploma from the United States Centennial Commission in 1876. He remained associated with Olmsted through about 1878. David Schuyler, "Jacob Weidenmann," in William H. Tishler, ed., *American Landscape Architecture — Designers and Places* (Washington, D.C.: The Preservation Press, 1989), pp. 44–47.

66. JHMP/MD-MHS, 544: 3, FLO to JHM, Oct. 7, 1876.

67. PFLO/LC, 16: 048, JHM to FLO, Oct. 16, 1876.

68. PFLO/LC, 16: 048, JHM to FLO, Oct. 16, 1876.

69. JHMP/MD-MHS, 544: 3, FLO to JHM, Oct. 18, 1876. (Based on rates that McHenry subsequently obtained from other unknown or less prominent "landscape gardeners," it does appear that Olmsted could and did command a higher than average fee, no doubt based on his renown and singular expertise).

70. Beveridge and Rocheleau, pp. 188–195.

71. JHMJ/MD-MHS, 544.1: 2 (Vol. 16), 1878 diary of JHM, entries of March 19 and 20, 1878.

72. A letter from Thomas Hill to McHenry, although undated, appeared to have been written during the time the McHenrys were abroad. Hill commented that he hoped that Mrs. McHenry "may continue to improve in health & with very best wishes for your health & that of the whole family," suggesting that Mrs. McHenry had been ill and the 1878 trip may have been for health reasons. The main thrust of Hill's letter involved property that McHenry owned in the city which Hill had been trying to sell without success. Hill urged McHenry to put up some small houses on the property "with a view to bringing them into productiveness," since "Baltimore is growing now…more rapidly than before…[and] I think it would result in a more **immediate** result than your pet idea of a suburban village. The latter must **ultimately** prove successful but it is a question of years before any beneficial result would be realized." JHMP/MD-MHS, 544: 4, undated page of a letter to JHM signed by Thos. Hill (emphasis in original). (Also among McHenry's letters from this period is one from C. H. Miller at the Office of Landscape Gardener, Fairmount Park, Philadelphia, addressed to John E. Howard, McHenry's cousin. (One explanation for this letter being with McHenry's correspondence is that McHenry might have asked his cousin to obtain information from Miller while McHenry was abroad). Miller responded to the inquiry regarding "the cost of laying out tracts of land for suburban and village lots," stating that a topographical survey would cost from $3 to $5 an acre, that plans were charged on a time basis, and that his charge for visits was $10 per day plus traveling expenses. Miller referred to "Bryn Mawr, on the Penna. R.R. as a place nicely laid out and planted under my supervision." Nothing further developed from this communication, but it evidences continuing inquiries about designing a suburban development in McHenry's papers. JHMP/MD-MHS, 544: 3, C.H. Miller to JHM, May 27, 1878).

73. JHMP/MD-MHS, 544: 4, JHM notes, Dec. 9, 1879.

74. JHMP/MD-MHS, 544: 4, JHM notes, Feb. 6, 1880.

75. JHMP/MD-MHS, 544: 4, JHM notes, undated (but with notes of Feb. 6, 1880).

76. JHMP/MD-MHS, 544: 3, Undated notes, titled: "Mr. Roullier's Propositions" (referring to Roullier's letter of Oct. 6, 1880 and indicating that McHenry made notations on Oct. 14, 1880).

77. JHMP/MD-MHS, 544: 4, "Payments of 1881 to G. A. Roullier, surveyor for surveying & mapping part of Sudbrook." Undated notes of McHenry's in the same box contained "Mr. Roullier's Inventory of Property in Engineer's Office—Sudbrook," and jottings that appeared to be issues McHenry wanted to discuss with Roullier, such as "where [to] place drains & would roots of trees interfere with them if under driving road that must be torn up if it should be desired to get at drains; one small tunnel to hold water-gas-steam heating & drainage pipes; would not best place for trees be inside of lot line & require building to be set back 10–20 feet or make sidewalk 8 feet & plant trees on two feet nearest to the lot line; reservation of line for horse railway extended from Baltimore, Pimlico & Pikesville terminus on turnpike…"

78. JHMP/MD-MHS, 544: 3, G. A. Roullier to JHM, three letters dated November 10 and 18, and December 3, 1881, respectively.

79. OAR/LC, A23: 13, FLO & Co. to EB, Sudbrook Co., Sept. 1, 1892. (See also OAR/LC, A12: 7, FLO & Co. to John W. Linton, Baltimore, January 20, 1891: "The topographical map which we used in the preparation of our plan for the Sudbrook Land Company was satisfactory, except that it needed to show some more of the principal trees.")

80. JHMP/MD-MHS, 544: 3, undated draft of JHM.

81. JHMP/MD-MHS, 544: 3, Report to Stockholders of the Baltimore, Pimlico & Pikesville R.R. Co., July 1, 1881 (noting that the road "can manage to pay its way eight or nine months in the year, but in the three or four winter months it runs behind…. The road lacks about half a mile of reaching Pikesville, where it was intended to go, and where it could obtain many more passengers…but being about as far from Pikesville as the Steam Railway, many persons prefer taking the latter on account of its better time.") Apparently, the horse-car line did not survive its immediate crisis. A printed notice among McHenry's papers advertised "Trustee's Sale of a Valuable Suburban Horse Railway known as the Baltimore, Pimlico and Pikesville R. R. Co. on Monday, 28 Nov. 1881." The notice, by Samuel B. Mettam, Auctioneer, described the line as follows: "starts at Pennsylvania Ave. near Cumberland St. in City and runs to within 1/4 mile of Pikesville, being about 7 miles in length. Skirts Druid Hill Park, near Maryland Agricultural & Mechanical Fair Assoc. & the race course at Pimlico, terminus near the U. S. Arsenal in the flourishing town of Pikesville. At its other terminus, it makes immediate connection with the Baltimore City Passenger Rwy & the Citizens' Passenger Rwy." JHMP/MD-MHS, 544: 4 (Nov. 1881).

82. Farrell, p. 45 (stating that the tracks ran "from Reisterstown Road, near Fulton Avenue, alongside the [Reisterstown] turnpike as far as what is now Park Circle and then cross country over what became Park Heights Avenue to the Confederate Soldiers' Home in Pikesville (the present State Police Headquarters)." In July 1892, the line was electrified, making it one of the earliest electrified lines in the Baltimore area. Farrell, p. 45).

83. *Maryland Journal* (Towson), June 30, 1883. I thank John McGrain for bringing this article to my attention.

84. Additional undated notes relating to suburban development among McHenry's papers include a "Mem. of some requirements for a town" which also has a rough sketch showing what appear to be three roads, and a separate page listing various issues or questions (it has no title or date). The Memorandum is a laundry list of items that includes, among other things, "R. Road passenger station — telegraph office, express office; Horse car station & stables; Water works; gas works; Sewerage; Stone quarries & stone breaking machines; Nursery & greenhouse — sale room of plants & seeds — cut flowers; Surveyors & agents & architects offices: Hotel/s (2); Livery stable & track for extension; Bakery (2), Refreshment rooms — Restaurant; Churches —Parsonages; Cemetery; Post office; Public school houses — Gymnasium; Playground for ball & other games — skating pond; Working men houses separate — also lodging houses for single men & women; Picnic house and grounds — trout pond; Law regulating property in roads & management of public grounds." The other page, which does not appear to be in McHenry's handwriting, includes: "Should there be any reservation of ground for churches — hotels — club house &c — shops -; [and] Regard should be had to easy drainage by the roads."

85. In another undated draft, McHenry wrote to an H. Clay Dallam to suggest through him to the commissioners authorized to sell the Greenbrier White Sulphur Spring Property in West Virginia, "the preparation and adoption of a plan…with which the Mineral Springs and a liberal allotment of land would be reserved and placed under suitable management for public use and enjoyment, in the shape of parks, drives, sites for buildings, etc., another allotment ... shall be laid off in Avenues and building lots with the intention of offering such lots for sale separately, whilst the more distant lands might be sold in large tracts." McHenry compared the potential to that which he observed around "some of the most noted Springs in Europe and this Country" and mentioned Baden-Baden and Wiesbaden in Europe and Saratoga in New York, among others. JHMP/MD-MHS, 544: 3, JHM to H. Clay Dallam, undated draft. (McHenry's interest in suburban village and township development must have been common to a number of estate owners of that time. In addition to topics such as "The Best Method of Treating Barn Yard Manure," "Cultivation of Corn" and "The Most Economical Employment of Farm Labor in Winter," the Garrison Farmers' Club agenda regularly included discussion of such topics as "County Roads," the "Township System" and "Mending and Making Roads." Garrison Forest Farmers' Club Minutes, MD-MHS, 381 (Vol. 1, April 23, 1874 — December, 1876)).

86. McHenry's death was caused by the bite of his favorite St. Bernard dog. After having been bitten, he was able to go to Bar Harbor the summer of 1888, but blood poisoning set in and he died on September 25. The McHenry Family History.

Chapter 3: The Sudbrook Company

1. Articles of Incorporation of Sudbrook Company of Baltimore County (March 16, 1889), Box WMI #2, pp. 309–311, CR 4260, Maryland State Archives No. CM141, Baltimore County Circuit Court. All incorporation information is taken from these Articles. (Additional purposes were "for the procuring, preparing for market, transportation, and selling of lumber, timber, wood, and other products of Land [and] for opening and working quarries of minerals or mineral substances in the State of Maryland." The Company had an agreement with the McHenry executors permitting it to obtain stone from a quarry on the property).

2. Seven hundred and fifty shares of stock, at a value of $100 per share, were issued. George R. Webb, George W. Haulenbeck, Edward J. Silkman and Hugh L. Bond, Jr., all residents of Baltimore City, and George Dobbing Penniman, a resident of Howard County, were listed as incorporators. The only name that is of continuing interest is that of Hugh L. Bond, Jr., also a director and the president of the Company. The other men, some of whom worked in the same building as Hugh Bond, Jr., may have been his friends or business associates. (The incorporators of a business frequently serve a purely functionary role, signing for the sole purpose of filing the Articles of Incorporation. Except for Bond, none of the five incorporators was ever heard from or mentioned again. A review of R.L. Polk's *Baltimore City Directory* for 1889 lists George W. Haulenbeck as a stenographer (he was also a notary public who notarized later Sudbrook Company deeds). Two persons named George R. Webb are listed, one a general agent (the more likely incorporator) and the other a salesman. The same directory indicates that both Edward J. Silkman and George D. Penniman were lawyers with offices at the B&O Central Building, where Hugh L. Bond, Jr., also a lawyer, was employed by the B&O Railroad. Also, while it may be coincidence rather than a family tie, it is possible that George Penniman was a cousin of Bond's — Hugh Bond's mother was the daughter of William Penniman, "a native of Boston, removed to Baltimore, where he was an agent for northern manufacturers." (See *Baltimore: Its History and Its People,* Vol. II (New York: Lewis Historical Publishing Co., 1912), p. 597.)

3. Of the seven original Directors, almost nothing is known about Charles Hill or John Geigan. A review of R.L. Polk's *Baltimore City Directory* for 1889 shows listings for two men named Charles G. Hill, one a cabinetmaker and the other a physician (the more likely director). John H. Geigan's business is listed as Geigan & Co. In addition to being a director, Geigan appeared to be a stockholder in the Sudbrook Co. In 1898, a guardian for one of the heirs of the Geigan estate requested financial information from the Sudbrook Company and inquired, apparently, about selling Geigan's stock. (BR&AB/MD-MHS, 131: 4: 4, pp. 356 and 358, EB to Stuart Kearney and C.W. Woolford, respectively, March 2, 1898). The Boston directors, Richard Weld and Robert Winsor, both were stockholders and Winsor was involved actively in the design phase of the project. The only Philadelphia director was James D. Winsor; there is a strong likelihood that he also was a stockholder. Baltimore directors Eugene Blackford, a long-standing friend of McHenry's, and Hugh L. Bond, Jr., both became principal players in developing Sudbrook Park.

4. BR&AB/MD-MHS, 131: 3: 1, p. 136, EB to G.C. Wilmer, Feb. 18, 1892, and p. 123, EB to N.L. Hipsley, Jan. 18, 1892. Blackford also noted: "It is our objective to attract residents of the best class, by offering every inducement that has been introduced by similar enterprises around Phila. & Boston, which have been taken as models." The inducements referred to included lots of not less than an acre, "macadamized roads with side walks of gravel & trees planted in an intervening strip," each house "required to be drained by the Waring absorption plan," and "a four inch water main…laid in each road, giving an unlimited supply of the purest water."

5. McHenry appeared interested in developing a much larger portion of his estate than the Sudbrook Co. purchased. Roullier surveyed 700 acres at least and the 1883 *Maryland Journal* article noted that McHenry had a plan for an 850-acre suburban community. The Sudbrook Co. purchased 204 acres, and held an option on another 100 acres that it never exercised.

6. BR&AB/MD-MHS, 131: 3: 1, p. 394, EB to Edwin Howland/Boston, July 5, 1893. No other names or lists of Boston stockholders have been found.

7. **Robert Winsor (1858–1930)**, listed in the 1897–1942 *Who Was Who in America,* was the son of Dr. Frederick and Anne B. (Ware) Winsor of Winchester, Massachusetts. He attended Phillips Exeter and graduated from Harvard in 1880, where he was a member of the Hasty Pudding Club. He became a member of Kidder, Peabody & Co. that same year and remained with the firm for fifty years. According to his obituary (*Boston Herald,* Jan. 8, 1930), his "first great coup was the reorganization, with Col. William A. Gaston [a classmate and fellow graduate of Harvard 1880], of the old West End Street Railway into the Boston Elevated Railway Company" (he was one of a few men who conceived the idea of an elevated line to relieve congestion in the business district) and he also merged "the several Greater Boston gas companies into the Boston Consolidated Gas Co." He was a director of numerous corporations, including U.S. Steel Corp., Rockland & Rockport Lime Co., N.E. Coal & Coke Co., Boston Consol. Gas Co., Boston Elevated Ry. Co., Union Mills, Bigelow-Hartford Carpet Co., Kidder Peabody Acceptance Corp., Lawrence Bldg. Inc., Winchester Repeating Arms Co., Waltham Watch Co., Mystic Iron Works, Peabody Trust Co. and the Sudbrook Co. He was also a trustee of Mass. Gas Cos. and the Brooks Cubicle Hosp., Boston Dwelling House Co. At his death, numerous tributes poured in, including one from the Governor of Massachusetts, the Secretary of the Navy and other prominent leaders. Attorney William H. Coolidge, a long-time friend, recalled Winsor's "indomitable will" which he first saw when they played a baseball game in college. Bob Winsor caught "without mask, gloves or other protection" and "Harvard beat Yale largely through his courage. He was not a regular catcher. He was a marvelous football player, and was known in his day as 'the prince of goal-kickers.' I remember his kicking five goals from the field in one game. He was popular with the student body, and whenever he made up his mind to do anything, he did it. He entered the senior year with 11 conditions, passed them all off, took the regular course and got his degree with Theodore Roosevelt and Robert Bacon. The day after his graduation in 1880, he secured employment with Kidder, Peabody & Co. as office boy at a salary of $100 a year. The following Christmas his bonus was larger than the bonus of any other employee of the firm, because they believed he had been the most useful man they had." An article about Winsor when he was forty-five described him as "medium height, erect, well though sparely built, dark moustache, alert black eyes" and noted "the secret of his success has been work, work, work…[but] in spite of a phenomenal amount of work — golf, his love of outdoors, and his habits of life have kept him young." Winsor married Eleanor May Magee in 1883 and they had four children. His home "Chestnut Farm" was in Weston, Mass. He died suddenly following a heart attack on Jan. 7, 1930, while on a business trip. (Robert Winsor's brother, Frederick, a prominent educator, was one of the organizers and the first headmaster (1897–1900) of the Country School for Boys in Baltimore (now Gilman School)). (Information about Robert Winsor was compiled from *Who Was Who in America,* Vol. 1, 1897–1942 (Chicago: E.A.N. Marquis Company, 1942), p. 1367 (hereafter referred to as *Who Was Who in America*), and the following articles provided by the Harvard University Archives: "Funeral Services will Be Held Tomorrow for Winsor" in the Jan. 8, 1930, *Boston Herald;* "Robert Winsor Dies in New York Hotel," *Boston Transcript,* Jan. 7, 1930; and clippings dated 1903–04 with no citation given. (Information about Frederick Winsor from *Who Was Who in America,* p. 1367, and courtesy of Liz Dausch, Gilman Development Office).

Robert Bacon (1860–1919), also listed in *Who Was Who in America,* was born in Boston, attended Hopkinson's school and entered Harvard in 1876 at the age of sixteen, graduating in the class of 1880. While at Harvard he began a friendship with Theodore Roosevelt that continued through life. Six feet tall with broad shoulders, Bacon was captain of the baseball team, captain of the university football team and a member of the university crew team. While he "displayed no particular bent in his studies and perhaps not more than an average ability in them," he was "popular with everybody" — first marshal and permanent president of his class, president of the Harvard Glee Club, and a member of the Hasty Pudding Club. After graduation, he was employed by the Boston banking house of Lee, Higginson & Co. for two years. In 1883, he became a member of E. Rollins Morse & Bro. until 1894, when he became a member of J. P. Morgan & Co. and moved to New York. He became an unofficial consultant to his old classmate and friend Theodore Roosevelt, who took over as President of the United States in 1901 when William McKinley was assassinated and who was reelected as President in 1904. On Jan. 1, 1903, Bacon retired from J.P. Morgan, "the strain of his work at 23 Wall Street [having] brought him to the verge of a breakdown." He and his wife went to Europe for a rest. President Roosevelt appointed him Assistant Secretary of State from 1905–1909 and he served as Secretary of State for a brief time in 1909. From 1909–1912, Bacon served as ambassador to France, having been appointed by President Taft. When he resigned, he was elected a Fellow of Harvard College. At the outbreak of the European war, he made repeated trips to France to organize an ambulance service and other projects to support the allies. He declared himself "strictly unneutral" in the war and urged Americans to take "vigorous measures against Germany." He was commissioned in the reserves and served with Gen. Pershing's staff in France until 1918, attaining the rank of Colonel. He returned, determined to take a rest, but died on May 29, 1919, from blood poisoning caused by mastoiditis. Bacon was survived by his wife and four children. His estate, consisting primarily of stocks and bonds, was valued at over seven million dollars. (Information was compiled from *Who Was Who in America*, p. 42, and the following articles provided by the Harvard University Archives: "Robert Bacon, '80" by William Roscoe Thayer, '81, in the *Harvard Alumni Bulletin*, June 26, 1919; "Colonel Robert Bacon," *Boston Transcript*, May 31, 1919; "Robert Bacon Estate Valued at $7,585,565," *New York Times*, July 29, 1920; and clippings with no citation given.)

Henry Bainbridge Chapin (1857–1910) was born in Springfield, Massachusetts. His grandfather and an uncle had been presidents of the Boston & Albany Railroad. Chapin attended Harvard College, where he and Theodore Roosevelt became friends. After graduating in the class of 1880, he traveled abroad for a year and a half. Upon his return, he accepted a position in the freight department of the Boston & Albany Railroad; two months later he was appointed General Freight Agent and in 1898 was named General Traffic Manager. He resigned in 1903 to start the Boston firm of Schirmer, Chapin & Emmons, bankers and brokers, and he remained there until May 3, 1910, when he resigned for health reasons. He was a director in the Boston Consolidated Gas Company, Boston & Albany Railroad, Mass. Bonding and Insurance Company, Taunton & New Bedford Copper Company, and President and Director of the Ware River Railroad Co. He was also a Trustee of the Faulkner Hospital and Adams Nervine Asylum. Chapin married Susan Torrey Revere and they had two sons. The younger of Chapin's two sons, named for his father, was killed in an accident in 1908. Chapin's Harvard obituary notes: "This great sorrow, which he bore so manfully, may have had some connection with his illness. He appeared to maintain his robust health until a few months ago, when an operation disclosed a cancer in the abdomen, which was incurable." Chapin was survived by his wife and older son, John, a student at Harvard at the time of his father's death. Among Chapin's pallbearers were Robert Winsor, William A. Gaston, and C. Minot Weld, all graduates of Harvard, class of 1880. [Robert Bacon was in France at the time, but his son served as an usher]. (Information was compiled from the following articles provided by the Harvard University Archives: "Henry B. Chapin Dead," in the *Boston Globe* and also in the *Boston American*, May 8, 1910, and clippings with no citation given).

Richard Harding Weld (1835–1908), also from Boston, attended Harvard, graduating with the class of 1856. After college, he worked with Cunningham Bros. in Boston for two years, when he entered business with his father, Aaron D. Weld, who was an importer of Russian merchandise. When the Civil War began, Mr. Weld served as captain of the Forty-Fourth Massachusetts Regiment. He married Laura Townsend Winsor, daughter of Alfred Winsor, in 1866 and again joined his father in business. The name of the firm was changed to Aaron D. Weld & Sons, merchandise brokers, and later was changed to Aaron D. Weld's Sons. He remained with the family business throughout his lifetime, serving as head of the company for almost thirty-four years. Weld was also director and vice president of the Market National Bank and the Ludlow Manufacturing Associates, and president of the Sweetwater Fruit Company. He was survived by his wife and two sons, Richard H. Weld, Jr. and Alfred Winsor Weld. (Information was compiled from the following articles provided by the Harvard University Archives: "Richard H. Weld Dead," *Boston Herald*, Mar. 31, 1908; "Deaths. Richard H. Weld," *Springfield (Mass.) Union*, April 2, 1908; *Textile World*, Boston, May, 1908; Harvard biographical information on graduates (1906) and clippings with no citation given; in addition, some biographical information about Weld was provided courtesy of Gary Boyd Roberts of the New England Historic Genealogical Society, telephone interview on June 27, 1996). [Note: Also graduating from Harvard in 1880 was a Christopher Minot Weld of Boston, who became a financier. C.M. Weld was President of Mass. Gas Cos. and Robert Winsor, his classmate, was a director of Mass. Gas Cos. Both C.M. Weld and Robert Winsor served as directors on the boards of some of the same corporations. It is not known whether C.M. Weld was related to Richard Weld, but if so, his friendship with Winsor might have been the link which resulted in the more senior Weld's investing in the Sudbrook venture. Of course, Richard Weld also was married to Laura Winsor, who may have provided the link. And one of J. Howard McHenry's relatives, Mary Sophia Read, married an Arthur L. Weld; they lived in Howard County, Maryland and visited McHenry with some regularity. Whether Arthur Weld might have been related to the Boston Welds, and been one of the connections between the McHenry property and the Boston investors, is not known.]

8. It is not known whether Laura Winsor Weld was related to either Robert Winsor or James D. Winsor, but it is quite possible that she was.

9. *Who Was Who in America*, p. 1367.

10. **James D. Winsor (1843–1921)** was the son of Henry Winsor and Mary Ann Davis. His family owned the Winsor Steamship Line, with offices in Boston, Philadelphia and New York. Born in Boston, James later moved to Philadelphia to run the offices there. He married Rebecca Chapman, who was known as a "formidable woman," in Philadelphia. They had five children — Mary, Henry, Ellen, James D. Jr. and Rebecca. Winsor died at his "Glen Hill" estate in Haverford, Pennsylvania. (Biographical information courtesy of Amb. Curtin Winsor, Jr., telephone interview, Feb. 8, 1996, and subsequent correspondence; other information from Alfred Decker Keator, ed., *Encyclopedia of Pennsylvania Biography* (Philadelphia: Lewis Historical Publishing Co., 1923), pp. 122–124).

11. Curtin Winsor and James D. Winsor IV, grandsons of James, both thought that Robert and James D. Winsor were cousins. Telephone interviews, Feb. 8, 1996. This was confirmed by Curtin Winsor, Jr., who has done significant family research. It is not certain whether they were second or third cousins. Telephone interviews with Curtin Winsor, Jr. on Feb. 8 and Aug. 4, 1996.

12. Nathaniel and Rebecca (Biddle) Chapman had two children, Emily and George. Emily Chapman married John Montgomery Gordon; they had five daughters, but only one, Rebecca Chapman Gordon, survived. She married Eugene Blackford. Emily's brother George Chapman married Emily Marcou; their daughter Rebecca Chapman married James Davis Winsor. (Information from telephone interview with Curtin Winsor, Jr., Aug. 4, 1996, and an article by Douglas Gordon, "A Virginian and His Baltimore Diary," *Maryland Historical Magazine*, Vol. 49, No. 3 (September 1954). I am particularly grateful to Curtin Winsor, Jr. who provided the information necessary for me to verify this family connection).

13. Harvard University Archives (the 1903–04 news clipping, source not identified, states the following about Robert Winsor: "Again his name figures as a leading spirit in the organization of the Boston Steamship Co., the Boston and Philadelphia Steamship Co., and the New England Cotton Yarn Co.")

14. *Encyclopedia of Pennsylvania Biography*, p. 123.

15. The Sudbrook Co. records ended in 1907; from 1889 until the records ended, Blackford served as manager of Sudbrook Park.

16. Garrison Forest Farmers' Club Minutes, MD-MHS, Ms. No. 381. There are two volumes of minutes. Vol. 1, dating from 1874–1876, lists among its members Eugene Blackford of "Cleve" in Pikesville and James Howard McHenry of "Sudbrook" in Pikesville. Meetings were held monthly. Vol. 2, dating from 1877–1879, shows that McHenry was the Club Secretary and Blackford the Treasurer for the year beginning April 1877. Blackford remained Treasurer in 1878 also.

Chapter 4: Hugh Lennox Bond, Jr.

1. Information for this profile on Bond, Jr. from: *Transactions: Maryland State Bar Association, 28th Annual Meeting*, Report of Committee on Legal Biography (Baltimore: Maryland State Bar Association, 1923), pp. 25–26; Ella K. Barnard, "'Mount Royal' and Its Owners," *Maryland Historical*

Magazine, Vol. 26, No. 4 (December 1931), pp. 311–315; and information provided by the Harvard University Archives, including: "H.L. Bond, Jr., Dies; Ill Only One Day," *Baltimore Sun,* April 12, 1922; Obituaries, *Baltimore Sun,* April 13 and 14, 1922; and Harvard College obituary. Information on Judge Bond from: *Baltimore, Its History and Its People,* Vol. II (New York: Lewis Historical Publishing Co., 1912), pp. 597–599; and Walter M. Merrill, ed., *Letters of William Lloyd Garrison,* Vol. 5 (Cambridge, MA: Belknap Press of Harvard University Press, 1979) (letter to James Miller McKim from Wm. Lloyd Garrison, Sept. 14, 1865, pp. 293–94; p. 211, fn. 1). [Thanks to Charles Beveridge for bringing the Garrison letters information to my attention.]

Chapter 5: Eugene Blackford

1. Information about Blackford compiled from several sources: (1) original source research, book excerpts, biographical information and letters sent to me by Elisabeth Corddry, including the letter cited in the first indented quote and excerpts from William Willis Blackford, *War Years with Jeb Stuart* (New York: Charles Scribner's & Sons, 1945), pp. x–xi (Introduction by Douglas Southall Freeman, author of *Lee's Lieutenants)* and pp. 231–232; Charles M. Blackford, Campaign and Battle of Lynchburg, Virginia (Lynchburg: Warwick House Publishing, 1994), pp. x–xi and 73; and Robert K. Krick, *Lee's Colonels* (Dayton, Ohio: Morningside, 1992) (Corddry has compiled extensive research on the Blackford family in preparation for writing a book about Eugene Blackford's early years, and she kindly shared pertinent portions of her research with me); (2) the Blackford Record and Account Books, MD–MHS, Ms. No. 131; (3) the Garrison Forest Farmers' Club Minutes, MD-MHS, Ms. No. 381; (4) Dawn F. Thomas, *The Green Spring Valley, Its History and Heritage,* Vol. One, *A History, Historic Homes* (Baltimore: Maryland Historical Society, 1978), pp. 90, 91 and 175; and (5) obituaries in the *Baltimore News,* February 5, 1908, and the *Baltimore Sun,* February 5, 1908. Information about John Montgomery Gordon from Douglas Gordon, "A Virginian and His Baltimore Diary," *Maryland Historical Magazine,* Vol. 49, No. 3 (Sept., 1954), pp. 196–204 (the second indented quote about Cleve is from this article, p. 203).

Chapter 6: John Charles Olmsted

1. Most of the information for this profile was excerpted from a section on John Charles Olmsted by Arleyn A. Levee (see William H. Tishler, ed., *American Landscape Architecture — Designers and Places* (Washington, D.C.: The Preservation Press, 1989), pp. 48–51). Unless otherwise noted, all quotations are from that source. [Author's Note: Although John was adopted by his uncle, Frederick Law Olmsted, Sr., he is often referred to as Olmsted's "stepson" to distinguish him from Olmsted's biological son, Frederick Law Olmsted, Jr. Since this seems the common practice, I have continued it.]
2. Beveridge and Rocheleau, p. 258.
3. Beveridge and Rocheleau, p. 260. See also Beveridge and Rocheleau, pp. 125 and 259–260, for information about John Olmsted's involvement in Druid Hills and the Seattle park system.

Chapter 7: Olmsted's Sudbrook

1. The surviving letters indicate that Hugh Bond, Jr. was the primary correspondent for the Sudbrook Co., although Robert Winsor, the stockholder/director who lived in Boston, was also involved in the planning phase. In 1891 and 1892, there were isolated letters between the Olmsted firm and Eugene Blackford, the manager of the development.
2. Although the design was completed in August 1889 and the Sudbrook Company had the final blueprint from which to work, some minor details (the boarding house lot line) and typographical errors had not been corrected. These remaining details were not attended to until early 1890, at which time the corrected version of the plan was lithographed for use in sales circulars.
3. Some possible scenarios include the following: (1) that Bond, with his interest in botany and architectural design, might have been acquainted with Olmsted's reputation and sought his expertise; (2) that Robert Winsor of Boston might have been familiar with Olmsted's work in the Boston area and sought his services for their venture; or (3) that McHenry himself, before his death, might have re-initiated contact with Olmsted and/or suggested that Olmsted be employed in the event that anyone followed through on his desire to develop his property.
4. Based on signature reproductions, it appears that John C. Olmsted (JCO) was the firm's correspondent with the Sudbrook Company, although his letters also clearly evidence Frederick Law Olmsted's on-going involvement.
5. During 1889, Frederick Law Olmsted (FLO) was involved in demanding and formidable work on the design of the Biltmore estate grounds near Asheville, North Carolina. In addition, because the commissions coming into the Olmsted firm increased significantly around 1889, FLO was no longer able to carry the entire workload himself.
6. OAR/LC, A3: 483, JCO to HLB, April 12, 1889.
7. In the April 12, 1889, letter to Bond, JCO mentioned that he "went to town to see Mr. Winsor…. He was out of town, so I lost the day." Brookline, where FLO lived and had his offices, was just a short distance from Boston. If Winsor was the initiating force in choosing Olmsted, or the initial contact person with Olmsted, it may be that preliminary contacts and discussions were held face-to-face, and that could explain why there are no letters addressing the routine preliminary matters that necessarily precede the commencement of work on a design plan.
8. OAR/LC, 1054: B75: R54, HLB to JCO, April 15, 1889. The Olmsteds did change the location of the bridge, moving it a little further from the station than the location chosen by the surveyor. See, OAR/LC, A: 4: 604–607, FL&JCO to HLB, April 29, 1889.
9. These limitations accorded with the Company's agreement with the McHenry executors to provide one acre for a train station and that any plan include a freight siding, which was to be placed at the grade crossing.
10. Bond never identified "the Sudbrook Company's architects" by name. Subsequent letters of Eugene Blackford, manager, identify the Boston firm of Cabot, Everett and Mead as the architects of Cottages 1 and 2, built about the same time as the station, and imply that this Boston firm functioned as the Company's architects. The principals of the firm were Edward Clark Cabot, Arthur G. Everett and Samuel W. Mead. The firm practiced under the name Cabot, Everett and Mead until 1900. No firm records survive. Information about Cabot, Everett and Mead courtesy of Robert Sturgis, a Boston architect (telephone interview, July 2, 1996).
11. OAR/LC, 1054: B75: R54, HLB to JCO, April 15, 1889. One reason for building the area near the bridge and station first was to be able to transport into the community the needed materials for constructing roads and houses. The freight siding would have been integral to these early construction efforts.
12. The executors of the Last Will and Testament of James Howard McHenry were his wife Sally McHenry, his son Wilson Cary McHenry and McHenry Howard. McHenry's will was "absolutely ratified and confirmed" on April 8, 1890. JHMAB/MD-MHS, 544.2: 3, Will and estate ledger, pp. 40–47.
13. The cited provision also required that the Company build "no mean dwelling" and that liquor not be sold on the property. A second provision might also have placed an urgency on the Company to get the development underway. It stated that the executors "will not before July 1, 1891 sell any land within ¼ mile of the proposed Railroad station and will not before Jan. 1, 1894, sell any large tract of land out of said Sudbrook estate for the

purpose of starting an enterprise similar to that of the Sudbrook Company of Baltimore County aforesaid without first giving the said Company an opportunity to take the tract at the price offered by the would be purchaser or purchasers thereof." In addition to the two provisions noted, there were six other points to the agreement. These required (1) the executors to donate the land necessary "for the bed of an Avenue from the proposed Railroad station to the Reisterstown Turnpike at a point opposite to the Arsenal (as now actually laid out) for the use of the Sudbrook Company," with title to remain in the estate; (2) that the Sudbrook Company would have the right "at any time before the first day of January 1891 to purchase an additional one hundred acres of said Sudbrook estate lying to the south west of and adjoining said…tract hereby sold and fronting on the Seven Mile or Milford [Mill] Road, at the rate of three hundred dollars per acre;" [Note: the Company had purchased its 204 acres at $123.52 per acre.] (3) that the Sudbrook Company would "obtain the promise of the W.M.R.R. signed by its President to establish the Railroad station and to build a sufficient and attractive station building with freight siding and express and telegraph office" and would guarantee the establishment of the station and the erection of the station building; (4) that the Sudbrook Company would "build the said Avenue from the proposed Station to the Reisterstown Turnpike fifty feet wide with a thirty-foot road bed in the centre and before so doing [would] fence both sides thereof"; (5) that within three years the Company would open a road from the railroad station to the Milford Road (also called the Seven Mile or County Road) and the western corner of the property (and over the optioned land, if the Company exercised its option); and (6) that the Company would give the right-of-way "for a road from the proposed Railroad station through the triangular piece of the property which lies to the north east of the W.M.R.R., to the adjoining part of the Sudbrook estate lying to the north east of the said railroad…in order that access may be had from said adjoining part of the estate to the Railroad station." JHMAB/MD-MHS, 544.2: 3, Will and Estate Ledger, pp. 40–47.

14. In an August 29, 1868, letter to Calvert Vaux after having seen Riverside, Olmsted complained about the rushed schedule the developer, E. E. Childs, wanted the landscape architects to observe, lamenting: "He wants to put 2000 men at work within a week & wants us to manage everything." In order to prepare the Riverside plan at a time when he was over-committed with other work and Vaux was in Europe, Olmsted had to hire additional help to survey the land, to assist in determining an overall design and to do the drafting. See, Schuyler and Censer, ed., pp. 269–70 and p. 292.

15. OAR/LC, A: 4: 493, FL&JCO to HLB, April 15, 1889. Because Bond was anxious to begin selling lots immediately, the Olmsteds suggested that he could do so before a final plan was completed by using a short memorandum of sale. This agreement would refer to the block and lot number on the preliminary study already prepared, and would also note that the lot was being sold subject to restrictions that were to be dated, signed and kept with the preliminary plan. They asked again about this suggestion in a letter of April 25. Despite the pressure that the Sudbrook Company put on the Olmsted firm to hastily provide a plan or portion thereof so that the Company could make sales of lots, no lots were sold to outside purchasers in 1889 or 1890.

16. A May 1890 letter from Bond stated that the Company already had "a cottage and several lots under contracts of sale." (OAR/LC, C: 2 (unbound, general correspondence), HLB to JCO, May 14, 1890). However, early Blackford letters indicate that all nine original cottages were owned by the Company and there were no lot or cottage sales until Bond obtained title to Cottage No. 11 (1018 Winsor Rd.) in 1891 (the house had been built in 1890). If the Company had difficulty selling lots, this no doubt stemmed from the fact that when the community began, Sudbrook was considered by many to be too remote from the city to be a desirable location for a year-round home, as Sally McHenry had complained. While it may be difficult in today's world to imagine Sudbrook as an isolated outpost, consider that even when construction of the Baltimore beltway (located only a few miles west of Sudbrook Park) was completed in 1962, "fairly little damage was done to the built environment by the beltway [because] few suburban communities had been set up that far from the center city at the time." McGrain, p. 14 (noting, however, that the route cut "a swath through the great Queen Anne houses of Eden Terrace at Catonsville" and demolished Ashlyons, the home of nineteenth century cotton lord John Wethered. McGrain, p. 15).

17. In late nineteenth century America, "cottage" was a widely used term that related more to the style than to the size of a house. Cottages encompassed a variety of architectural types, but primarily reflected picturesque, quaint, comfortable and — compared to the grand and ostentatious country estates of the day — humble single family abodes, usually made of batten wood or shingle exterior. The term "cottage" implied a simplicity and closeness to the land; few cottages ever became a part of a truly urban setting. Many cottages of the period were built using the Shingle Style. As noted by architectural historian Vincent Scully: "The shingles were normally dark…later much lighter…. The houses were both new and old, freely serving and suggesting every kind of domestic relaxation while at the same time linking modern life with an American past seemingly more primordial than it had ever been in fact and endowed with a national history freshly valued and newly loved." Vincent Scully, introduction to *The Architecture of the American Summer: The Flowering of the Shingle Style,* Robert A. M. Stern, ed. (U.S.A: Rizzoli International Publishers, Inc., 1989), p. 6. (Thanks to Darragh Brady, A.I.A.).

18. OAR/LC, A: 4: 531, FL&JCO to HLB, April 19, 1889.

19. OAR/LC, A: 4: 573–583, FL&JCO to HLB, April 25, 1889 (explaining that the reason for requiring a map on a one hundred foot scale is that "if we enlarge our plan from the 200 foot scale there might be an error in the total length, which taking into account also the shrinking and stretching which paper is liable to, might be 50 or 100 feet when run out on the ground. With a fresh map plotted from notes of the actual survey, the error ought not (on the 100 foot scale) to exceed 5 or 10 feet.").

20. OAR/LC, A: 4: 536, FL&JCO to HLB, April 20, 1889.

21. OAR/LC, A: 4: 546, FL&JCO to HLB, April 22, 1889.

22. OAR/LC, A: 4: 573–583, FL&JCO to HLB, April 25, 1889. The Olmsteds wrote that "to make these radial curves…sufficiently accurate to be 'run out' at any time and time after time by any good surveyor on the ground, requires that they should be **measured on the ground** and careful notes kept and plotted. This is surveyor's work, which we do not do." (Emphasis in original). Two years later, Eugene Blackford wrote to Olmsted stating: "I have had great difficulty in securing engineers able to put your plat of Sudbrook Park upon the ground. I have been delayed in the development of the property on that account." Blackford claimed to have located an engineer who thought that he could "give satisfaction" and asked Olmsted for information about the meridian on the plat. BR&AB, MD-MHS, 131: 3: 1, p. 32, EB to FLO, Sept. 3, 1891. A short time later, Blackford complained to his friend and fellow director James Winsor: "I have furbished up my old knowledge of engineering, and am now laying down the balance of the plat upon the ground, thereby saving a good deal of money & much vexation, and we have never been able to find but one engineer who could work after Mr. Olmsted's plan, the data being very meager." BR&AB, MD-MHS, 131: 3: 1, p. 92, EB to JDW, Oct. 28, 1891.

23. OAR/LC, A: 4: 573–583, FL&JCO to HLB, April 25, 1889. As noted previously, Olmsted's roads of continuous curvature exasperated engineers and surveyors. Then, as today, the more common method of creating curves (and that favored by engineers) was a straight segment of road, followed by a curve, followed by another straight segment. This tangent/curve/tangent approach is quite different, in both form and effect, from the continuous curvature used by Olmsted in his designs. (Continuous curvature is more aesthetically appealing, and also tends to slow vehicles. It may even be safer, since drivers do not have to readjust from a straight-away to a curve). (Opinions are mine. Thanks to Catherine Mahan, ASLA, for suggesting the aptly descriptive phrase "roads of continuous curvature" and for information about differing methods of making curves).

24. OAR/LC, A: 4: 573–583, FL&JCO to HLB, April 25, 1889.

25. OAR/LC, A: 4: 573–583, FL&JCO to HLB, April 25, 1889 (emphasis in original).

26. OAR/LC, A: 4: 573–583, FL&JCO to HLB, April 25, 1889.

27. OAR/LC, 1054: B75: R54, HLB to FL&JCO, April 27, 1889. Shortly thereafter, Winsor wrote Olmsted that it was "unnecessary at present" to make drawings for the third 100 acres, "though I think the fact that we may take the other 100 acres should be borne in mind while laying out the first 200." OAR/LC, 1054: B75: R54, RW to "Mr. Olmstead [sic]," May 4, 1889. (It was not unusual, then or now, for persons to misspell Olmsted's name. Even Sudbrook Park has a street built in the 1940s, ostensibly named after its designer, but spelled "Olmstead Road.")

28. OAR/LC, 1054: B75: R54, HLB to FL&JCO, April 27, 1889. Bond stated that the station location on the preliminary plan was too far westward, and its location was to be one hundred feet or more eastward of the railroad grade crossing.

29. As noted in Chapter 1, Olmsted was interested in creating permanent healthfulness and permanent beauty in his residential communities.

30. OAR/LC, A: 4: 604–607, FL&JCO to HLB, April 29, 1889.

31. OAR/LC, 1054: B75: R54, HLB to FL&JCO, April 27, 1889.

32. OAR/LC, A: 4: 604–607, FL&JCO to HLB, April 29, 1889 (emphasis in original).

33. OAR/LC, A: 4: 604–607, FL&JCO to HLB, April 29, 1889. This dual boarding house suggestion was never pursued. The final plan located the boarding house nearer the station and reserved the Cliveden triangle for a church or other building.

34. OAR/LC, A: 4: 604–607, FL&JCO to HLB, April 29, 1889 (noting: "If, however, our 'study' has the station in the right place, it is probably right as to the bridge location. We moved the bridge a little further from the station than your surveyor had put it on the diagram, in order to get distance enough for a 5 per cent grade in the two roads between them. If the contours are a good guide as to the heights of the ground, the one of these bridge-station approaches which lies to the north of the railroad follows the surface as well as could be expected, while the other involves a 'cut' of four feet. If this amount of cutting brought the grade down into the rock, it might be necessary to make a wider detour, to save expense. These questions can probably be determined at the time we visit the grounds.")

35. OAR/LC, A: 4: 725–726, JCO to HLB, May 18, 1889. In a previous letter, Bond indicated that he had not realized that so much work would be needed to prepare a working drawing: "I supposed the curves were taken from forms which you had used elsewhere and on which your calculations were ready made, and under that impression, telegraphed you for the radii…. If I have put you to extra trouble, I am sorry." OAR/LC, 1054: B75: 54, HLB to FL&JCO, April 27, 1889.

36. OAR/LC, A: 4: 725–726, JCO to HLB, May 18, 1889. We do not know for certain to what John Olmsted was referring when he mentioned the "other causes of delay in getting your land on the market," but it seems likely he could have meant problems with the McHenry heirs and representatives of the estate, which were reflected in other letters.

37. OAR/LC, 1054: B75: R54, RW to "Mr. Olmstead [sic]," May 20, 1889.

38. OAR/LC, A: 4: 741–743, JCO to RW (with the salutation "Robert" inserted above "Mr. Winsor"), May 21, 1889.

39. OAR/LC, A: 4: 768, FL&JCO to HLB, May 24, 1889. (The area near the bridge was heavily wooded at the time).

40. See the following: OAR/LC, A: 4: 768, FL&JCO to HLB, May 24, 1889; A: 4: 773–775, FL&JCO to HLB, May 28, 1889; A: 4: 822–824, FL&JCO to HLB, June 5, 1889; 1054: B75: R54, HLB to FL&JCO, June 12, 1889; A: 4: 861, JCO to HLB, June 12, 1889; A: 4: 874, JCO to HLB, June 15, 1889; and A: 4: 926, JCO to HLB, July 8, 1889.

41. In May, JCO wrote to Bond, stating: "I think that as soon as the station is started we ought to study out a working drawing for grading the roads and paths and garden plots about it as it is quite a complicated problem." To do this, the Olmsteds needed a more detailed topographical survey of the vicinity of the station. OAR/LC, A: 4: 725–726, JCO to HLB, May 18, 1889. The same request was repeated to Bond in letters of May 24, June 5 and June 12, 1889. It appeared that the Olmsteds were still awaiting this topographical survey in July. OAR/LC, A: 5: 22–24, JCO to HLB, July 20, 1889.

42. OAR/LC, A: 5: 22–24, JCO to HLB, July 20, 1889.

43. OAR/LC, A: 5: 39–41, JCO to HLB, July 23, 1889.

44. OAR/LC, A: 5: 39–41, JCO to HLB, July 23, 1889.

45. OAR/LC, C: 2 (unbound, general correspondence), HLB to JCO, January 16, 1890.

46. OAR/LC, A: 5: 39–41, JCO to HLB, July 23, 1889.

47. JHMP, MD-MHS, 544: 2, S. Chew to JHM, March 6, 1875 (Chew apparently resided at Germantown and wrote the following to McHenry: "I was exceedingly glad to hear of your visit to Cliveden (you have the correct orthography of the name) and much regretting [sic] not seeing you there. You may remember that your grandmother was married there and that Gen. Washington made a memorandum in his diary of having dined there with the wedding guests.") McHenry was related to the Chews; his much esteemed Uncle Ben was Benjamin Chew Howard. JHMJ, MD-MHS, 544.1: 2 (Vol. 14), 1872 diary, entry of March 6, 1872. ("Cliveden" is now a National Trust Historic Site, with a colorful but somewhat convoluted history. The stone country home was built by Benjamin Chew (1722–1810), a successful Philadelphia lawyer, and named "Cliveden" after an estate he had seen in England. Information on Cliveden's history courtesy of Sandy Lloyd, Curator of Education, Cliveden of the National Trust).

48. JHMP, MD-MHS, 544: 4, Notes of JHM, July 15, 1876 (stating, in part, that James McHenry, JHM's grandfather, had been born in Ballymena County, Antrim, Ireland on Nov. 16, 1753; had come to America in 1771; studied medicine under Benjamin Rush of Philadelphia; joined the army at Valley Forge and was "present at the battle of Monmouth.") [The Battle of Monmouth, New Jersey, took place during the Revolutionary War on June 28, 1778, when Gen. George Washington attacked the British. Neither side won an advantage and the battle ended in a draw. *The World Book Encyclopedia,* Vol. 16 (Chicago: Field Enterprises Educational Corporation, 1977), pp. 260 and 266.]

49. Barnes, p. 62.

50. Carisbrook also is the name of a castle in the Isle of Wight, which may have had some meaning to McHenry from his travels, but I have found no information on this. (Thanks to Charles Beveridge).

51. A glade is an open space in a forest.

52. OAR/LC, C: 2 (unbound, general correspondence), HLB to FLO & JCO, January 16, 1890. While noting that "no important changes have been found necessary," Bond did point out that the location of the boarding house and two small cottages on Block 17 of the blueprint were only "approximately located," while the locations of the cottages in Blocks 15 and 16 (at 511 and 508 Sudbrook Lane, respectively) were accurate. In conclusion, he added: "I hope now that you can speedily have the sale plats printed,…of course, the sooner we can get them the better."

53. OAR/LC, A: 5: 39–41, JCO to HLB, July 23, 1889. The letter asked if the Company wanted to widen Milford, but it is clear from the full text of the letter and Olmsted's cross-sections that the Olmsteds were not asking about widening the roadbed itself, but were referring to increasing the total right-of-way to include sidewalks. (There may well have been a wall along Milford Mill Road at the time. The Olmsteds and later letters of Blackford make reference to it, without going into any detail. Since Milford was the County Road, it is possible that McHenry had built a wall along it. A resident who moved to Sudbrook in 1939 recalled seeing two gate posts at what is now Sudbrook Lane and Milford Mill Road, as well as fences and a bridle path along Milford. Telephone interview with Stella Hazard, July 28, 1996).

54. OAR/LC, C: 2 (unbound, general correspondence), HLB to Messrs. J.C. Olmsted & Co. [sic], January 27, 1890.

55. OAR/LC, A :5: 39–41, JCO to HLB, July 23, 1889. Bond apparently did not get around to providing anything except the proposed location of the boarding house, the station, the water tower and four cottages which are shown on the General Plan for Sudbrook dated August 24, 1889. On a second lithograph dated 1890, only one badly deteriorated copy of which has been located and which is not among the lithograph collection at the Frederick Law Olmsted National Historic Site ("Fairsted"), the Plan and the station remain the same but the boarding house and all nine of the original cottages built by the Sudbrook Company and rented out beginning the summer of 1890 are shown in their actual locations as identified in Blackford's correspondence.

56. Corrections to the proof of the plan were still being made in February 1890, when Bond wrote to correct the corporate name (noting it was not the Sudbrook "Land" Company) and the distance to Pikesville (from $^1/_2$ to $^1/_3$ mile). OAR/LC, C: 2 (unbound, general correspondence), HLB to FLO, February 14, 1890. [Note: the location of the boarding house and two small cottages near it are not accurate on the Aug. 24, 1889, plan; in fact, the

boarding house is situated on a lot line. JCO noted this in a Jan. 24, 1890 letter to Bond, who replied that a dotted line should be used to show that lot line. The mistake was corrected in a subsequent lithograph (see fn. 55, immediately above)].

57. The letter noted that the drawing did not show the detail of construction but only the surface arrangements and discussed that the Olmsteds' recommendation to make "the whole width of the road of a side hill in a 'cut' was not economical in construction but justifiable in not injuring the value of the down hill side of roads for selling." OAR/LC, A: 4: 773–775, FL&JCO to HLB, May 28, 1889.

58. OAR/LC, A: 4: 822–824, FL&JCO to HLB, June 5, 1889 (noting that the trees should have "a hole dug for each one, 3 feet square and two feet deep, which should be filled with good topsoil. This is usually done after the street is built, but it would be cheaper to do it at the time of construction.") Although the sidewalks are no longer visible, Cliveden Road provides an example of a road that had an eighteen foot roadbed, a ten-foot planting space and six-foot sidewalks (the graveled remnants of which can still be uncovered). (Thanks to John Leith-Tetrault and Michael Sotir for their assistance in locating the old sidewalks).

59. Quote from "Cross-sections for Roads" [orig.] (June 5, 1889), National Park Service — Frederick Law Olmsted National Historic Site: 1054–5 (The Sudbrook Land Co. of Baltimore Co.).

60. OAR/LC, A: 4: 822–824, FL&JCO to HLB, June 5, 1889 (adding, with respect to the turf strips: "As you must be very economical in road building, we think that a depth of **three** inches of top soil will do in the turf strips **when they are on a fill** and **six** inches in depth when **in a cut.**") (Emphasis in original.)

61. Macadam was popular "in less-traveled residential and suburban routes" in the late nineteenth century. Asphalt and concrete became available about this time, but their use did not become widespread until later in the twentieth century. Jackson, p. 164. Jackson also noted that while macadam worked well for carriages and horses, the suction of automobile tires tore it to pieces. Although the Sudbrook Co.'s letters and advertisements in the 1890s and early 1900s touted their "paved" roads, residents who recalled the community in the 1920s talked of "dirt" roads. It is quite possible that, with the advent of the automobile around 1908 and its increased usage between 1913 and 1923 (see Jackson, pp. 160–162), and without continual upkeep, the macadamized roads reverted to dirt roads.

62. Little seems to have been written about the condition and surfacing of Baltimore's roads in the 1890s, but in 1809, Baltimore's three important turnpike roads — Frederick, York and Reisterstown — were twenty feet wide and stoned twelve inches deep. Even after 1900, when Baltimore County had a thousand miles of roads, only about a third were graveled, the rest were dirt. See Sherry H. Olson, Baltimore, *The Building of An American City* (Baltimore: The Johns Hopkins University Press, 1980), pp. 47 and 289.

63. It is ironic that, as important as sidewalks were in Olmsted's scheme, none have survived in the older-house section of Sudbrook Park. Perhaps because they were graveled and not made of cement, they have disappeared into the ground. But remnants can still be found in many yards. The fact that the older section of Sudbrook Park now lacks sidewalks belies Olmsted's intention and the Sudbrook Company's efforts.

64. Although I did not locate any Sudbrook planting lists, there is Olmsted correspondence in 1890 with Franklin Davis & Co. in Richmond about other jobs. Franklin Davis & Co. apparently had both a Richmond, Va. office/nursery and a Baltimore office/nursery. Blackford ordered trees and shrubs from Baltimore's Franklin Davis & Co. Since Blackford made numerous references to the planting that the Company did along the roadways and on individual properties prior to occupancy, it seems almost certain that additional orders must have been placed or plant materials obtained even though records have not survived.

65. BR&AB, MD-MHS, 131: 3: 1, p. 178, EB to Messrs. Franklin, Davis & Co., April 6, 1892 (This order was canceled by Blackford since he had not heard from them and "I fear it is too late to send out trees.... I lost so great a percentage of trees and shrubs sent me by you last year that I'd not care to run any risks again." MD-MHS, 131: 3: 1, p. 194); 131: 4: 3, p. 137, EB to Franklin, Davis & Co., October 12, 1895; 131: 4: 2, p. 415, EB to Mr. J.W. Saper, April 2, 1901. (Blackford may have misspelled "pisardi," which should have been spelled "Pissardi." It is "one of the best of all small purple-leaved trees, holding much of its color in the American summers. It seems to be hardy wherever the common Plum will stand." Liberty Hyde Bailey, et. al., *Hortus Third, A Concise Dictionary of Plants Cultivated in the United States and Canada,* (New York: Macmillan Publishing Company, 1976), p. 920 and L. H. Bailey, *Cyclopedia of American Horticulture* (London: Macmillan and Co., Limited, 1900), p. 1447. (Thanks to Charles Beveridge). (It is also possible that Blackford, in his efforts to economize, transplanted various trees and shrubs growing naturally in the area. We have no direct evidence of this, but his letters indicated that he used the existing woods to provide fuel for the water system boiler initially and that he tried to economize whenever possible).

66. OAR/LC, A: 4: 498, JCO to HLB, April 16, 1889.

67. *Riverside in 1871...,* p. 13. These restrictions are similar to the initial four mentioned to Bond. There may have been other restrictions in the Riverside deeds, but I was not able to obtain an actual deed and thus rely on the brochure of the Riverside Improvement Company.

68. OAR/LC, A: 4: 501, FL&JCO to HLB, April 17, 1889.

69. OAR/LC, A: 4: 500–518, FL&JCO to HLB, April 17, 1889. (In the later Druid Hills development, eleven restrictions were suggested. While similar to many of Sudbrook's restrictions, they were not as extensive or as detailed). (See also OAR/LC, A: 4: 493, FL&JCO to HLB, April 15, 1889, suggesting that any preliminary agreements for the sale of lots should also reference and contain restrictions "to be afterwards more fully written out in the deed.")

70. OAR/LC, A: 4: 500–518, FL&JCO to HLB, April 17, 1889.

71. Maryland first passed a State Zoning Enabling Act in 1927 (Chapter 705 of the Acts of 1927, subsequently codified as Article 66B of the Annotated Code of Maryland (1957, 1988 Repl. Vol., 1994 Cum. Supp.), but as a charter county, Baltimore County was exempt from many of the provisions in Md. Code Art. 66B (see Md. Code Art. 66B Section 7.03 which states: "Except as provided...this article does not apply to the chartered counties of Maryland."). Cromwell v. Ward, 102 Md. App. 691, 651 A. 2d 424 (1995). As noted in Chapter One, fn. 52, it was not until 1941 that the State legislature passed zoning regulations that applied to all of Baltimore County. McGrain, p. 6).

72. The Olmsteds seemed to anticipate that some prospective purchasers might balk at restrictions. In a May 18, 1889, letter to Bond, JCO sent a copy of a recent deed showing examples of the type of restrictions recommended and commented: "These examples may help you to persuade intending purchasers that there is nothing unheard of or impracticable in such restrictions and clear the way for a strong argument in favor of the **neutrality** of the benefit which is intended to be derived from them." OAR/LC, A: 4: 725–726, JCO to HLB, May 18, 1889 (emphasis in original).

73. Beveridge and Rocheleau, p. 141.

74. Beveridge and Rocheleau, p. 141.

75. BR&AB, MD-MHS, 131: 3: 1, p. 175, EB to John Cowan, April 4, 1892 (these three houses had just been built and were being painted).

76. For example, in 1894, Oscar Webb, who had been renting Cottage No. 9 (501 Sudbrook Lane) in Sudbrook since 1890, wanted the Sudbrook Company to enclose part of the porch on the house. Blackford wrote to John Cowan, the builder, saying: "I do not think it wise to make the alteration, & do not wish to antagonize him. It would be best if you were to dissuade him from it by failing to find any satisfactory way of overcoming the difficulties. Apart from the disfiguring appearance of the change proposed, I would never consent to darken the hall & cellar, which would be the result...." BR&AB, MD-MHA, 131: 3: 1, p. 78, EB to Jno. Cowan, Dec. 4, 1894.

77. OAR/LC, A: 4: 861, FL&JCO to HLB, June 12, 1889. Waring's subsurface irrigation system apparently required a system of sewer pipes that would remove the disposed materials through a water flushing procedure to an outlet or to reserved land, sufficient in size and drainage capability to safely absorb any organic matter and far enough removed from the village population so as not to present any health or sanitary problems. See Waring,

pp. 314–332. Blackford's letters do not indicate the layout of Sudbrook's sewer system. During the planning process, JCO had written to Bond that before the Company sold any lots on the low land, "the future policy as to sewerage ought to be determined, as it may be necessary to get an outlet for sewage or to reserve land for a subsurface irrigation ground." OAR/LC, A: 5: 22– 24, JCO to HLB, July 20, 1889.

78. BCLR, Liber J.W.S. 181, folio 478, Sudbrook Company of Balto. County Deed to Mercantile Trust & Deposit Co. of Balto., September 19, 1890 (giving the bank a first mortgage on all of the Company's Sudbrook property, including "a boarding house with stable, gas plant and out buildings.") By 1903 Sudbrook's boarding house (hotel) had electric lights on the first floor, but lighting for the bedrooms, kitchen, pantries and basement still was "by a Kemp gasoline gas generator" with the tank located fifty yards from the hotel and five feet underground. BR&AB, MD-MHS, 131: 4: 4, p. 300, EB to Messrs. Baldwin & Frick, June 9, 1903). Residents who heated or illuminated with gas may have had to purchase and install their own gas tanks and generators.

79. Electricity was not readily available from Reisterstown Road to Glyndon until 1910; natural gas reached Sudbrook Park by 1929. Neal A. Brooks and Richard Parsons, *Baltimore County Panorama* (Norfolk/Virginia Beach: The Donning Company Publishers, 1988), p. 126. (The Riverside Improvement Co. not only provided roads, walks, water and sewers, but also manufactured gas on the premises and supplied it to its buildings, roads, roadway gas lights and park areas. *Riverside in 1871…*, p. 15.

80. OAR/LC, A: 9: 77, JCO to Col. Geo. E. Waring, July 22, 1890 (responding to Waring's letter of the previous day asking for copies of regulations or restrictions "on use, building, etc. — for the government of residence parks." OAR/LC, C: 2 (unbound, general correspondence), Geo. E. Waring, Jr. to F.L. Olmsted & Co., July 21, 1890).

81. OAR/LC, A: 9: 109, JCO to Col. Geo. E. Waring, July 26, 1890. John Olmsted sent Waring a copy of the form of deed adopted by the Sudbrook Company. Waring thanked him for the document "showing the restrictions and regulations under which sales are made," noting that it "will answer my purpose admirably." OAR/LC, C: 2 (unbound, general correspondence), Geo. E. Waring, Jr. to J.C. Olmstead [sic], July 28, 1890. It is interesting to speculate whether Waring shared the copy of Sudbrook's deed with Roland Park's developers with whom he would work the following year. Roland Park's early deeds contained some similar, but not nearly as extensive, restrictions.

82. For example, the wording of one of the Olmsted provisions provided that only one dwelling could be erected if a lot was less than two acres, but if larger, that one dwelling could be erected on each full acre. The Sudbrook Company reworded that provision to say that "one dwelling only shall be erected on the lot if the lot is one acre or less," and retained the wording as to lots over two acres. (The Olmsted plan included not only lots of one acre or more, but a number of lots that ranged from .4 to .9 acre, as well as some lots of .2 or .3 acre or less). The wording of item No. 14 regarding permissible sewage disposal was changed rather early in the deeds to delete "a leaching cesspool" and leave only "by subsurface irrigation or shall be removed to a safe distance." Other minor wording changes were made which did not affect the substance of any provision. Also, wording was added to provision No. 10 to include "that no wine, distilled or fermented liquor or intoxicating drink of any kind shall ever be sold or offered for sale…." In addition, Olmsted's provision (not numbered) that required that the Sudbrook Company not sell any land abutting on either side of any lot conveyed or directly facing it, without embodying in the deeds all of the same restrictions, did not apply to land adjoining and lying in the rear of the land conveyed. The Sudbrook Company modified that provision to state that: "…this shall not be held to apply to land adjoining the land hereby conveyed and lying in the rear of the same, **except as to the 8th, 10th, 11th, 12th, 13th and 14th restrictions above….**" (emphasis added; see Appendix A for the text of the cited restrictions).

83. Some examples of deeds listing $2,500 as the minimum price: Liber L.M.B. 193, folio 230, Aug. 4, 1892 (deed to George Coursen); Liber L.M.B. 203, folio 48 (deed to Sophie L. Graves); and Liber L.M.B. 205, folio 334, June 26, 1894 (deed to John Glenn, Trustee). A deed listing $3,000 as the minimum price: Liber L.M.B. 199, folio 250, July 1, 1893 (deed to George M. Shriver).

84. BCLR, Liber J.W.S. 188, folio 11, The Sudbrook Co. of Balto. Co., et. al, Deed to Hugh L. Bond, Jr., Aug. 20, 1891. Eugene Blackford served as Acting President of the Sudbrook Company in executing this deed.

85. See for example deeds in the Baltimore County Land Records' Office to Edgar H. Bankard, Liber L.M.B. 295, folio 45, Aug. 1, 1892, and to George M. Shriver, Liber L.M.B. 199, folio 250, July 1, 1893 (both containing the provision) and to George H. Coursen, Liber L.M.B. 193, folio 230, Aug. 4, 1892 and to Sophie L. Graves, Liber L.M.B. 203, folio 48, Dec. 12, 1893 (neither containing the provision).

86. OAR/LC, A: 4: 498, JCO to HLB, April 16, 1889 (stating with regard to the suggested restrictions: "of course when you get them you will have to improve the legal phraseology. I have authority in deeds actually recorded for almost all the suggestions, but some of them you may think best to embody in a separate, unrecorded agreement.") As an attorney, Bond may have decided it inappropriate, from a strict legal interpretation, to include a provision in a deed requiring a purchaser of the property to build within two years. While this would apply to the first purchaser of a vacant lot, subsequent purchasers technically would be similarly bound, but obviously a second dwelling would not even be permissible. Since the provision is referred to as a requirement throughout the Blackford letters, it seems that the Company must have retained the provision, but moved it to a separate, unrecorded agreement.

87. These provisions are contained in the first three paragraphs immediately following the suggested 16th restriction. A full text of the suggested restrictions is contained in Appendix A.

88. From a brochure of the Sudbrook Company (undated, but approximately 1891) advertising the new development of Sudbrook Park. Similar provisions can be found in early deeds.

89. OAR/LC, A: 7: 327, JCO to HLB, April 23, 1890. (Although not identified in this letter, the Denver project most probably was the Denver & Lookout Mountain Resort Co. project near Golden, Colorado, which the firm was involved with at that time. Thanks to Charles Beveridge for information on this project.)

90. OAR/LC, A: 8: 536, JCO to HLB, May 15, 1890.

Chapter 8: Sudbrook's Beginning Years: 1889–1893

1. BCLR, Liber J.W.S No. 181, folio 475, Sudbrook Co. of Balto. Co. Deed to Western Maryland Railroad, September 19, 1890. A memorandum of survey of the lands of the Sudbrook Company listed the Company as having 204.01 acres, "of which 2.27 acres is used for R.R. purposes & 1 acre is to be used for a R.R. Station." (BR&AB, MD-MHS, 131: 3: 1, pp. 74–76, October 10, 1891). Only one acre was deeded to the railroad, with a provision that if ever the land ceased to be used for station purposes, it would revert back to the Company. The Sudbrook Company's architects, who designed the station, apparently were the Boston firm of Cabot, Everett and Mead.

2. From the one surviving photograph, Sudbrook's waterworks system was strictly utilitarian and not a highly decorative landmark, as were the water towers at Riverside, Chicago and Baltimore's later developed Roland Park, both of which have survived as ornamental reminders of a past time. Sudbrook's water tower, which was located at the corner of Cliveden West and Upland, is long gone. (While Sudbrook's water tower may not have been an architectural achievement, its water supply was prized by many. An early letter asked Blackford to send some Sudbrook water, and he replied: "I will send Mrs. Toliffe some of the Sudbrook water as soon as I can provide some bottles in which to put it, and hope that it may do her good, tho' I attribute more virtue to the air at Sudbrook Park than to the water." BR&AB, MD-MHS, 131: 3: 1, p. 39, EB to Jas. A. Randall, Sept. 9, 1891).

3. BCLR, Liber J.W.S. No. 181, folio 468, Sally N. McHenry, et. al., Deed to the Sudbrook Co. of Baltimore County, Sept. 18, 1890 (conveying 204 acres of land). In addition to the usual conveyance language, the deed contained four provisions, similar in whole or in part to some of the seven

provisions set forth in the McHenry estate's "Report of Sales of Real Estate," discussed previously in Chapter 7 and its footnotes. Under the first of the provisions in the deed, the executors of the McHenry estate would donate the land for an avenue from the railroad station to the Reisterstown Pike "at a point opposite to the arsenal as said avenue is now actually laid out" and both the Sudbrook Company and the estate would have use of this avenue. The second stated that the Sudbrook Company would "permit no mean dwelling to be erected on the land" and "no store in which liquor is sold except for medicinal use." The third set a time limit of two years from the date of the deed for the Sudbrook Company to open a road to provide access for the remaining Sudbrook property "from the present railroad station to the Seven Mile or Milford Road and the western corner of the property." The fourth required the Sudbrook Company, if requested, to give a right-of-way for a road to the estate's adjoining land lying to the northeast of the station.

4. Both the deed for the property and the McHenry estate's "Report of Sale of Real Estate" recite that the Company **had purchased** the property. See BCLR, Liber J.W.S. 181, folio 478, Sudbrook Company of Balto. County Deed to Mercantile Trust & Deposit Co., Sept. 19, 1890; and "Report of Sale of Real Estate," J. Howard McHenry Executors to Sudbrook Company, Liber B.W.A. 13, folio 117–124, April 8, 1890.

5. OAR/LC, C: 2 (unbound general correspondence), HLB to JCO, May 14, 1890.

6. Although Sudbrook Park did not have electricity yet, many of its cottages had battery operated "electric" bells; some cottages also were wired during construction to facilitate future connections to electrical service. (Batteries in this period were often assembled from multiple, large glass jars; gasoline engines were used to charge the batteries.) Thanks to James Wollen, A.I.A., John McGrain and Michael Sotir for information on early batteries, electric bells and wiring of Sudbrook houses.)

7. BR&AB, MD-MHS, 131: 3: 1, p. 283, EB to Thos. Hill, September 7, 1892. In 1892 the prices for Cottages No. 1 and 2, unfurnished, were $5,800 and $4,800, respectively. We do not know if Nos. 1 and 2 were the only cottages of the original nine designed by Cabot, Everett and Mead, but they are the only ones that Blackford specifically attributed to the firm. (A few years later, Blackford used the firm again to design his own house at 1008 Winsor Road).

8. On a partial map of Sudbrook among the historical records of the late Dorothy Cox, and in a history she compiled which referenced this map (as well as in later articles), "the first ten cottages" and the boarding house were discussed, but the 1913 map showed only nine cottages numbered 1 to 10, with no Cottage No. 3 (long thought to be the "missing" or "mystery" cottage). See Dorothy Cox, *History of Pikesville, Maryland,* Vol. 2, "Sudbrook Park," pp. 33–45 (unpublished, n.d.). A copy is available at the Pikesville branch of the Baltimore County Public Library. [All references to Cox are to Vol. 2, which contains the section on Sudbrook Park.] With the discovery of the Blackford letterpress volumes in 1995, it was learned that the Company initially built only nine cottages (Nos. 1,2,4,5,6,7,8,9 and 10) along with the boarding house, and that Blackford consistently identified the boarding house (later called the hotel) as the long missing "No. 3."

9. Another house was built where Cottage No. 5 had been, and that house was also razed by the State Highway Administration in the early 1960s, in connection with the planned expressway. Telephone interviews with Dorothy Cox Liebno and Newell Cox, Jr., June 29–30, 1997.

10. BR&AB, MD-MHS, 131: 3: 1, p. 136, EB to G.C. Wilmer, February 18, 1892 (noting that the Company amended its own rule "in a certain tract adjoining the Inn, where there is a strong demand for small houses.") The Olmsteds' seventh suggested restriction stated that "one dwelling only shall be erected on the lot if the lot is less than two acres in extent...but if larger than two acres one dwelling may be erected in each full acre." The Sudbrook Company changed the provision to read: "That one dwelling only shall be erected on the lot if the lot is one acre or less...but if larger than two acres, one dwelling may be erected on each full acre." The Company's rewording left a gap by not addressing lots that were over one acre but under two acres (of which there were quite a few on the Olmsted Plan and which the Olmsted wording more clearly addressed). In practice, however, the Company applied its seventh restriction as Olmsted had envisioned (only one house could be built on any lot less than two acres), except in the instances specifically cited. Cottages No. 4, 5 and 10 were smaller than the other six the Company built and were constructed at a cost of $2,500 each. Hugh Bond owned Cottage No. 11 and built Cottages No. 13, 14 and 15 in the vicinity of the Inn. All were on lots of slightly less that an acre, although the lots for Nos. 11 and 14 were intended to have less than an acre (.9 and .8 acre, respectively) on the Olmsted Plan. (The lots on which Cottages 13 and 15 were built are shown containing 1.07 and 1.2 acres, respectively, although the Company sold Bond just under an acre of land for each of these, no doubt because of his position as Company President and his willingness to build houses in the struggling community). Initially these four houses were built without kitchens, which were added a few years later. All other houses in Sudbrook came equipped with kitchens and, to the extent ascertainable, were built either for year-round occupancy or piped and equipped for the installation of furnaces.

11. No. 6, a year-round residence from early on, was leased for several years by W.G. Clemons and his wife, who sublet it when Clemons was transferred to Cleveland. John A. Barker purchased it in March 1895. Barker, a realtor, still lived in the house in 1913.

No. 7, leased by Joseph Whyte and his family for the 1890 and 1891 seasons, was rented to Mrs. Eliza C. Miller beginning in 1892 and purchased by her in February 1894. While the Company installed a furnace in 1893 for a winter tenant, Mrs. Miller used it only from May to October (although she sometimes rented it out during the winter). Mrs. Miller's estate owned the home from 1903 to 1907 or later. By 1913, George Sellman had purchased No. 7.

No. 8 was leased to Mrs. Miller's son, D.H. Miller, Jr. from 1890 through 1900. Miller only used it during "the season." Starting in 1901, B. Deford Webb leased No. 8 and later purchased it.

No. 9 was leased to Oscar Webb from 1890 through 1897 and appeared to be occupied year-round from 1892 on. Webb bought property at 709 Cliveden Road in 1896 and moved into his own house there in 1898.

12. BR&AB, MD-MHS, 131: 4: 4, p. 460, "Inventory of the Property of the Sudbrook Company," November, 1905 (containing the description of the Inn). In 1892 the Company built an adjoining house for the help. In 1898 construction began to add a billiards room. The Inn burned in 1926. (Cox noted that "Langdon and Company, architects from Boston, were employed to design a large frame hotel." Cox, p. 1 [no citation provided]. I was unable to locate any information about Langdon and Company, either in Blackford's records or from listings of Boston architectural firms of that period. The only Boston architectural firm named by Blackford was Cabot, Everett and Mead, which we know designed Cottages No. 1 and 2, and which Blackford seemed to designate as the Company's architects. It is not known whether they designed the hotel, although "the Company's architects" did design the station.)

13. Somehow, the Inn accommodated larger numbers than its forty-five rooms suggest. The following summer, a local newspaper article stated that there "are nearly 200 guests at the hotel and cottages in the park grounds, besides the dwellers in the neighboring homesteads and summer cottages." "Sudbrook Park — How the Young and Old Folk Enjoy Themselves Out There," *Baltimore Sun,* July 18, 1893. (Occupants of the summer rental cottages near the Inn may have been included in calculating guests at the hotel.)

14. BR&AB, MD-MHS, 131: 3: 1, p. 123, EB to N. L. Hipsley, Jan. 18, 1892. Mrs. Thomson's name is spelled with a "p" as "Thompson" in the Company's 1891 brochure and by Cox (Cox had a copy of this brochure among her records). But in all five volumes of Blackford's letters, it is spelled as "Thomson," the spelling used in this book. This latter spelling is reinforced by the fact that Mrs. Thomson's son, Maynard, is mentioned in Meredith Janvier's book, *Baltimore in the Eighties and Nineties,* (Baltimore: H. G. Roebuck & Son, 1933) p. 59 and photo facing p. 156, and in that book, the name is spelled without a "p." Mrs. Thomson was a long-term resident of Sudbrook, running the Inn each season and renting various houses during the out-of-season months. Blackford's letters mentioned that Mrs. Thomson's daughter, Louisa, married William Ross Howard, Jr. (a descendant of John Eager Howard) in November 1902. The couple rented in Sudbrook for a number of years and later bought 607 Sudbrook Road, where they lived for many years. Even today, many long-time residents are aware that 607 Sudbrook was once "the Howard house." (Interestingly, James Howard McHenry knew Howard, Jr.'s parents; one of his diary entries stated "...paid evening visit to the bride, Mrs. William Ross Howard [Sr.]...." JHMJ, MD-MHS, 544.1: 2 (Vol. 15), 1873 diary, entry of Dec. 10, 1873.)

15. Although there are gaps in the documentation, it is clear that some of the McHenry heirs loaned money toward the initial and ongoing development of Sudbrook Park (either strictly as an investment or to help bring to fruition J. Howard McHenry's long-desired suburban village). Various records indicate that loans to the Sudbrook Company were made "out of money in the hands of the Trustee [Mercantile], forming part of the trust estate devised and bequeathed to it by the will of James Howard McHenry." In connection with a subsequent $4,000 loan, for example, "$3,000 was held by the Trustee under the Will in Trust for the use of Sophia McHenry Stewart, one of the daughters of the testator…and $1,000 for the use of Ellen McHenry Keyser [also one of McHenry's daughters]." See, e.g., BCMR, Liber NBM 204, folio 350, Sudbrook Company of Baltimore County Mortgage to Mercantile Trust & Deposit Co., Dec. 30, 1898. Not only is it highly unlikely that two of McHenry's daughters would have suddenly decided to loan money to the Sudbrook Company for the first time in 1898, but there is evidence that several of the heirs funded the initial 1890 loan of $30,000. In all of these loans, Mercantile served as Trustee and received an administrative fee for its services.

16. BCLR, Liber J.W.S. 181, folio 478, Sudbrook Company of Balto. County Deed to Mercantile Trust & Deposit Co., Sept. 19, 1890. [Note: It is not known whether a second mortgage securing a $10,000 loan to the Company to extend its water supply was funded by the bank or by the McHenry heirs. BCMR, Liber L.M.B. 161, folio 344, Sudbrook Co. of Balto. Co Deed to Mercantile Trust & Deposit Co., August 9, 1892.]

17. The Olmsted letters and the early deeds referred to Olmsted's "General Plan for Sudbrook dated August 24, 1889" and never mentioned the name "Sudbrook Park."

18. Olmsted, Vaux & Co.'s "Preliminary Report Upon the Proposed Suburban Village at Riverside, Near Chicago, " (1868) put forth the idea (p. 26) that the "essential qualification" of a park was "range" and to that end all buildings and artificial constructions should be subordinated, whereas the "essential qualification" of a suburb was "domesticity" and habitation, and to that end anything that favored movement should be subordinated. To Olmsted, parks were different in purpose, design and function from suburban villages. The two did not, and were not meant to, overlap. Regardless of these finer theoretical points, the Company began calling the community "Sudbrook Park" and soon residents were abbreviating this to "the Park." This book will use all three of the appellations — Olmsted's "Sudbrook," the Company's "Sudbrook Park," and the colloquial "the Park." (The one 1890 lithographed General Plan by F. L. Olmsted & Co. that has been found, which shows the correct locations of the hotel and first nine cottages, contains the name "Sudbrook Park," but the lettering looks quite different from the lettering on the rest of the plat prepared by the Olmsted firm. It is possible that the Company had "Sudbrook Park" stenciled in, but exactly what transpired is unknown, since none of the surviving letters addresses the name change to Sudbrook Park).

19. A number of Blackford's 1891 letters do indicate the names of several of the occupants of the cottages during the 1890 season, however.

20. Sudbrook Company brochure, "Sudbrook Park" (undated, but about 1891). This date is based on the brochure's references to the previous season as having been the first. Photographs in the brochure show foliage on trees and include a number of children, so probably were taken between May and October 1890, with the brochure being printed early in 1891 and available before that season. Although photocopies of the brochure were with Mrs. Cox's memorabilia and records, the only surviving brochure that has been located belonged to Mrs. Margaret Newcomb, who preserved it over many years and more recently gave it to another Sudbrook resident, Roger Katzenberg. The brochure had been given to Mrs. Newcomb by another long-time resident, Mrs. Traband. (Note: Sudbrook's distance from the city in all references other than this brochure was stated as eight, not seven, miles. Perhaps the Company thought it would gain some advertising advantage by claiming to be only seven miles from the city).

21. While the Company's brochure clearly promoted sales and referred to permanent suburbs outside New York, Philadelphia and Boston, it also tacitly acknowledged that some people might want to buy for summer use rather than as a year-round residence.

22. Waring's 1876 book, *The Sanitary Drainage of Houses and Towns* (Ch. 1, fn. 56) discussed more than one method for the disposal of sewage, none of which he specifically labeled as his "system of subsurface drainage." One method that Waring discussed at length under "irrigation" was developed by a Mr. Denton in Wales and called "Intermittent Downward Filtration:" "A gravelly soil is thoroughly underdrained at a depth of six feet, and is divided into two separate plots to which the sewage is applied alternately. After a certain amount has passed through one field the supply is turned on to the second, and the first is allowed to become thoroughly aerated, and so cleansed by the oxidation of the organic matters that it has taken up, as to be ready again to serve its purpose as a filter." This may have been the sewerage system referred to and used at Sudbrook, since the other system discussed by Waring was "Artificial Purification," and Sudbrook had no purification facility. Waring, p. 316. As for "house slops, etc.," so long as there was "a gradual incline from the house to the garden," Waring proposed to "let all the slops fall into a trapped sink, the drain from which to the garden should be of glazed socket pipes, well jointed, and emptying itself into a small tank…. The surplus rain-water from the roof may also enter this. Out of this tank, lay three inch common drain-pipes, eight feet apart, and twelve inches below the surface…. The liquid oozes into the cultivated soil; and the result is something fabulous…. There is no smell, no possibility of any foul gas to poison the atmosphere…." Waring, p. 329.

23. No. 11 was rented out for the summer seasons of 1891 and 1892 to E. deKay Townsend; seasonal rental was $375. Other tenants were Edward Norris (1893), George Cator (1894), William P. Robinson (1895 through 1897), and Dr. Herbert Harlan (1898 through 1906). Dr. Harlan then purchased another cottage in Sudbrook Park at 722 Howard Road. Cottage No. 11 was raised 25 inches above its original foundation in 1896 and placed on an elevated stone foundation, because of water problems. In 1899–1900, a servant's w.c., a kitchen, a pantry and a porch were added.

24. BR&AB, MD-MHS, 131: 3: 1, p. 13, EB to JDW, Aug. 1, 1891.

25. BR&AB, MD-MHS, 131: 3: 1, p. 21–22, EB to Jos. Whyte, August 22, 1891; pp. 23–24, EB to D. H. Miller, Jr., Aug. 22, 1891; pp. 25–26, EB to Albert Hughes, Aug. 27, 1891; pp. 28–29, EB to H. K. Darby, Aug. 31, 1891; pp. 35–36, EB to Louis Oudesluys, Sept. 7, 1891; see also p. 44, EB to Jno. Cowan (builder), Sept. 15, 1891.

26. While the conspicuous assertion of social superiority is offensive today, it was not unusual in the context of those times. This was, after all, 1891, when, according to one Baltimore resident-author: "Classes were still definitely and happily divided, wealth and position held their place and were respected." Janvier, p. 19. (The Sudbrook Company's 1891 brochure pointedly had assured interested purchasers that "great care will also be taken to prevent sales to persons who might prove undesirable neighbors.").

27. BR&AB, MD-MHS, 131: 3: 1, p. 21, EB to Jos. Whyte, August 22, 1891.

28. BR&AB, MD-MHS, 131: 3: 1, p. 23, EB to Decatur H. Miller, Jr., August 22, 1891. (The proposition to D.H. Miller, Jr. was identical except that the cottage he had occupied, No. 8, was valued at $4500, with the lot value estimated to be $900. Miller did not purchase, but continued to rent No. 8 each season through 1900. His mother, Mrs. Eliza C. Miller, began renting Cottage No. 7 in 1892 and purchased No. 7 in 1894.)

29. BR&AB, MD-MHS, 131: 3: 1, p. 31, EB to Fitzhugh Goldsborough, Sept. 3, 1891.

30. BR&AB, MD-MHS, 131: 3: 1, p. 40–42, EB to JDW, September 9, 1891.

31. BR&AB, MD-MHS, 131: 3: 1, p. 48–49, EB to HLB, September 22, 1891.

32. This presented certain problems under Sudbrook's deed restrictions or contractual requirements, which stipulated that owners had to build on their property within two years of purchase. Owners who wished extra acreage were expected to purchase two or more adjoining acres and could satisfy the restrictions by building only one house on the larger acreage. As it developed, Mrs. Miller did later buy Cottage No. 7. She did not purchase the lot across the street, but did buy additional property adjoining her lot.

33. BR&AB, MD-MHS, 131: 3: 1, p. 92, EB to JDW, October 28, 1891. (Blackford's letters indicate that it was not unusual for a family with an unoccupied bedroom to have relatives or friends stay with them, or for couples or smaller families to share the rental of a cottage for the season.)

34. The one sale had been Hugh Bond's purchase of Cottage No. 11, 1018 Winsor Road, by deed dated Aug. 20, 1891. George Coursen's deed was dated Aug. 4, 1892, although he moved into 515 Sudbrook Lane in May 1892. See BR&AB, MD-MHS, 131: 3: 1, p. 197, EB to G. H. Coursen,

April 30, 1892, stating: "Your house is ready for you, except that the last coat of oil has not been put on the floors. I sent word today to the painter to finish these at once;" and p. 204, EB to Messrs. W. E. Arnold & Co., May 10, 1892, asking for samples of curtain goods and instructing them to show the same "to Mr. Coursen in No. 12, a large newly furnished house."

35. BR&AB, MD-MHS, 131: 3: 1, p. 81, EB to Capt. E. deKay Townsend, October 15, 1891.

36. BR&AB, MD-MHS, 131: 3: 1, p. 96, EB to Joseph Whyte, November 11, 1891.

37. BR&AB, MD-MHS, 131: 3: 1, p. 283, EB to Thos. Hill, September 7, 1892 (Hill had been McHenry's agent). Around this time, the technology of house building was changing in significant ways as a result of the industrial revolution and the mass production of materials, which could be transported to building sites by train, eliminating the need to mill everything at the work site. Various aspects of Sudbrook's houses that Blackford touted were not in common use yet, and were mentioned to indicate that the houses reflected above average construction and the newest methods. "Double floors" referred to the use of both a subfloor and the finished floor, standard practice now, but prior to and during the 1890s, floors were commonly laid as a single layer. "Paper lined" meant the application of a tar paper under the exterior shingles, which had not been used in earlier times, but was introduced as a wind stop, and to control air and heat loss. These techniques, common to Sudbrook houses, were just coming into usage and were indicative of better than average construction practices of that time. Thanks to James T. Wollen, A.I.A. for this information about construction techniques in the 1880s and 1890s (Telephone interview with James Wollen, September 13, 1996. Wollen is chairman of Baltimore's Historic Architects Roundtable).

38. *Baltimore American,* October 2, 1891, p. 5. (Blackford's records indicated that a Mr. and Mrs. Joseph Whyte rented Cottage No. 7 for the seasons of 1890 and 1891. Most probably the news article incorrectly spelled their name as "White" but was referring to the Joseph Whytes mentioned by Blackford).

39. See for example, BR&AB, MD-MHS, 131: 4: 2, EB to [addressee unidentifiable], December 31, 1892, noting: "I go into Baltimore [403 N. Charles St.] for the winter on Monday."

40. BR&AB, MD-MHS, 131: 3: 1, p. 54, EB to John M. Hood, September 26, 1891 (noting that after October 15, "all but the occupants of four cottages will have gone away").

41. BR&AB, MD-MHS, 131: 3: 1, p. 39, EB to John M. Hood, September 9, 1891; p. 66, EB to John M. Hood, October 1, 1891.

42. BR&AB, MD-MHS, 131: 3: 1, p. 77, EB to G.H. Slaughter, October 13, 1891; p. 100, EB to E. deK. Townsend, November 30, 1891. Slaughter was treasurer of the Sudbrook Company until the fall of 1897. The only thing known about him is that he had an office at the B&O Central Building, where Hugh Bond, President, also had an office. He was replaced by C. W. Woolford, about whom there is no information.

43. BR&AB, MD-MHS, 131: 3: 1, p. 123, EB to N.L. Hipsley, Jan. 18, 1892. As 1891 drew to a close, Blackford wrote to a friend in Washington, D.C. who was a realtor and had visited Sudbrook Park, stating that "the time has come to put the property in the market." He noted that, in addition to "the unanimous & enthusiastic voice of all who resided at the Park last summer…we can point to what has been done, not what we intend to do," which may have been a reference to other developments of the time that had little more than stakes in the ground to show prospective purchasers. BR&AB, MD-MHS, 131: 3: 1, p. 97, EB to E.L. McClelland, November 17, 1891.

44. BR&AB, MD-MHS, 131: 3: 1, p. 120, EB to HLB, January 12, 1892. The ball to which Blackford referred probably was the January 6 "leap-year german" mentioned in two newspaper articles. It was given by "the young ladies of Pikesville and Green Spring Valley" on Jan. 6 at the Woodland Inn, Sudbrook. The committee in charge included Miss Sophie McHenry and Miss Emily Blackford, and "[i]t is anticipated that quite a number of the prominent society people of Baltimore will attend. There will be a special train leaving Baltimore, which will be under the chaperonage of Mrs. C. Ridgely Goodwin and Mrs. Thomas B. Harrison. It will be strictly a leap year affair, the ladies having full privileges. Green's orchestra will furnish the music…." *Baltimore American,* Sunday, Jan. 3, 1892. See also "The World of Society," *Baltimore American,* Jan. 6, 1892, announcing the event and noting that a "special train leaves Union Depot at eight o'clock, returning after the dance." [A "german" was a dancing party at which the german — consisting of capriciously involved figures intermingled with waltzes — was danced. C.T. Onions, ed., *Oxford Universal Dictionary on Historical Principles,* 3d ed. revised with addenda, revised (London: Oxford University Press, 1955)].

45. BR&AB, MD-MHS, 131: 3: 1, p. 122, EB to G. Coursen, January 15, 1892. Blackford wrote again to Coursen on February 1, 1892 (p. 128) asking if he had seen the ads and adding: "they are very fetching, I think." [Unfortunately, I was unable to locate any of these ads.]

46. BR&AB, MD-MHS, 131: 3: 1, p. 170, EB to Mrs. G. P. Tiffany, March 29, 1892.

47. BR&AB, MD-MHS, 131: 3: 1, pp. 152 and 153, EB to John M. Marshall, Secretary, Merc. Safe Dep. & Trust, March 5, 1892. (See also p. 297: "Most of the cottages at Sudbrook Park are rented by those who go into town in the winter." EB to Mrs. E.L. Deringer, October 7, 1892).

48. BR&AB, MD-MHS, 131: 3: 1, pp. 152 and 153, EB to John M. Marshall, Secretary, Merc. Safe Dep. & Trust, March 5, 1892.

49. BR&AB, MD-MHS, 131: 3: 1, p. 167, EB to Geo. Coursen, March 23, 1892. "Rotten rock" was partly decomposed rock. Onions, *Oxford Universal Dictionary*

50. In each instance, Bond agreed to invest the money for the requested additions only if the tenant was willing to enter into at least a three-year lease. No. 14 (503 Sudbrook Lane) was leased to Charles Crane from 1894 to June 1897, when he had to give up his lease due to his wife's poor health. That same month, Clarence Shriver moved in under a lease-purchase arrangement; title passed to him in January 1901. B. T. Stokes leased No. 15 (721 Cliveden Road) from 1894 until June 1901, after which various individuals rented it until it was purchased in 1907 by Kate P. (and B. Deford) Webb, who had rented No. 8 (now 505½ Sudbrook Lane) from 1901–1907. It was quite common for renters who had lived in Sudbrook Park for some period of time to purchase either the same cottage they were renting or another cottage in the community, or to purchase a lot after renting for many years and build to their own specifications. Some of those who followed this pattern were Arthur Poultney, Eugene Blackford, John Littig, James McEvoy, Oscar Webb, Dr. Herbert Harlan, C. W. Linthicum, Clarence Shriver, William R. Howard, Judge Henry Harlan, Judge H. Arthur Stump, William H. Stellmann and George Cator.

51. BR&AB, MD-MHS, 131: 3: 1, p. 247, EB to Chief Eng. Thom Williamson, July 7, 1892, stating: "We have a large collection of…plans, and by alterations made to suit the taste of the owner, can suit almost any one…."

52. Houses which were built from the same design, or have similar design characteristics, are: 505 and 505½ Sudbrook Lane (same plan; see fn. 53 below and corresponding text); 1016 Winsor and 610 Upland (same plan, with some alterations at the latter house); 1017 Winsor and 724 Howard (porches); 721 and 708 Cliveden (similar Dutch Colonials); and 500, 503 and 515 Sudbrook Lane and 1018 Winsor (which all may have been designed by George Coursen, who owned 515 Sudbrook). [No. 515 Sudbrook Lane originally had a large porch but that and the front of the house were badly burned in a fire in the 1920s. The house was salvaged, but the front design elements and the porch were not restored. In addition, the house was converted into a duplex after the fire. Telephone interview with Martha Volz Kaufman, June 1, 1997).

53. BR&AB, MD-MHS, 131: 3: 1, p. 110, EB to Thomas E. Bond, Dec. 22, 1891. Cottages No. 6 and 8, which now stand next to each other at 505 and 505½ Sudbrook Lane, clearly were built from the same plan.

54. While the 1891 promotional brochure and numerous letters make clear that certain portions of the Company's property were heavily treed from the start, additional trees and shrubbery were added in the planting strips, in the open land and around new cottages. As noted previously, no one has located any Olmsted planting lists for Sudbrook, although correspondence with the Olmsteds did discuss where on the roads to plant trees and the proper method of planting. In addition, the cross-sections of roads prepared by Olmsted give some information about the planting spaces.

55. BR&AB, MD-MHS, 131: 3: 1, p. 162, EB to HLB, March 11, 1892.

56. BR&AB, MD-MHS, 131: 3: 1, p. 211, EB to John Hood, May 23, 1892.

57. The lots that were purchased and subsequently built upon:

717 Cliveden Road (No. 16) was purchased by John Glenn, trustee for Horatio G. Armstrong. (Nothing is known about Armstrong except that he was in the *Society Visiting List* for the season of 1893–94 and subsequently). There were some delays in building, partly because of the trust arrangement. The house was designed by Thomas Buckler Ghequier, a local architect, and completed in April 1895. [T. Buckler Ghequier (1854–1910) was the grandson of Robert Cary Long, Sr. (1760–1833), generally considered Baltimore's first native professional architect. Long's son, Robert Cary Long, Jr. (1810–1849) was well-known in his time as one of the most important architects in the development of the profession. Long's daughter Sarah married Louis J. Ghequier in July 1853. T. Buckler Ghequier worked for J. Crawford Nelson for five years and then, apparently, worked on his own. Ghequier was a life-long active member of St. Paul's Church. Ghequier designed a number of Baltimore houses and churches, and the Parish House at St. Paul's Church. His style evolved with the times and included Romanesque, Gothic and Queen Anne. He is buried in St. Paul's cemetery. Biographical information about Ghequier courtesy of James T. Wollen, A.I.A.].

710 Cliveden Road (No. 18) was purchased by E.H. Bankard, who began construction in the fall of 1892. Edgar H. Bankard was a purchasing agent for the B&O Railroad. (His father, Henry Nicholas Bankard, owned a real estate office at 5 St. Paul Street and was said to have "largely contributed towards building up the suburban portion of the city." See Scharf, Part II, pp. 774–775 for biographical information on H. N. Bankard). Interestingly, E.H. Bankard originally bought Lot 5, Block 15 (which later became 706 Cliveden) by deed dated Aug. 1, 1892 (Liber L.M.B. 200, folio 227). By another deed dated Sept. 12, 1892 (Liber L.M.B. 295, folio 45), Bankard reconveyed that property back to the Sudbrook Company and purchased Lot 3, Block 15 (which became 710 Cliveden Road).

607 Sudbrook Road (No. 19) became the home of George M. Shriver, an attorney who worked for the B&O Railroad and took over as 2nd Vice President when Hugh Bond resigned that position in 1910. The deed to Shriver (Liber L.M.B. 199, folio 250) was dated July 1, 1893. It appears that the house was built, the yard graded, seeded, etc. and the home occupied by November 1893. According to former Sudbrook resident William B. Merrick in his "Memories of Sudbrook Park," (unpublished, undated recollections kindly made available to me by Stewart McLean, Mr. Merrick's grandson) and referred to hereafter as "Merrick's Memories," the Shrivers had five children. Merrick recalled that George Shriver used to join in games with the children in the evening and "no one who ever attended the Shrivers' 4th of July parties will ever forget them." When the Shrivers moved from Sudbrook, they built a large house on Old Court Road called "Alsenborn." (See *Social Register-1915* (Vol. XXIX, No. 14, Nov. 1914). William Ross Howard, Jr. and his wife were subsequent purchasers of 607 Sudbrook Road.

600 Sudbrook Road (No. 20) was built by William H. and Ann Isabel Trego, who contracted with the Sudbrook Company but never appeared to have held a deed to the property (see fn. 73, below). At the time, the house they contracted for was the most extravagant house built in Sudbrook Park. No expense was spared. Designed by George Archer and built by John Cowan, the house was on two acres. The Tregos took occupancy in the spring of 1893. For reasons unknown, the house was for sale by June 1893, for $7,000. J. Hume Smith purchased it in October 1893 and took title by deed dated May 2, 1894 (Liber L.M.B. 204, folio 324). By deed dated Oct. 3, 1905 (Liber W.P.C. 291, folio 2), the property was conveyed by Robert H. Smith, a court-appointed trustee, to Frederick B. Beacham for $5750. Beacham conveyed the property to James L. Sellman by deed dated Jan. 17, 1914 (Liber W.P.C. 421, folio 514). [George Archer (1848–1920) was born in Harford County, where generations of his family had lived. Educated at Princeton, Archer was first employed by George A. Frederick, a well-known Baltimore architect of the day. (Frederick had trained with Edmund G. Lind, who had designed McHenry's Sudbrook house). Archer opened his own office in 1875 and designed buildings for the Johns Hopkins hospital, churches, residences, banks, educational institutions, businesses and industrial structures. He exhibited design competence in a variety of styles: Gothic, Renaissance, Romanesque, Queen Anne, Colonial, and Palladian. Archer designed three houses in Sudbrook Park — 600 Sudbrook Road, 706 Cliveden Road and 709 Cliveden Road. Biographical information about Archer courtesy of James T. Wollen, A.I.A., from a paper by Wollen and Irma Walker].

726 Howard Road (No. 22) was built in 1893. The first cottage on Howard Road, it was designed by local architect J. Appleton Wilson for Roswell (alternately spelled Rosewell or Rosswell) W. and Sophie L. Graves. The Graveses, and later their daughter Sophie, lived in the home until the 1960s. [John Appleton Wilson (1851–1927) was a member of the fourth generation of a wealthy Baltimore family. They were devout Baptists and Wilson's religious and social connections played a role in his professional life. Wilson studied architecture at MIT. He formed his own practice in 1877. Wilson designed about forty houses in the city's Belvidere neighborhood in the 1880s, as well as churches and a wide range of commercial and industrial buildings. From the 1890s on, he designed many houses in the suburbs of Baltimore. Wilson's Sudbrook designs were 726 Howard Road and 507 Sudbrook Road. Many of Wilson's papers and photographs were donated to the Maryland Historical Society by his daughter. Biographical information about Wilson courtesy of James Wollen, A.I.A., from a 1993 paper by Charles Duff, an architectural historian. See also Dorsey and Dilts, pp. 289–290].

Nos. 17 and 21 on Blackford's list were the livery stable and a tenant house, not cottages.

[NOTE: When purchasers did not rely on the Sudbrook Company to oversee construction of their house, the Company records contain little or no information about that house. Information is most plentiful about those houses owned by the Company and those built for private use where Blackford managed the construction and/or handled the rental.]

58. BR&AB, MD-MHS, 131: 3: 1, p. 170, EB to Mrs. G.P. Tiffany, March 29, 1892.

59. BR&AB, MD-MHS, 131: 3: 1, p. 177–178, EB to Rev. Dr. J.W.M. Williams, April 5, 1892.

60. BR&AB, MD-MHS, 131: 3: 1, p. 252, EB to HLB, July 12, 1892. As mentioned previously (see Profile of Eugene Blackford, Chapter 5), Blackford had obtained "Cleve" in a similar manner, as a gift from his father-in-law after his marriage.

61. BR&AB, MD-MHS, 131: 3: 1, p. 247, EB to Chief. Eng. Thom. Williamson, W.N.S. [no date given but approximately July 7–12, 1892]. This was a time when cholera, smallpox, influenza, tuberculosis, typhoid, typhus, and similar diseases were common and justifiably feared.

62. BR&AB, MD-MHS, 131: 3: 1, p. 247, EB to Chief. Eng. Thom. Williamson, W.N.S. [no date given but approximately July 7–12, 1892].

63. BR&AB, MD-MHS, 131: 4: 4, p. 105, EB to Wm. P. Chunn, November 6, 1900.

64. BR&AB, MD-MHS, 131: 3: 1, p. 274, EB to HLB, August 22, 1892.

65. BR&AB, MD-MHS, 131: 3: 1, p. 321, EB to HLB, December 7, 1892.

66. One commentator claimed that "the depression of the 1890s may rank behind only the Great Depression of the 1930s in severity. Between 1894 and 1897, unemployment averaged 15 percent. Farmers reeled from falling prices. In 1891, a bushel of wheat sold for 96 cents; by 1895, the price was 60 cents." Robert J. Samuelson, "The Message from 1896?," *Newsweek*, Aug. 12, 1996, p. 51. The depression also affected Baltimore: "Eighteen ninety-three turned out to be a bad year, a year of financial panic, spreading outward from bank crashes to railroad bankruptcies and layoffs, the collapse of farm prices, and foreclosures nationwide…. In Baltimore…construction workers were laid off. Men on city contracts begged to be kept at work and take their pay later. By 28 December observers estimated that seventy-five hundred residents were out of work. The most careful estimates suggest ten thousand by New Year's Day, then thirty thousand…. Three hundred destitute were housed in the police stations every night…. During the season of 1893–94 prices fell by half, and all wages accordingly." Olson, pp. 228–229.

67. Olson, pp. 242–243 and information from pp. 241 and 332. (Hugh Bond was one of those appointed as a receiver for the B&O system. Later, the B&O named a tugboat after Bond, in accord with its custom of naming tugboats after railroad officials. Information about the Bond tugboat, courtesy of Herb Harwood, telephone interview on Aug. 12, 1996).

68. Block 14, lot 10 (709 Cliveden) was purchased by Oscar Webb in December, 1896. Lot 11 (711 Cliveden) originally intended for Blackford's son-in-law, was sold to F.C. Tyson in 1904.

69. BR&AB, MD-MHS, 131: 4: 2, pp. 44–46, EB to Chas. A. Keyser, June 27, 1893. It is questionable whether Blackford would have known even **if** Olmsted so regarded Sudbrook, since Blackford's few communications with the Olmsted firm seem to have been confined to administrative matters.

70. This June 27, 1893, letter to Keyser is the only time that Blackford stated that sidewalks were five feet rather than six feet wide. In all other letters, and there are many of them, he described the sidewalks as being six feet wide. Whether this letter simply contained an error, or whether the sidewalks at 600 Sudbrook Road were a foot smaller than elsewhere, is not known. The electric line to which Blackford referred was the Baltimore, Pimlico & Pikesville Railway (previously the horse-car line on whose board McHenry had been a Director), but it now was an electric trolley line. Its Pikesville terminus was actually farther away than Blackford indicated — probably about 1 to 1.5 miles from 600 Sudbrook.

71. BR&AB, MD-MHS, 131: 4: 2, pp. 44–46, EB to Chas. A. Keyser, June 27, 1893. In building his house, Trego also insisted that "the entire house is to be covered with boards shaped to a uniform thickness nailed on diagonally with 2 nails in each stud…[and] building paper & shingles." BR&AB, MD-MHS, 131: 3: 1, p. 331, EB to Wm. Trego, Dec. 28, 1892. (Nailing boards on diagonally behind the exterior walls provided additional strength when diagonal bracing was no longer a customary way to frame houses. As noted previously, these techniques, common to Sudbrook houses, were just coming into usage and were indicative of better than average construction practices of that time. Thanks to James T. Wollen, A.I.A., for this information).

72. BR&AB, MD-MHS, 131: 4: 2, pp. 44–46, EB to Chas. A. Keyser, June 27, 1893.

73. The property was not deeded over to James Hume Smith by the Sudbrook Company and Mercantile Trust & Deposit Company of Baltimore, Trustee, until May 2, 1894 (Liber L.M.B. 204, folio 324; this deed contained the Olmsted restrictions). A concurrent short deed from William Hopps and Wf. to James Hume Smith can be found at Liber L.M.B. 204, folio 330. It appears that the Sudbrook Co. contracted with and sold the property to Ann Isabel Trego by agreement dated Nov. 30, 1892 (see, Ann Isabel Trego & husband, deed to William Hopps made Jan. 8, 1894, Liber L.M.B. 202, folio 271). The Tregos began building their grand house almost immediately after the sale, moved in about April 1893, and the house was for sale by June 1893. Hume apparently contracted to buy the house in October 1893. In January 1894, Ann Isabel Trego and her husband granted to William Hopps all right, title and interest in the property. Hopps conveyed his interest to Hume in May 1894, on the same day that the Sudbrook Co. conveyed the land to Hume. It appears that the Sudbrook Co. never actually deeded the land over to the Tregos; no deed to them is referenced in subsequent deeds or has been located. (Also, the deed to Hume contained the customary language releasing the property from Mercantile's lien and making payment to the sinking fund; had the property been deeded to the Tregos, it already would have been released from the lien). Thus, it seems that the Tregos began building after the land was contracted for but before the property was deeded to them, and that the Tregos then had some problem, perhaps financial, and never took title to the land. They transferred to Hopps their contractual right to the property plus their financial interest in the house; Hume bought Hopps' rights for $5,250 and took title from the Sudbrook Co.

74. "Sudbrook Park — How the Young and Old Folk Enjoy Themselves Out There," *Baltimore Sun*, July 18, 1893. The article described Sudbrook as "a beautiful little summer village," and commented that the "lack of regularity to the arrangement of the roads and grounds is one of the chief attractions, for the carriage roads and pathways run in and out and round-about with delightful unexpectedness, and wherever a sufficient expanse of ground is enclosed by them a pretty cottage is dotted, without fence or gate to separate it from its neighbors." Commenting that the "usual dearth of men noticeable so often at summer resorts is happily not a characteristic of Sudbrook Park," the article attributed this to the fact that fathers and brothers, while occupied in the city during the day, returned on the afternoon trains and were "met by welcoming womankind." It also stated that Sudbrook was planning a casino of its own, with a bowling alley, swimming pool and other attractions, to be built "next season." The location would be "where the tennis courts now are." Since Blackford's early letters mention no tennis courts, it is not known whether the ones referred to in this article were located near the hotel, near the bridge on the Howard Road side (where we know that tennis courts later existed), or in some other location.

Chapter 9: Location is Everything: 1892–1893

1. "Suburban Developments, How Baltimore is Forging to the Front," *Baltimore Daily News,* February 18, 1892 (hereafter referred to as "Suburban Developments…"); Waesche, p. 55 (Waesche's book is both an excellent read and a documented study recounting how the stage was set for Baltimore's suburban development, how Edward Bouton ably managed the development of the named suburbs, and the lasting impact these suburbs have had on the Baltimore area).

2. Waesche, pp. 44 and 56. Roland Park's official "opening day" was June 15, 1892, five months after the article appeared. (The first plat of Roland Park was designed by landscape architect George E. Kessler of Kansas City. While it included a few curving streets, the predominant form of block arrangement was straight and angular, so that the total Plat exhibited only occasional variations from a typical grid design. (See reproduction of Plat One, Waesche, p. 54, and plat shown in "Monumental City Suburbs, They Cannot Be Eclipsed Anywhere in the Union" *Baltimore Sunday Herald,* April 30, 1893, (hereafter referred to as "Monumental City Suburbs"), p. 26; or, as another commentator noted: "The street plans produced by Kessler for Plat One of Roland Park were not especially dramatic…" Harry G. Schalck, "Mini-Revisionism in City Planning History: The Planners of Roland Park," *Journal of the Society of Architectural Historians*, Vol. 39, No. 4 (December 1970), p. 348). Plats Two and Three were designed in the Olmsted tradition by the firm (then, Olmsted, Olmsted & Eliot) after 1897, with credit for the design generally attributed to Frederick Law Olmsted, Jr. (although John C. Olmsted also was involved until his death in 1906). Plat Two was opened to the public in 1901. Waesche, pp. 69–70).

3. Realizing, as Sudbrook's developers had, that it must build some typical houses on speculation to "show" prospective purchasers what life in Roland Park would be like, the Roland Park Co. began constructing several houses in the fall of 1892. Waesche, pp. 56–57.

4. "Suburban Developments…" Although Baltimore's suburban movement began to pick up greater momentum in the 1890s, it would take another decade or two for permanent suburban living — in contrast to summering in the suburbs and wintering in the city — to become fashionable. It would take even longer, until the 1940s or later, for permanent migration to the outlying suburbs to become commonplace in the Baltimore area. The greatest revolution — the automobile — was still to come.

5. This lack of convenient and efficient transportation has been cited by a number of historians and writers as contributing to Baltimore's lag in suburban development as compared to other large cities in the East. See for example, Joseph L. Arnold, "Baltimore's Neighborhoods, 1800–1980," (pp. 76–98) in *Working Papers from the Regional Economic History Research Center* (Wilmington, Delaware: Eleutherian Mills-Hagley Foundation, Spring 1980), pp. 88–90, (cited with permission of the author and hereafter referred to as "Arnold, Baltimore's Neighborhoods").

6. "Suburban Developments…" The paper estimated that investments in cable and electric roads in Baltimore in 1891–92 would total nearly $10 million in the aggregate, and upon completion, Baltimore would have one hundred miles of rapid transit.

7. Farrell, p. 13 (see pages 13–21 regarding the efforts required to gain permission to operate the first horse car line).

8. Train fares varied by distance, carrier, etc., but to commute to the city from Sudbrook Park on the Western Maryland Railroad cost about ten cents each way in 1892. Additional fares were required to transfer to a horse rail line or taxis to get around the city. For laborers who earned a dollar a day, five days train fare was equivalent to a full day's wages.

9. In mid-August 1885, Leo Daft's system (using electric motor cars to pull passenger cars), began operating in Baltimore. Although claimed to be the "first electric railway in America built for regular passenger service," neither this venture nor an earlier short electric line in Cleveland (1881) was really successful. In 1888, however, an electrified trolley system developed by Frank Sprague and installed in Richmond would "revolutionize the entire street railway industry." Farrell, pp. 53–58.

10. The word "elevated" appeared to be somewhat misleading. Only a small section of the line was elevated in order to go above the lines of all the other street railway companies that had gotten there first. Farrell, p. 69.

11. Harry G. Schalck, "Planning Roland Park, 1891–1910," *Maryland Historical Magazine,* Vol. 67, No. 4 (Winter 1972), p. 421, noting that "contrary to popular belief, the Roland Park Company was never a financial success." Schalck pointed out that the Roland Park Company's general manager and then president, Edward H. Bouton, "could never bring himself to cut costs in providing community amenities or in the construction of houses. Thus the community's beauty paid off for the private homeowners rather than for the corporate investors." Waesche's account confirms that there were financial difficulties early on. By December 1892, the Roland Park Company was in debt and having problems obtaining local loans "with only 17 houses under construction and none occupied." The bankruptcy in September 1893 of Jarvis and Conklin, the Kansas City managers of the Roland Park Co., was potentially disastrous. But the subsequent purchase of the Roland Park Co. by a Baltimore syndicate combined with Bouton's skilled management saved the early enterprise. The Roland Park Co. continued active operations until the 1940s; it was dissolved and liquidated in 1959. Waesche, pp. 58–60 and 115–116. Although it may not have been a highly profitable investment for its stockholders, the community of Roland Park has been a success for its residents and the city (which annexed the area in 1918). For more than a century, it has remained prime residential property, retaining consistently high property values. Some factors contributing to this long term success were the Olmsted firm's picturesque design, Bouton's attention to detail and strong direction in implementing the plan, the incorporation into deeds of restrictive covenants and controls that are still in effect, and the foresight to develop a sizable area (buttressed by the Roland Park Company's later development of Guilford and Homeland) just north of the city (the direction of earliest expansion).

12. Baltimore was nicknamed the "Monumental City" because it was one of the first American cities (in the early nineteenth century) to conceive and erect monuments (primarily the Washington Monument and the Battle Monument) that had no function other than commemoration. Olson, p. 42.

13. "A belt of twenty-three square miles on the north and west of the city was annexed in 1888." Olson, p. 209.

14. It is possible that Sudbrook Park was considered too remote at the time, although St. Denis Park in the Relay section was featured in the article, and it, too, was remote from the city. Other established suburban villages, such as Mt. Washington (one of the earliest with an 1854 plan), and Lutherville (dating from the 1850s), also were not mentioned. Although Mt. Washington had a population of 1,200 and Lutherville a population of 500, their reputations were primarily as places of summer residence for the wealthy until after 1900. (John R. Bland, ed., *Maryland Directory and State Gazetteer* (Baltimore: The Baltimore Publishing Co., 1887), pp. 102, 105). Mt. Washington still had dirt roads in 1886; by 1892, it had electric lights; around 1900, more permanent residents began to move in after the resort era. Mark Miller, *Mount Washington* (Baltimore: GBS Publishers, Division of Gordon's Booksellers, 1980), pp. 35, 51. (Dixon's Hill in Mt. Washington apparently had several families in residence in the 1880s, a number of whom were employed in downtown Baltimore and had "no other residential address." Dorsey and Dilts, XLI. But, as a later newspaper article observed: before the introduction of electric railway lines, only "the better-heeled Baltimoreans had been able to afford the luxury and inconvenience of a home in the suburbs." "Time and the Automobile Remap Baltimore Town," *Baltimore Evening Sun,* October 10, 1955).

15. Lansdowne, for example, had sold over 700 of its 1,032 lots and had seventy-five cottages by April 1893, while Sudbrook had a mere eighteen cottages (both suburbs were begun in 1889). Another major difference was that Lansdowne's individual lot prices were in a low to moderate price range for the times ($80–$300), and its lots were significantly smaller than Sudbrook's (about .087 acre compared with lots of about an acre in Sudbrook). Rosedale, a forty-acre row house suburb adjoining Irvington on Frederick Road, advertised lots priced as low as $100. It had sold one-third of its lots the first week the property was on the market, openly inviting investors and speculators as well as home-builders.

16. Concept from presentation on October 15, 1996 by Kenneth I. Helphand, FASLA (University of Oregon), at conference sponsored by the National Association for Olmsted Parks in Chicago, titled "Exploring American Landscape Design in Planned Communities." Using nineteenth century and current advertisements for suburban communities, Professor Helphand demonstrated themes of striking commonalty, including the appeal of bucolic and wooded settings (then and now, the most desired houses have woods or a nature-enhanced setting on at least one side), convenient access to the city combined with physical and psychological distance from it, the explicit or implicit promise of something better, and the attraction of owning a private domain that also offers connectedness as part of an idealized "community."

17. Communities at the turn of the century vied for the highest elevation. High elevations were considered healthier and more able to "catch cool breezes." Today, few people living in these same suburbs think of them as having particularly high elevations, because extensive construction in suburban areas has eliminated the views that undeveloped land once offered. To regain some of that perspective, consider a few facts from the *Baltimore Sunday Herald* article: discussing Tuxedo Park, elevation 390 feet, it noted that such an elevation was 300 feet higher than Mt. Vernon Place and 115 feet higher than the top of the Washington Monument on Charles Street in downtown Baltimore.

18. The city's 1888 annexation of twenty-three square miles along its northern and western boundaries, along with the incorporation of cable railway companies, "jointly provoked a wave of speculation and a sharp increase in the sales of real estate, which bore fruit in 1893." Olson, p. 209

19. Waesche, p. 61. (It is sobering to compare the prevalent prices for lots and houses in these new suburbs with wages and housing costs for those not yet a part of the "middle class." From 1885–1900, wages for unskilled laborers remained relatively constant at $1.25 a day. Wage rates for skilled workers ranged from $1.75 to $3.00 a day, increasing somewhat over the period. After the crisis years of 1893–1896, prices in Baltimore began to spiral upward and rents definitely increased. The average cost of housing for a family went from $78 a year in 1885 to over $100 in 1902. A survey in 1903 of twenty "typical Baltimore workingmen's families" showed that only two owned their own homes and only two were able to save anything from their earnings. Eight were in debt. Eight had annual incomes of less than $300; the average earnings for a whole family (sometimes three to five persons) was a little more than $600 a year. Charles Hirschfeld, *Baltimore, 1870–1900: Studies in Social History* (Baltimore: The Johns Hopkins Press, 1941), pp. 64–65).

20. Olson, p. 212. The designated terms are Olson's. Arnold also identified "two radically different types of neighborhoods" which essentially correspond to Olson's. These were: (1) "the architecturally homogenous working-class neighborhood adjacent to major employment centers" (basically, the industrial suburb), and (2) the "middle-and upper-class neighborhood where land use is limited to residences…[located] increasingly distant from the sources of employment upon which its families depend and [which is]…characterized by a romantic, semi-rural ideal based upon nineteenth-century concepts of family life and child nurture, as well as a strong desire to have a miniature landed estate" (the commuter suburb). Arnold: Baltimore's Neighborhoods, p. 87.

21. Advertisement for Rosedale, *Baltimore Sunday Herald,* April 30, 1893, p. 26.

22. South Baltimore Harbor/Curtis Bay was situated south of the city on the line of the Baltimore and Ohio railroad. Lots were small and manufacturing concerns were welcome (already there was "a sugar refinery, barrel factory, car works, foundry, and nut and bolt manufactory. Many more are either in process of erection or under contemplation.") An electric railway was also nearby. "Monumental City Suburbs," p. 25. (A family that later lived in Sudbrook Park owned significant amounts of property in this area and played a role in its development. The South Baltimore Harbor and Improvement Company, together with the related Curtis Bay Company, were under the direction of William S. Rayner, and later his son, who became Senator Isidor Rayner. "Dreams of Enterprising Brooklyn-Curtis Bay Pioneers Nearly Realized," *Baltimore Sun,* December 12, 1937 (noting that the biggest residential boom in the area did not come until 1916, when Brooklyn Park was born). Senator Rayner and his family became the first occupants of 605 Upland Road in Sudbrook Park, where they lived for a number of years).

23. Orangeville was located about a half mile from the city limits on the east side, two and a half miles from City Hall. Two years old, the development had twenty-two occupied cottages and "many others being constructed." Lots 25 feet by 100-to-190-feet were priced $200 to $350. In addition to being "entirely free from malaria," the suburb would soon be illuminated with electric lights (an advantage that Sudbrook Park could not claim until a decade later). "Monumental City Suburbs," p. 26.

24. The article stated that the "inexhaustible ore and paint banks, which form the background of Lansdowne, will probably be the field of operation of the new enterprise." "Monumental City Suburbs," p. 25.

25. Begun in 1889 using Philadelphia and Baltimore capital, Lansdowne was being developed on ninety acres of an old Linthicum homestead. The development was located on the Baltimore and Ohio railroad with thirty-five daily trains each way; the four mile train ride to City Hall took ten minutes. Free transportation was provided to view the community. Already, it had sold over two-thirds of its 1,032 lots at prices ranging from $80 to $300.

26. Situated within the city limits, Rosedale had city water, gas, railways, schools and free mail delivery — "all the city conveniences." The article noted that Rosedale sold a third of its lots in its first week, and commented that it was easy to find purchasers "at the remarkably low figures [as low as $100] at which [the lots] are being offered." "Monumental City Suburbs," p. 25. Although lots sold quickly, development moved at a much slower pace. An 1896 map of the area showed only a handful of houses, while the 1906 map still evidenced more vacant than built lots. As shown on a 1914 topographical survey of the City of Baltimore, the area was mostly built by that time. (Thanks to Edward Orser, Professor of American Studies at the University of Maryland Baltimore County, for providing me with maps of this area).

27. There were to be a total of 581 building lots, 50 feet by 125 feet and larger.

28. Olson, p. 212.

29. Six or more of Walbrook's 1893 lot owners were listed in the *Social Register*. Waesche, p. 43.

30. Minimum front footage for a lot was fifty-feet, but nothing smaller than seventy-feet front had been sold and 100-feet front was the average at that time. At $16 to $50 per front-foot, lots would have ranged from $800 to $5,000 or more.

31. In 1892, an existing rail line which had operated along a portion of North Avenue as the North Avenue Railway Company combined with the Lake Roland Elevated under the latter's name. This line served both Walbrook to the west of the city and Roland Park, to the north. "City's Northwest Area Keeps Serene," *Baltimore Sun*, November 7, 1937.

32. In 1867, George M. Pullman formed the Pullman Car Company to design "a system by which passengers could be carried in luxurious [railroad] cars of uniform pattern, adequate to the wants of both night and day travel." Pullman's Company developed comfortable sleeping cars, dining cars and drawing-room cars, setting the standard for the ultimate in first-class train travel. Horace Porter, *Railway Passenger Travel, 1825–1880* (Charles Scribner's & Sons, September 1888; repr. Maynard, Massachusetts: Chandler Press, 1987), no page numbers listed.

33. Annexation permitted Walbrook's residents to be served by the city's water service and gas company at city prices. The community also received fire protection and a city-installed fire plug. Many outlying areas lacked these desirable protections in an age when most structures were of wood and fire was a dreaded threat.

34. West Arlington was the property of the Baltimore Traction Company, one of the early horse railway companies that later electrified its lines. It had no houses yet but would soon start to sell its 260 acres, situated five miles from City Hall. "Monumental City Suburbs," p. 25.

35. The news article listed George R. Webb and Charles G. Hill among the residents of West Arlington. Interestingly, Webb was one of the incorporators of the Sudbrook Company; Hill was one of the Company's original directors.

36. The article noted, more than once, that the portion of the city being developed most rapidly was toward the north, the direction of both of these suburbs. (The northwesterly direction, in which Sudbrook was located, did not develop as quickly as did the northern corridor. Atlases in 1905 showed Pikesville with about 400 lots, but only about 100 built houses; Sudbrook Park had about fifty houses at the time. West Arlington, also in the northwest corridor and closer to the city than Sudbrook, was described in 1915 as showing "signs of life near the Reisterstown road, but was far from being thickly settled." Clearly, the development of Roland Park was aided because the predominant outward movement from the city was in a northerly direction. "Growing Northwest Baltimore Absorbs 'The Country'," *Baltimore Evening Sun*, Oct. 17, 1955).

37. The Roland Park Co. was reputed to have spent over a million dollars on the purchase and development of its property (this figure may have included some of the costs to extend the electric rail line that would serve the community). "Monumental City Suburbs," p. 26.

38. Waesche, p. 57.

39. Waesche, pp. 57–58.

40. Although settled at a much faster pace than Sudbrook Park, even Roland Park had to cope with the reluctance of Baltimoreans to give up their winter homes in the city. Waesche, p. 71 (and see Chapter 12).

41. As noted previously, this requirement was suggested by Olmsted and imposed on purchasers to prevent buying on speculation.

42. The article touted Ruxton Heights' "cozy" cottages, well-kept grounds and beautiful landscape, proclaiming that "here, anyone of respectability but modest means can enjoy the same comforts and convenience as the wealthy neighbor at really less expense than the cost of a city residence." "Monumental City Suburbs," p. 26.

43. There was a maximum $150 bonus on houses costing over $3,000.

44. The Relay Station, like Sudbrook's, provided telegraph, express, mail, etc.

45. The town of Catonsville was three and a half miles from St. Denis Park. In 1887, Catonsville was considerably more settled (about 2,500 population) than was the village of Pikesville (about 450 population) near Sudbrook Park. Catonsville also had a theatre, a library, and a newspaper. Bland, ed., *Maryland Directory and State Gazetteer*, pp. 83–84 and p. 109. (The *Gazetteer* also listed the price of an acre of land in Catonsville as ranging from $200–$1,000, while an acre of land in Pikesville averaged $125. Although this was several years before Sudbrook Park got a foothold, it may have been more difficult to sell lots in Sudbrook at the higher than average rates for the area that the Sudbrook Company was asking).

46. Edward Orser and Joseph Arnold, *Catonsville, 1880 to 1940: From Village to Suburb* (Norfolk: The Donning Company Publishers, 1989), pp. 38–45. (This book provides excellent documentation of the development of Catonsville).

47. "Monumental City Suburbs," p. 26. Eden Terrace was situated between Edmondson Avenue and Frederick Road. It was within "a few minutes walk" of both the Paradise and Catonsville stations of the Catonsville Short Line Railroad. It was also served by the Union Line horse cars (about to be electrified), while the Edmondson Avenue Electric Railway would soon be added. A development called Paradise Park was located to the south of Eden Terrace, on the opposite side of Frederick Road; it had twenty residences at that time.

48. An October 10, 1892 article in *The Argus* announced that houses in the Eden Terrace development would range from $3,500 to $12,000 and that the Eden Construction Company would "probably erect fifteen houses at once, and offer them for sale on reasonable terms." Victor Bloede, the developer, built the most lavish home in the subdivision, estimated to cost $13,000. Orser and Arnold, pp. 38 and 39.

49. Several of Eugene Blackford's letters, as manager of the Sudbrook Company, hint of competition between Sudbrook and Roland Park for the same people. A number of affluent Baltimoreans lived, at alternate times, in both of the communities. The other two suburbs were similar enough also to provide some competition. In April 1896, for example, John Barker, a realtor and resident of Sudbrook Park, claimed a commission on the sale of a lot in Sudbrook to Dr. Samuel Kemp Merrick, "as Dr. Merrick was prevented by [Barker's] advice, sought as an expert in real estate matters, from buying at the Relay." (Relay appeared to refer to St. Denis Park and the Relay Station area). BR&AB, MD-MHS, 131: 4: 3, p. 173, EB to G.B. Howard, April 13, 1896.

50. In 1897, the Western Maryland Railroad rescinded these passes.

51. Eleanor Stephens Bruchey, *The Business Elite in Baltimore 1880–1914* (Dissertation submitted to the Johns Hopkins University, 1967; repr. North Stratford, N. H.: Arno Press, 1976), pp. 246– 253 (page references are to reprint edition). Bruchey adopted the *Social Register*, an elite listing first published in 1887 of the most prominent American families, as the test of upper class membership; she considered the *Society Visiting List*, which

appeared in 1889–1890, a somewhat more liberal guide. (Significant numbers of residents of both Sudbrook Park and Roland Park also were listed in these social registers; this is addressed more fully in subsequent chapters).

52. It does not appear that Sudbrook Park had gas lamps lighting its streets, as did many of these early suburbs.

53. "Monumental City Suburbs," p. 26 (referring to Ruxton Heights).

54. Fares on electric lines tended to be about five cents, versus a fare of ten cents for the same distance on a train. While these amounts seem minuscule today, the average laborer was paid only about a dollar a day. As a further comparison, Eugene Blackford's Day Book listed the following expenses (1891–93): hair cut — fifteen cents; shoes — $3.50; umbrella — $1.00; suit for Blackford's son — $11; shoes for Blackford — $4; wedding dress for Blackford's daughter — $24; wedding cake — $2; half-gallon of whiskey — $1.25; sale of calf — $3; hire of horse and cart — $8. BR&AB, MD-MHS, 131: 2 (Day Book, 1891–1893). Blackford's salary from the Sudbrook Company was $41.66 a month until December 1893, when it was increased to $83.33 a month.

55. The article described cars "so heavily constructed that they run with great smoothness and almost without noise, at an average rate of 12 miles an hour." "Monumental City Suburbs," p. 27.

56. Olson, p. 212.

Chapter 10: A Year of Renewed Vigor: 1894

1. While certain sectors of the economy showed improvement by this time, other sectors (many industries and laborers) felt the effect of the financial depression for several years after 1893. Segments of the nation's economy endured a depression from 1893 through about 1897, with a slight improvement in 1895. See "U.S. Prosperity and Depressions since 1790," *World Book Encyclopedia,* Vol. 5, p. 127.

2. BR&AB, MD-MHS, 131: 3: 1, p. 414–15, EB to Mrs. Eliza C. Miller, October 2, 1893 (Mr. O. B. Zantzinger and his wife, boarders at the hotel, wanted to occupy Cottage No. 7 for the winter months).

3. BR&AB, MD-MHS, 131: 3: 1, p. 428–29, EB to Col. W.A. James, January 4, 1894.

4. BR&AB, MD-MHS, 131: 3: 1, p. 433–35, EB to Lynn R. Meekins, January 26, 1894 ("To my great surprise, Mrs. Miller has notified me of her intentions to buy the No. 7 Cottage for cash.")

5. BR&AB, MD-MHS, 131: 3: 1, p. 433–35, EB to Lynn R. Meekins, January 26, 1894. It is apparent from Blackford's letters that Mrs. Miller, a widow, consulted her son about her purchase and relied on his advice; he most certainly was the Decatur H. Miller that Blackford referred to in this letter.

6. Although Mrs. Miller purchased the cottage in her own name (Eliza C. Miller), Blackford more frequently corresponded with her son, Decatur H. Miller, Jr. (see for example BR&AB, MD-MHS, 131: 3: 1, p. 433, EB to D. H. Miller, Jr., January 26, 1894: "I shall write to Mr. Meekins today informing him of your mother's determination to take the house."). Blackford almost always directed his correspondence to men, usually husbands, even when it clearly should have gone to a woman (for example, when a wife was the purchaser of property or had been the one to initiate contact with Blackford about some problem).

7. BR&AB, MD-MHS, 131: 3: 1, p. 433–35, EB to Lynn R. Meekins, January 26, 1894.

8. The Meekins family called their Sudbrook home "Lyndhurst," according to their listing in the *Society Visiting List* for the season of 1897. Years later when the Alexander R. Early family obtained the house, they renamed it "Chudleigh." See *Social Registers* of 1913 and 1915.

9. Although the cottage numbers assigned by Blackford correlated with the sequence in which lots were purchased, and many numbers accurately reflected the chronology of building, not all did. Here, the lot had been purchased in 1892 (thus receiving the No. 16 designation), but the house was not built until 1894, after construction already had commenced on the cottage numbered 23. (Also, since the community's livery stable and the foreman's farmhouse were among Blackford's numbered buildings, not all cottage numbers corresponded to the number of actual cottages built at the time).

10. BR&AB, MD-MHS, 131: 3: 1, p. 460, EB to W.R. Stone, Road Master, May 8, 1894.

11. BR&AB, MD-MHS, 131: 3: 1, p. 464, EB to H.G. Armstrong, May 15, 1894.

12. BR&AB, MD-MHS, 131: 3: 1, p. 465, EB to Jesse L. Cassard, May 20, 1894.

13. BR&AB, MD-MHS, 131: 3: 1, p. 479, EB to Messrs. Dorksrader & Considine, August 24, 1894.

14. BR&AB, MD-MHS, 131: 3: 1, p. 478, EB to Mrs. Frank H. Norman, August 22, 1894.

15. At the request of tenants who wanted to occupy two of the summer cottages year-round and agreed to pay a higher rent, Bond winterized cottages Nos. 14 (503 Sudbrook Lane) and 15 (721 Cliveden). (A dining room, kitchen with range and furnace were added to No. 14, whereupon Charles Crane and his wife became permanent residents until Mrs. Crane's poor health required them to give up their lease three and a half years later, whereupon Clarence Shriver leased and subsequently purchased the property. Cottage No. 15 was enlarged with a kitchen, dining room, pantry, back porch and furnace; Bradley T. Stokes and his family lived there that winter and for the next seven and a half years. BR&AB, MD-MHS, 131: 3: 1, p. 494, EB to Charles Crane, September 28, 1894 and p. 490, EB to HLB, September 22, 1894, respectively).

16. BR&AB, MD-MHS, 131: 3: 1, p. 482, EB to HLB, September 4, 1894.

17. Waesche, p. 37 (showing a photograph of Walbrook's casino. Mount Washington also had, early on, a casino where couples waltzed and neighbors congregated; it was razed in 1958. Miller, p. 71).

18. BR&AB, MD-MHS, 131: 3: 1, p. 490, EB to HLB, September 22, 1894.

19. BR&AB, MD-MHS, 131: 3: 1, p. 493, EB to HLB, September 26, 1894.

20. It is unclear from Blackford's subsequent letters at what point Sudbrook's casino was fully implemented. Other letters that fall indicated that John Cowan began to build an addition for the casino based on a design he drew. After these letters, little more was said about the casino until 1898, when a pool table was put in the hotel. I have been unable to ascertain whether this was a second pool table or the one intended as part of the earlier casino, which might not have been installed until later.

21. BR&AB, MD-MHS, 131: 3: 1, p. 494, EB to J.E. Trippe, September 25, 1894.

22. BR&AB, MD-MHS, 131: 3: 1, p. 494, EB to J.E. Trippe, September 25, 1894 (emphasis in original).

23. Several years later, Archer designed Oscar Webb's house at 709 Cliveden Road. See fn. 57 in Ch. 8 for biographical information about George Archer.

24. BR&AB, MD-MHS, 131: 4: 3, p. 3, EB to J.H. Wilson Mariott, October 2, 1894. In this letter, Blackford talked about the Waring drainage, rather than sewerage, system. It seems clear that Waring's drainage system for roads, walks and house rainwater was implemented at Sudbrook. (See for example, BR&AB, MD-MHS, 131: 4: 3, p. 256, EB to Messrs. Ghequier & May, April 17, 1897). As well as I can ascertain, Sudbrook also used Waring's system for sewage disposal. See for example BR&AB, MD-MHS, 131: 4: 2, p. 19, EB to Geo. E. Waring, Jr., August 13, 1892: "Dear Sir, I have your postal of the 10th inst. offering to send me a copy of your 'Sewage Disposal at Wayne.' I write to say that I shall be very glad to have it, following your work as I do with much interest, and having adopted your system at the Suburban Settlement, of which I am manager. In this connection I would say that of the eight separate systems I have laid, not one has ever given the least trouble, nor has one received the least attention." Blackford never used the term "sewerage system," although his letters made clear that Sudbrook had indoor flush toilets, water closets and bathroom plumbing.

195

Blackford did write often that Sudbrook used the "Waring absorption system," most likely referring to Sudbrook's sewerage system, which appeared to be a home-by-home or interconnected septic system. (Typical home septic systems consist of "an underground, watertight container (the septic tank), a soil absorption drainage field (pipes buried in the ground, surrounded by gravel), and a box in between them that distributes liquid from the tank to the field." Karol V. Menzie and Randy Johnson, "A Happy Septic System is a Good Septic System," *Baltimore Sun*, November 3, 1996, p. 3L).

25. BR&AB, MD-MHS, 131: 4: 3, pp. 11, 15 and 18, EB to Nat. Architects Union in Phila., Messrs. J.C. Cady & Co. Architects in New York, and Messrs. Child & deGoll, Architects, in New York, October 11, 12 and 17, 1894, respectively.

26. Blackford did not identify by cottage number the house that Child & deGoll designed, but by a process of elimination, 724 Howard Road seems to be the most likely. The house at 708 Cliveden was a near duplicate of Bond's 721 Cliveden Road; 1016 Winsor came from a plan book (the "Westin house"); and 1017 Winsor did not fit Blackford's description of the Child & deGoll house, while 724 Howard did (in writing for "suggestions on which colouring" to use, Blackford noted that the "roof & gable end is of Maine Cedar shingles & will be left to colour naturally."). BR&AB, MD-MHS, 131: 4: 2, p. 99, EB to Messrs. Child & deGoll, March 11, 1895.

27. BR&AB, MD-MHS, 131: 4: 3, p. 25 and 29, EB to Cowan, November 7 and 15, 1894, respectively.

28. BR&AB, MD-MHS, 131: 4: 2, p. 79 and 84, EB to Cator and Webb, December 4 and 15, 1894, respectively. Blackford does not state where this private stable, the first of seven, was built. (Although convenience was one reason to build a private stable, another seemed to be that Sudbrook residents were not always happy with the operation of the community's livery stable. In March 1893, a committee of gentlemen representing fourteen houses "called upon [Blackford] to lease a piece of ground upon which to build a stable." They agreed not to press the issue if August Fowner, the livery manager, would accept seventy-five dollars and surrender his lease of the stable "to a party to be named by them.... Otherwise, they intend to build a stable & rent it to this man, who will care for their horses & keep others for them." Fowner surrendered his lease and the crisis was averted, perhaps in part because of Blackford's warning that "I have no doubt in my own mind but that they will succeed in getting every horse that comes to the place, and I would impress this fact upon you." BR&AB, MD-MHS, 131: 3: 1, p. 497, EB to Aug. Fowner, March 1, 1893).

29. Of these twenty-five cottages, Bond owned four individually, the Bond-Blackford syndicate owned four under construction and the Company had built nine (one of which had been sold).

Chapter 11: High Hopes: 1895–1907

1. BR&AB, MD-MHS, 131: 4: 3, p. 49, EB to R.H. Pollack, January 14, 1895.

2. Dr. and Mrs. S. K. Merrick built the house at 517 Sudbrook Lane, where they raised their family. Two of their sons, William and Robert, have contributed, albeit posthumously, to this book. William S. Merrick's unpublished memoirs ("Memories of Sudbrook") and the photograph of the family taken in about 1897 were shared with me by William Merrick's grandson, Stewart McLean. The major grant used to publish this book came from the Jacob and Annita France and the Robert G. and Anne M. Merrick Foundations. The late Robert G. Merrick's fondness for Sudbrook Park and willingness to contribute to its preservation was quite evident when I visited him in the early 1980s to request a contribution to efforts to save Sudbrook Park from the then-threatened rapid transit project. I was accompanied by long-time Sudbrook resident Edward B. Stellmann, who had known Merrick when the two of them were growing up in Sudbrook Park. They both enthusiastically recounted their recollections of boyhood fun and adventures in the young community.

3. BR&AB, MD-MHS, 131: 4: 3, p. 47–48, EB to Dr. S. K. Merrick, January 7, 1895.

4. BR&AB, MD-MHS, 131: 4: 3, p. 72, EB to HLB, April 2, 1895. Blackford's reference to "my house" here meant Cottage No. 2, which he still was renting from the Company.

5. When Blackford wrote asking that furnaces also be put in Cottages Nos. 24 and 25 (for Charles A. Webb and George Cator, respectively), he commented: "I had hoped that I would not need both of them, as they are to be occupied only in the summer, but the tenants are of that class which demands everything." BR&AB, MD-MHS, 131: 4: 2, p. 103, EB to Sexton & Sons, May 13, 1895.

6. BR&AB, MD-MHS, 131: 4: 3, p. 93, EB to John Hood, May 21, 1895.

7. It is not clear that there were long flights of wooden steps at the end of the pedestrian bridge. Judging from Blackford's letters, early photographs and the location of that bridge on the Olmsted Plan, it appears that those disembarking from the train would have had at most six steps on the station side and eleven steps on the Sudbrook side. There did not appear to be stairs up to the pedestrian bridge from the track level, which would have been at ground level on the Sudbrook side and appears to have been accessed on the station side by traversing the landscaped area east of the station.

8. Cox, p. 39. Unfortunately, many of the statements in this account cannot be authenticated. In addition, much of the information to which we now have access had not been uncovered when Cox wrote her history. Even though not all of the details in Cox's history are accurate based on newly discovered material, hers was for a long time the **only** account of the early community. As such, it became the basis of most of the newspaper and other articles written over the years (and still quoted) about Sudbrook. While it is important to correct the historical record, Cox deserves significant credit for compiling, preserving and sharing information about Sudbrook Park which otherwise most certainly would have been lost.

9. It is unfortunate that Blackford never enumerated the railroad's reasons, but he did comment to John Hood, President of the Western Maryland Railroad, that "while recognizing the force of your reasons for desiring the change...," it was in the Sudbrook Company's interest to leave the station in its original location. BR&AB, MD-MHS, 131: 4: 3, p. 93, EB to John Hood, May 21, 1895.

10. If the railroad's insistence on moving the station had been prompted by efforts to resolve complaints by residents of Sudbrook Park regarding the number of stairs to the pedestrian bridge, the Sudbrook Company certainly would have been in more of a quandary, since it would have been in the Company's interest, as well as the railroad's, to keep commuters satisfied. Moreover, all photographs of the relocated station show it at a much higher grade above the tracks than the original station, requiring residents to navigate more than thirty stairs in descending to and ascending from the train. Unfortunately, the earliest dated photograph is 1917. The railroad did lower the existing grade around 1906–07 when it laid double tracks; it is possible that there was less of a climb before that.

11. BR&AB, MD-MHS, 131: 4: 3, p. 93, EB to John Hood, May 21, 1895.

12. BR&AB, MD-MHS, 131: 4: 3, p. 147, EB to John Hood, January 27, 1896.

13. BR&AB, MD-MHS, 131: 4: 3, p. 147, EB to John Hood, January 27, 1896.

14. BR&AB, MD-MHS, 131: 4: 3, p. 172, EB to HLB, April 6, 1896. Blackford's concern that the McHenrys might prohibit passage across the lot seemed to stem from the fact that Sudbrook residents using the Company's pedestrian bridge would have had to cross the abandoned station property either going to or returning from Pikesville.

15. BR&AB, MD-MHS, 131: 4: 3, p. 178, EB to Hood, April 25, 1896. A few years later, Blackford again used Mr. Spicknall to raise the Sudbrook water tower five feet in an effort to increase water pressure.

16. Cox, p. 39. Most likely, the station was taken across the tracks at the freight siding, which was west of the station and at ground level, and from there transported to its new location on Howard Road.

17. As noted above in fn. 15, Blackford later used Spicknall to raise the water tower. The relationship between Spicknall and Cox may have been that of contractor and subcontractor, respectively.

18. Efforts to keep the new station area attractive were on-going. In January 1899 Blackford wrote the railroad asking for a car load of coarse limestone for use at the station, because "at the season of alternate freezing & thawing the approaches to the Station are very muddy, and visitors who

come to view the property have at the first step a bad impression." BR&AB, MD-MHS, 131: 4: 3, p. 475, EB to Vandervanten, January 24, 1899. In August 1900 Sudbrook resident George Coursen contacted John Hood, President of the Western Maryland Railroad, about the unsightly condition of the station grounds. Blackford followed up on this with Hood. In a cooperative effort, the railroad and the Sudbrook Company widened the path to seven feet, covered it again with rolled gravel, provided a galvanized box for waste paper and a sign printed: "Vehicles are forbidden to stand here." The sign was placed on the porte-cochere, where it was "the custom for horses to stand for hours gnawing the rail of the enclosure & making the waiting room unpleasant by their droppings." BR&AB, MD-MHS, 131: 4: 4, pp. 68, 70, and 71, EB to Hood, August 15, 16 and 28, 1900, respectively.

19. Purchasers not connected with the Company owned eleven of the twenty-six cottages. The Sudbrook Company still owned seven cottages, of which three (Nos. 4, 5 and 10) were for summer use. (No. 4 was at 1020 Winsor Road; Nos. 5 and 10 have not survived). Bond owned four rental cottages, of which two (Nos. 11 and 13, at 1018 Winsor and 500 Sudbrook Lane) were for summer use. The Bond-Blackford syndicate owned four, all equipped for winter use.

20. BR&AB, MD-MHS, 131: 4: 3, p. 140, EB to Prentiss Ingraham, Nov. 14, 1895.

21. A few years later, Blackford wrote that there were about twenty Sudbrook men who went to town daily in the winter, and about sixty to seventy-five in the summer. The more-than-doubling of Sudbrook's population each May through October seemed to perpetuate its "summer community" reputation despite a growing core of permanent residents. BR&AB, MD-MHS, 131: 4: 3, p. 451, EB to First Assistant Postmaster General, Washington, D.C., October 31, 1898.

22. BR&AB, MD-MHS, 131: 4: 3, p. 151, EB to HLB, February 5, 1896 and BR&AB, MD-MHS, 131: 4: 3, pp. 156 and 160, EB to William P. Robinson, February 17 and 27, 1896, respectively. Whether Bond's stated reason was the real reason is questionable. He had just spent over $17,000 to build the four syndicate houses (Nos. 24, 25, 26 and 27) and might have objected to **any** additional expense. Even more pertinent, No. 11 was one of five cottages (three owned by the Company, two by Bond) built in close proximity to the hotel — all intended as summer cottages for "boarders" who would take all of their meals at the hotel. Mrs. Thomson, who ran the hotel, was given a discount in rent if any of the cottages for boarders went unoccupied, a situation that did not occur until 1904, when one summer rental sat vacant. Bond did, however, agree to make changes to No. 11 in later years to satisfy renters. In 1899 he added a servant's w.c. on the first floor; in 1900 he added a kitchen, pantry and porch; and in 1904 the defective drainage system was replaced. No. 11 was rented by Dr. and Mrs. Herbert Harlan from 1898 through 1906. Records indicate that the cottage must have been winterized before the winter of 1903–04, since Mrs. Thomson who ran the hotel occupied it during that winter.

23. It is possible that Mifflin Coulter was related to John Mifflin Hood, President of the Western Maryland Railroad. Hood's mother, Hannah Mifflin Hood, was the daughter of Alexander Coulter of Baltimore. For information about John Mifflin Hood, see Scharf, Part 1, p. 357.

24. In October 1898 the Coulters wanted an addition to their house. Bond's response, relayed by Blackford, was that the addition they wanted might benefit a family constituted like theirs, but might prove undesirable for most people. (Apparently, they had an adult daughter, Nannie Coulter, living with them and so wanted the house modified so that it would "suit two parties of the same family.") Bond agreed to make the addition if the Coulters would purchase the nine room house for $4,500. This they appeared to be doing, and the addition was made. Then, sometime between the spring of 1899 and March 1900, after the house had water in the cellar which the Sudbrook Company drained, the Coulters vacated the house. It seemed that the final purchase papers never had been signed by Mifflin Coulter. See BR&AB, MD-MHS, 131: 4: 3, pp. 445, 447 and 448, EB to Miss Nannie G. Coulter, October 17 and 25, 1898, respectively, and BR&AB, MD-MHS, 131: 4: 3, pp. 484 and 485, EB to M. Coulter, March 3 and 6, 1898, respectively. (Mifflin Coulter is listed with a Sudbrook Park address in the *Society Visiting List* and the *Social Register* from 1894 through 1899. He, together with Mr. and Mrs. Albert Gambrill (Nannie G. Coulter), are listed in the 1904 *Social Register* as living at "Valley View," St. Denis, Maryland).

25. BR&AB, MD-MHS, 131: 4: 3, p. 178, EB to Messrs. Gittings & Reynolds, April 25, 1896. Another letter trying to sell No. 29 states: "This house was built in the best manner possible — of Ga. pine, when exposed — double sheathed & covered with paper, over which white cedar shingles are laid & left to weather stain." BR&AB, MD-MHS, 131: 4: 3, p. 183, EB to Dr. J. Harvey Hill, May 9, 1896.

26. The main problem, Blackford felt, was the deplorable condition of the road that passed his farm and went from Randallstown to the Pikesville train station. He had written to county officials on numerous occasions imploring them to do something about the road. He again wrote, noting: "I have twice lost the chance of selling this farm to parties, who would not spend money upon it solely on account of the road. Nor am I able to rent the house except at a very reduced rate for the season." BR&AB, MD-MHS, 131: 4: 2, p. 126, EB to Frank George, Feb. 25, 1896.

27. BR&AB, MD-MHS, 131: 4: 3, p. 173, EB to G.B. Howard, April 13, 1896.

28. BR&AB, MD-MHS, 131: 4: 3, p. 179–180, EB to C.P. Knight, April 25, 1896.

29. BR&AB, MD-MHS, 131: 4: 4, p. 143, EB to Reuben Foster, April 8, 1901.

30. "Suburbs and County. Sudbrook Park," *Baltimore Sun*, July 7, 1896. The article listed persons occupying cottages as well as some of those staying at the Woodland Inn. A large number of those named were listed in either or both the *Social Register* or the *Society Visiting List* Among the cottagers were the families of James McEvoy, Dr. Herbert Harlan, Bradley T. Stokes, Dr. Garland Davison, D. Howard Miller, Jr., Lynn R. Meekins, Joseph Whyte, Dr. George Thomas, Henry Ward, Byrd Thompson, William Rayner, Joseph Trippe, James Corner, Mifflin Coulter, Alexander Early, Franklin Cator, W.P. Robinson, Charles Webb, Oscar Webb, Charles Crane, John Barker, Dr. S.K. Merrick, Eugene Blackford, Eugene Poultney, J. Hume Smith, Clarence Shriver, E. B. Bankard, Charles Linthicum, James Shriver, and William Stellmann. Hotel guests included the Adrian Oudesluys, Beauregard Howard, the Jesse Cassards, the Albert Gambrills, and several Webbs and Duvals, among others. (Thanks to John McGrain for finding this article and forwarding it to Beryl Frank, who sent it to me.)

31. BR&AB, MD-MHS, 131: 4: 2, p. 165, EB to HLB, October 2, 1896.

32. BR&AB, MD-MHS, 131: 4: 2, p. 168, EB to John Hood, October 13, 1896.

33. BR&AB, MD-MHS, 131: 4: 3, p. 225, EB to James McEvoy, December 11, 1896. The digging of a new artesian well commenced in the summer of 1895, but did not get far. The man hired was to dig to a depth of 100 feet. He had trouble digging and lost his drill; after other difficulties, Blackford agreed to release him when he got to 32 feet. A second man was hired to complete the job, got to 38 feet and then "threw up the job." Chances are it was the extensive rock underlying much of Sudbrook Park that presented the problem. Blackford frequently used dynamite to blast rock so that cellars could be prepared, and often commented that he could not use a compass to survey, measuring by angles and courses instead, since the land had so much iron ore. The new well was completed in 1896, however. (Blackford's enthusiasm in the letter to McEvoy just cited belied the letter immediately following it. That letter related problems with the boiler, which leaked badly and "was too small to turn the pump for which it was intended." BR&AB, MD-MHS, 131: 4: 3, p. 225, EB to Messrs. Thom. K. Carey & Bros. Co., December 11, 1896. Despite the new well, the Company continued to experience problems with water pressure and had to raise the water tower five feet the following year).

34. While sales during this period were better than during the Company's prior years, they lagged far behind what was needed to generate sufficient profit to sustain long-term success. The sale of twelve properties over a three-year period amounted to about one sale every three months.

35. BR&AB, MD-MHS, 131: 4: 2, p.323–24, EB to Mrs. Jas. Hewes, Oct. 27, 1899.

36. BR&AB, MD-MIIS, 131: 4: 3, p. 317, undated Request for Proposal (between two letters dated Nov. 7 and 8, 1897). In a subsequent request for permission to use Baltimore County's steam roller in the road work, Blackford stated that 4,600 feet of the road he wanted to roll extended from the Reisterstown turnpike, opposite the Soldier's Home, to Milford [Mill] Road, and about the same length of the road was within the limits of Sudbrook Park. BR&AB, MD-MHS, 131: 4: 3, p. 321, EB to President, Board Commissioners of Baltimore County, November 15, 1897. As for the size of

stones needed, Blackford had earlier written one supplier that they should "not be larger than hickory nuts." To another he wrote that "there are some 5 miles of roads. Of this amt. about 2 miles have been finished with furnace slag, covered with limestone of the size represented by chestnuts." BR&AB, MD-MHS, 131: 4: 3, p. 101, EB to Decarbonate Lime Co., Waynesboro, Pa., June 6, 1895, and pp. 108–109 to Messrs. Hoke Bittinger & Co., Hanover, Pa., June 27, 1895.

37. In order to increase water pressure for residents, a number of whom had complained, Blackford in June 1897 gave Spicknall the specifications for raising the water tower five feet. BR&AB, MD-MHS, 131: 4: 3, p. 282, EB to Spicknall, June 24, 1897 (the specifications are at pp. 280–81).

38. BR&AB, MD-MHS, 131: 4: 3, pp. 342–343 and 348–350, various letters of EB to prior tenants and new prospects, February 19–25, 1998.

39. BR&AB, MD-MHS, 131: 4: 3, p. 345–347, EB to Sam. S. Keighler, undated (based on chronological sequence written in February 1898). Blackford exaggerated slightly. Each acre would have contained about 7.26 lots measuring 40'x150' (6,000 square feet). Even if each of the seven sold for $250, the per acre price would have been $1,815, not $2,000.

40. Blackford's letters reveal him to have been a diligent, perhaps "workaholic" personality, who seemed to put in hours that greatly exceeded the standard work week and who often worked on holidays like Thanksgiving and Christmas.

41. BR&AB, MD-MHS, 131: 4: 3, p. 367, EB to John M. Hood, March 16, 1898.

42. A golf course/Club House had not been a part of the Olmsted Plan. The golf course began to show signs of neglect during the 'teens and by 1920, "the club house had been torn down and the fairways had become fields of wildflowers." Cox, p. 41. As recounted by another resident: "When World War I came the golf club fell upon evil days and the owners of the property tried to force the property owners to purchase it, but with the war on, little interest could be aroused for such a procedure and the Club faded out of existence." Merricks "Memories." The golf course acreage was part of the land developed by the William F. Chew Company in the 1940s (see Chap. 14 for more information on this development).

43. BR&AB, MD-MHS, 131: 4: 3, p. 367, EB to John M. Hood, March 16, 1898. Blackford stated: "I find it impossible to drain the bath room on the flat lot next [to] the Station, where the [Club] house must be built." Having heard nothing from Hood on this matter, Blackford later repeated the request and pledged that the Sudbrook Company would "remove the [sewer] connection at anytime on demand from the R.R. Co." BR&AB, MD-MHS, 131: 4: 3, p. 385, EB to Hood, April 6, 1898.

44. BR&AB, MD-MHS, 131: 4: 3, p. 367, EB to Coursen, March 16, 1898 (It is not known whether this implied that the casino idea first advanced in 1894 (as an addition to the hotel) had not been successful, or whether Blackford contemplated two casinos. In fact, no casino ever developed around the Club House, which no longer survives).

45. The golf course was immediately popular. Blackford wrote to the railroad in May asking them to lay off the approach from the station to the Club House, which had not yet been completed, because "parties are already arriving by train to play." BR&AB, MD-MHS, 131: 4: 3, p. 409, EB to Vandervanter, May 31, 1898.

46. Waesche opined that the "masterstroke" of Edward Bouton, who directed the development of Roland Park, "was his 1898 transformation of the [Roland Park] Golf Club into the Baltimore Country Club. It was the move that would guarantee Roland Park's ascendancy as Baltimore's premiere suburb." Waesche, p. 68. This observation was astute and accurate. As other commentators have pointed out, "country clubs were first and foremost social instruments and only secondarily dedicated to sport and leisure pursuits. They existed to draw lines between ethnic, class, economic, and social groups, and quickly became registers of social prominence in themselves…. Indeed, country clubs and the institutions surrounding them — the country day school, summer resort, elite university, exclusive suburban enclave — were the most important barometers of power and prestige in elite circles during the era of capitalist consolidation [following the panic of 1893 and extending into the beginning of the twentieth century]." Mark Alan Hewitt, *The Architect & the American Country House, 1890–1940* (New Haven: Yale University Press, 1990), pp. 10–11.

47. The Sudbrook Co. originally agreed to build the house with just a two and a half-year lease agreement — perhaps in desperation after a year with no sales whatsoever. The Company was cautious about Duncan, a builder with whom it had no experience. Apparently, Duncan had supervised the erection of houses at Normandy Heights, beyond Roland Park. Duncan quit work on Cottage No. 36 after the Sudbrook Co. refused to pay his workmen when it learned that he owed his subcontractors more than he was still due.

48. Hooper owned a business that was assigned to creditors at one point, and then made a comeback — at which point the Company agreed to give him a one-year option for purchase of the house at $7,000. Meanwhile, other prospective purchasers were turned down. The house was sublet to William B. Rayner (who had wanted to purchase it) in 1900 and to Dr. Hiram Woods in 1902. After the sale to Hooper fell through in 1902, the asking price went to $7,500. Hooper was still listed as lessee on the Company's records in 1907. By 1913, a family named Pendleton was in the house. The grand cottage with electric lights no longer stands at 520 Sudbrook Lane; it burned in the 1920s and another house was subsequently built.

49. BR&AB, MD-MHS, 131: 4: 2, p. 390, EB to Hoffman, Dec. 18, 1900. Appleton Wilson had also designed No. 26, the Graves' house at 726 Howard Road, which subsequently had water problems. When Graves complained, Blackford had written to remind him that he had advised against such a flat roof, but Graves' architect had insisted. Perhaps elevating the house a foot above ground level was Wilson's added insurance against water problems that plagued a number of Sudbrook houses, despite Blackford's "almost perfect" (at least by his accounting) drainage systems. Other houses that had problems with cellar water were Nos. 14 (503 Sudbrook Lane) and 30 (722 Howard). Blackford resolved the problems by ditching around the houses and adding additional drains.

50. Although Blackford often referred to Rayner as a U.S. Senator, this office came after he was living in Sudbrook, although he had been an elected official for some time. Isidor Rayner (1850–1912) represented the second district of Baltimore County in the state legislature during terms beginning in 1878 (House) and 1886 and 1888 (Senate); served three terms in the United States House of Representatives (1887, 1891 and 1893); served a term as Maryland's Attorney General beginning in 1899; and served four terms in the United States Senate (1905, 1907, 1909 and 1911). Edward C. Papenfuse, ed., *Archives of Maryland, An Historical List of Public Officials of Maryland,* Vol. I (Annapolis: Maryland State Archives, 1990), pp. 359 and 494.

51. BCMR, Liber N.B.M. 225, folio 103, Sudbrook Company of Baltimore County Mortgage to Isidor Rayner, made Sept. 18, 1901. Under the terms of the mortgage, Rayner advanced $6,000 to the Sudbrook Company and was to be repaid the full principal amount on April 1, 1907, with interest at five and a half percent per annum, payable quarterly from April 1902. The Sudbrook Company's debt was secured by a mortgage Rayner held on the property (approximately two acres in Block No. 22, Olmsted's Plan of Sudbrook). The Sudbrook Company was responsible for all taxes and insurance. The Company paid Rayner in full and the mortgage was released on October 20, 1910 (BCMR, Liber W.P.C. 352, folio 248, Isidor Rayner Release to Sudbrook Company of Baltimore County, referring to the original 1901 mortgage as well as a second mortgage of May 21, 1903 (Liber N.B.M. 236, folio 156)).

52. Described as "one of Baltimore's most talented architectural firms," Wyatt and Nolting designed Roland Park's Country Club, the Roland Park shopping center, numerous houses (many in Roland Park) and many other noteworthy buildings. Dorsey and Dilts, pp. XLV and 241.

53. BR&AB, MD-MHS, 131: 4: 4, p. 179, EB to HLB, Sept. 9, 1901. Blackford's letters indicated that William B. Rayner, who had rented No. 27 (708 Cliveden) and No. 36 (the original house at 520 Sudbrook Lane), was Senator Rayner's son. While Blackford welcomed the prominence of a U.S. Senator, he was not happy when, in 1906, Rayner had a number of unauthorized repairs made and billed the Company after the fact. For diplomacy's sake, however, Bond allowed the expenses, agreeing with Blackford "that a snit would be undesirable." BR&AB, MD-MHS, 131: 3, Sudbrook Company Day Book, 1903–1908.

54. Although the cottages numbered up to thirty-nine, there were only thirty-five cottages for residents by 1907. No. 3 was the hotel; No. 17 was the Company's livery stable; No. 21 was the farm or tenant house located at lot 9 of Block 13; and No. 35 was the (golf) Club House, erected in 1898.

Chapter 12: The Promise Fades: 1907–1910

1. The Sudbrook Company retained its legal status as a Maryland corporation until at least 1922. According to documents in the Baltimore County Land Records office, Bond signed documents as President of the Company up to March of that year; he died the following month. For all practical purposes, however, the Sudbrook Company faded out of the picture in connection with Sudbrook Park in November 1910, when it conveyed to others all of its remaining land and property in Sudbrook Park. (The Company never appears to have filed articles of dissolution, even after 1922. Its Articles of Incorporation had stipulated a forty year corporate existence, to 1929).

2. BR&AB, MD-MHS, Ms. No. 131, Vols. 1–5, 1891–1907.

3. Historian Joseph L. Arnold cited four factors as contributing to Baltimore's lag in suburban development as compared to other large cities in the East: (1) the transit and utility systems ("until the 1890s Baltimore's transit system was, by all local reports, one of the worst in the nation and was a substantial retardant to outward migration. In addition, the outlying sections of the city were very badly served with basic utilities like water, gas and electricity;" (2) the nature of the housing and land development market (noting a reluctance of moneyed landowners to sell large estates for middle-class dwellings), as well as inferior county schools and police and fire protection; (3) the architectural conservatism and preference for elegant town houses among the city's home buyers and renters ("even among those who could, and did, own suburban summer cottages. Not until 1910 or 1920 did the preference of the upper middle classes swing decisively toward the detached house and the romantic, rural setting embodied in areas such as Roland Park."); and (4) combined factors associated with Baltimore's "Southernlyness" that held people in the old sections of the city longer than occurred in cities to the North or West (Baltimore never had as large a foreign-born population as cities like Philadelphia, New York or Boston, so that the middle-class here did not feel such an urgent need to "escape" from the city. In addition, the largest ethnic group in the city was German, "the group that made the easiest transition to middle-class status"). Arnold, "Baltimore's Neighborhoods," pp. 88–90.

4. Schalck, "Planning Roland Park," p. 419. Schalck incorrectly stated in his article that Sudbrook Park was "intended" as a summer resort.

5. Waesche, p. 71.

6. "Suburbs Blazed By Lone Woman," the *Baltimore Sun*, Dec. 5, 1937 (noting that those adventuresome enough to live year-round in Baltimore's early suburbs were considered hardy pioneers).

7. See Ch. 9 and "Monumental City Suburbs," cited therein.

8. According to streetcar historian Farrell, "The Baltimore, Pimlico & Pikesville is another of those companies that was organized to serve a purpose more imagined than needed." Farrell, p. 37.

9. Farrell, 45. Thanks also to Herbert H. Harwood, Jr., author of *Baltimore and Its Streetcars* (New York: Quadrant Press, 1984) and a contributor to the Farrell book, for information he kindly shared in a telephone interview on July 12, 1996, regarding the Pimlico & Pikesville Railroad, the Western Maryland Railroad and train vs. electric rail travel in the late 1880s.

10. BR&AB, MD-MHS, 131: 4: 3, pp. 47–48, EB to Dr. S.K. Merrick, January 7, 1895. In this letter, Blackford also pointed out that a "broad, macadamized avenue leads to the electric road and the Reisterstown turnpike." This would have been the current Sudbrook Lane, which was designed by Olmsted and constructed by the Sudbrook Company. The road's width would appear to have been about twenty feet, based on Olmsted's cross-section drawings.

11. BR&AB, MD-MHS, 131: 4: 3, pp. 46, EB to C.P. Knight, January 9, 1895.

12. Ultimately, Blackford's failure to fully anticipate and adapt to some of the changes that were being thrust onto his late nineteenth century world may have contributed to his inability to promote Sudbrook Park in a more dynamic manner.

13. BR&AB, MD-MHS, 131: 4: 2, p. 54, EB to Robt. B. Chapman, November 10, 1893 (despite his professed distaste for electric street rail travel, Blackford goes on to say that he might invest in the electric line road, adding: "Of course my place is near enough to the R.R. to enable one to make use of it, yet, I would regard its value as greatly enhanced were a good electric road to pass by it.")

14. Blackford later wrote that Sudbrook was "promised a nearer approach [of the Pikesville electric line], but of this I know nothing certain." BR&AB, MD-MHS, 131: 4: 3, p. 453, EB to Richard H. Woodward, November [8], 1898. No nearer terminus was ever implemented.

15. In a subsequent letter to John Hood, President of the Western Maryland Railroad, Blackford noted that his own sons often had to take the electric cars to Sudbrook in the fall and winter, since they did not get off work until after the Western Maryland train had departed, "but they are country bred & can stand the walk, but others cannot or will not." BR&AB, MD-MHS, 131: 4: 4, p. 12, EB to Hood, September 29, 1899. Also, while many electric line waiting stations were quite decorative and ornamental, they were, for the most part, open-air rather than enclosed structures in the early years. This made them less pleasant than fully enclosed train stations in inclement weather. Later, enclosed waiting stations were built, particularly along the Lake Roland Elevated Line. See generally Farrell.

16. "Monumental City Suburbs…" *Sunday Herald*, April 30, 1893.

17. General information about the Western Maryland Railroad courtesy of train historian Herb Harwood, telephone interview on July 12, 1996.

18. BR&AB, MD-MHS, 131: 4: 3, p. 235, EB to Hood, February 13, 1897.

19. BR&AB, MD-MHS, 131: 4: 3, p. 254–255, EB to Hood, April 7, 1897.

20. BR&AB, MD-MHS, 131: 4: 3, p. 254–255, EB to Hood, April 7, 1897.

21. BR&AB, MD-MHS, 131: 4: 3, p. 254–255, EB to Hood, April 7, 1897. Blackford's letter apparently moved Hood, who asked for Blackford's suggestions about scheduling and when best to resume service. Blackford took the opportunity to present his views and to expound on the relative disadvantages of electric rail travel again — the "disagreeable waiting for cars without shelters; the disturbance as to seats when once under way; the sideways motion, &c, &c.— soon drive off the class of people most desirable for us & for you, viz., those who have means & inclination to travel." He suggested that to develop suburban traffic, the railroad should have trains to suit laborers who had to travel to the suburbs early in the morning, businessmen who went from the suburb into the city to work, ladies who wished to shop or visit and return before lunch, and those who wanted to go to dinner, the theatre or balls in the evening. BR&AB, MD-MHS, 131: 4: 3, p. 257–258, EB to Hood, April 19, 1897.

22. BR&AB, MD-MHS, 131: 4: 3, p. 303, EB to Hood, September 13, 1897.

23. BR&AB, MD-MHS, 131: 4: 3, p. 319, EB to Hood, Nov. 9, 1897; pp. 336 and 337, EB to Griswold, Jan. 17 and 27, 1898, respectively.

24. BR&AB, MD-MHS, 131: 4: 3, p. 435, EB to Hood, September 13, 1898. We only have Blackford's letters, not Hood's responses, so we do not know for certain whether Blackford's request was granted. But usually when a response is unfavorable, Blackford either writes again or informs Bond. In the absence of such letters, we probably can assume that Hood has provided Blackford with what he wanted.

25. BR&AB, MD-MHS, 131: 4: 4, p. 12, EB to Hood, September 29, 1899.

26. BR&AB, MD-MHS, 131: 4: 4, p. 93, EB to Hood, October 2, 1900.

27. BR&AB, MD-MHS, 131: 4: 4, pp. 281 and 282, EB to Griswold, Feb. 9 and 13, 1903, respectively.

28. BR&AB, MD-MHS, 131: 4: 4, p. 381, EB to F.M. Howell, June 18, 1904.

29. BR&AB, MD-MHS, 131: 4: 4, p. 462–63, EB to HLB, November 3, 1905.

30. Since the 1970s, Sudbrook Park's community association has fought what seems a never-ending battle with Baltimore County to rehabilitate and preserve this bridge, which is now marked as "one-lane." The bridge was an integral part of the Olmsted design for the community and thus is historic in function and purpose.

31. BR&AB, MD-MHS, 131: 4: 3, p. 232, EB to E.A. Griffith, January 28, 1897. According to Blackford, there was a chance Mrs. Thomson might agree to electric lights only in the dining and sitting rooms to avoid the heat from gas. BR&AB, MD-MHS, 131: 4: 3, p. 245, EB to Jas. H. Couper, March 3, 1897.

32. BR&AB, MD-MHS, 131: 4: 4, p. 90, EB to C.M. Kemp Mfg. Co., September 28, 1900. Soon after, Blackford responded to someone who had seen and was interested in 508 Sudbrook Lane (Cottage No. 2), adding that in addition to a full cellar and furnace, the house had "electric bells & speaking tubes throughout & telephone connection. The house is also piped for gas. The current for electric lighting is only 50 yds. distant." BR&AB, MD-MHS, 131: 4: 4, p. 98–99, EB to J. Scott Anderson, October 18, 1900.

33. BR&AB, MD-MHS, 131: 4: 4, p. 162, EB to W.L. Burk, Kikson Hydro-Carbon Lighting Co., June 6, 1901.

34. BR&AB, MD-MHS, 131: 4: 4, p. 247, Blackford to Lloyd Speero Real Estate Co., July 8, 1902 (emphasis added); p. 300, EB to Messrs. Baldwin & Frick, June 9, 1903. It does not appear that the Sudbrook Company ever installed a central gas generating system for the community; the hotel and some of the houses had their own underground gas tank and piping system. Other houses appeared to be lit by separate gas or oil lamps not connected to a complete system.

35. "Monumental City Suburbs…" *Baltimore Sunday Herald,* April 30, 1893.

36. BR&AB, MD-MHS, 131: 4: 3, p. 437, EB to Hood, Sept. 16, 1898, and BR&AB, MD-MHS, 131: 4: 2, p. 294, EB to D.H. Miller, Jr., April 12, 1899.

37. Waesche, p. 69.

38. BR&AB, MD-MHS, 131: 4: 4, p. 40, EB to HLB, March 7, 1900.

39. BR&AB, MD-MHS, 131: 4: 4, pp. 175 and 242, EB to C.W. Linthicum, Aug. 20, 1901 and June 11, 1902, respectively. In the latter letter, and by way of explanation, Blackford also noted that the Sudbrook Company had gone to the expense of raising the water tower by five feet to address water problems that residents were having.

40. BR&AB, MD-MHS, 131: 4: 2, p. 334, EB to Redmond C. Stewart, February 15, 1900.

41. BR&AB, MD-MHS, 131: 4: 4, p. 9, EB to Wm. P. Robinson, March 7, 1902.

42. Olson, pp. 246–47.

43. BR&AB, MD-MHS, 131: 4: 4, p. 351, EB to Mrs. Geo. Harlan, March 3, 1904; BR&AB, MD-MHS, 131: 4: 3, p. 358, EB to Mrs. Thomson, March 18, 1904; and BR&AB, MD-MHS, 131: 4: 3, p. 360, EB to Dugan & Nephew, March 22, 1904.

44. Except where noted, the source of all background information about Roland Park is James F. Waesche's book, *Crowning the Gravelly Hill.*

45. While well-meaning, Blackford may have been slow in adopting certain measures which might have been cost efficient for the Sudbrook Company. One striking example of this was the Company's eventual installation of water meters to stem residents' over consumption of water. Although it appears that Blackford had considered using water meters since about 1890, he did not seriously begin gathering information until 1902; the meters were installed in 1903. By that time, Sudbrook Park's need for them was glaring. In July of 1902, for example, Sudbrook's 34 cottages consumed 1,500,000 gallons of water while Roland Park's 269 cottages used about 2,600,000 gallons (and this included water used in flushing their drains). (Sudbrook's water usage in June and July 1902 had exhausted the subterranean basin from which the supply was drawn). BR&AB, MD-MHS, 131: 4: 4, p. 264, EB to E.H. Bankard, Sept. 30, 1902. When water meters were installed in Sudbrook Park, the Company paid for all expenses and bought the best meters then available. The new policy was to charge residents for any usage over 40,000 gallons, at the rate of twenty cents per 1,000 gallons. A number of residents protested and passively resisted the water meter system at first, causing Blackford a good deal of anguish. BR&AB, MD-MHS, 131: 4: 4, pp. 288 and 289, EB to various tenants and residents, March 4 and 9, 1903. The effect of the water meters in Sudbrook Park was that "only one half as much water was consumed…[the] summer [of 1903] as was during the previous one." BR&AB, MD-MHS, 131: 4: 4, p. 327, EB to Clarence Shriver, Dec. 2, 1903.

46. Bouton was Secretary the first ten years, and became President in 1903 when the Roland Park Company reorganized. Waesche, pp. 44, 87.

47. Waesche, p. 44 and BR&AB, MD-MHS, 131: 4: 4, pp. 113 and 116, EB to Chas. H. Grasty *(Balto. News),* December 28, 1900 and January 15, 1901, respectively. (Grasty apparently wanted to rent Cottage No. 1 at 511 Sudbrook Lane, which still was under lease by a Dr. George Shattuck. Blackford responded that he could only give him priority if it became available. It is not known whether Grasty ever resided in Sudbrook Park).

48. Waesche, p. 44 and BR&AB, MD-MHS, 131: 4: 2, p. 335, EB to Hiram Woods, February 20, 1900. See also BR&AB, MD-MHS, 131: 4: 4, p. 225, EB to Dr. Hiram Woods, April 30, 1902. Dr. Woods was subletting the Hooper cottage at 520 Sudbrook Lane for the year of 1902. (City directories from those years list both a Hiram Woods and a Dr. Hiram Woods. One inquired about renting at Sudbrook; the other lived in Sudbrook for a year).

49. BR&AB, MD-MHS, 131: 4: 3, p. 453, EB to Richard H. Woodward, Roland Park, [date unreadable but another letter on the same page is dated November 8, 1898].

50. BCMR, Liber L.M.B. 161, folio 344, Sudbrook Company Mortgage to Mercantile Trust and Deposit Co., August 6, 1892 (securing the $10,000 loan and giving Mercantile, which was also the holder of the first mortgage, a second mortgage on the Company's land). Under the original terms of the 1892 second mortgage, the $10,000 principal was to be paid in full in five years, using a sinking fund mechanism (based on the sale of lots) to accumulate the principal. Interest at six percent per annum was due semi-annually. The bank apparently agreed to extend the term of the loan when sales did not materialize as expected; the mortgage was not released until 1901. BCMR, Liber A.B.M. 220, folio 270, Mercantile Trust & Deposit Co. Release to Sudbrook Company, January 15, 1901.

51. BR&AB, MD-MHS, 131: 4: 3, pp. 356 and 358, EB to Stuart Kearney and C.W. Woolford, respectively, both March 2, 1898. Blackford was responding to a request for information from "the guardian of one of the heirs of the late John H. Geigan," who had been an original director and apparent stockholder. Ibid.

52. BCMR, Liber N.B.M. 204, folio 350, Sudbrook Company Mortgage to Mercantile, Dec. 30, 1898 (stating that the loan was "out of money in the hands of the Trustee forming part of the trust estate devised and bequeathed to it by the will of James Howard McHenry." Specifically, $3,000 of the total was from money being held in trust for Sophia McHenry Stewart and $1,000 from money being held in trust for Ellen McHenry Keyser). The bank held the lien on the property (lot 7, Block 17 of the Olmsted Plan). The term of the loan was three years; the Company issued fourteen promissory notes for the principal and eighteen promissory notes for interest due at various times. In 1910, the bank still held the lien on the property, indicating that the loan had not been paid or released.

53. The Company borrowed the $6,000 from Senator Rayner, who held the mortgage. BCMR, Liber N.B.M. 225, folio 103, Sudbrook Company Mortgage to Isidor Rayner, Sept. 18, 1901. The original terms required the Company to repay the principal to Rayner on April 1, 1907, with interest payable quarterly from April 1902 at five and a half percent per annum. This loan was not repaid and released until 1910. BCMR, Liber W.P.C. 352, folio 248, Isidor Rayner Release to the Sudbrook Company, October 20, 1910.

54. BR&AB, MD-MHS, 131: 4: 5, p. 82–83, EB to James Winsor, May 11, 1904.

55. See for example, BR&AB, MD-MHS, 131: 4: 3, p. 453, EB to Richard H. Woodward, November [8], 1898.

56. BR&AB, MD-MHS, 131: 4: 4, p. 462–463, EB to HLB as President of the Sudbrook Co., Nov. 3, 1905. In addition to the undeveloped land, the Company in 1905 owned Cottages Nos. 1, 2, 4, 5, 8, 9, 10, 29, 30, 36, and 38; the hotel, the golf club house, two wells & pumping stations "complete with pumps and boilers," one well without machinery and a livery stable "containing 20 stalls and room for 20 carriages." (Blackford's numbers add up to 207 acres, the first time that this number has appeared in the Company's records. There is no explanation as to how he arrived at 207, an additional three acres above the 204 acres originally purchased and always referred to previously).

57. BR&AB, MD-MHS, 131: 4: 4, p. 462–463, EB to HLB as President of the Sudbrook Co., Nov. 3, 1905. If the Sudbrook Company spent $155,792.33 from 1889 to 1905 and yet in 1905 the total valuation, albeit a conservative one in Blackford's own words, was only $152, 600.00 (without valuing the water supply, which cost over $10,000 to install, or road work), then its investment had not appreciated much.

58. A few weeks later, another letter to Bond indicated that Judge Harlan, who had been renting Cottage No. 27 on a seasonal basis since 1900, wanted to purchase it. Blackford provided Bond with the expenses attributable to the cottage, adding that he was biased toward the sale "because the tenant is a personal friend whose residence here, with his attractive wife, adds much to the charms of the place, and I should much regret seeing him depart, tho' of course he is liable to go at any time, without regard to any one…." BR&AB, MD-MHS, 131: 4: 5, p. 129–130, EB to HLB, Nov. 15, 1906. Although Judge Harlan never purchased the house, which Hugh Bond's widow sold in 1923 to Annie Offutt Parlett, memoirs of residents indicate that Judge Harlan and his family resided in Cottage No. 27 (708 Cliveden) until at least 1920. Merrick's "Memories." See also, BCLR, Liber W.P.C. 575, folio 310, Jessie V.R. Bond Deed to Annie Offutt Parlett, August 10, 1923.

59. "Maj. Blackford's Funeral," *Baltimore News*, Wednesday, February 5, 1908. Blackford commanded the sharpshooters of the Fifth Alabama Regiment (not a battalion of the Fourth Regiment). (Correct information courtesy of Elizabeth Corrdry). In addition, Blackford moved to Baltimore at least four or five years before 1875, the date stated in the obituary. James Howard McHenry's journals confirm that Blackford was residing at his Pikesville home, Cleve, by 1871.

60. "U.S. Prosperity and Depressions Since 1790," *World Book Encyclopedia*, Vol. 5, p. 127. (This chart also indicates that the country had a couple years of depression around 1903–04. The 1907 depression appeared to last about two years; less intense depressions followed in about 1911 and again in 1914–15).

61. We know that the Sudbrook Park Improvement Association was formed in 1908 from information on the Association's letterhead after it incorporated in 1941. The late Edward B. Stellmann mentioned the Association to me in various conversations about Sudbrook Park. Because the Association left no records that have been located, we do not know the specific purposes for which it was formed or the role it played in maintaining Sudbrook Park after Blackford's death.

Chapter 13: The Changes Begin: 1910–1939

1. Blackford was intent on preserving the attractiveness of the community and expected fellow residents to cooperate in this endeavor. When someone cut down a small tree opposite the golf course Club House, Blackford immediately wrote to the President of the Pikesville & Sudbrook Park Golf Club to ask that the Club take steps to see that "enthusiastic golfers" not wreak further destruction, lest "all the trees on the links may gradually be destroyed." Blackford admonished: "Knowing how important it is to increase the beauty of the grounds you will, I trust, try to do something to prevent further damage." BR&AB, MD-MHS, 131: 4: 4, p. 67, EB to Wm. P. Robinson, August 2, 1900. Other more mundane but bothersome matters also arose in the early community, and Blackford always attended to them. When Sudbrook resident Clarence Shriver complained to Blackford that William R. Howard was letting fowls run at large, Blackford wrote to his friend Willy: "If your chickens are the offenders, I know I can count on you to abate the nuisance. The deeds for property here require the management to do all in its power to prevent this trouble." BR&AB, MD-MHS, 131: 4: 4, p. 27, EB to Wm. R. Howard, July 27, 1904. Similarly, when Horatio Armstrong accumulated piles of dirt on lots in the rear of his yard, Blackford wasted no time in asking him to remove them, as "they are very unsightly, and if removed now will permit the grass to grow." BR&AB, MD-MHS, 131: 4: 3, p. 396, EB to H. G. Armstrong, May 3, 1898.

2. In addition to continual oversight, Blackford and the Sudbrook Company had provided numerous services to residents, such as snow removal, pick-up of trash and ashes, maintenance of the station area, the roads and sidewalks, on-going landscaping, and repair and maintenance of communal facilities (such as the water works). Thomas Ross, who had assisted Blackford, seemed to assume many of these responsibilities after Blackford's death, but how long he continued in this capacity is unknown.

3. The Company sold a portion of lot 1, Block 16 (now 504 Sudbrook Lane) to Louise B. Cassard. BCLR, Liber W.P.C. 354, folio 464, The Sudbrook Co. Deed to Louise B. Cassard, Feb. 28, 1910.

4. Bond sold two cottages in 1907: Cottage No. 15 at 721 Cliveden Road (BCLR, Liber W.P.C. 311, folio 234, Hugh L. Bond & wf. to Kate P. Webb, February 20, 1907) and No. 13 at 500 Sudbrook Lane (BCLR, Liber W.P.C. 320, folio 374, Hugh L. Bond & wf. Deed to Oliver Carroll Zell, Nov. 1, 1907; see also Liber W.P.C. 332, folio 464, between the same parties on Sept. 28, 1908, to correct the earlier deed's lack of definiteness in describing the property. As part consideration, Zell assumed a $2,000 mortgage dating from June 18, 1892 from the Bonds as mortgagors to Lennox Birkhead, a relative of Hugh Bond's).

5. BCLR, Liber W.P.C. 368, folio 532, The Sudbrook Co. Deed to Patrick Casey, November 1, 1910. That same day, Bond and his wife transferred one of their remaining Sudbrook properties to Joseph Berman and Charles Stein; see, BCLR, Liber W.P.C. 368, folio 536, Hugh L. Bond & wf. Deed to Joseph Berman, et. al, November 1, 1910 (conveying Cottage No. 30 at 722 Howard Road, subject to a mortgage from the Bonds to the Sudbrook Company).

6. BCLR, Liber W.P.C. 368, folio 538, Patrick Casey Deed to Joseph Berman et.al., November 2, 1910.

7. Stein and Berman's occupations obtained from listings in *Polk's City Directory, 1911*. Their names pepper Baltimore County land records transfers in this general time period, and transfers in the city also are mentioned.

8. BCMR, Liber W.P.C. 352, folio 69, Patrick Casey Mortgage to the Sudbrook Company of Baltimore County, Nov. 1, 1910. There is no record of this mortgage being assigned until 1922, when the Sudbrook Company assigned the mortgage (together with the $20,000 balance of the mortgage debt) to A. Herman Siskind, attorney, and Joseph Berman, S. Victor Jelenko (who lived at 1014 Windsor Road from 1913 to 1934) and Louis Croner (President of the Sudbrook Development Company, incorporated in 1917). See BCMR, Liber W.P.C. 614, folio 271, Assignment of Mortgage from the Sudbrook Company of Baltimore County to A. Herman Siskind, et.al, March 23, 1922. Siskind, et. al immediately assigned the mortgage to the Union Trust Co. of Maryland, which ten months later issued a full release to the Sudbrook Development Co., in whom the property had become vested by mesne conveyance. BCMR, Liber W.P.C. 614, folio 272, Assignment of Siskind to Union Trust, March 23, 1922; and BCMR, Liber W.P.C. 641, folio 150, Union Trust Co. Release to Sudbrook Development Co. of Maryland, Jan. 2, 1923.

9. Berman appeared to be the one most involved (1910–1923) with the sale of property in Sudbrook; Stein had a lower profile after he transferred his interest in the property to Berman in 1911, but was the attorney on some of the transactions. Although Stein and Berman are listed on 1913–1915 maps and plats of Sudbrook along with other property owners, there is no evidence that either ever lived in Sudbrook Park. Deeds designate both men as living in Baltimore City; it is likely that they were work-out specialists. Stein repurchased from Berman the property at 520 Sudbrook Lane and an undeveloped parcel next to 520 Sudbrook. He sold 520 Sudbrook to Nathan Pendleton the same year and never developed the adjoining parcel. Four brick neo-colonial houses (512, 514, 516 and 518 Sudbrook Lane) built in the 1940s now stand on the property.

10. Casey is linked to Berman and Stein as a pass-through for other conveyances also, as is a Mary Casey, described in deeds as "single." See for example BCLR, Liber W.P.C. 365, folios 400, 406, 407 and 409, all Sept. 16, 1910. A Patrick Casey is listed as being a clerk in *Polk's City Directory, 1911*. Although purely conjecture, Casey may have been a clerk in Stein and Berman's office; it was not uncommon for secretaries or clerks to be paid a small fee to serve as straw parties in real estate transactions. *Polk's City Directory, 1911* lists two other Patrick Caseys — one a watchman and one a shoemaker. It seems more likely that the Casey listed as a clerk was the one involved in the Sudbrook land transfers. [Although all assumptions and

opinions are mine, I am indebted to attorneys David Belcher, Tom Lewis, Michael Mannes, and Jerry Sopher, all of whom provided information that assisted me in understanding various aspects of the Sudbrook Company's 1910 deed and mortgage transactions].

11. It is also possible that Casey assigned the mortgage to Berman and Stein in an unrecorded transaction, or that they indemnified him against any personal liability.

12. The debt may have been $40,000 or more, because it appears that Mercantile may have taken over the $6,000 mortgage from the Sudbrook Company to Senator Rayner. Although Rayner released the Sudbrook Company in October 1910 (BCMR, Liber W.P.C. 352, folio 248, Oct. 20, 1910), the property became a part of the Casey mortgage, to be released upon the payment of $7,000.

13. There are several reasons why Mercantile might have agreed not to foreclose on the Sudbrook Company. For one, Mercantile was still managing the trusts of the McHenry heirs under the late J. Howard McHenry's will, and so would have been sensitive to the family's situation. Since some of the McHenry heirs still lived on other portions of the Sudbrook estate, they may have preferred a more orderly work-out to an auction. Also, Hugh L. Bond, Jr. was a prominent Baltimore attorney in 1910, and some of the other Sudbrook stockholders were nationally prominent at the time (see fns., Ch. 3). Foreclosure might have been a public embarrassment that everyone wanted to avoid if possible. Lastly, such a work-out arrangement may have been advantageous to the bank, if it did not want the Sudbrook Park land on its own hands but had no ready means of disposing of it. Under the arrangement that seems to have been made, each time a parcel of land was sold, dual deeds were issued: first, Mercantile would deed the property to Berman (or the then-title holder) and release it from the first lien upon payment of the requisite amount to the bank, and then the title-holder would deed the land to the new purchaser.

14. *Transactions, Maryland State Bar Association, 28th Annual Meeting* (1923), p. 26 ("Hugh L. Bond").

15. BCLR, Liber W.P.C. 386, folio 258, Charles F. Stein & wf. to Joseph Berman & wf., Oct. 20, 1910.

16. BCLR, Liber W.P.C. 414, folio 285, Jos. Berman & wf. Deed to Jennie Miller Hysan & hsb., June 27, 1913.

17. BCLR, Liber W.P.C. 454, folio 487, Gilbert Panitz (agent) Deed to Milburn Realty Co., January 13, 1916.

18. BCLR, Liber W.P.C. 502, folio 111, The Milburn Realty Co. Deed to the Sudbrook Development Co., May 6, 1918; and BCMR, Liber W.P.C. 641, folio 151, Jones Herman Realty Co. Mortgage to Sudbrook Development Co., Jan. 5, 1923 (referring to a deed of even date in which the Sudbrook Development Co. conveyed all of the land to Jones Herman Realty Co., no Liber/folio numbers given. The mortgage indebtedness was $45,500; Jones Herman individually guaranteed repayment in five years at six per cent interest per year).

19. The lack of extensive development may have helped preserve portions of the Olmsted Plan. In a 1913 transfer of the property that is now 1014 Windsor Road, Joseph Berman reserved the westernmost fifty feet of the lot for a roadway from Windsor to McHenry Road, on the condition that the road was constructed and opened within ten years. This would have been a major modification of the 1889 plat. The road was not installed and the reservation became null and void. BCLR, Liber W.P.C. 408, folio 237, Jos. Berman & wf. Deed to Gustav Geisler & wf., Feb. 8, 1913.

20. BCLR, Liber W.P.C. 369, folio 330, Charles F. Stein, et al. Deed to Carrie C. Harlan, November 7, 1910 (the property at 722 Howard Road was "subject to the conditions and restrictions contained in a deed from the Sudbrook Company of Baltimore County to Hugh L. Bond, Jr., dated August 20, 1891." These were the Olmsted/Sudbrook Company restrictions). See also BCLR, Liber W.P.C. 371, folio 483, Charles F. Stein, et al. Deed to Arthur Poultney, December 17, 1910 (conveying Cottage No. 2 at 508 Sudbrook).

21. BCLR, Liber W.P.C. 381, folio 190, Charles F. Stein, et al. Deed to Emma Middleton, June 28, 1911 (for property originally identified as 1011 Windsor Road and now known as 1007 Windsor Road). See also BCLR, Liber W.P.C. 380, folio 282, Charles F. Stein et al. Deed to Clarence Reynolds, June 8, 1911 (conveying property at 506 Sudbrook Lane).

22. The Sudbrook Company had bound itself to enforce the restrictions as long as it maintained its corporate existence. Although it appeared to maintain its status as a Maryland corporation until at least 1922, it did not enforce the restrictions after selling the Sudbrook property in 1910.

23. See for example BCLR, Liber W.P.C. 417, folio 210, Agreement Joseph Berman and Salzman Bros., et al., June 11, 1912 and various plats filed. (Coogan's 1912 survey and subdivision of Sudbrook Park is referred to in many deeds, but the plat he prepared apparently was not filed (although it most likely was the model for the subdivided areas of Sudbrook Park shown on the 1915 Bromley Atlas of Baltimore County). Judging from references in various deeds to lots (i.e., lot 3, Block P) on the Coogan survey for parcels whose location I can ascertain, his survey/plat seems to have been similar to later plats subdividing Sudbrook Park that are on file in the land records office, such as one filed with the deed from Elizabeth Slagle to the Onlee Realty Company, 1928).

24. See for example BCLR, Liber W.P.C. 417, folio 213, Agreement Joseph Berman and Louis Levy, June 10, 1912; folio 216, Joseph Berman Agreement with William Salzman, June 11, 1912; and folio 219, Joseph Berman Agreement with Philip Salzman, June 11, 1912.

25. About six houses were built over the next ten years on the fifty-foot-wide lots along or close to the south side of Upland Road near Cliveden. Large areas of the community still lacked roads and water supply, and so would have been expensive to develop, especially for only one or two homes. Several 1911 deeds of undeveloped land gave purchasers the right to connect "by means of proper pipes to the most convenient pipe line of the water system." (See for example deeds to Clarence Tucker and Emma Middleton, cited previously). One of the larger parcels that was conveyed contained 18.2 acres — from the Western Maryland Railroad tracks along the undeveloped side of Howard Road to Upland and back along the track to Howard — essentially much of the golf course area, which remained undeveloped for more than forty years. See, plat dated February 7, 1913, filed in the Baltimore County Land Records Office to accompany a deed "from Joseph Berman & wf. to August Mehr."

26. See for example BCLR, Liber W.P.C. 417, folio 210, Agreement Joseph Berman and Salzman Bros., et al., June 11, 1912. (Unfortunately, such racial — and later religious and ethnic — restrictions were incorporated in many deeds of that period, until later declared unenforceable and unconstitutional. For example, like Sudbrook's, Roland Park's early deeds contained no racial restrictions, but later deeds did. Both Guilford (1913) and Homeland (1922) inserted a racially restrictive covenant into a "Deed and Agreement that covered all the separate properties within the development." Waesche, pp. 67 and 113. Dumbarton, a Pikesville subdivision developed beginning in the early 1920s, also contained a racially restrictive covenant. Beryl Frank, *A Pictorial History of Pikesville, Maryland* (Towson, Maryland: Baltimore County Public Library, 1982), p. 78.

27. See for example BCLR, Liber W.P.C. 417, folio 210, Agreement Joseph Berman and Salzman Bros., et al., June 11, 1912.

28. As noted previously, there is no indication that Berman or Stein ever lived in Sudbrook Park, and various *Polk's City Directories* show them living either in the city (Stein eventually lived in Roland Park) or in Randallstown (Berman eventually moved there). None of the other investors or principals to whom the land was transferred ever seemed to live in Sudbrook Park either. One person among several to whom the Sudbrook Company in 1922 assigned its mortgage from Casey, however, did live in Sudbrook: S. Victor Jelenko lived at 1014 Windsor Rd. from about 1913 to 1934. His time as a mortgagor was fleeting; the mortgage was immediately re-assigned to Union Trust Co.

29. BCLR, Liber W.P.C. 369, folio 330, Chas. F. Stein, et al. Deed to Carrie C. Harlan, Nov. 7, 1910.

30. BCLR, Liber W.P.C. 369, folio 326, Chas. F. Stein, et al. Deed to Ella M. Emery, Nov. 7, 1910.

31. BCLR, Liber W.P.C. 369, folio 328, Chas. F. Stein, et al. Deed to Mary R. Hoffman, Nov. 7, 1910. The property purchased is identified only through a metes and bounds description, making it difficult to ascertain exactly which lot was purchased. From the description of nearby lots, it may have been lot 5, Block 16 (now 510 Sudbrook Lane).

32. BCLR, Liber W.P.C. 372, folio 88, Chas. F. Stein, et al. Deed to Thomas R. Ross, Dec. 5, 1910.

33. BCLR, Liber W.P.C. 373, folio 61, Chas. F. Stein, et al. Deed to Willoughby Hall, Dec. 10, 1910; and Baltimore County real estate transactions, *Daily Record*, Dec. 30, 1910 (Hall to H. Arthur Stump).

34. BCLR, Liber W.P.C. 371, folio 483, Chas. F. Stein, et al. Deed to Arthur Poultney, Dec. 17, 1910.

35. BCLR, Liber W.P.C. 372, folio 266, Chas. F. Stein, et al. Deed to Wm. E.R. Duvall & wf., January 3, 1911.

36. BCLR, Liber W.P.C. 374, folio 142, Chas. F. Stein, et al. Deed to Ezra Whitman & wf., January 16, 1911.

37. Information about Tucker's occupation from Merrick's "Memories."

38. BCLR, Liber W.P.C. 377, folio 44, Charles F. Stein, et al. Deed to Clarence A. Tucker & wf., April 17, 1911 (the deed referred to a separate contract giving Tucker the option to purchase the remaining property on the triangle, to the rear of what he had purchased). As the Sudbrook Company became more desperate for sales from 1900 on, it made evident its willingness to sell the 2.3 acre lot that was to have been reserved for a church or other public building. A number of people had inquired about and were interested in the lot while Blackford kept records. BR&AB, MD-MHS, 131: 4: 4, p. 244, EB to Frank F. Peard, June 1, 1902 (offering the site for $2,500, "the finest site we have") and p. 380, EB to Philip H. Hoffman, June 15, 1904 (offering the land for $2,000, for one dwelling only, "the most desirable lot we have, but the architecture should of course accord with the nature of the lot.").

39. BCLR, Liber W.P.C. 380, folio 282, Chas. F. Stein, et. al Deed to Clarence I. Reynolds, June 8, 1911. (Reynolds and his wife, Anita, lived in Sudbrook Park until 1927. Reynolds was active in the community; he died about 1930).

40. Information about Reynold's occupation from Merrick's "Memories."

41. BCLR, Liber W.P.C. 381, folio 190, Chas. F. Stein, et al. Deed to Emma Middleton, June 28, 1911. The house at 1007 Windsor Road was designed for Emma Middleton in August 1911 by Laurence Hall Fowler (1876–1971), a locally distinguished architect. He gained prominence after winning a competition for designing Baltimore's War Memorial and Plaza, but primarily designed private houses. Between 1906 and 1941, he designed about sixty houses and ten cottages in the Baltimore area, working actively with the Roland Park Company in Guilford. No. 1007 Windsor was the only house he designed in Sudbrook Park. Fowler was apparently a personal friend of Emma Middleton and her family. When Miss Middleton died several years later, her nephew Benjamin Read inherited the house and retained Fowler to design an addition to accommodate his family. Fowler's records (which list the address as 1011 Windsor) show additions dated August 1914 and November 1918. Many of Fowler's plans and some correspondence can be found at Evergreen House. [See Egon Verheyen, ed., *Laurence Hall Fowler, Architect (1876–1971)* (Baltimore: The Johns Hopkins University Press, 1984). Beryl Frank's research many years ago turned up the initial information about Emma Middleton and that Laurence Hall Fowler designed the house. See also Dorsey and Dilts for more information about Fowler. Information about the Middleton-Fowler friendship from telephone interview with Benjamin Read's granddaughter Mrs. Mary Cadwalader on July 18, 1996.]

42. BCLR, Liber W.P.C. 385, folio 220, Chas. F. Stein, et al. Deed to Nathan S. Pendleton, Sept. 14, 1911. (The Hooper house at 520 Sudbrook Lane was destroyed by fire in the 1920s. Subsequently, another house was built on the property).

43. William R. Howard, Jr. was a descendant of John Eager Howard. Howard's wife was the daughter of the hotel proprietress, Mrs. Thomson. The Howard's children were raised in Sudbrook Park. One of them, William III, served in the Maryland House of Delegates in the 1930s. In 1943 he married the actress Dorothy Lamour, whose presence in Sudbrook introduced a touch of Hollywood glamour to the neighborhood (Bob Hope and Bing Crosby, among others, visited at 607 Sudbrook). Howard III died in 1978. "William Ross Howard 3d Dies in California at 70," *Baltimore Sun*, February 16, 1978.

44. The deed history on several of these parcels is quite convoluted, and it is impossible to tell solely from the deeds when a house was built (it was boilerplate language to state that the property was being transferred together with any "buildings and improvements;" such language did not necessarily indicate that any structure existed). Most of these properties appear to have had houses by 1913.

45. "New Trolley Line To Tap Northwest," *Baltimore News*, Saturday, May 3, 1913.

46. Advertisement, *Baltimore News*, Saturday, May 3, 1913. (Merrick noted that at some point before 1920, two tennis courts were added near the golf course's Club House somewhere in the vicinity of the station. In addition, between 1905 and 1940, there were numerous private tennis courts in Sudbrook. Houses at 515 Sudbrook, 520 Sudbrook, 507 Sudbrook, 718 Howard, 708 Cliveden, and 1014 Windsor all installed tennis courts. (Information about tennis courts courtesy of Sarah Sener, telephone interview on July 24, 1996; John Leith-Tetrault, interview April 25, 1997; and from Merrick's "Memories").

47. Recollections from Merrick's "Memories."

48. Cox, p. 41.

49. The new residents included Emma Middleton, the Yearley sisters, and the families of Frederick Beachum, Nathan Pendleton, Walter Duvall, William E.R. Duvall, George Sellman, James L. Sellman, O.C. Zell, John C. Legg, William Hayden, S.B. Austin, S.V. Jelenko, A.H. Bishop, Clarence Reynolds and Ezra Whitman. We have only limited information about most of these people. According to Merrick, John C. Legg was a member of the New York Stock Exchange firm of McCubben, Goodrich & Co.; William Mozart Hayden was President of the Eutaw Savings Bank; James L. Sellman was in the real estate business; William E.R. Duvall was Treasurer of Fidelity & Deposit Co.; and Nathan Smith Pendleton was paymaster of the B&O Railroad. (Merrick's "Memories"). Sidney B. Austin was listed as proprietor of the Austin Adding Machine Company in *Polk's Directory, 1911*.

50. Long-time residents included the Oscar Webbs, Mrs. Charles Linthicum, Dr. and Mrs. Herbert Harlan, the William Stellmanns, the R.W. Graves, the B. Deford Webbs, the E.H. Bankards, Judge Henry Harlan and family, the Clarence Schrivers, the John Littigs, the John A. Barkers, the Frederick Hoffmans, Judge H. A. Stump and family, the William Howards, Dr. Samuel K. Merrick and family, the Arthur Poultneys, the George Cators, the Alexander Earlys, and the family of Eugene Blackford. (According to Merrick, John Littig was President of the Marine Bank; Frederick Hoffman was Treasurer of the Savings Bank of Baltimore; Clarence Shriver was the local agent for Ericson Line Steamboats to Philadelphia; and Arthur Poultney was in the coal business).

51. William H. Stellmann to his son, Edward B. Stellmann (who was traveling abroad), June 2, 1913 (mispelling Mrs. Thomson's name as Thompson was a common mistake). Stellmann mentioned several families at the Park, including the Yearleys, Oliver C. Zell and his bride, Mr. & Mrs. Bissell ("she was Miss Clara Littig, and only just married"), the Haydens, and the Duvalls. It appears that a number of cottages were still being rented to others for the summer; Stellmann noted: "The Watmoughs, Hamiltons & Austins all went up on Saturday to New Windsor. Fentons have Watmoughs' house [possibly 610 Upland], Mr. Geo. P. Thomas has Hamiltons' house [706 Cliveden West] (you know the house Miss Lou Yearley used to occupy), and Mr. Littig has taken Austins' house [1017 Windsor]. The Whitman Cottage [501 Sudbrook Lane] has also been rented but I don't know who has it." Letter courtesy of William and Elizabeth Stellmann. (The Stellmanns had long resided at 724 Howard Road. When this letter was written, Mrs. Stellmann and her son, Edward, were in Europe and Mr. Stellmann was temporarily staying at the Sudbrook hotel).

52. The Articles, filed October 27, 1913, stated that Duvall and Reynolds were "both of Sudbrook Park." McEvoy must still have been a summer resident, since he was listed as being "of the City of Baltimore." The Articles also provided that there be ten directors but name only nine: William E.R. Duvall, Edgar H. Bankard, Oscar E. Webb, James L. Sellman, Frederick Hoffman, Eugene Blackford (son of Sudbrook's late manager), Oliver C. Zell, William M. Hayden and Matthew S. Brenan. All of the named directors except Matthew Brenan were known to occupy cottages in Sudbrook in 1913. (Note: Blackford's son went by the name "Eugene Blackford" and did not use the appellation "Jr.").

53. In the following excerpt from her account, Cox did not correctly identify the hotel's owners or mortgagee, but did describe its fate generally: "In 1914, the Sudbrook Hotel was sold to Miss Annie Slicer, who lived on Sudbrook Lane, for $13,000 — subject to a mortgage held by the Helfrick Lumber Company. Subsequently, ownership changed several times until the 'Inn' was sold in 1922 to Carville Benson, who renovated the building and opened it to guests for the summer season with a big dinner and dance…." Cox, p. 43. There is no record of the persons named ever having any interest in the hotel property.

54. BCLR, Liber W.P.C. 414, folio 285, Jos. Berman & wf. Deed to Jennie Miller Hysan & husb., June 27, 1913. (Prior to this transfer, the land

had gone from the Sudbrook Company to Patrick Casey; from Casey to Berman and Stein; and from Stein & wf. to Berman & wf., as set forth and cited previously).

55. BCLR, Liber W.P.C. 421, folio 296, Jennie Miller Hysan & husb. Deed to Sudbrook Hotel Co., Dec. 18, 1913. BCMR, Liber W.P.C. 426, folio 130, Sudbrook Park Hotel Co. Mortgage to Jennie Miller Hysan, Jan. 15, 1914 (noting that the Hotel Co. assumed a prior mortgage from Wm. H. Baker, Jr. to the German Savings Bank of Baltimore City).

56. BCLR, Liber W.P.C. 520, folio 228, Sudbrook Park Hotel Co. Deed to Milburn Realty Co., Feb. 8, 1919. BCMR, Liber W.P.C. 478, folios 96 and 102, Sudbrook Hotel Co. Mortgages to Eugene Blackford and Max Cohen, respectively, March 3, 1916.

57. BCLR, Liber W.P.C. 520, folios 230, The Milburn Realty Co. Deed to Wilsie W. Adams & wf, January 28, 1920. BCMR, Liber W.P.C. 565, folios 237, Wilsie W. and Alice M. Adams Mortgage to Joseph Berman, January 28, 1920.

58. BCLR, Liber W.P.C. 573, folios 312, Max Cohen, assignee, Deed to Oregon R. Benson, Jr., May 25, 1923. Benson also built a house in Sudbrook Park in the early 1920s. Originally located at 753 Howard Road, east of the bridge, it was moved across the street to avoid demolition during construction of the rapid transit. The current address of the house is 401 Sudbrook Lane. [Information, in part, from telephone interview with Mrs. Robert Leland Bart, July 29, 1996].

59. BCLR, Liber W.P.C. 573, folios 312, Max Cohen, assignee, Deed to Oregon R. Benson, Jr., May 25, 1923; BCLR, Liber W.P.C. 573, folios 315, Oregon R. Benson, Jr. & wf. Deed to George M. Henderson, widower, May 25, 1923; BCLR, Liber L.McL.M. 875, folios 501, George M. Henderson & wf. Deed to Alfred F. Walker & wf., March 31, 1931. (The 2.51 acre parcel was subdivided in 1951).

60. The advertisement for the opening read: "The Best Summer Hotel in Maryland. All Kinds of Amusements — Tennis, Dancing, Croquette, Quoits, Swings, Baseball. Room and Board Within the Reach of All. Make Reservations Early. Call Vernon 3181. Elizabeth G. Durm, 903 St. Paul Street." Maryland Historical Society, Prints and Photographs Department, Broadsides Collection, c. 1924; and Cox, p. 44.

61. Cox, pp. 43–44. The charred remains of the hotel sat on the site for years and many of the children who grew up in Sudbrook Park in the 1930s and 1940s played amidst the hotel's ruins. In the 1950s, the site was cleared and four brick Cape Cod style homes were erected. [Information about hotel ruins from Sarah Sener, a long-time Sudbrook Park resident, telephone interview on July 24, 1996, and Betty O'Connell Erwin, telephone interview on June 1, 1997. Erwin also recalled watching the fire as a young girl from the porch of her Aunt May Gavin's house at 721 Cliveden Road. Sener's parents, Mr. and Mrs. Pyle, moved to "the Cator Cottage" at 1016 Windsor Road in about 1920. At first they rented but later bought the house, where Sener, her sister and brother grew up. As did many Sudbrook residents, she purchased her own house in the Park in 1949 and has remained a resident. Mrs. Sener's sister, Melissa Donaldson, also resided in Sudbrook Park until her death several years ago].

62. The information in this paragraph came from a combination of several sources: my transcription and analysis of letters in all five volumes of the Blackford Record and Account Books (BR&AB, MD-MHS, Ms. No. 131), Merrick's "Memories," and information contained in the *Social Registers* cited.

63. Bruchey, pp. 408–416. Bruchey relied on listings in the *Social Register* as being more indicative of the elite than the *Society Visiting List,* which was less exclusive. In determining whom to include in the business elite of Baltimore, she looked at club membership, residence, recreation and religion.

64. Scharf, Part I, p. 379 (Charles Webb, whose son of the same name lived in Sudbrook, is also featured, pp. 183–184).

65. BR&AB, MD-MHS, 131: 4: 3, p. 453, EB to Richard H. Woodward, Nov. [8], 1898 (Perhaps Blackford intended to convey some degree of disparagement by his comment).

66. BR&AB, MD-MHS, 131: 4: 4, p. 247, EB to Mssrs. Lloyd Spears Co., July 8, 1902 (Blackford's prejudice against Jews is perhaps even more ironic given that Pikesville, where Sudbrook is located, ended up being identified primarily with Baltimore's Jewish community).

67. See fn. 26 above regarding racial and religious restrictions.

68. This description of life in Sudbrook is an amalgamation of information from my research (primarily the five volume BR&AB, MD-MHS, Ms. No. 131), Merrick's "Memories," Cox's history, conversations with the late Edward Stellmann and discussions with former and current residents.

69. Quotation from Merrick's "Memories." The Sudbrook Company constructed the "avenue" (now Sudbrook Lane) from Sudbrook Park to Reisterstown Road. Blackford maintained it as an attractive approach and threatened to take legal action against a man named Grogan, who wrote Blackford of his intentions to cut down the honeysuckle vines along the avenue, claiming that they obstructed his view. Blackford responded: "I can scarcely believe that you seriously contemplate entering on the property of another, and committing an outrageous action so spoiling the appearance of a road, upon the beauty of which so much care & money has been expended." He later wrote to Bond: "That idiot, Grogan, has cut down the vines along the Sudbrook road and lest something is done, will cut the trees, I fear." (BR&AB, MD-MHS, 131: 4: 3, p. 405, EB to Grogan, May 30, 1898, and BR&AB, MD-MHS, 131: 4: 2, p. 256, EB to Bond, June 2, 1898).

70. Quotation from Merrick's "Memories." (Beginning in 1907, the hotel was no longer managed by Mrs. Thomson and Miss Henrietta M. Trippe took over. Mrs. Thomson may simply have decided to move on or to retire, but Blackford's earlier letters had hinted that two significant events might cause her to relinquish her proprietorship of the hotel: (1) Her daughter Lulu had married William R. Howard, Jr. in 1902, and while the couple continued to live in Sudbrook Park, LuLu was no longer living with her mother, and (2) Mrs. Thomson's son Maynard died in 1904 after a long illness).

71. Had the Sudbrook Company used the reserved triangle on Cliveden Road for a church or school as intended by Olmsted, it would have added an important element of institutional infrastructure, increasing the stability of the area and providing an attraction for many people.

72. As remembered by William Merrick, there were three morning trains into the city: the 7:00 a.m. train was for the "workers," the 7:43 a.m. train was for the "clerkers," and the 8:06 a.m. train was for the "shirkers." Merrick commented that the shirkers seemed to be in the majority at Sudbrook.

73. Merrick's "Memories."

74. A few years later, Stellmann wrote: "I had a little ride in an automobile yesterday morning and enjoyed it very much indeed, only it did not last long enough. A friend of mine, who has just bought one, came through Sudbrook and saw me on the hotel porch and asked me to go along with him and give him some pointers on the operation of the machine which I was very pleased to be able to do." William H. Stellmann to Edward Stellmann, June 2, 1913. (Letter courtesy of William and Elizabeth Stellmann).

75. All information in this paragraph from Merrick's "Memories."

76. In addition to the hotel property and the Sudbrook Company's land that changed hands frequently, as described previously, certain other parcels had a complex history. As one example, the property now known as 510 Sudbrook Lane went through several early transfers as well as two public sales (after mortgage defaults in 1915 and 1937). BCLR, Liber W.P.C. 448, folio 562, John H. Duncan, attny, Deed to the Saratoga Building & Loan Corp., Aug. 11, 1915; and BCLR, Liber C.W.B., Jr. 1014, folio 252, Arthur E. Griffith, Assignee, Deed to Dorothy R. Vohden, Oct. 26, 1937 (both deeds giving details of the public sales).

77. Waesche, p. 105 and pp. 86–116, generally.

78. According to Cox, "[b]y 1912, the Park was in the hands of the Sudbrook Development Company with the Realty Mart as Sales Agents." Cox, p. 43. Since the Sudbrook Development Company did not incorporate or come into existence until 1917, it seems that Cox may have been mistaken in her date.

79. Information about the Reads courtesy of Mrs. Mary Cadwalader, telephone interview on July 18, 1996.

80. As noted in fn. 46 above, houses at 515 Sudbrook, 520 Sudbrook, 507 Sudbrook, 718 Howard, 708 Cliveden and 1014 Windsor all had private tennis courts.

81. Merrick's "Memories."

Chapter 14: New Development: 1939–1954

1. Even in the period from 1898 to 1913, the increase in automobiles was astounding. According to historian Kenneth Jackson, there was only one automobile in operation for every 18,000 Americans in 1898, but there was one automobile to every eight people by 1913! Automobile ownership received a further boost when Henry Ford reduced the price of his Model T from $950 in 1910 to $290 in 1924. By the 1920s, ownership of a private car, originally a luxury of the wealthy, had become a necessity — an essential part of life for middle class Americans. Jackson, pp. 157–163.

2. Interestingly, Foster Fenton spent a part of his childhood in Sudbrook Park. According to Merrick, Mr. and Mrs. Matthew C. Fenton moved into Cottage No. 29 at 610 Upland Road when Judge Stump and his family left. The Fentons had five boys — Matt, Jr., Ed, Glenn, Foster and Randolph. Foster became "a very successful builder & businessman and later owner of the Chesapeake Cadillac agency." Merrick does not say how long the Fentons lived at 610 Upland Road, nor do relatives of the Fentons recall. (Merrick's "Memories"). The same Foster Fenton mentioned by Merrick did, however, develop a portion of Sudbrook Park. (Confirming information about Foster Fenton courtesy of Matthew C. Fenton III and Matthew C. Fenton IV, telephone interviews, July 28, 1996).

3. The configuration of streets and lots implemented by Fenton and Chew bore a resemblance but was not identical to that plotted in 1912 by Coogan and shown in the *1915 Bromley Atlas of Baltimore County*, and a plat filed in April 1928 with a "Deed from Elizabeth Slagle to The Onlee Reality Co." (mentioned at the end of Chapter 13).

4. Information courtesy of Stella Hazard, telephone interview on July 28, 1996. The Hazard's were the third family to buy a house and take up residence on Monmouth Road in 1939.

5. Because of later in-fill development, there are now nineteen houses on this section of Sudbrook Lane.

6. In 1939, there were two gate posts on old Monmouth and Milford, as well as fences and a bridle path along Milford Mill Road. Several of Blackford's letters referred to a stone wall (which apparently did not survive) and gate near the Milford entrance (at what was then Monmouth). (Telephone interview with Stella Hazard on July 28, 1996).

7. Residents who moved to Sudbrook before or in the early 1940s recalled the street still being named "Monmouth." Stella Hazard moved to a house on what was then still Monmouth in 1939. She recalled that various residents did not like the sound of "Monmouth" and so initiated procedures to change the name in the 1940s. (Information courtesy of Dorothy Diehl and Stella Hazard, telephone interviews on July 27 and 28, 1996, respectively). An early edition of the community newsletter noted, perhaps tongue-in-cheek, that some areas of the Park had "detachable road signs" and "it depends entirely upon your point of view whether you live on Sudbrook Rd., Monmouth Road or Sudbrook Avenue. But after all, what's a little thing like a name…between friends. It might mean something to a foreigner from Pikesville or Villa Nova, but out here in the Park — what's the difference?" *The Sudbrook News, Official Newspaper of the Sudbrook Park Improvement Association,* (hereinafter referred to as *The Sudbrook News* or *The News)* Vol. 1, No. 2, November 1943. A later newsletter stated that "Sudbrook Avenue appears on the original plats as Monmouth." *The Sudbrook News,* Vol. I, No. 4, April 1944. By the 1950s, the street was called Sudbrook Lane by most, but not all, of those who lived on it (some residents continued to list their address as Sudbrook Road when surrounding neighbors on the same street listed their address as Sudbrook Lane). (Information from membership records of the Sudbrook Club, Inc. and telephone interview with Sylvia Finifter, April 13, 1997).

8. *The Sudbrook News,* Vol. 1, No. 2, November 1943, stated that the name "Adana" was created by melding the names of the two daughters — Ada and Anna — of "the gentleman who named our streets." It is questionable whether this was the genesis of the street's name. The 1912 Coogan survey and plat included an Adana Road, which was referenced in some 1919 deeds, but the name sat dormant until the street was developed in 1940. Rumor had it that Foster Fenton might have named the street, but the name preceded him and he had no daughters. (Telephone interview with Matthew Fenton, III, July 28, 1996). The genesis of the name Adana remains unknown.

9. From sales brochure owned by Sudbrook resident Dorothy Diehl, who moved to Adana Road in September 1940. She and Betty Anton, who moved to Adana Road in November 1940, each purchased their home, the Chase, for $3,825, a special "early sale" inducement. I am grateful to Mrs. Diehl for providing the brochure, and to her and Mrs. Anton for general background information about the 1940s development in Sudbrook Park.

10. According to a 1940s sales brochure, Fenton's development company was the County Engineering Company with offices at the Real Estate Trust Building, Charles & Chase Sts. in Baltimore. The company's field office was located in Sudbrook Park at what is now 914 Adana Road. (Sales brochure and information courtesy of Dorothy Diehl, telephone interview August 12, 1996). (Fenton also was president of Land Mortgages, Inc., which was listed on some 1930 deeds and agreements in connection with Sudbrook Park. BCLR, Liber C.W.B., Jr. 952, folio 576, Land Mortgages, Inc. et al. Deed to Hugh A. Marshall, June 15, 1935; and BCLR, Liber C.W.B., Jr. 1092, folio 58, Land Mortgages, Inc. Deed & Agreement with Foster T. Fenton, December 28, 1939).

11. The monthly payment covered $22.66 for F.H.A. principal, interest and insurance; $6.00 toward taxes; sixty-four cents for fire insurance and $7.00 for ground rent. (Information from sales brochure in the collection of Dorothy Diehl).

12. BCLR, Liber C.W.B., Jr. 1092, folio 58, Land Mortgages, Inc. Deed & Agreement with Foster T. Fenton, December 28, 1939 (these covenants were to be binding until January 1, 1965, after which they would be automatically extended for successive periods of ten years "unless by a vote of the majority of the then owners of the lots it is agreed to change the said covenants in whole or in part.")

13. Although several 1912 and 1913 deeds for subdivided parcels in Sudbrook Park contained a racial restriction, it was not until the new development began in 1939 that racial, ethnic and religious exclusions became part of a large number of Sudbrook Park deeds.

14. Waeshe, pp. 67 and 113, and Frank, p. 78.

15. Shelley v. Kraemer, 334 U.S. 1 (1948). The U. S. Supreme Court held that the Fourteenth Amendment did not bar private parties "from entering into racially restrictive covenants, which exclude blacks from buying or renting homes in 'covenanted' neighborhoods," but that it did "prohibit state courts from enforcing such covenants," which would constitute state action denying equal protection of the laws. Elder Witt, ed., *The Supreme Court and Its Work* (Washington, D.C.: Congressional Quarterly, Inc., 1981), p. 212.

16. The initial board was composed of the following persons: A. Hamilton Bishop (1013 Windsor Road), James A. Miller (704 Cliveden Road West), George S. McCreedy (520 Sudbrook Lane), J. Roberts Wilson (507 Sudbrook Lane), Charles E. Caltrider (714 Howard Road), Kenneth B. Boyd, M.D. (1007 Windsor Road) and C. G. K. Carroll (704 Carysbrook Road). (All but Carroll lived in the older section). Bishop, McCreedy and Wilson served as incorporators. By 1944, Andrew MacDonald (916 Adana Road) was Secretary and Editor of *The Sudbrook News,* and L. M. Bates (Adana Road) was in charge of the Roll of Honor project for members of the community serving in the armed forces.

17. Incorporation information is from a State Tax Commission document retained by the community association. Dues information is taken from a Nov. 1, 1941, letter of George S. McCreedy, Secretary of the Association, to Mr. Pearson. It was reportedly another Secretary of the Association, Andrew MacDonald, who started *The Sudbrook News.* MacDonald served as its editor through at least 1954, according to information in *The News.* The documents referred to in this footnote, as well as the old newsletters, are in the archives of the community association (currently called Sudbrook Park, Inc.). They were retained over the years and made available to me by Dorothy Collins, who has served as historian of the community association for several years. Her help and assistance in this regard and on innumerable aspects of this project have been greatly appreciated.

18. "Sudbrook Park Residents Want to Abolish 'Unsightly' Dump," *Baltimore Sun,* January 18, 1942; and "County Unit Uses Greenwood Dump," *Baltimore Sun,* January 19, 1942 (claiming that the county roads department was one of the groups using the dump — for leaves, dead branches and tree stumps).

19. "Sudbrook Park Residents Want to Abolish 'Unsightly' Dump," *Baltimore Sun*, January 18, 1942. (Blackford would no doubt have been appalled. Of course, under his watchful eye, the situation never would have progressed to such an advanced stage).

20. "Will Clear Dump in Sudbrook Park," *Baltimore Sun*, January 30, 1942. Although the use of the area as an open dumping ground by garbage and county roads trucks ended, the community still must monitor trash dumping along both sides of the S-curve on Greenwood Road entering Sudbrook Park, and schedules periodic community clean-up days to collect litter and other debris left in that area.

21. *The Sudbrook News*, Vol. 1, No. 2, November 1943. Although intended to honor its designer, Sudbrook Park's "Olmstead" Road spells his name incorrectly.

22. "Ten Years Ago," *The Sudbrook News*, October 1954, p. 4.

23. *The Sudbrook News*,, Vol. 1, No. 2, January 1944.

24. *The Sudbrook News*,, Vol. 1, No. 2, April 1944. Civil Defense readiness drills continued into the 1950s. In Sudbrook Park, as in other areas, Block Officers, armbands and identification cards were considered part and parcel of preparedness. *The News* kept residents informed. A 1954 advisory notice stated that a "nation-wide surprise alert will be held during the three days of Nov. 8, 9, or 10. The alert may come without previous warning any time during the night or day."

25. This area was still undeveloped, although building development after the war was to be centered "south and west of the Park, with new homes going up on both sides of Milford Road." *The Sudbrook News*, Vol. 1, No. 2, January 1944.

26. Information courtesy of Betty Anton and Dorothy Diehl, telephone interviews on July 27 and 28, 1996.

27. *The Sudbrook News*,, Vol. 1, No. 2, April 1944. With spring in the air, this same edition of *The News* asked residents of Sudbrook: "The birds like Sudbrook Park and why not? What other community welcomes them and feeds them as much high grade grass seed as we do. Where else, outside of the penitentiary, do the residents dig rocks year after year...?" The latter question still resonates with Sudbrook Park residents who engage in any gardening or landscaping.

28. Vanik was said to have been the main carpenter for the Bata Shoe Company in Czechoslovakia. When the war was heating up in the late 1930s, the Company moved a factory to Maryland and brought Vanik and his family with them. He worked for Bata Shoe until the end of World War II. After the War, he and his grown sons went into house building. Vanik built 612 and 614 Cliveden, and may have built other houses on vacant lots in Sudbrook. One former owner noted that Vanik "used some of the finest structural techniques that I've seen in the Baltimore area." Information about Vanik courtesy of Robert M. Schaller, Sr., telephone interview July 29, 1996.

29. As discussed in Chapter 7, Olmsted designed roads of continuous curvature while the typical subdivision uses a tangent-curve-tangent method to create a "curved" street. It is the latter method that was used in the streets developed in Sudbrook in the 1940s and 1950s, although some newer roads (such as Carysbrook, McHenry and a large portion of Olmstead) more closely emulate a Olmstead continuous curve — perhaps because the developers attempted to follow or invert, at a slightly changed location, the curvature of the road on the 1889 plat.

30. Many families at that time had only one car and the Western Maryland Railroad was still the choice for many men who worked downtown. Women also used the train to go into the city, often with their children.

31. In an item titled "Ten Years Ago," the Improvement Association in its newsletter of October 1954 noted that at its October 6, 1944 meeting, it had instructed its Secretary "to check and see if ladies would like to form a social club."

32. The date of organization was stated on a booklet titled "Revised Constitution and By-Laws" of the Sudbrook Club. The object of the group as stated in the 1946 By-laws was "to unite and utilize the combined influence and efforts of the members to further social, recreational and educational activities within the community and to promote the general good and welfare of the residents." Articles of Incorporation of The Sudbrook Club, Inc. were filed on June 1, 1956. Beulah M. Swindell (908 Windsor Road), Margaret R. Harrison (900 Windsor Road) and Alice L. Smith (700 Cliveden Rd. West) acted as incorporators.

33. Karen Hyneckeal, "Sudbrook Park Keeps Serenity, Aloof to Surging Suburbia," *Baltimore Evening Sun*, May 20, 1964 (noting that the first elected president of the Sudbrook Club was Mrs. Prunetta Owens).

34. Although the 1946 By-laws indicated that membership was open to any "adult residents of Sudbrook Park," the Sudbrook Club remained solely a women's group into the early 1970s. Program topics from meetings in the 1950s included "Dance Lesson by Ted Cochell," "Talk on Child Psychology," "Floral Arrangements for Christmas," "Hats for Milady," "Easter Egg Dyeing and Decorating by International Centre," "Gift Wrapping," "Chef's Night" (by the Chef for the Sheraton-Belvedere), "Foreign Exchange" (by foreign exchange students of Milford Mill High School) and "Around the World in 80 Slides."

35. For many years the Christmas tree lighting was held around a seventy-five foot tree on the Howard Road and Sudbrook Lane triangle, which reportedly was "the tallest community Christmas tree in Baltimore County." (Newspaper article (marked only "1950s") in the Sudbrook Park, Inc. Archives). Children were given small cone candles to hold as they sang carols; residents collected donations and canned goods which were donated to the needy. Santa would arrive on a fire engine amidst the clanging of bells, and hot cider and cookies were provided. It was, and still is, an event enjoyed by young and old. Since at least the early 1970s, it has been held at the Windsor/Sudbrook triangle. (Information about the tree lighting from Sally Gracie, who grew up in Sudbrook Park (telephone interview, December 4, 1996), and from the author's personal experience).

36. Robert Highton, "Residents of Sudbrook Park to Mark Twelfth Night," *Baltimore Evening Sun*, January 4, 1961. The community held its first tree-burning ritual on January 6, 1946. According to the article, Epiphany celebrations had a 300-year history and the day had been marked for years along the Eastern Shore, but Sudbrook Park was apparently responsible "for reviving the burning-of-the-greens in Maryland." (Information about where the practice started and spread to also from this article). A subsequent news article noted that: "Caroling is also a popular Yuletime tradition in Sudbrook and families are asked to join the club's annual serenade around the Park. Judging of the best decorated home takes place shortly after Christmas with prizes being awarded at the Twelfth Night celebration." Hyneckeal, "Sudbrook Park Keeps Serenity."

37. Information about Sudbrook's tree burning from telephone interviews with Sally Gracie and Dorothy Diehl, December 4, 1996, as well as from the author's personal experience attending the event.

38. Hyneckeal, "Sudbrook Park Keeps Serenity." Cliveden Green, intended by Olmsted to be preserved as a permanent open space and playground, had been subdivided and was being developed at this time.

39. In 1978, the Greenwood Road site was officially deeded back to First National Bank of Maryland and Elsie White, as Trustees under the Will of John O. White and William R. MacCallum.

40. The houses that were constructed on McHenry were in the area that the Olmsteds and the Sudbrook Company had called the "low lands." During major hurricanes (David and Agnes) in the early 1970s, some of the houses on McHenry were hard hit by flooding.

41. *The Sudbrook News*, October 1954, p. 3.

42. Olson, p. 314. Increased private automobile ownership had a profound effect on public transportation systems. According to Olson (p. 359): "When the shortages of rubber and steel ceased [after the war], households bought automobiles in startling numbers. The mass transit system disintegrated. Streetcar ridership plummeted after VJ-day. The Baltimore Transit Company collapsed financially, and was bought out by a Chicago group, indirectly connected with General Motors, who converted the transit system to diesel buses and sold out to the city....Trains and electric commuter lines sold off their rights of way. Pennsylvania Station became a half-deserted hulk...[and] Mount Royal Station...was converted into an art school."

43. Olson, p. 360. Olson commented (p. 361): "Like the railroads before them, the expressways provided the prime basis for land speculation — a struggle to capture prize sites as springboards to private wealth…. Road building gave value to the suburban county ring, then to the great corridors, and above all to the nodal properties where they crossed."

44. *The Sudbrook News,* October 1954, p. 2. Also in the 1954 *News* were two additional items that previewed continuing pressures the community would face. One item noted that a Traffic Committee was working on a petition and a proposal "to ban heavy trucks using the Park as a thru way." The other item announced that while there were "no zoning issues before the Association at this time," persons "at the junction of Greenwood and Church Lane have had to form an Improvement Association in an effort to curb expansion of the present industrial development along the railroad tracks and to prevent projected development of new factories." The days when Sudbrook Park was a remote outpost were fast becoming a thing of the past.

Chapter 15: Saved by Preservation: 1955–Present

1. The proposed route, starting at Patterson Avenue in the city and going to Reisterstown, covered a distance of about 12.4 miles. See Report No. FHWA-MD-EIS-73-01-F, Relocated U.S. Route 140 (Northwest Expressway), Baltimore City Line to Reisterstown, and Phase I Rapid Transit, Baltimore City Line to Owings Mills in Baltimore County, Maryland, Administrative Action — Final Environmental Impact Statement/Section 4(f) Statement of the U.S. Dept. of Transportation and the Maryland Department of Transportation, officially signed on March 16, 1976 and Jan. 27, 1977 (hereinafter referred to as the Environmental Impact Statement or EIS), pp. A-1, A-5. Baltimore County's Department of Public Works, acting at the behest of the county's Planning Commission, wrote the June 16, 1948 letter to the SHA. EIS, p. A-1.

2. The proposed expressway was also referred to as "Wabash extended" and "Relocated Route 140."

3. The Northwest Expressway was to be a six-lane dual highway, "consisting of a 36-foot roadway and 10-foot paved shoulder in each direction, separated by a variable width median. The typical right-of-way width would be 300 feet." EIS, p. A–8.

4. At that point, the planners deemed it too expensive to condemn the businesses and pay to move them elsewhere. Sudbrook's historic landscape, historic houses and other homes in the community, however, had been deemed expendable by state and county officials. In addition to losing its entranceway bridge, triangles and greenspaces, Sudbrook would have lost as many as forty homes under plans for the expressway. Larry Singer, "N.W. Residents to Fight to the End of the Road," (Pikesville) *Northwest Star,* June 5, 1975.

5. Telephone interviews on June 28–29, 1997 with James Barrett, Newell Cox, Jr., William T. Cox and Sarah Sener.

6. EIS, p. A-1.

7. By January 1976, the state had acquired approximately 85% of the necessary right-of-way from the Baltimore City Line to the Beltway, 5% from the Beltway to Painters Mill Road, and 16% from Painters Mill Road to U.S. Route 140. EIS, p. A-1.

8. Telephone interviews on June 29–30, 1997 with Newell Cox, Jr., Jackie Cox and Dorothy Liebno. Cottage No. 5 had been purchased by Thomas Ross, a jack-of-all-trades who had helped Eugene Blackford maintain the community. Ross' daughter, Stella Ross Finnerty, had been living on the property before the state leveled it. Telephone interview with Newell Cox, Jr. on June 29, 1997.

9. Telephone interviews on June 28–30, 1997 with James Barrett, Delores Bennett, Newell Cox, Jr., William T. Cox, Bayard Hochberg, Donna MacLean, Mary H. Mosner and Sarah Sener.

10. The community did not mobilize to fight the project when it was first proposed and rumors were circulating for several reasons. One reason seems to be that during the fifties and sixties few people "fought City Hall" and even fewer won. Moreover, especially in the early years, but even into the 1970s, it was difficult for residents and community groups to get reliable information, or any information, about the SHA's plans. In a 1975 news article, the President of the Sudbrook Club charged that the state had "deliberately withheld information about its plans from citizens." Among those documents difficult to obtain were the preliminary and final EIS, the transcript of public hearings on the project and the "Historic District report." Martin Sussman, "Sudbrook Club Nixes Highway; Agrees to Rapid-Rail System," (Randallstown) *Community Times,* June 4, 1975.

11. The protections afforded by the National Historic Preservation Act of 1966 were not commonly known until well into the 1970s.

12. In 1957 when the Western Maryland Railroad stopped its passenger service, "the trip took 30 minutes and cost 48 cents." James D. Dilts, "Another Expressway, Another Battle," *Baltimore Sun,* April 16, 1972. A number of citizens suggested to the state that it reactivate the Western Maryland Railroad's passenger service rather than spend hundreds of millions of dollars to construct an entirely new system. No one with authority in the bureaucracy ever seemed to take these suggestions seriously. There may be a number of reasons. First, bureaucratic planners seem to have a preference for building new structures rather than reviving old ones. Second, large numbers of state, county and related private industry jobs depend upon devising and continuing major new public works projects. Third, at one point, the rapid transit was planned to be a complete system, with four or five spokes from the central city to outlying areas. However, by the time the line was being built to Reisterstown Plaza, costs had escalated and federal funding for a comprehensive system looked unlikely, not to mention that there was community opposition from many different areas. Still, the MTA nurtured the hope that once the first leg all the way to Owings Mills was operational, other areas would also want a line. This has not happened. Today, the MTA operates a light rail line from northern Baltimore County to the city, but the rapid transit line still consists of a single spoke from Owings Mills, extended now to The Johns Hopkins Hospital in the eastern section of Baltimore city. There is little or no talk of ever establishing a rapid transit "system."

13. See for example Dilts, "Another Expressway, Another Battle," (noting that Sudbrook's opposition to the expressway and transit line was comparable to the opposition of residents of Fells Point, who had filed suit against the 3-A expressway system through their area), and Olson, p. 361 ("From 1942 to 1972 engineers repeatedly proposed crosstown routes [major radials to connect with the Beltway], while neighborhoods passed the ball back and forth from year to year to resist demolition, isolation, expropriation, or environmental nuisance.")

14. By 1972, a group of Sudbrook residents had begun to actively fight the expressway and transit line. Dilts, "Another Expressway, Another Battle." Sudbrook resident Linda Powell began the effort to mobilize others to take on the state and county bureaucracies. She, Jack Dowell and others in the Sudbrook Club waged a major battle in the early 1970s against the expressway and transit line. Telephone interviews with Jack Dowell, June 28 and 29, 1997.

15. In 1973 the Sudbrook Club prepared a Petition in Opposition to the proposed Northwest Expressway and Rapid Transit System. Through a door-to-door effort, it obtained over 500 signatures in two weeks. Miriam Otterbein, "Transit Project Draws Criticism from Residents," (Randallstown) *Community Times,* April 5, 1973. The petition argued that the proposed project would create various problems for the community, including increased surface water run-off (affecting the Gwynns Falls flood plain), increased traffic through and adjacent to Sudbrook, overloaded sewerage facilities, and objectionable air pollution, noise levels, and visual impact.

16. The Sudbrook Club's by-laws never actually limited membership to women. I have not been able to find out exactly when the Improvement Association ceased operating, although it must have been after 1954, since the group still produced a newsletter that year. As to why it stopped functioning, the consensus of residents who recall the Association seems to be that, with the women's group doing so much, there was not enough reason to continue the Improvement Association.

17. The reconstituted organization was immediately consumed with the urgent expressway issues hanging over the community's future, but it also continued to sponsor holiday parades and festivities, as well as other long established traditions.

18. Women in the community, most of whom were not employed outside the home at that time, found great satisfaction participating in the Sudbrook Club's busy calendar of activities. The group provided a social outlet while also doing good works for the immediate and larger community.

Although many women were alienated by the abruptness of the change and the implication that what the group had been doing was of lesser value, time has shown that both the social and civic functions of the community association were and are crucial. The women's group was vital in preserving and instituting important traditions that imparted the sense of community spirit so important to Olmsted, while had the community **not** mobilized to fight the expressway, it would have been irreparably destroyed.

19. The urgency to get a nomination completed did not allow time to do careful, documented research. Even if it had, many of the documents, including the 1889 Plan of Olmsted, had not been discovered or were not known or readily available to researchers in the early 1970s. The major emphasis of the 1973 nomination was on the architecture of various houses. The nomination cursorily mentioned Olmsted as the designer of the community and even misspelled his name. Deed restrictions were mentioned but were attributed to the Sudbrook Company rather than Olmsted. The nomination form also included the erroneous information that Sudbrook had been designed as a summer community and implied that it always had a golf course, swimming pool and tennis courts.

20. The National Register nomination's emphasis on architecture reflected a still common viewpoint that the community hopes to correct by someday expanding the historic district's boundaries to reflect the importance of Olmsted's landscape design plan.

21. An open cut is a section that lies below and is visible looking down from the surface; it is not covered.

22. EIS, p. A-3.

23. An MTA representative expressed the opinion that the historic value of Sudbrook Park had already been "taken into consideration" in drafting the preliminary EIS and "the consultants did not feel that the proposed project alternate routes [which then included a 200–300 foot cut through Sudbrook for the combined expressway/transit line] would affect that area 'to any appreciable degree'." He noted, however, that this "in no way means the Department of Transportation feels the same way." (Miriam Otterbein, "Transportation Fight Bolstered — Sudbrook Park Wins National Historic Status," (Pikesville) *Northwest Star*, July 12, 1973.) Not everyone agreed. State Delegate Richard Rynd was concerned about the possible destruction of the "beauty and general environment of the Sudbrook Park area which was recently claimed as a national historic site." ("Del. Says: Communities Jeopardized by Transit Plans," (Pikesville) *The Star-Northwest*, Nov. 15, 1973.) Rynd arranged a meeting with Secretary of Transportation Harry Hughes, his staff, project consultants and members of affected community groups. At that meeting, it was "revealed that discussions between the Department of Transportation and the Maryland Historical Trust [have] led to the strong probability that any construction [of the expressway] in the Historic Sudbrook area would be done in an underground tunnel." (Jeffrey Pollack, "Transportation Dept. Restudies Expressway," (Pikesville) *The Star-Northwest*, Dec. 20, 1973.) In the end, the SHA abandoned as too costly the idea of tunneling a six-lane expressway through Sudbrook.

24. Miriam Otterbein, "Transit Project Draws Criticism from Residents," (Randallstown) *Community Times*, April 5, 1973; Craig Roberton, "To Love or Not to Love the N.W. Expressway," (Pikesville) *Northwest Star*, February 21, 1974; Larry Singer, "N.W. Residents to Fight to the End of the Road," (Pikesville) *Northwest Star*, June 5, 1975; Marcia Wagner, "Residents of Old Court Area Protest New X-Way Proposals," (Pikesville) *Northwest Star*, Aug. 6, 1975; and "Willow Glen Proclaims Opposition to Northwest Expressway Proposal," (Pikesville) *Northwest Star*, Aug. 7, 1975.

25. The area between Sudbrook and Gwynnvale was part of the Gwynns Falls watershed, which had experienced severe flooding during tropical storm Agnes (1972). The Gwynnvale community claimed that the run-off from heavy rains in August 1984 was made worse by construction of the MTA's Old Court Station. An MTA attorney countered that the MTA construction did not cause the flooding and that the agency could not "tak[e] the heat for developer Victor Posner's 1957 decision to build [Gwynnvale] homes in the flood plain." Larry Carson, "Gwynnvale Group Opposes MTA Bridge," *Baltimore Evening Sun*, September 11, 1984.

26. "[Fourth District Democratic] Club [of Greater Reisterstown, Owings Mills and Glyndon] Disturbed at Expressway Delay," 1973 newspaper clipping describing this group's letter to Governor Marvin Mandel, no date or identification of the paper listed on the clipping; "That Road," editorial in (Pikesville) *Northwest Star*, Dec. 19, 1974.

27. Martin Sussman, "Sudbrook Club Nixes Highway; Agrees to Rapid Rail System," (Randallstown) *Community Times*, June 4, 1975; Joyce Price, "Northwest Citizens Ask Expressway Not Be Built," *Baltimore News American*, June 15, 1975; and "N.W. Expressway Urged Apart From Beltway," *Baltimore News American*, July 21, 1975.

28. Martin Sussman, "Final Route Still Uncertain For Expressway," (Randallstown) *Community Times*, June 18, 1975.

29. "County Planner Agrees with Residents to Nix Expressway Within Beltway," (Pikesville) *Northwest Star*, July 10, 1975. The article noted that these recommendations were sent to Baltimore County Executive Ted Venetoulis, who then had to decide whether to ask the state to modify its plans or ask the Task Force to make further compromises. It appeared that Sudbrook representatives believed that, if the Task Force's plan was adopted, "there will probably be no homes destroyed in the Sudbrook Park area." This did not prove to be the case. In addition to the homes demolished in the 1960s, about fifteen homes on Westover Road were later demolished for the rapid transit construction.

30. Although not mentioned in the news articles, the transit route chosen was **not** Alternate 9, which Sudbrook had agreed to, but Alternate 7, a less expensive alternate that required the transit line to leave the Western Maryland Railroad tracks and veer into Sudbrook Park. "M-DOT Drops Sudbrook Park from Expressway," (Pikesville) *The Star-Northwest*, June 3, 1976. See also David Collins, "Citizens Meet on X-way Expansion," *Baltimore News American*, June 17, 1975 (regarding Alternates 9 and 7, estimated in 1975 to cost $46 million and $31 million, respectively. Both cut off the expressway at the beltway, but in Alternate 9, the transit line ran parallel to the Western Maryland Railroad bed all the way to Owings Mills, whereas in Alternate 7, the transit line ran through "a different part of the community, including Sudbrook.")

31. The dedication ceremony was held on September 24, 1978. As noted in the Preface, Sudbrook's historical marker incorrectly states, among other things, that the community was designed in 1891 (it was 1889), and that it was designed as a summer community.

32. Peter Ruehl, "Finally, An Answer for Sudbrook Park," *Baltimore Sun*, July 30, 1978 (Sunday Real Estate Section, p. 1).

33. EIS, pp. B-32—B-35 and Memorandum of Agreement March 1976, signed by representatives of the Advisory Council on Historic Preservation, the Department of Transportation/Federal Highway Administration, and the Maryland State Historic Preservation Officer. No agency charged with preserving historic districts, and intent on doing so, could have in good faith signed off on what the SHA/MTA and related agencies were proposing in Sudbrook. The only possible explanation is that the historic preservation agencies that gave their approval did not understand the importance of Olmsted's greenspaces to his entire Plan or did not fully comprehend the SHA/MTA's proposal and the irreparable devastation it would wreak.

34. The Maryland Historical Trust did support Sudbrook in a number of ways. MHT representatives attended a number of meetings, adding clout to Sudbrook's position. The MHT also cooperated by placing an easement on 726 Howard Road before the MTA disposed of it. And the Trust actively supported and worked with Sudbrook representatives to assure adequate and appropriate re-landscaping by the MTA.

35. Paul Riede, "Transit Worries Again Plague Sudbrook Park," (Pikesville) *The Star-Northwest*, June 7, 1979 (written some months after the meeting).

36. The alternate routes described in the EIS for the combined expressway-transit project included a cut-and-cover tunnel proposal, although it was not the alternative that was chosen. In addition, apparently even state Delegate Howard Needle at one point had proposed a 900 foot tunnel through Sudbrook Park, although his idea was buried in a small local news article and garnered no major publicity. In addition, it is not clear whether his proposal was intended to address the combined expressway/transit project or only the rapid transit alternative. "Tour-bus," (Pikesville) *Northwest Star*, February 20, 1975.

37. Written surveys were distributed to the approximately 500 families living in Sudbrook Park. Two hundred sixteen responses were in favor of

retaining the narrow bridge. Eight preferred a new bridge. A return rate of forty-three percent on such surveys is extremely high.

38. Kenneth T. Berents, "MD May Build Rail Tunnel as Help to Historic District," *Baltimore Evening Sun,* January 3, 1980, p. E 1.

39. In the months following this meeting, the county posted the Sudbrook bridge as a "one-lane bridge." Although narrow by the standards of current two-lane bridges, with a sixteen-foot four-inch roadway, Sudbrook's bridge had been a two-lane bridge since 1907. The bridge was and still is owned by the railroad — previously the Western Maryland Railroad and now CSX. Baltimore County, however, inspects the bridge every two years and appears to have maintained it for years.

40. The Sudbrook Club retained A. G. Lichtenstein & Associates, Inc., Consulting Engineers from Fair Lawn, New Jersey. Bridge consultation services took place from about May to August 1980. (The county initially proposed replacing Sudbrook's bridge with one that was multi-laned and fifty-four feet wide. After a community outcry, the county reduced the width to thirty-four feet. That, too, met with community opposition. Both plans called for the widening and straightening of Sudbrook Lane on both sides of the bridge. Sudbrook is continuing to fight to preserve the historic function of its bridge — which was intended by Olmsted to be a constricted "gateway entrance" after which five major roads branch out, and also to slow traffic coming into the residential area. The community has insisted that the county make no changes to Sudbrook Lane on either side of the bridge; Sudbrook Lane was also designed by Olmsted and implemented by the Sudbrook Company from Reisterstown Road to Milford Mill Road.

41. The Milford Mill station was so costly not only because of its size and the clearing of so many acres of forested land, but also because of water retention issues, the relocation of Milford Mill Road and the construction of a new bridge on relocated Milford Mill Road.

42. These studies and meetings spanned a ten-year time period (about 1974–1984), and they constituted an important but small segment of the many issues that confronted Sudbrook and other communities affected by this project. One of the persistent difficulties that communities have is finding volunteers able and willing to make the huge investment of time required to monitor and remain involved in projects and meetings that go on for years.

43. It is possible that MTA Administrator Kimball's cut-back of the tunnel for Sudbrook and his hard-line attitude stemmed from pressure he was feeling from legislators and officials because of the MTA's deficits. The MTA in 1979 had projected a deficit of $206 million between 1981 and 1986. In 1980, it had to increase its deficit projection for that time period to $342 million, a sixty-six percent increase. The MTA's annual deficit was projected to be $20.4 million for FY 1981 but turned out to be $33 million. (Michael J. Himowitz, "MTA Sees Gusher of Red Ink: Deficit of $342 Million," *Baltimore Evening Sun,* Nov. 21, 1980). Mr. L. A. "Kim" Kimball was the Administrator of the MTA from 1979 to September 1981. Kimball left to run the Denver area transit agency. Thomas Hasler, "Mass Transit Chief Lured Away by Denver Job," *Baltimore Evening Sun,* August 1, 1981.

44. The Sudbrook Club attempted to publicize having been awarded a grant from the National Trust for Historic Preservation. Both the *Sun* and the *News American* ran articles, but seemed to have their own agendas as to the topics included. The *Sun's* article never even mentioned the grant and also failed to identify the Executive Director of the National Association of Olmsted Parks and Landscapes who was in an accompanying photograph. The *Sun* did publish a later Letter to the Editor from the community association correcting these oversights. Joel McCord, "Residents of Sudbrook Don't Mind Trains, But They Don't Want Them So Close to Home," *Baltimore Sun,* December 14, 1980; Letter to the Editor, "Sudbrook Park," *Baltimore Sun,* Jan. 19, 1981; and Michael Powell, "Sudbrook Suburb Resists Siege by Subway Noise," *Baltimore News American,* Dec. 10, 1980.

45. Michael J. Himowitz, "Budget Cuts Threaten Subway," *Baltimore Evening Sun,* February 18, 1981.

46. Robert Timberg, "Second Leg of Rapid Rail System Put on Hold," *Baltimore Evening Sun,* April 13, 1981.

47. For examples of the two differing opinions, see, "Finish the Subway," Editorial in *Baltimore Sun,* March 1, 1981; Tom Welshko, "Federal Funds Dry Up — Baltimore's Dismal Mass Transit Picture," op-ed in *Baltimore Evening Sun,* June 4, 1981; and Eric Garland, "M is for Metro, Baltimore's New Subway. E is for Eight Hundred Million Dollars, Which It Will Cost. T is for Tracks, Which Run Only Eight Miles. R is for Riders (How Many Will There Be?). O is for Its Operating Deficit (and Who Will Pay for It?). Put Them All Together, and They Spell Mistake," *Baltimore Magazine,* August 1981.

48. Robert Timberg, "Second Subway Leg Backed; No Funds" and "U.S. Said to Support Subway," *Baltimore Evening Sun,* April 21, 1981. Both of Timberg's articles noted that Maryland was seeking federal funding of eighty percent of the $190 million cost of building the second leg of the transit line.

49. News articles about the storm: Kelly Gilbert and Michael Shultz, "Trees, Power Lines Mark Storm's Path," *Baltimore Evening Sun,* June 22, 1981; and Robert Hilson, Jr. and Kelly Gilbert, "135,300 Homes Lose Power in Storm/Winds Lead to Heavy Damage," *Baltimore Evening Sun,* June 26, 1981.

50. Brian Sullam, "Lewis Backs Link Tying BWI, I-95," *Baltimore Sun,* July 30, 1981; Tom Linthicum, "$200 Million for I-70 May Go to Subway Line," *Baltimore Sun,* September 5, 1981; and Michael J. Himowitz, "Second Phase of Subway Moves a Step Closer to Being Funded," *Baltimore Evening Sun,* September 5, 1981.

51. Paul D. Mindus, "Metro Gets $7 Million for 2nd Leg," *Baltimore Evening Sun,* November 13, 1981.

52. At the same meeting, three historic houses with changes and additions larger than the original "historic" portion were approved for nomination to the National Register. Yet Sudbrook, whose Olmsted design had some changes, but still exemplified and preserved Olmsted's key design principles and intent, was denied.

53. A major concern of persons whose homes were located closest to the alignment was possible structural damage from the MTA's blasting. Part of the pre-construction survey process involved taking photographs so that any damage could be documented as caused by the blasting and the owner appropriately compensated.

54. The first year after re-landscaping, Sudbrook lost eighty percent of its new trees. Many died as a result of a drought and some were lost through theft. Sudbrook representatives worked with the MTA on a second re-planting plan, which was implemented successfully.

55. The other two bids were $11,501 and $17, 801, which probably represented more realistic values in light of the enormous expense necessary to rehabilitate the house. Many residents of Sudbrook found it unconscionable that the state was able to profit from the rental and sale of 726 Howard Road when its benign neglect had created the problem.

56. Seven houses remained in 1995, since 726 Howard Road had previously been purchased and another house on Howard Road was turned over to The Chimes, Inc. Over the years, Sudbrook Club representatives had insisted that the MTA include provisions in the deeds stipulating that the houses, when purchased, must be owner-occupied for at least the first five years. This was to prevent speculators from doing minimal work to houses already in dilapidated condition and then re-renting them. Clauses of this nature were inserted in the deeds. As this book goes to press, one house on Howard Road still remains under MTA ownership, although hopefully, it too will be returned to private ownership soon.

57. Recently the MTA again proposed selling air rights over certain transit stations. Many of these issues will return again and again. Jay Apperson, "Owings Mills Transit Hub Seeks Growth," *Baltimore Sun,* Jan. 29, 1996, and Jennifer Brennan, "Metro Site Development Considered," *Owings Mills Times,* Feb. 8, 1996.

58. According to news articles, pressure to revive the old Northwest Expressway through Sudbrook came from the Valleys Planning Council, apparently intent on reopening the possibility of an expressway that would devastate Sudbrook Park in an effort to keep new or expanded cross-country roadways out of the Greenspring, Worthington and Caves valley area. Larry Carson, "Sudbrook Residents Worry About Plan to Extend I-795," *Baltimore Evening Sun,* Feb. 2, 1990; and Alyssa Gabbay, "Council Removes Threat to Sudbrook," *Baltimore Jewish Times,* Feb. 8, 1990.

59. The study to relieve beltway traffic will look at the area from I-83 to U.S. Rte. 40. The proposal to amend the County's 1990–2000 Master Plan also removed the word "widening" from a Milford Mill Road capital project, indicated no support for air rights over the Metro station at Old Court Road, and supported establishing a Cultural Arts Center in Pikesville. Letter from Baltimore County Councilman Melvin Mintz (Second District) to

the Sudbrook Club, February 8, 1990.

60. The community often considered developing a comprehensive plan, but formal action to develop one began in October 1996 with a resolution introduced by Councilman Kevin Kamenetz with the community's support. Councilman Kamenetz was Chair of the Baltimore County Council at the time and represented the Second District, where Sudbrook Park is located.

61. BR&AB, MD-MHS, 131: 4: 3, p. 438, EB to Jas. McEvoy, September 26, 1898.

Epilogue

1. After extolling the lasting contribution of Olmsted and some of his contemporaries to urban planning and the preservation of open spaces, historian Lewis Mumford questioned whether anything like Olmsted's work had been accomplished since and admonished: "The point is that Olmsted attended to first things first…. If we still defile the possibilities of the land, it is not for lack of better example." Lewis Mumford, *The Brown Decades, A Study of the Arts in America 1865–1895* (New York: Harcourt, Brace and Company, 1931; repr. New York: Dover Publications, 1955 and 1971), p. 43.

2. Our failure to learn from the lessons of the past condemns us to a vicious and expensive cycle: poor planning and a lack of preserved open space creates ugly places where no one wants to live, shop or work; citizens who can afford it continue to move farther out, continuing the spiral of suburban sprawl; municipalities struggle to revive dying cities and older suburban neighborhoods and to "re-beautify" areas made ugly by uninformed and poor planning. Using the all too common "penny-wise and pound-foolish approach," we create the very problems that we later have to raise new tax dollars to rectify.

3. Alexander Garvin, *The American City, What Works, What Doesn't* (New York: McGraw-Hill, 1996), p. 252.

4. Garvin, p. 282.

5. Quotes in this paragraph from Olmsted, Vaux & Co., Preliminary Report, pp. 7 and 16.

6. Christopher Tunnard, *The City of Man* (New York: Charles Scribner's Sons, 1953), pp. 195–196.

7. Mumford, pp. 94–95.

8. Alexander Allport, "Inside Fairsted," Vol. 1, No. 5, *National Association of Olmsted Parks Newsletter* (1980/81).

9. Quote taken from the author's notes made during an October 15, 1996 presentation about Riverside by Ann Nowotarski, Architect, Riverside Historical Commission, at the National Trust for Historic Preservation's 50th National Conference in Chicago, "Preserving Our Nation's Historic Communities."

Appendix A

1. OAR/LC, A: 4: 500–518, FL&JCO to HLB, April 17, 1889.

BIBLIOGRAPHY

MANUSCRIPT SOURCES

Advertisement for Sudbrook Inn, 1924. Broadsides Collection, Prints and Photography Department, Maryland Historical Society, Baltimore, Maryland.

Architectural drawings by J. Appleton Wilson for 507 Sudbrook Lane, about 1900. In the private collection of Deana and Chris Karras.

Baltimore County Land and Mortgage Records, Baltimore County Land Records Office, New Courthouse Building, Towson, Maryland.

Blackford Record and Account Books, Ms. 131, Manuscript Division, Maryland Historical Society, Baltimore, Maryland.

Bromley Atlases of Baltimore County, 1898 and 1915. Philadelphia: G. W. Bromley Co., 1898, 1915.

Cox, Dorothy. "Sudbrook Park," pp. 35–44, in *History of Pikesville, Maryland,* Two Vols., unpublished and n.d. A copy is available in the Pikesville Branch of the Baltimore County Public Library.

Cromwell v. Ward. 102 Md. App. 691, 651 A. 2d 424 (1995).

Duff, Charles. "J. Appleton Wilson." Unpublished paper available from the author or from the Baltimore Historic Architects Roundtable.

Garrison Forest Farmers' Club Minutes, Vols. 1 and 2, Ms. 381, Manuscript Division, Maryland Historical Society, Baltimore, Maryland.

Incorporation Records, Maryland State Archives, Annapolis, Maryland.

James Howard McHenry Account Books, Ms. 544.2, Manuscript Division, Maryland Historical Society, Baltimore, Maryland.

James Howard McHenry Journals, Ms. 544.1, Manuscript Division, Maryland Historical Society, Baltimore, Maryland.

James Howard McHenry Papers, Ms. 544, Manuscript Division, Maryland Historical Society, Baltimore, Maryland.

Merrick, William. "Memories of Sudbrook Park." Unpublished memoirs of author's life in Sudbrook Park around the turn of the century, n.d. In the private collection of Stewart McLean.

Olmsted Associates Records, Manuscript Room, Library of Congress, Washington, D.C.

Papers of Frederick Law Olmsted, Manuscript Room, Library of Congress, Washington, D.C.

Rhine, C. Stewart. "A Backward Glance." Unpublished paper on the origins of the Western Maryland Railroad. In the private collection of Mr. Rhine.

Sanborn Insurance Maps, Map Room, Library of Congress, Washington, D.C.

"Sudbrook." Unpublished paper in a McHenry-Stewart family album ("The McHenry Family History") compiled by Marjorie Ober Keyser McHenry, 1959.

"Sudbrook Park" brochure prepared by the Sudbrook Company of Baltimore County, n.d. (about March 1891). In the private collection of Roger Katzenberg; a copy is among the records of the late Dorothy Cox.

Sudbrook Park sales brochure prepared by The County Engineering Company, n.d. (about 1940). In the private collection of Dorothy Diehl.

Stellmann letter. Unpublished letter from William H. Stellmann to Edward Stellmann, June 2, 1913. In the private collection of William and Elizabeth Stellmann.

Wollen, James T. "T. Buckler Ghequier." Unpublished paper available from the author or from the Baltimore Historic Architects Roundtable.

Wollen, James T. and Walker, Irma. "George Archer." Unpublished paper available from the authors or from the Baltimore Historic Architects Roundtable.

Working drawings and plans of the Sudbrook Land Company of Baltimore County, Job No. 1054, National Park Service, Frederick Law Olmsted National Historic Site ("Fairsted") in Brookline, Massachusetts.

BOOKS

Atlas of Baltimore County, Maryland. Surveyed & Published under the Direction of G. M. Hopkins, C. E. Reproduced from 1877 originals and reprinted 1971, Baltimore County Records Management Division.

Bailey, L. H. *Cyclopedia of American Horticulture.* London: Macmillan and Co., Limited, 1900.

Bailey, Liberty Hyde, et al. *Hortus Third, A Concise Dictionary of Plants Cultivated in the United States and Canada.* New York: Macmillan Publishing Company, 1976.

Baltimore, Its History and Its People. Vol. II. New York: Lewis Historical Publishing Co., 1912.

Barnes, Robert. *The Green Spring Valley, Its History and Heritage.* Vol. Two, *Genealogies.* Baltimore: Maryland Historical Society, 1978.

Beveridge, Charles E. and Rocheleau, Paul. *Frederick Law Olmsted, Designing the American Landscape.* New York: Rizzoli International Publications, Inc., 1995.

Blackford, Charles M. *Campaign and Battle of Lynchburg, Virginia.* Lynchburg: Warwick House Publishing, 1994.

Bland, John R., ed. *Maryland Directory and State Gazetteer.* Baltimore: The Baltimore Publishing Co., 1887.

Brooks, Neal A. and Parsons, Richard. *Baltimore County Panorama.* Norfolk/Virginia Beach: The Donning Company Publishers, 1988.

Bruchey, Eleanor Stephens. *The Business Elite in Baltimore, 1880–1914.* North Stratford, N.H.: Arno Press, 1976.

Dorsey, John and Dilts, James D. *A Guide to Baltimore Architecture.* 2d ed. Centreville, Maryland: Tidewater Publishers, 1981.

Farrell, Michael R. *The History of Baltimore's Streetcars.* Sykesville, Maryland: Greenberg Publishing Company, Inc., 1992.

Frank, Beryl. *A Pictorial History of Pikesville, Maryland.* Towson, Maryland: Baltimore County Public Library, 1982.

Freeman, Douglas Southall. Introduction to *War Years with Jeb Stuart* by William Willis Blackford. New York: Charles Scribner's Sons, 1945.

Garvin, Alexander. *The American City, What Works, What Doesn't.* New York: McGraw-Hill, 1996.

Hewitt, Mark Alan. *The Architect & the American Country House, 1890–1940.* New Haven: Yale University Press, 1990.

Hirschfeld, Charles. *Baltimore, 1870–1900: Studies in Social History.* Baltimore: The Johns Hopkins Press, 1941.

Jackson, Kenneth T. *Crabgrass Frontier, the Suburbanization of the United States.* New York: Oxford University Press, 1985.

Janvier, Meredith. *Baltimore in the Eighties and Nineties.* Baltimore: H. G. Roebuck & Son, 1933.

Keator, Alfred Decker, ed. *Encyclopedia of Pennsylvania Biography.* Philadelphia: Lewis Historical Publishing Co., 1923, pp. 122–124.

Krick, Robert K. *Lee's Colonels.* Dayton, Ohio: Morningside, 1992.

Malone, Dumas, ed. *Dictionary of American Biography,* Vol. X, Part I. New York: Charles Scribner's Sons, 1936, pp. 456–67.

McLaughlin, Charles Capin and Beveridge, Charles E., eds. *The Papers of Frederick Law Olmsted.* Vol. 1, *The Formative Years, 1822–1852.* Baltimore: The Johns Hopkins University Press, 1977.

Merrill, Walter M., ed. *Letters of William Lloyd Garrison.* Vol. 5. Cambridge, Mass.: Belknap Press of Harvard University Press, 1979.

Miller, Mark. *Mount Washington.* Baltimore: GBS Publishers, Division of Gordon's Booksellers, 1980.

Mumford, Lewis. *The Brown Decades, A Study of the Arts in America 1865–1895.* New York: Harcourt, Brace and Company, 1931; repr. New York: Dover Publications, 1955 and 1971.

Olson, Sherry H. *Baltimore, The Building of An American City.* Baltimore: The Johns Hopkins University Press, 1980.

Onions, C. T., ed. *Oxford Universal Dictionary on Historical Principles,* 3d ed. revised with addenda, revised. London: Oxford University Press, 1955.

Orser, Edward and Arnold, Joseph. *Catonsville, 1880 to 1940: From Village to Suburb.* Norfolk: The Donning Company Publishers, 1989.

Papenfuse, Edward C., ed. *Archives of Maryland, An Historical List of Public Officials of Maryland,* Vol. 1. Annapolis: Maryland State Archives, 1990.

Polk's, R. L. *Baltimore City Directory.* (For 1889, 1910, 1911 and 1913). Microfilmed by Research Publications, Inc., New Haven, Connecticut.

Porter, Horace. *Railway Passenger Travel, 1825–1880.* Charles Scribner's & Sons, September 1888; repr. Maynard, Mass.: Chandler Press, 1987.

Remington, Caroline P., comp. *Society Visiting List.* Baltimore: Thos. E. Lycett & Co., 1889–90; Guggenheimer, Weil & Co., 1890–1897; Lucas Brothers, 1907–1916.

Roper, Laura Wood. *FLO — A Biography of Frederick Law Olmsted.* Baltimore: The Johns Hopkins University Press, 1973; repr. Johns Hopkins Paperbacks edition, 1983.

Scharf, J. Thomas. *History of Baltimore City and County,* Parts I and II. Philadelphia: Louis H. Everts, 1881; repr. Baltimore: Regional Publishing Company, 1971.

Schuyler, David. *The New Urban Landscape.* Baltimore: The Johns Hopkins University Press, 1986.

Schuyler, David and Censer, Jane Turner, ed. *The Papers of Frederick Law Olmsted,* Vol. VI, *The Years of Olmsted, Vaux & Company 1865–1874.* Baltimore: The Johns Hopkins University Press, 1992.

Scully, Vincent. "Introduction" in Robert A.M. Stern, ed. *The Architecture of the American Summer: The Flowering of the Shingle Style.* U.S.A.: Rizzoli International Publishers, Inc., 1989.

Shivers, Frank R., Jr. *Walking in Baltimore: An Intimate Guide to the Old City.* Baltimore: The Johns Hopkins University Press, 1995.

Social Register, Baltimore. Vol. XI, No. 5 (1896); Vol. XII, No. 5 (1897); Vol. XIII, No. 6 (1898); Vol. XVIII, No. 7 (1903); Vol. XXVII, No. 12 (1912); Vol. XXIX, No. 14 (1914). New York City: Social Register Association, 1896–1914.

Thomas, Dawn F. *The Green Spring Valley, Its History and Heritage.* Vol. One, *A History, Historic Homes.* Baltimore: Maryland Historical Society, 1978.

Tishler, William H., ed. *American Landscape Architecture, Designers and Places.* Washington, D.C.: The Preservation Press, 1989.

Tunnard, Christopher. *The City of Man.* New York: Charles Scribner's Sons, 1953.

Verheyen, Egon, ed. *Laurence Hall Fowler, Architect (1876–1971).* Baltimore: The Johns Hopkins University Press, 1984.

Waesche, James F. *Crowning the Gravelly Hill, A History of the Roland Park-Guilford-Homeland District.* Baltimore: Maclay & Associates, 1987.

Waring, George E. Jr. *The Sanitary Drainage of Houses and Towns.* New York: Hurd and Houghton, 1876.

Who Was Who in America. Vol. 1, 1897–1942. Chicago: E.A.N. Marquis Company, 1942.

Witt, Elder, ed. *The Supreme Court and Its Work.* Washington, D.C.: Congressional Quarterly, Inc., 1981.

JOURNAL AND MAGAZINE ARTICLES

Archer, John. "Country and City in the American Romantic Suburb." *Journal of the Society of Architectural Historians,* Vol. 42, No. 2 (May 1983), pp. 139–156.

Barnard, Ella K. " 'Mount Royal' and Its Owners." *Maryland Historical Magazine,* Vol. 26, No. 4 (December 1931), pp. 311–361.

Beveridge, Charles E. "Frederick Law Olmsted's Theory of Landscape Design." *Nineteenth Century* (Summer 1977), pp. 38–43.

Dehler, Katherine. "Mt. Vernon Place at the Turn of the Century: A Vignette of the Garrett Family." *Maryland Historical Magazine,* Vol. 69, No. 3 (Fall 1974), pp. 279–292.

Garland, Eric. "M is for Metro, Baltimore's New Subway. E is for Eight Hundred Million Dollars, Which It Will Cost. T is for Tracks, Which Run Only Eight Miles. R is for Riders (How Many Will There Be?). O is for Its Operating Deficit (and Who Will Pay for It?). Put Them All Together, and They Spell Mistake." *Baltimore Magazine,* August 1981.

Gordon, Douglas. "A Virginian and His Baltimore Diary." *Maryland Historical Magazine,* Vol. 49, No. 3 (September 1954), pp. 196–213.

Karp, Walter. "The Central Park." *American Heritage,* Vol. 32 (April–May 1981), pp. 81–97.

McLaughlin, Charles Capen. "The Environment: Olmsted's Odyssey." *Wilson Quarterly,* Vol. VI, No. 3 (Summer 1982), pp. 78–87.

Miller, Samuel H., ed. "Civil War Memoirs of the First Maryland Calvary, C.S.A." *Maryland Historical Magazine,* Vol. 58, No. 2 (June 1963), pp. 137–170.

"Re-Creation of Grey Rock, Baltimore County." *Maryland Historical Magazine,* Vol. 50, No. 2 (June 1955), pp. 82–92.

Robinson, Michael. "The Suburban Ideal: 19th Century Planned Communities." *Historic Preservation,* Vol. 30, No. 2 (April–June 1978), pp. 24–29.

Samuelson, Robert J. "The Message from 1896?" *Newsweek,* August 12, 1996, p. 51.

Schalck, Harry G. "Mini-Revisionism in City Planning History: The Planners of Roland Park." *Journal of the Society of Architectural Historians,* Vol. 39, No. 4 (December 1970), pp. 347–349.

Schalck, Harry G. "Planning Roland Park, 1891–1910." *Maryland Historical Magazine,* Vol. 67, No. 4 (Winter 1972), pp. 419–428.

REPORTS AND PAMPHLETS

Arnold, Joseph L. "Baltimore's Neighborhoods, 1800–1980." *Working Papers from the Regional Economic History Research Center.* Wilmington, Delaware: Eleutherian Mills-Hagley Foundation, Spring 1980, pp.75–98.

Beveridge, Charles E. and Hoffman, Carolyn F., comps. *The Master List of Design Projects of the Olmsted Firm 1857–1950.* Boston: National Association for Olmsted Parks, in conjunction with the Massachusetts Association for Olmsted Parks, 1987.

"James McHenry, Soldier-Statesman of the Constitution." A Bicentennial Series Pamphlet. CMH Pub. 71–4, n.d. Available from the Ft. McHenry Historical Site.

McGrain, John W. *Master Plan History — Modern Planning; Master Plan Working Paper.* Towson, MD: Baltimore County Office of Planning and Zoning, 1989.

Office of the Riverside Improvement Company. *Riverside in 1871, With a Description of its Improvements, Together with some Engravings of Views and Buildings.* Chicago: D. & C. H. Blakely, Printers, n.d. Available from the Riverside Historical Commission.

Olmsted, Vaux & Co. *Preliminary Report upon the Proposed Suburban Village at Riverside, Near Chicago.* New York: Sutton, Bowne & Co., Printers, 1868.

Transactions: Maryland State Bar Association, 28th Annual Meeting. Report of Committee on Legal Biography. Baltimore: Maryland State Bar Association, 1923, pp. 25–26.

Report No. FHWA-MD-EIS-73-01-F, "Relocated U.S. Route 140 (Northwest Expressway), Baltimore City Line to Reisterstown, and Phase I Rapid Transit, Baltimore City Line to Owings Mills in Baltimore County, Maryland, Administrative Action — Final Environmental Impact Statement/Section 4(f) Statement of the U.S. Dept. of Transportation (Federal Highway Administration and Urban Mass Transit Administration) and the Maryland Department of Transportation (State Highway Administration and Mass Transit Administration)," officially signed on March 16, 1976 and January 27, 1977.

"The Charms of Mt. Vernon — A Walking Tour Guide to Baltimore's Most Historic and Elegant Neighborhood." Downtown Partnership of Baltimore, Inc., n.d.

NEWSPAPER ARTICLES

Advertisement for Sudbrook Park. *Baltimore News,* May 3, 1913.

Advertisement for Rosedale. *Baltimore Sunday Herald,* April 30, 1893, p. 26.

Allport, Alexander. "Inside Fairsted." *National Association of Olmsted Parks Newsletter,* Vol. 1, No. 5, 1980–81.

Apperson, Jay. "Owings Mills Transit Hub Seeks Growth." *Baltimore Sun,* January 29, 1996.

Berents, Kenneth T. "Md. May Build Rail Tunnel as Help to Historic District." *Baltimore Evening Sun,* January 3, 1980.

Blitz, John. "Sudbrook Park Marking 75th Anniversary." *Baltimore Evening Sun,* April 29, 1964.

Brennan, Jennifer. "Metro Site Development Considered." *Owings Mills Times,* February 8, 1996.

Carson, Larry. "Gwynnvale Group Opposes MTA Bridge." *Baltimore Evening Sun,* September 11, 1984.

Carson, Larry. "Sudbrook Residents Worry About Plan to Extend I-795." *Baltimore Evening Sun,* February 2, 1990.

Clippings files. Harvard University Archives, Pusey Library, Cambridge, Massachusetts.

Collins, David. "Citizens Meet on X-way Expansion." *Baltimore News American,* June 17, 1975.

"County Planner Agrees with Residents to Nix Expressway within Beltway." (Pikesville, Maryland) *Northwest Star,* July 10, 1975.

"County Unit Uses Greenwood Dump." *Baltimore Sun,* January 19, 1942.

"Del. Says: Communities Jeopardized by Transit Plans." (Pikesville, Maryland) *The Star-Northwest,* November 15, 1973.

Dilts, James D. "Another Expressway, Another Battle." *Baltimore Sun,* April 16, 1972.

"Dreams of Enterprising Brooklyn-Curtis Bay Pioneers Nearly Realized." *Baltimore Sun,* December 12, 1937.

Editorial, "Finish the Subway." *Baltimore Sun,* March 1, 1981.

Editorial, "That Road." (Pikesville, Maryland) *Northwest Star,* December 19, 1974.

"[Fourth District Democratic] Club [of Greater Reisterstown, Owings Mills and Glyndon} Disturbed at Expressway Delay." [Clipping from unidentified newspaper, 1973]. Collection of the author.

Gabbay, Alyssa. "Council Removes Threat to Sudbrook." *Baltimore Jewish Times,* February 8, 1990.

Gardner, Kay. "Antiques, Rare Furniture on Tour Display." *Baltimore American,* April 25, 1960.

Gardner, Kay. "Sudbrook Park on Tour." *Baltimore American,* April 24, 1960.

Gilbert, Kelly and Shultz, Michael. "Trees, Power Lines Mark Storm's Path." *Baltimore Evening Sun,* June 22, 1981.

"Growing Northwest Baltimore Absorbs 'The Country'." *Baltimore Evening Sun,* October 17, 1955.

Hasler, Thomas. "Mass Transit Chief Lured Away by Denver Job." *Baltimore Evening Sun,* August 1, 1981.

Highton, Robert. "Residents of Sudbrook Park to Mark Twelfth Night." *Baltimore Evening Sun,* January 4, 1961.

Hilson, Robert, Jr., and Gilbert, Kelly. "135,300 Homes Lose Power in Storm; Winds Lead to Heavy Damage." *Baltimore Evening Sun,* June 26, 1981.

Himowitz, Michael J. "Budget Cuts Threaten Subway." *Baltimore Evening Sun,* February 18, 1981.

Himowitz, Michael J. "MTA Sees Gusher of Red Ink: Deficit of $342 Million." *Baltimore Evening Sun,* November 21, 1980.

Himowitz, Michael J. "Second Phase of Subway Moves a Step Closer to Being Funded." *Baltimore Evening Sun,* September 5, 1981.

Hyneckeal, Karen. "Sudbrook Park Keeps Serenity, Aloof to Surging Suburbia." *Baltimore Evening Sun,* May 20, 1964.

Letter to the Editor from Melanie Anson, Civic Committee Chair, Sudbrook Club, Inc. "Sudbrook Park." *Baltimore Sun,* January 19, 1981.

Linthicum, Tom. "$200 Million for I-70 May Go to Subway Line." *Baltimore Sun,* September 5, 1981.

McCord, Joel. "Residents of Sudbrook Don't Mind Trains, But They Don't Want Them So Close to Home." *Baltimore Sun*, December 14, 1980.

"M-DOT Drops Sudbrook Park from Expressway." (Pikesville, Maryland) *The Star-Northwest*, June 3, 1976.

Mindus, Paul D. "Metro Gets $7 Million for 2nd Leg." *Baltimore Evening Sun*, November 13, 1981.

Moberly, Elizabeth H. "Baltimore's Barbara Fritchie." [Clipping from unidentified newspaper, n.d., in The McHenry Family History].

"Monumental City Suburbs, They Cannot Be Eclipsed Anywhere in the Union." *Baltimore Sunday Herald*, April 30, 1893.

"New Trolley Line To Tap Northwest." *Baltimore News*, May 3, 1913.

Notices. "Sudbrook Park." (Towson, Maryland) *Maryland Journal*, June 30, 1883.

"N.W. Expressway Urged Apart from Beltway." *Baltimore News American*, July 21, 1975.

Obituaries, Robert Bacon. "Colonel Robert Bacon," *Boston Transcript*, May 31, 1919; "Robert Bacon, 1880," by William Roscoe Thayer, '81, *Harvard Alumni Bulletin*, June 26, 1919; and "Robert Bacon Estate Valued at $7,585, 565," *New York Times*, July 29, 1920.

Obituaries, Eugene Blackford. *Baltimore Sun*, February 5, 1908; and "Major Blackford's Funeral," *Baltimore News*, February 5, 1908.

Obituaries, "H. L. Bond, Jr., Dies; Ill Only One Day." *Baltimore Sun*, April 12, 1922, and *Baltimore Sun*, April 13 and 14, 1922.

Obituaries, Henry B. Chapin. *Boston American*, May 8, 1910; and "Henry B. Chapin Dead," *Boston Globe*, May 8, 1910.

Obituaries, Richard H. Weld. Boston Textile World, May 1908; "Richard H. Weld Dead," *Boston Herald*, March 31, 1908; and "Deaths. Richard H. Weld," *Springfield (Mass.) Union*, April 2, 1908.

Obituaries, Robert Winsor. "Robert Winsor Dies in New York Hotel," *Boston Transcript*, January 7, 1930; and "Funeral Services will be held tomorrow for Winsor," *Boston Herald*, January 8, 1930.

Otterbein, Miriam. "Transit Project Draws Criticism from Residents." (Randallstown, Maryland) *Community Times*, April 15, 1973.

Otterbein, Miriam. "Transportation Fight Bolstered — Sudbrook Park Wins National Historic Status." (Pikesville, Maryland) *Northwest Star*, July 12, 1973.

Pollack, Jeffrey. "Transportation Dept. Restudies Expressway." (Pikesville, Maryland) *The Star-Northwest*, December 20, 1973.

Powell, Michael. "Sudbrook Suburb Resists Siege by Subway Noise." *Baltimore News American,* December 10, 1980.

Price, Joyce. "Northwest Citizens Ask Expressway Not Be Built." *Baltimore News American,* June 15, 1975.

Real Estate Transactions. Baltimore *Daily Record,* December 30, 1910.

Riede, Paul. "Transit Worries Again Plague Sudbrook Park." (Pikesville, Maryland) *The Star-Northwest,* June 7, 1979.

Roberton, Craig. "To Love or Not to Love the N. W. Expressway." (Pikesville, Maryland) *Northwest Star,* February 21, 1974.

Ruehl, Peter. "Finally, an Answer for Sudbrook Park." *Baltimore Sun*, July 30, 1978.

Singer, Larry. "N.W. Residents to Fight to the End of the Road." (Pikesville, Maryland) *Northwest Star,* June 5, 1975.

Society Note. *Baltimore American,* October 2, 1891 and January 3, 1892.

"Suburban Developments, How Baltimore Is Forging to the Front." *Baltimore Daily News,* February 18, 1892.

"Suburbs and County. Sudbrook Park." *Baltimore Sun*, July 7, 1896.

"Suburbs Blazed By Lone Woman." *Baltimore Sun*, December 5, 1937.

"Sudbrook Park - How the Young and Old Folk Enjoy Themselves Out There." *Baltimore Sun*, July 18, 1893.

"Sudbrook Park Residents Want to Abolish 'Unsightly' Dump." *Baltimore Sun*, January 18, 1942.

Sullam, Brian. "Lewis Backs Link Tying BWI, I-95." *Baltimore Sun*, July 30, 1981.

Sussman, Martin. "Final Route Still Uncertain for Expressway." (Randallstown, Maryland) *Community Times,* June 18, 1975.

Sussman, Martin. "Sudbrook Club Nixes Highway; Agrees to Rapid-Rail System." (Randallstown, Maryland) *Community Times,* June 4, 1975.

The Sudbrook News, Official Newspaper of the Sudbrook Park Improvement Association, Vol. I, No. 2, November 1943; No. 4, April 1944; and October 1954.

"The World of Society." *Baltimore American,* January 6, 1892.

Timberg, Robert. "Second Leg of Rapid Rail System Put on Hold." *Baltimore Evening Sun,* April 13, 1981.

Timberg, Robert. "Second Subway Leg Backed; No Funds." *Baltimore Evening Sun,* April 21, 1981.

Timberg, Robert. "U.S. Said to Support Subway." *Baltimore Evening Sun,* April 21, 1981.

"Time and the Automobile Remap Baltimore Town." *Baltimore Evening Sun,* October 10, 1955.

"Tour-bus." (Pikesville, Maryland) *Northwest Star,* February 20, 1975.

Wagner, Marcia. "Residents of Old Court Area Protest New X-Way Proposals," (Pikesville, Maryland) *Northwest Star,* August 6, 1975.

Welshko, Tom. "Federal Funds Dry Up — Baltimore's Dismal Mass Transit Picture." *Baltimore Evening Sun,* Op-Ed, June 4, 1981.

"Will Clear Dump in Sudbrook Park." *Baltimore Sun,* January 30, 1942.

"William Ross Howard 3d Dies in California at 70." *Baltimore Sun,* February 16, 1978.

"Willow Glen Proclaims Opposition to Northwest Expressway Proposal." (Pikesville, Maryland) *Northwest Star,* August 7, 1975.

TELEPHONE INTERVIEWS BY AUTHOR

Anton, Betty Ann. July 28, 1996.

Barrett, James. June 28, 1997.

Bart, Mrs. Robert Leland. July 29, 1996.

Beachley, Priscilla. June 29, 1997.

Bennett, Delores. June 29, 1997.

Bride, Marjorie McHenry. August 22, 1996.

Cadwalader, Mary. July 28, 1996.

Cox, Jackie. June 30, 1997.

Cox, Newell, Jr. June 29 and 30, 1997.

Cox, William T. June 28, 1997.

Diehl, Dorothy. July 27, August 12 and December 4, 1996.

Dowell, John L. June 29 and 30, 1997.

Erwin, Betty O'Connell. June 1, 1997.

Fenton, Matthew C., III. July 28, 1996.

Fenton, Matthew C., IV. July 28, 1996.

Finifter, Sylvia. April 13, 1997.

Gracie, Sally. December 4, 1996.

Harwood, Herbert H., Jr. July 12, 1996.

Hazard, Stella. July 28, 1996.

Hoblitzell, Joan McHenry. June 27, 1996.

Hochberg, Bayard. June 28, 1997.

Humphrey, Jerrold R. June 3, 1997.

Kaufman, Martha Volz. June 1 and 9, 1997.

Leith-Tetrault, John. April 25, 1997.

Liebno, Dorothy. June 30, 1997.

MacLean, Donna. June 30, 1997.

McGrain, John. September 23, 1997.

Mosner, Mary H. June 29, 1997.

Quisgard, Joan. June 29, 1997.

Roberts, Gary Boyd. June 27, 1996.

Schaller, Robert M. July 29, 1996.

Sener, Sarah. July 24, 1996; June 29 and 30, 1997.

Sturgis, Robert. July 2, 1996.

Watts, Juliana. August 15 and 30, 1996.

Winsor, Curtin. February 8, 1996.

Winsor, Curtin, Jr. February 8 and August 4, 1996.

Winsor, James D., IV. February 8, 1996.

Wollen, James T. September 13, 1996 and September 22, 1997.

(Italicized page numbers indicate photographs)

228

ABOUT THE AUTHOR

A resident of Sudbrook Park since 1970, Melanie Anson is a free-lance writer who began researching the community's history almost two decades ago. Since 1978, she has been continually active in the community association, serving as a member of the Board of Directors, Historian, Chair of Civic Affairs and President.

In the 1980s, Ms. Anson led the community's efforts to preserve key elements of Olmsted's design plan, to expand the boundaries of the National Register Historic District and to mitigate the adverse impact of a proposed transit line through Sudbrook Park. She served on the board of Friends of Maryland's Olmsted Parks and Landscapes from its inception in 1986 to 1990. She currently serves on the Board of the National Association for Olmsted Parks.

Ms. Anson received an M.S.W. from the University of Maryland School of Social Work and Community Planning, and a J.D. from the University of Maryland School of Law, where she was an assistant editor of the *Maryland Law Review*. She practiced law for ten years with the Baltimore firm of Semmes, Bowen and Semmes and served on the Editorial Advisory Board of the *Maryland Bar Journal* for several years. She has four sons and a grandson.